FURTHER EDUCATION, GOVERNMENT'S DISCOURSE POLICY AND PRACTICE

Further Education, Government's Discourse Policy and Practice
Killing a paradigm softly

SANDY CRIPPS
University of East London, UK

Taylor & Francis Group
LONDON AND NEW YORK

First published 2002 by Ashgate Publishing

Reissued 2018 by Routledge
2 Park Square, Milton Park, Abingdon, Oxon OX14 4RN
711 Third Avenue, New York, NY 10017, USA

Routledge is an imprint of the Taylor & Francis Group, an informa business

Copyright © Sandy Cripps 2002

The author has asserted her moral right under the Copyright, Designs and Patents Act, 1988, to be identified as the author of this work.

All rights reserved. No part of this book may be reprinted or reproduced or utilised in any form or by any electronic, mechanical, or other means, now known or hereafter invented, including photocopying and recording, or in any information storage or retrieval system, without permission in writing from the publishers.

Notice:
Product or corporate names may be trademarks or registered trademarks, and are used only for identification and explanation without intent to infringe.

Publisher's Note
The publisher has gone to great lengths to ensure the quality of this reprint but points out that some imperfections in the original copies may be apparent.

Disclaimer
The publisher has made every effort to trace copyright holders and welcomes correspondence from those they have been unable to contact.

A Library of Congress record exists under LC control number: 2001099941

ISBN 13: 978-1-138-73636-8 (hbk)
ISBN 13: 978-1-138-73631-3 (pbk)
ISBN 13: 978-1-315-18598-9 (ebk)

Contents

List of Figures		vi
Acknowledgements		vii
Abbreviations		viii
Preface		x
1	The Dynamic Context of Change	1
2	The Government's Right to Change Things: Policy-making and its Legitimacy	9
3	Chameleonic Policy Process Dynamics: Landmarks in the History of Further Education II	23
4	Vision or Mission?	55
5	The Archaeological System of Knowledge and its Discursive Roots	93
6	The Archaeological System of Knowledge: A Broad Panoramic Sweep	152
7	Mastering the Paradoxes: Regulation as Problematic	179
8	The Roots of Competitive Advantage	202
9	The Cast	217
10	Genesis of a New Theme	262
Bibliography		271
Index		290

List of Figures

Figure 1	Language coding themes	157
Figure 2	Document language themes	157
Figure 3	Word frequency type: new	158
Figure 4	Word frequency type: growth	159
Figure 5	Word frequency type: decline	160
Figure 6	Word frequency type: inconsistent but recurrent	160
Figure 7	Word frequency type: death/life	161
Figure 8	Word frequency type: life/death	161

Acknowledgements

My special thanks go to my family, whose love makes everything worthwhile: to my mother for her words of encouragement; to my husband Robert for his love and understanding; and finally to my son Toby and my daughter Jenni for being proud of me.

A work of this kind is largely dependent on the work of others in the past and my debt to them is acknowledged in the endnotes and bibliography. My thanks also go to Pat FitzGerald for her painstaking proofreading.

Abbreviations

ACACE	Advisory Council for Adult and Continuing Education
AFC	Advanced Further education
AMS	Annual Monitoring Survey
BEC	British Education Council
BFED	Burnham Further Education Funding Document
BTEC	Business and Technical Education Council
CBI	Confederation of British Industry
CEO	Chief Executive Officer
CNAA	Council for Academic Awards
CPVE	Certificate of Prevocational Education
CSE	Certificate in Secondary Education
DES	Department of Education and Science
DfEE	Department for Education and Employment
EEC	European Economic Community
FASB	Financial Accounting Standards Board
FEFC	Further Education Funding Council
FESC	Further Education Staff College
FESR	Further Educational Statistical Record
FEU	Further Education Unit
FT	full-time equivalent
GCSE	General Certificate in secondary Education
GNVQ	General National Vocational Qualification
HMI	Her Majesty's Inspectorate
HND	Higher National Diploma
ILEA	Inner London Education Authority
LEA	Local Education Authority
MoE	Ministry of Education
MSC	Manpower Services Commission
NAB	National Advisory Body for Higher Awards
NATFHE	National Association of Teachers in Further and Higher Education
NEC	National Economic Council
NCVQ	National Council for Vocational Qualifications
NJC	National Joint Committee
NUT	National Union of Teachers

NVQ	National Vocational Qualifications
PCFC	Polytechnics and Colleges Funding Council
PPBS	Planning Programming Budgeting System
QM	quality management
ROI	Return on Investment
TEC	Technical Education Council
TUC	Trades Union Congress
TOC	Training Occupation Classification
TQM	total quality management
TVEI	Technical and Vocational Education Initiative
UDACE	Unit for Development of Adult Continuing Education
UFC	University Funding Council
WFTE	weighted full-time equivalent students
YTS	Youth Training Scheme

Preface

This work explores the link between public policy-making and its implementation. It adds to the policy–action process debate by raising awareness of the power which governmental discourse can have in determining action. In view of the complexity of the subject, the research was narrowed to four further education colleges, one of which is a private college. It investigates how far the values and priorities sought by government since the 1988 and 1992 Education Acts are internalised or resisted in those colleges. This work thus tracks the impact of increased government regulation and its effect on risk behaviour in those colleges.

On the macro level, it was postulated that the state may have the power to influence what is considered 'acceptable' to the wider public and thus bring about changes to social values in order to smooth the passage of legislation and its implementation. At the meso/micro level it was anticipated that discourse analysis would contribute to the understanding of the policy implementation process within the organisations for whom the policy change was intended. The task of this work is to show that the use of language can be an important tool in any attempt to use power. Understanding the battle for power can be elaborated by linking it with the battle for power over discourse.

It tracks the historical development of the further education sector from 1943 – further education colleges in particular – via government documentation and legislation. Thus it provides a benchmark against which public policy making in the 1990s can be evaluated; illuminates debate about the association between increased regulation and risk at the institutional level; explains how power over language themes can be used to bring about radical change; and finally introduces emotional intelligence as a key factor in professionals' decision-making. Analysing this narrative reveals several themes representing a journey towards modernising democracy and underlying themes that consistently temper attempts towards radical change. Further, a paradigm shift from the pursuit of educational effectiveness, based on equality and the notion of social responsibility, to the pursuit of educational efficiency is revealed. The panoramic of the narrative reveals that the vision of the welfare state was subjected to the theme of inadequacy and rationalisation, which in combination explain the mobilisation of bias and the way in which society can embrace radical changes such as equal opportunity, yet do little to attain them. It thus traces the factors that influenced the debate about further education such that the political consensus portrayed in the Education Act 1944 failed to maintain its momentum.

It is argued that government's language themes challenged and altered the professionals' language and thus their right to decide, but rendered the newly-incorporated colleges less able to manage the high risk environment in which it was placed by them. In contrast, the private college, operating with professional autonomy as key to its success, shows that professional autonomy and commercial success are not mutually exclusive. Using state-of-the-art management discourse, I am able to show that this approach has much in common with new trends in management.

The evaluation of successive governments and their language themes provides a contribution to the policy–action debate at the macro governmental level and the micro organisational level. At the macro level, identifying the significant language themes affecting the further education sector over a 50 year period offers a panoramic view of governmental discourse, which explains the second-rate position of further education and its identity in the education sector today. Analysis of root metaphors explains how the language of caution and non-radicalism allowed the government to say one thing while doing another. Further analysis of the narrative offers a description as to how governments can espouse equal educational opportunity, and indeed have a history of policies to achieve it, yet it remain a problem in the 1990s.

At the micro organisational, level, it shows how a theme of demonisation of professional practice smoothed the change process within the colleges. It thus provides some insight into the way in which increased government regulation of this sector caused the principals of the colleges to adopt a more risk averse management style and the professionals to toe the line, even when their hearts and minds resisted.

Chapter One

The Dynamic Context of Change

For me, the most interesting contributions made by social scientists are those that attempt to unravel the dynamics of public policy-making. This is because public policy-making can be seen as demand-pull, expressing the value system of a society, or viewed as a story about the expression of a covert power structure in society somehow influencing those values.

Choice of policy direction in any economy tends to reflect the perspective of the government in power as it seeks to obtain what it believes to be the 'right' goals. It could be argued that government simply sets out to do its best, assumptions about what is 'right', however, are incredibly value laden. Indeed, Hammersley (1993, p. 8) states, 'the language of "acceptability" can serve to provide a rhetoric through which selectors define the "good sense" of their decision-making ...'. Investigation of government's power to implement its policy is thus particularly pertinent if what is deemed 'right' for society, albeit value laden, can become part of our accepted social order and appear rational and beyond question. Understanding why some issues in society become acceptable and others not is crucial if you wish to unravel the story about how decisions are made in society and who makes them.

The power a government has to ensure its set of beliefs are dominant in society is dependent on the power that it has over decision-making all the way down to the institutional level where its intentions are implemented. Looking at any government's policy implementation processes offers, therefore, an opportunity to shed more light on how/if a democratically elected government can exert its will.

In the simple model of how a democratic society operates it is argued that power cannot be accumulated by the few because it is shared amongst many.[1] Those critical of this pluralist model emphasise the role social structure can play in covertly suppressing conflict and limiting the boundaries of what is deemed discussible in the public domain. They suggest the role of the state as a political power player should be made explicit in decision-making (Wolfe, 1977; Ham and Hill, 1987).

Early studies of policy-making tended to unpack the context that surrounded a policy decision or choice. Pressman and Wildavsky (1973) played a key role in demonstrating that policies often brought little lasting change, this refocused interest in study to the implementation of policy. In one of the early studies of policy implementation Hall, Land, Parker and Webb (1975) drew attention to legitimacy as a limiting feature of the capacity of a policy to move from the drawing board into practice.[2] Yet government may be able to redefine the limits of legitimacy; indeed, it is argued by some that in the 1980s Mrs Thatcher's government managed to do just this. For those of us interested in expressions of power there is thus a need to understand better whether this can be achieved, and if so how and in what circumstances.

Public policy debate embraces the notion of non-decision-making; thus the discourse about power includes a distinction between issues that fail to appear because they are suppressed by those who hold power and those which fail to appear because of inaction on behalf of those who hold power (Bachrach and Baratz, 1970).

This story is about public policy-making and the effect of that policy-making on the development of further education colleges and their identity. It uses discourse as a way of investigating the possibility that power games are determinants of action. If there is a battle for power its study could be enhanced by thinking about the role discourse plays in forming the boundaries of the legitimate. I thus set out to discover whether discourse was key in legitimising and facilitating the implementation of radical policy changes in the further education colleges,and, if so, how skewing discourse – the covert or overt power to shift debate and change legitimacy to control – could be used by the government to change educational practice in the colleges. In terms of policy implementation analysis, discourse analysis might also help to explain some of the dynamics involved in the policy/action relationship.

If the government can use discourse to influence what is considered 'acceptable' to the wider public it can smooth the passage of its legislation and implementation within the organisations for whom the policy change is intended. In such a situation, alternative discourses become simply marginalised or worse become undiscussable or invisible, in which case democracy becomes a nebulous notion.

Organisations, however, are not policy-centred: they are power systems that have their own discourse (Gouldner, 1964; Crozier, 1964; Benson, 1983). Indeed, Barrett and Fudge (1981) suggest that policy change is often a process of interaction and negotiation between the policy implementers and those who are expected to take action. Developing this notion, to ensure that its policy and intention is implemented, government must influence organisations' decision-making processes. The way government asserts its political ideology within institutions is thus dependent on the way it manages compliance at the organisational level.

Organisational Discourse: The Case of Further Education

As a result of the social reconstruction programme in the 1940s, common perception highlighted state intervention in the system of education as morally superior to private provision. Legitimisation of state intervention relied on public support for a continued growth towards the establishment of egalitarian principles. This was coupled with a belief that economic growth was positively related to an educated workforce.

Education thus commonly became seen as a 'merit' good: in other words, society as a whole placed a value on it that exceeded that of its individual consumption. In the case of further education, however, a general problem of individual underinvestment in education was endemic. Individuals did not recognise, value or were excluded from the possibility of valuing the collective social effect. Government intervention thus came about in order to correct the general trend of individual underinvestment in education and took on the task of establishing an education system that would ensure economic growth (Burns, 1991, in Maclure, 1993).

Further education colleges are not simply involved in education, however; they also provide training. There is a separate case for the national trend towards underinvestment in general training. Individual employers lacked an incentive to offer education of a general kind because this increased their employees' transferable skills, thus potentially increasing their staff turnover. Those who did offer training therefore tended to concentrate on job-specific training, but even this was small scale compared to economic development needs (ibid.). More common was the process of 'learning with Alice', which circumvented any need for a training budget. General training thus evolved often as an unnecessary extra, making it the remit of individual rather than organisational responsibility. However, individuals often did not have the resources to invest in either their education or training. Further, social exclusion processes placed limits on aspiration.

Historical social processes seem to have created a reinforcing vicious cycle of events. In 1944 a coalition government created a reactionary social reconstruction programme that placed the responsibility for individuals' education and training in the hands of government. Despite this, the UK continues to lag behind vocational training developments in Europe. Indeed

Bennet, Glennerster and Nevison (1995) argue that there remains much to suggest that we are still witness to a market failure in education and training in the UK.[3]

There can be a tension between central government intervention that is based on priorities with a broad consensus and those priorities that develop from local needs. While the relationship between local and central government should be a partnership, if local authorities are ideologically in conflict with central government negotiation through a field of tensions becomes the norm – thus further education colleges, serving both national and local education and training needs, found themselves caught in the middle, between two eminent power players who were often in conflict.

By the 1980s a college's portfolio of courses reflected both a response to wider societal needs, interpreted by central government, and the broader educational needs of the local community. They had become control agencies, they were labour-intensive, bureaucratic and delivered direct to the customer (Dunleavy, 1989b). Because they attracted super-programme budgets, government retained potential control over these colleges through regulation.[4] Despite working within these limits, in practice the colleges enjoyed considerable freedom in managing and controlling their operations and innovation strategies. In the 1980s the problem for government, who had a preference for reducing government interventionalism, became how to steer the further education sector towards their way of thinking.

Government Initiatives: Post-1979

The question of whether state intervention could remain justified on moral grounds emerged as a debate in the 1970s. Advocates of change pointed to the failure of the post-1944 system to deliver the vision of equal opportunity. Those in support of a reduction in welfare provision suggested that subjecting the education system to market conditions was morally and socially defensible, as long as safety nets were in place (Vallance, 1995; Tooley, 1996). The market argument is, of course, not new and is rooted in the psychology, or political dogma, of self-interest and utility maximisation.[5] The Education Act introduced by Kenneth Baker in 1988 began a process of change for further education colleges that was far from value-free. Refined in the 1992 Further and Higher Education Act, these initiatives implied revolutionary change to the strategic direction and management of operations of further education colleges.[6]

It is clear that the fairly unproblematic introduction of changes to the curriculum in schools had demonstrated to government that a 'macho' approach worked. It could use tight control to bring about reforms in areas that had previously been thought untouchable (Maclure, 1993).

Not surprisingly, March 1991 saw the introduction of an independent sector for post-16 further education provision: further education colleges were on the road to becoming independently-managed incorporated bodies. Whilst these colleges were used to responding to demand in terms of their local community needs, government now added a new facet of competition, namely, entrepreneurialism.

At the same time legislation made the colleges governing bodies responsible for the general direction and management of the incorporated colleges. Previously this responsibility had been within the remit of the local education authority (LEA). Half of this new governing body had '... to be, or to have been, engaged or employed in business, industry or any profession or in any other field relevant to the activities of the institution' (Education Reform Act 1988, section 152). Exemplifying the government's ideology, the governance of the colleges was to be biased towards the views of the business environment.

A White Paper in 1991 had made clear that funding for further education was to be distributed by the government via a new statutory funding council – the Further Education Funding Council (FEFC). 'The funding regime will consist of a basic annual budget together with an element dependent on the numbers actually enrolled' (DES, 1991, Vol. 2, 4.6). Coupled with this, an increase in funding from sources other than government became part of the change agenda (ibid., Vol. 2, 4.10). Mirroring increased marketisation, long-term pay negotiations with staff were to become localised in order to provide greater market flexibility (ibid., Vol. 2, 7.18).

In 1989 the Confederation a British Industry (CBI) Report had once again identified the paucity of skills development in the UK. It set targets for addressing the skill shortage. It also highlighted the need to bridge the gap that had developed between academic and vocational qualifications (CBI, 1989). Adding to the changed environment in which the colleges functioned, in 1991 a National Council for Vocational Qualifications (NCVQ) was set up to reduce the 'hotch-potch' of existing examining bodies. National Vocational Qualifications (NVQ) were introduced with the intention that they would be fully operational by 1994 (DES, op. cit., Vol. 1, 1.5).

This introduction of NVQ qualifications was a signal that training, not education, was the way forward. Whilst the NCVQ did not have statutory powers of influence, it was given the power to withhold funding to colleges, particularly if they did not add NVQs to their portfolio of courses. The government also made clear its intention that some funding for colleges would be associated with demand: training credits were to be created which students were free to spend (ibid., Vol. 2, 4.10). This caused colleges to look carefully at the income-generation of their range of courses.

In the 1980s the government attempted to increase control over local revenue, increasing pressure through rate-capping and, later, council tax capping. The balance of power between local and central government became increasingly dynamic.

Outcomes of the Initiatives

The incorporation process removed the colleges from the public sector and placed them in a market-oriented environment. The change in the funding methodology introduced competition among those educational institutions. Similarly, it increased competition within the colleges through enforcement of devolved budgets. All this was in common with changes made to the public sector in general. The foundations for competitive tendering had been laid down in the Local Government and Planning Act 1980 and the Local Government and Housing Act 1988. Large parts of the public sector began to separate core and margin activities, outsourcing as many margin activities as possible.

The new boards of governors within the colleges, which were biased towards the business environment, had the potential to alter the role of the professional in decision-making within the colleges. The introduction of NVQs had the potential to limit a college's control over the content and delivery of its courses and reduced choice in the selection of examining bodies.

Policy direction thus subtly began to challenge the professional educationalists' right to decide on its practice. However, these professionals are not powerless because they hold legitimate authority to resist external attempts to change their working environment. Compared to the compulsory education sector, further education's story is less well known, but professional resistance seemed a possibility. If so, the Conservative government's problem was how to control the change process at the institutional level – alternatively, how to gain control over the professional groups.

Since both financial incentives and the nature of the language used by policy-makers changed, and both interact and reinforce one another, it is impossible to state that either one or the other is ultimately the more important.

Faced with potential resistance, however, what better tools are there to use to convince a profession than the language it uses, and which is used, about its activities, in combination with financial control? I thus to set out to examine the way these two spheres of influence have been used in combination to affect change in the further education colleges. The object of this story is simply to show that discourse can be an important tool in any attempt to use power, to increase understanding of the government's problem in reforming this sector and to question the right of the state to enter the discourse and challenge the professionals and tell them what to do.

Notes

1. Pluralist writers emphasise power as shared amongst many, often competing, groups. Those who write about elite power or class relations, on the other hand, argue that there is a concentration of power in the hands of a particular economic group.
2. They found legitimisation, feasibility and government support for a policy is flexible. They argue authorities use political tactics or counter moves as technique of decision avoidance. Attaching a score to three general components of changes in policy issue priority, its comparative strength, its characteristics and its basic criteria, they evaluated how the scores changed and why. They found that changes to issue priority comprised alterations to the characteristics of the issue rather than fundamental alterations of the general criteria (Hall, Land, Parker and Webb, 1975, pp. 487–506).
3. Their research suggests that, at the minimum school-leaving age, inadequate returns to low-level vocational qualifications in comparison to that of higher or no qualifications act as disincentive to participation (Bennet, Glennerster and Nevison, 1995).
4. Government could control local authority borrowing through limiting local authority capital programmes and, to some extent, local authority current spending through restrictions on central grants.
5. This is the conception of individual liberty under the law developed from writers such as David Hume, Adam Smith and Edmund Burke. This interpretation of liberalism recognises the limits of human reason, the spontaneous order of social interaction and supports the enforcement of just rules of conduct. They argue that just conduct provides the protection of an individual at the same time as it allows maximisation of individual expression. Social rules outline what must not be done but individuals are free to determine their own action: any limit to this freedom of action is deemed to destroy liberal order. As individuals interact in order to achieve maximum individual benefit, they also create a wider social order which is of benefit to society as a whole. Government's task is to ensure the enforcement of abstract rules that develop in order to provide reciprocity from the summation of an individual's just conduct – any action on behalf of government to alter the spontaneous order of society, for example welfare economics in order to provide social justice, is seen only to be appropriate in a simple society where there is a single hierarchy of ends and any such rules can be applied to all. In a complex system the market mechanism acts to provide an optimum position by many players joining in a

game of skill and chance – government's task, therefore, is only to enforce the law to ensure free competition (Hayek, 1967).
6   We will return for a more in-depth discussion of these influences later in this work. Here we simply offer a flavour of the changing climate for the further education sector.

Chapter Two

The Government's Right to Change Things: Policy-making and its Legitimacy

Further education colleges became part of the social reconstruction programme following the Education Act 1944. Establishing such public sector services relied on regulating, constraining and sometimes influencing and controlling diverse stakeholder needs. Such state intervention has become a common feature of developed democratic industrialised economies and the state now provides a plethora of services on which an individual relies. The legitimacy of the government to make decisions on behalf of the polity in this way relies on those regulated and controlled trusting its right to make the rules.

There are three basic choices of organisational mechanisms for mediation or control in an economy, namely markets, bureaucracies and clans. Each is based on a different set of assumptions related to the transaction process.[1] The demand for reciprocity and equity, implicit in all complex exchange mechanisms, creates a transaction cost (Ouchie, 1980). If the objectives of the transacting parties are congruent transaction cost will be low since reciprocity and equity can be met. On the other hand, any ambiguity will cause transaction cost to rise. The mechanism for mediation in society should be one that best reduces the cost of transaction.

Where difference is endemic in a democratic society, rules and procedures can be seen to bring about conflict resolution, thereby reducing transaction cost.[2] Organisation of the market has thus come to represent the expression of moral order, above that of natural order, because it is a mechanism through which society's development can be achieved.[3] The growth of state apparatus, structures, procedures and rituals can, therefore, be seen to 'excite and preserve the reverence of the population' made up of autonomously acting individuals (Crossman, 1963, p. 34). On the other hand, it can be seen as the result of economic necessity driven by structural power inequalities.[4] The role that government does, or should, have in organising social action thus provides the basis for many debates.

The structure of society that developed post 1944 was based on evident market failure. There was a recognition that a society organised on market principles could waste resources and fail to provide some goods and services.[5] The reconstruction of the system of education was part of a radical rethink about how society should function – it altered tradition. Indeed, Giddens argues that the recreation of tradition at this time was essential to the legitimisation[6] of the scale of state intervention and authority over individual rights that began post 1944.[7] The opportunity for a change of agenda developed from the failure of traditional values and social norms.

The national education system that developed post 1944 appeared to rest on a new consensus about the type of educated individual that society needed to create. Different skills and different specialised manpower were thought essential for the UK to compete better in the global context. Alongside this, increased education was known to be related to social stratification, the government's task stemmed from the recognition that there was wastage of working class talent. A more in-depth analysis of why this occurred must be left until later in this work, but the task of the state-run education system was that of delivering an educated population.

As the system of education grew, institutions that acted as intermediate bodies were created to carry out practical tasks from which government distanced itself.[8] Left alone, these institutions became powerful in their own right; expert knowledge became a form of authority, so that these institutions became clothed with legitimacy. Briault (1976) suggests that the relationship which developed between these power players is best described as 'a triangle of tensions' – each competing over resources and pursuing different objectives.[9]

By the 1970s, however, it was clear that the system of education had not fulfilled expectations. Readjustment of the system became central to government debate. In 1979 Mrs Thatcher used the dissatisfaction debate to bring about a system of education more closely linked to market needs. In order to legitimise its right to steer society in a different direction the government had to be able to convince the polity that the system had indeed failed. The intermediate institutions, however, held significant power over the decision-making process within the education system. Coupled with this, the further education colleges had developed a tradition of autonomy. In order to change the system of education the government had also to be able to influence these powerful institutions.

In a democracy government needs support from the polity to legitimise its right to change existing patterns of behaviour. The role that authority, power, consent and social order play in decision-making is thus central to understanding a government's right to bring about social change – to explain why people might accept the authority of the state to alter tradition.

A democratic system is said to exist where power is generally dispersed through a participate decision-making process, now commonly expressed through election processes and pressure groups (Dahl, 1961). The state emphasises public power over individual power: to do this it depersonalises the use of power through the rules and procedures of its institutions.[10] In general, governmental bodies and officials are deemed to act in the public interest but there is the potential for some to exploit their power over others, in which case Etzioni suggests that 'decisions ... would reflect the decisions of the most powerful and organised interests in society, while the interests of the under-privileged and politically unorganised would be neglected' (Etzioni, 1961, p. 10). Governmental power could thus be used to mask the desired outcomes of a minority interest.[11] At its worst, public policy-making could be organised by a dominant elite, reflecting that elite's own values and reinforcing its power.

At the centre of the justification for the democratic process to bring about change is the intellectual discourse about the variety of sources of power and the way in which they can be played out in decision-making. To understand the use of power it is also important to understand the debate about an individual's potential to determine, or be determined by, social interaction.

The story about the use of power in society is dependent on the political views of the storyteller, whose perception alters the relationship between actors. In order simply to express divergent political perceptions about how the role of politics and the state works, how power should be dispersed and indeed whether it is possible for democracy to deliver liberalism, Lukes' labels of liberal, reformist and radical are adopted here (Lukes, 1977, p. 127). While there are dangers inherent in a simplification process of this kind, it has the benefit that differences between the perspectives are better exposed.[12]

The need for a system of education developed from a social 'predicament' – new rules were needed to bring about a resolution and ensure progress towards society's betterment (Finer, 1970). In this role, government activity imposes a unitary perspective even though conflict and complexity was known to exist, social development of this kind is thus often at the cost of individual choice. This paradox creates the dichotomy that is evident in intellectual debate and its sets of imaginings about policy-making.

Lukes (1993) suggests that the discourse about the use of power in society can be separated into three understandable dimensions, namely, open conflict which is based on an adaptation of the classical liberal tradition, now imagining intermediary groups as representing popular sovereignty, and the reformist and radical views, which imagine different features of structured power inequality. Power can thus be expressed covertly, exercised through non-decision-making and/or through the mobilisation of bias that skews individual's preferences.[13] The point is that what happens outside the observable arena of political behaviour is also of concern in the study of the exercise of power.

Government policy-making develops in three stages: the initiation stage, the processing stage and the implementation stage. It is the initiation stage of policy-making that is particularly important to the proponents of the liberal perspective because they see policy-making as resulting from open competition between rival groups.[14] The government's role becomes one of passive interaction with interest groups so that it can better represent the views of the people.[15] Individuals are believed to collectively or individually pursue their own interests and the state simply mediates any competing pressures.[16]

In the liberal's set of imaginings, the power state institutions have over individuals is legitimised because individuals freely release their individual power to authority, with the result that conflict is resolved by the application of abstract impersonal rules. All individuals are then personally free but subject to control in their social and work obligations through the application of those abstract rules.[17] Organisational systems and structures, therefore, become important custodians of those rules, while at the same time they reinforce the legitimacy of those rules.

Central to the liberal approach is a belief in an individual's capability to alter the social system, latterly including pressure group membership,[18] although more recently elections are regarded as the competitive forum.[19] The processing stage of policy-making is seen as a process of mutual adjustment.[20]

To a certain extent the reformist view accepts much of the liberal view; the proponents of this view also believe in popular sovereignty, but competition to influence policy-making is perceived as unequal. One approach suggests that individuals may not be able to act in their own interests because of the expression of unequal power in the socialisation process. Another approach suggests some individuals are unable to understand their rights and thus cannot make effective decisions on their own behalf or influence government in their favour. In this set of imaginings the role of professionals and experts is important because they are deemed to act on behalf of the uninformed.

The reformists' thus view the role of government in society differently.[21] In this case, the government and its institutions maintain law and order and steer society's betterment. Social inequalities are readjusted by government and welfare intervention.[22] Ham and Hill (1987, pp. 31–47) suggest that the development of the state educational system is evidence of such steering.[23]

The radical theorists imagine that power is held over the many by the few. They highlight the historical development of society, in particular the power that social structure can have in constraining and directing the development of society. Individual freedom, these theorists argue, is moulded by macro structures.

Indeed, Bravermann (1974) argues that the pursuit of profit in a capitalist economy ensures that ultimate power in the system belongs to the owners of capital because the production process determines the social process.[24] The capitalist class can align policy-making with its own interests, ensuring its survival.[25] The role of government is to foster capitalism, never to question its suitability.[26] Nor is government concerned with pursuing popular sovereignty.[27] Transforming society into a universal market place, government legitimates the accumulation of profit and the unequal production relationship, thus ensuring the process of inequality.[28]

Adopting this perspective, political activity is at best peripheral to the power structure of society. Indeed, individual action is limited by socialisation processes resulting from class dominance – bureaucracies are also seen as instruments of class domination because they institutionalise the mechanism for transmitting that set of social relationships. Elite power thus determines that what is considered legitimate is 'right'; denigrating, or making invisible, viable alternatives. Policy-making is thus a process of action and inaction (Ham and Hill, 1987).

In this set of imaginings the state education system is not identified as a radical rethink of social processes but as another means to tighten social control. The only route for the expression of individual liberty from this perspective is through membership of a fraternity fighting to change the capitalist mode of distribution, a coalition of class consciousness.[29]

The labels of liberal, reformist and radical perspectives are a simple but useful way of looking at the use of power in society. Each offers different sets of imaginings about why individuals may accept the authority of the state to change social relationships. Each is based on different assumptions about the exercise of power and thus the role of the state and an individual's capacity to collectively or individually influence the policy process.

Some suggest that the growth in government and its institutions is a demonstration that government is now distanced from the control of capital. Similarly, some suggest that the growth in the specialisation and division of the work task is an example that power is dispersed amongst many different groups. Indeed Hall (1994) suggests that class has fragmented to such an extent that no clear class identity remains.[30] As the growth in skills and professionalisation has taken hold, the working class no longer has a common reality (Parkin, 1979). This has led some theorists to suggest that the radical's philosophical position is untenable.

However, there is no reason to assume evidence of social disaggregation is evidence of defusing elite power – indeed the case has been made that it may provide the very route for its survival. It may be in the capitalists' interests for government to exert some discretion in meeting needs of other classes, espousing caring capitalism to bring about compliance – as long as capitalism remains king in the long run.[31] 'The marriage of capitalism and democracy was strictly one of convenience which could be dissolved by the dominant partner at any time it felt its interests threatened', Sweezy (1980, p. 16) suggests. If the process of democracy leads to questioning the rules of capitalism, a different picture of activity might emerge.[32]

Government intervention in the education system can be seen as a way of neutering class conflict, with economic growth helping to hide the real differences between the classes (Coates, 1986). Even in a recession the power of the masses can be seen as neutralised by their dependence on unemployment benefits (Bradshaw, 1986).

However, the distinction between the exercise of legitimate or illegitimate power by government is increasingly difficult to identify because of the economic conditions and the structures and authority that exist.[33] To make the analysis even more complex, as the protagonists from the radical perspective argue, traditional ways of doing things might deliberately create this fuzziness.

Given the former discussion, exploring a government's ability to implement goals, particularly in difficult economic conditions and against opposition from powerful interest groups, will tell us much about whether the state itself is a source of power.[34]

While independent institutions may be desirable and intended outcomes of reform,[35] critics of state intervention argue that the disassociation of government from its institutions has caused professionals and technocrats to have more power to decide than elected representatives.[36] These institutions are thus free to change or alter the rules independent of the elected government's, and thereby the polity's, wishes.[37]

The mandate for change in the 1980s, led by Mrs Thatcher, did not attack the right to welfare services but focused on the inability of the state and its machinery to deliver an efficient and effective service.[38] The New Right thus challenged the legitimisation of reformism – they argued that the legitimate power relationships encompassed in the vision of 1945 was outmoded and a new set of imaginings was needed.[39] As proponents of the liberal perspective, they argued that the system had to return, as Friedman (1962, p. 30) succinctly expresses it, to 'freedom as the ultimate goal and the individual as the ultimate entity in the society'. Government intervention in order to bring about equal opportunity had failed – it had to stop.[40] Central to New Right philosophy is thus the belief that nationalisation and welfarism are the causes of the decline in Britain.[41]

Given this political vision it was inevitable that the system of state education would be problematised, alongside the role of the intermediate institutions and the professionals' right to choose.[42] The government proceeded to increase its authority over local government and interest groups, in particular the Trades Union Congress (TUC) and the Confederation of British Industries (CBI).[43] Its protagonists argued this was not a new approach to democratic politics; it was retrenchment to the classical liberal tradition.[44]

My research task was thus to investigate why educational goals are changing and who has power to do the changing, in order to test whether the power to decide lies in the hands of the few. It is at the implementation stage of national policy-making that the power of the government to exert its will is tested – particularly if that policy is radical. An investigation of policy implementation at the institutional level had the potential to provide some insight into the government's power to steer society because the management of organisational change is an expression of the policy/action relationship.

Policy Implementation

Pressman and Wildavsky (1993, p. 38) suggest that 'implementation may be viewed as a process of interaction between the setting of goals and actors geared to achieving them'. With a network of interests at play it is not surprising to find that policies are rarely clearly articulated mandates. If policy is resourced and its mandate clear, conflict tends to be at a minimum (Hargrove, 1983). Poor policy definition provides a gap, an opportunity for different interpretations (Barrett and Fudge, 1981).

At the implementation stage of policy-making several levels of governmental power come together. This creates an interactive field of tensions, altering the policy context. Indeed, all players may have legitimate power to act yet different objectives (Pressman and Wildavsky, 1973). At the organisational level, the operational stage of policy becomes a complex chain of activity, any ambiguity in this chain providing ever more opportunities to increase implementation deficit (Bachrach, 1969, p. 44; Barratt and Fudge, 1981; Bishop, 1981).

At the organisational level, policy implementation deficit is a problem; even more so where it involves professionals, because they can exercise discretion in interpreting the rules of society. Ethical decisions represent a law of conscience, which is separate from the law of the land.[45] Professionals still hold power even though more recently it has been seen as causal to individuals acting as passive receivers.[46] In reality, however, only subdued resistance has been met in public service bureaucracies, as they have become privatised.[47] Nevertheless, to implement its policies the government had to appeal to the electorate, to legitimise its right to alter control traditionally held by the educationalists.

The continuance of tradition centred on a previously undisputed truth – that the social benefits of the welfare system outweighed the social costs.[48] The discourse of the 1980s led by the New Right treated intervention and professionals as inadequate. Mrs Thatcher's approach to change management was confrontational. However, current educational practices had developed in response to individuals and interest group interaction and been popular over a period of time. Similarly, organisations are interactive systems that are not easy to change or influence (Lindblom, 1968). At the micro level the government's problem became that of how to bring about change within the further education colleges so that their strategic direction mirrored policy intention. Could such an approach be enough to alter traditional conditioning and would those systems be so transformed that the conditional influences would be changed?

In a democratic society open debate should consider whether there are better ways of doing things. Indeed Giddens (1996, pp. 234–51) suggests that modernising the state could be ethically desirable and indeed necessary to ensure the legitimacy of government.[49] But could the government set out to transform the facts so that the professionals' traditional reasoning and discourse became illegitimate?[50] The government's attempt to control the policy implementation process within the further education colleges could be viewed as a direct challenge to the right of professionals to choose and determine their own vocabulary.[51]

If there is a causal link between thought, knowledge and action, control of the discourse would then change professional behaviour – social changes being simply a process of redefining the way in which that control is instituted. On the other hand, if the ability to reason, consider and improve is relative, meaning becomes subordinated to social trends (Giddens, 1987). Knowledge is simply a product of the here-and-now and thus illusory and changeable (Bloor, 1988). Within this context, universal theories become invalid (Lyotard, 1992, pp. 9–19).

To understand the Conservative government's attempts to change education institutions further and the resultant compliance with, or resistance to it, I set out to unravel the 'chameleonic flux' of policy-making to shed light on who determines the new era and/or how it is determined.[52]

Notes

1. In a market transactions take place between the buyer and the seller, the process being mediated by price. Competition in the market reassures both parties that the terms of exchange are equitable. In a bureaucratic relationship transactions are enacted through a corporate body that mediates the process by placing a value on each contribution compensating it fairly. Legitimate authority is implicit. Where individual's roles are congruent with some others it is possible to use the clan structure. This is based on cooperation as a process of mediation and control.
2. Williamson (1975) argues that organisations came about because markets failed.
3. Organisations become 'courts of appeal before which policy and practise appear as plaintiffs or defendants in an evolving trial of promise and performance' (Halsey, 1981, p. 21).
4. Indeed, Foucault (1977) suggests that surveillance techniques perfected in small organisations became subsumed into large organisations as society developed, thus creating bureaucratic organisations with hierarchical power. Pastoral power is thus simultaneously individualising, totalising and normalising because as government attempts to improve society, it intensifies regulatory control.
5. Market failure arises where benefits cannot be individualised, thus user charges are difficult to determine, or where a sole supplier controls resource allocation by price, thus supply need not reflect demand. Many suppliers may duplicate provision wasting resources and creating a high average cost. Government intervention tends to be used where monopolies are the most efficient mode of production but where price needs to be controlled in order to maximise social benefit. If these public services are then moved into the private sector some economists argue they would have to be regulated to maximise social benefit.
6. State power is perceived as legitimate where authority is established by the consent of the governed.
7. Giddens (1996, pp. 15–30) suggests that traditions are preserved through ritual and beliefs constructed by authority figures – rituals provide reasons for tradition to continue. However, he suggests that institutions and constitutions are continually renegotiated – truths become re-identified and this weakens identity and meaning of social norms, enabling change.
8. Namely the DES (Department of Education and Science), responsible for the general direction of education policy, the LEA (Local Education Authority) which organised local provision and the teachers. Later the MSC (Manpower Services Commission), responsible for national training policies, also influenced the strategic direction of some educational institutions.

9   The belief was that these institutions agreed about the intrinsic value of education. Briault (1976, p. 429), however, found their values and objectives to be unstructured and often in tension with one another.
10 The exercise of legitimate power involves person 'A' in influencing person 'B' to do what 'A' wants. Legitimate power within bureaucratic organisations is expressed as authority: this entitles 'A' to get 'B' to fulfil the task as 'B' accepts that 'A' has the authority to request it (Thurton, 1991).
11 Djilas (1957) argues that the state is autonomous where it can control organisations and political institutions.
12 The liberal perspective can be seen to include conventional pluralism, neo-pluralism and the New Right; the radical perspective includes conventional Marxism and structural Marxism (Potter, 1986).
13 Lukes defines the liberal approach as a one-dimensional view of power, addressing only observable behaviour in decision-making. He feels that it fails to address the structures of power in which these decisions are made and thus ignores mobilisation of bias – less visible ways in which power can be used. The two-dimensional view addresses potential and observable conflict, recognising that power can covertly control public agenda issues. However, he argues, because it concentrates on specific issues it personalises those issues and thus fails to address complexities of institutional power and the inactivity of leaders. He suggests investigation of the inactivity of leaders and the exercise of institutional power as a way to study political inactivity because an individual may be unaware that power is being exercised over him. Action may simply be 'A' affecting 'B', who retains control to act. If open conflict does not occur, it would be better to set out to justify a counterfactual, to explain why individuals may not act in their own interests. This would reveal unarticulated and non-individualised ideologies permeating social consciousness. 'By shaping their perception, cognition and preferences in such a way that they accept their role in the existing order of things' (Lukes, 1993, p. 24).
14 Dahl (1957, p. 203) describes power as follows: 'A has power over B to the extent that he can get B to do something that B would not otherwise do.' Thus any group can exert power to influence the system. A proponent of pluralist theory, he believes that power in industrialised societies is dispersed amongst many competing agents – power is not equally dispersed but fragmented and thus non-cumulative.
15 This developed from the modernist movement, which held that society could be steered and improved. Jones (1992, pp. 20–22). argues this transformed the political forum to a centralised nation state, increased bureaucratic administration, systematic forms of surveillance and democratic political party systems and brought about cultural changes that emphasised scientific and technical knowledge.
16 In classical liberal social order, universal rules of just conduct protect individual action and enable order from spontaneous social interaction – government enforces the application of the rules. However, the demand for technical and expert knowledge meant experts could exert unfair pressure on the government.
17 Max Weber (1864–1920) criticised classical liberal tradition for its inability to account for the sociopolitical power of administrative machinery. He argued that authority was necessary to equitable transaction and identified three types, namely charismatic, traditional and rational legal. He postulated that the modern state was based on rational-legal authority. Charismatic power relies on B admiring A's characteristics and wishing to emulate them. Traditional and charismatic authority, he argued, could limit individual freedom because

it separated the individual from control over the means of production and limited individual knowledge to job specification and rule obedience. He thought a bureaucratic system based on rational-legal authority was superior because it used abstract rules and individual acquiescence to authority's right to implement those rules – obedience from impersonal order. Bureaucracies, he thus argued, are a necessary, though not sufficient, condition for efficiency (Andreski, 1965, p. 324).

18 Because government needed support from the pressure groups they held a bargaining position causing a more collectivist approach to dominate policy-making. Including competing groups in the analysis separates liberal individualism from pluralism (Beer, 1965).

19 The bargaining power of pressure groups ensures that political parties are aligned with their interest because they need to maximise support at elections (Downs, 1967).

20 Because government and business are caught in a feedback loop of economic growth, coercion can be a reality of apparent consensus. Dahl (1985) sees the reformist and liberal perspective as linked by an imperfect democracy, which developed in order to explain their model of power as society developed.

21 Giddens (1987, pp. 17–26) describes this perception of power as designed 'to influence for the better the human condition', which he suggests led to problem diagnosis and cures.

22 Cheal (1991) makes the point that to challenge tradition, the individual had to be able to act rationally.

23 Indeed, proponents of the corporatist thesis argue that the role of the state had to change because of international pressures. In the 1970s government and major interests groups drove capital accumulation and enabled it to balance national and consumer need. 1979 heralded a return to central control: indeed, some elitist theorists point to the state's dominant power over institutions as an example of a ruling class.

24 The radicals argue that the production system creates players with competing needs: problem resolution is achieved through unequal power.

25 Weber and Marx identified individuals as autonomous actors but Marx thought class relationships lead to conflict whereas Weber thought political authority and rational law brought about equity. Weber perceived the separation of the worker from the means of production as an application of rationalism but Marx identified this separation as central to the use of power. Paradoxically, Weber thought individuals had the potential to exhibit irrationality if action was associated with ethical stands and substantive rationality (Andreski, 1965).

26 The state thus supports industrial capitalism by enriching the monopoly power of the capitalist classes by generating their economic surplus. Labour time becomes an input to create an output and therefore an instrument of capital.

27 In industrial capitalism ownership of the means of production determines the social dimensions of class, status and power – hierarchy of class ensures inequality within the system (Marx and Engels, 1988, pp. 1861–6).

28 'The introduction of free competition is therefore the public declaration that henceforward the members of the society are only unequal in so far as their capital is unequal, that capital has become the decisive power and therefore the capitalists, the bourgeoisie, have become the first class in society ... proclaimed itself to be the first class in the political sphere ... by establishing the representative system, which rest upon the bourgeois ... equality before the law and the legal recognition of free competition' (Bravermann, 1974, p. 11).

29 Weber argues that class identity is not dependent on property ownership alone; class stratification includes individual ability, educational advantage and unique skills. Since class and status are not mutually dependent an individual, he argues, can alter his/her status – expert knowledge and officialdom become the basis of the power of capitalism and dependent upon it. Class identification is not unitary it contains similarities: historical change cannot, therefore, be achieved through 'class consciousness' (Andreski, 1965, p. 425).

30 Hall (1994, pp. 49–60) argues that class consciousness does not explain the many forms of social stratification. Individuals have multiple identities created by the different roles they have to play in society.

31 The state is identified as a unified organisation; any diffusion of power is simply to diffuse the power of the working classes (Dunleavy, 1981).

32 Poulantzas (1993, pp. 69–85) argues that state executive controls social development through increased bureaucratisation and the dominance of two players in the democratic process, where the winner dominates the decision-making process. This explains the rise of the power of the executive and the demise of democracy. Poulantzas thus argues that representative politics no longer has effective control.

33 An elite can covertly suppress revolutionary change by influencing the choice of issues that are open to debate (Bachrach and Baratz, 1970). Lukes (1993) takes this a step further and suggests that the possibility exists for the values and attitudes of the majority to be moulded by the ideology of the few.

34 Skocpol (1993, pp. 86–100) argues that the liberal and radical views have treated the state as if it were moulded by society. He suggests that the state may be an autonomous actor, in which case civil servants have significant influence over policy-making even where they are reliant on interest group support. It is thus the interrelationship between the state and the context in which it operates that determines its strength.

35 'State is a highly generalising, integrating and legitimating concept that identifies the leading values of the political community with reference to which authority is to be exercised; emphasises the distinctive character and the unity of the "public power" finds its embodiment in one or more institutions and one or more public purposes which thereby acquire a special ethos and prestige and an association with the public interest or general welfare; and produces a socio-cultural awareness of [and sometimes dissociation from] unique and superior nature of state itself' (Dyson, 1980, p. 206).

36 Crisis is inevitable if spending to maintain legitimation exceeds accumulation. The government is then faced with increasing taxation in order to maintain the level of provision or cutting back on welfare expenses. Following the Marxist tradition they view individuals as controlled by structure thus ultimately unable to influence government because the structure of domination limits the extent of legitimate power (Clegg and Dunkerley, 1980).

37 Hayek (1960) describes liberalism as being concerned with the extent of governmental power, democracy as concerned with who holds the power. Using the opposite of liberalism and democracy, totalitarianism and authoritarianism, he argues that it is possible for a democratic government to be totalitarian and for an authoritarian government to act on liberal principles – thus the pursuit of unlimited power of the majority is anti-liberal. The aim of economic power should never be to achieve results for particular individuals because this relies on a unitarist perspective, which is absent in any complex economy. Planning cannot adjust in the way markets do. Bureaucratic organisation is a problem, social justice inhibits liberty and must be replaced by a moral order – justice attributed to individual conduct.

38 Public ownership is an international trend. Mrs Thatcher and Chancellor Kohl in Germany followed President Reagan's approach in the United States, which is to regulate these industries in the private domain. Concerns were expressed that government spending effectively crowded out private enterprise. Rules and regulations were also seen as contributing to increasing diseconomies of empire.

39 Niskanen (1971) argues that managers of public monopolies, free from profit-making, can pursue organisational growth in order to fulfil their own needs and wants. He argues that monopoly power leads to a loss of social benefit. Using the same argument, Tullock (1993, pp. 110–20) suggested that the competitive arena in state-run bureaucracies would force them to produce more efficiently, either by contracting out or through devolved responsibility and budgets.

40 The key issue for the proponents of New Right philosophy is that the political arena is driven by the need to compete to satisfy interest groups, which in turn increases the state's role as the giver of concessions (Auster and Silver, 1979).

41 The attack on socialism is not new: in 1915 Michels (1987) argued that expert power could be used to control nonprofessionals.

42 Ham and Hill (1987, p. 42) suggest that research examining the power of the state at the local level has not revealed a common rule – the power relationship therefore remains unclear. Yet the New Right choose to back the urban power thesis.

43 During the 1960s and 1970s the CBI and TUC had become the representatives of the two sides of industry. The DES represented the professional educationalists at the national level and the LEAs represented local needs.

44 Rhetoric was about the return to popular sovereignty, which had been eroded by the unitary process of democracy – common purpose. It was led by an economic theory created by Adam Smith, who rejected the pursuit of common purpose in favour of universal rules of just conduct and spontaneous order. Smith favoured a system governed by law – abstract rules – which he argued protected individuals and their values through prohibition. Government's task was to ensure the process of law. Individuals pursuing self-interest increased the production possibility frontier, because they created new jobs and opportunities: free markets thus led to better resource allocation. The New Right began to re-establish popular sovereignty. Mrs Thatcher choose Sir Berry Burns, a follower of Freidman, to be Chief Economic Advisor to the Treasury. The role of government became focused on the control of natural monopolies and public goods not the ownership of them (Hayek, 1960).

45 The outcome of the Ploughshares case demonstrates this.

46 Meaning for Weber involves combining 'actually existing' meaning and 'ideal type meaning'. Andreski suggests that for Weber the ability an individual has to associate meaning to an act is the difference between meaningful action and simple reactive behaviour. Where the individual has observational (which Weber calls 'actually existing' meaning) as well as explanatory understanding (which Weber calls 'ideal type') the individual can act proactively and alter the context of meaning (Andreski, 1975, p. 88). Professional behaviour contains both a high degree of freedom of will, personally rational, and a maximum of predictability and understandability for the general public, abstract rationality, hence the freedom of will exerted by the professionals is seen as socially acceptable and thus is legitimised. For Weber subjectivity occurs where the individual actor responds to her own stimuli, created by observable actual patterns of conduct, but also to the ideals on which society is based, but he fails to describe how this takes place

and why unusual behaviour becomes labelled as deviant (Henderson and Parsons, 1947, pp. 13–29).

47 Those acting bureaucracies, the New Right argued, were maximising their own interests at the expense of the organisation or society. Resistance to the removal of these excesses would be opposed.

48 The legitimate right to circumvent the bureaucratic rule relies on a social set of beliefs which maintain that professionals act altruistically. Growth in the knowledge base led to the belief that only experts could fully understand issues about their discipline. While professionals have expert knowledge, and therefore power, it is believed that their knowledge is applied in the interest of community. Actions are thus value-free. Professional discretion thus permits the practitioner to interpret the rule to suit the client's needs best. Paradoxically, a homogenous group of actors, who share unique characteristics, also has the potential to be a threat to the individual freedom of others because they can exploit their joint power (Andreski, 1975, p. 392).

49 The process of democracy should become a process of open controversial dialogue rather than an exercise of power.

50 Foucault's (1990) work is the antithesis to modernity. He says (p. 43): 'Scientific knowledge is not powerful because it is true: it is true because it is powerful.'

51 Solidarity is explicit in communal language but it is not a sufficient condition of community – 'it is only with the emergence of a consciousness of difference from a third person that speaks a different language that the fact that the two persons speak the same language, and in that respect share a common situation, can lead them to a feeling of community and to modes of social organisation consciously based on the sharing of a common language' (Henderson and Parsons, 1947, p. 136).

52 The third dimension of power allows investigation of political inactivity so that we can attempt to explain that which did not arise in the political arena (Lukes, 1993).

Chapter Three

Chameleonic Policy Process Dynamics: Landmarks in the History of Further Education II

The story of the development of further education colleges is a complicated one to unravel because there seem to be so many drivers and levers that have affected and created further education colleges as we see them today. The task of this chapter is thus simply to outline some of the most significant drivers and levers. The aim is to deconstruct each of the drivers/levers into its constituent parts, to understand better how further education colleges do what they do and are what they are.

The identity and division of the sector are hazy, hence it is very difficult to separate one part from another. Indeed, such has been the degree of fuzziness around these definitions that the Crowther Report (1959) suggested the term 'further education' as used in official documents and statistical references had become something of a term of art. This is partly because the UK does not have a written constitution: in consequence, O'Hara (1988) argues, there is very little clear delineation between government, the levels of government, or their relationship with individual colleges. Another significant factor has been the change in the use of the term 'further education' over time. Initially it was a loose term commonly used to describe all post-compulsory education but it is now more commonly used to describe a distinct sector within the education industry.

The further education sector is very complex. It includes a plethora of institutions, namely: agriculture and horticulture colleges; art, design and performing arts colleges; general further education and tertiary colleges; sixth form colleges, mainly concerned with non-advanced education courses; and universities, although they are mainly concerned with post-compulsory advanced education. This book concentrates on telling a story of government intervention through the experience of four general further education colleges.

The division of post-compulsory further education into segments is in historical terms a fairly recent event. As the system of post-compulsory education developed, two distinct market sectors evolved, each serving academically differentiated student populations. The two distinct sectors became relabelled as 'higher education' and 'further education'. How, why and on what evidence this outcome emerged is part of the evolving story of the development of public education in this country. Perhaps more importantly, how society came to identify one as better than another is part of a story about the socialisation process within the UK.

Nevertheless, programmes of study, the primary task in post-compulsory education institutions, have become divided into two distinct academic levels, namely advanced and non-advanced. In the main, higher education institutions are now responsible for delivering advanced courses while further education institutions, in the main, deliver non-advanced. Despite the apparent divisions of the primary task within the post-compulsory sector, higher and further education institutions' portfolios have continued to overlap, particularly at the periphery.

However, non-advanced further education is defined in the Annual Monitoring Survey as that comprising all courses not defined as higher education up to and including A level and BTEC National. Nevertheless, universities often include HND in their course portfolio. Similarly, further education colleges have a tradition of balancing portfolios that include advanced and non-advanced education. Indeed, there is an increasing trend currently for further education colleges to provide franchise services to universities; thus it would not be unusual to find a further education college's portfolio including BTEC Higher National and the first years of Bachelor degree courses.

While no formal constitution exists, two forms of legislation do affect further education colleges. These are Act of Parliament (primary legislation) and statutory instruments (secondary legislation). An Act of Parliament often results from a government decision which becomes formalised when the Bill receives the Royal Assent. Primary legislation that is targeted at the education sector has immediate impact. Most of the legal requirements imposed on further education colleges, however, arise from the statutory instruments mainly imposed through the regulations.[1]

There are two other formal communication channels used by central government to communicate with the colleges: circulars and administrative memoranda. Through these communication channels the Secretary of State and the Department of Education and Science offer guidance, rather than instruction. Such guidance is not enforceable in law. Nevertheless, circulars and administrative memoranda tend to have considerable impact on further education colleges because experience has shown that noncompliance often results in some form of sanction, conditioning the colleges' activities. Further education colleges are not alone in this; indeed, it has been argued that the growth in government activity since 1945 has culminated in the division between civil servants and politicians becoming blurred (Heclo and Wildavsky, 1974).

Added to these influences, extra-governmental institutions, as well as other interest groups, can influence parliamentary procedure and thus further education colleges; Green Papers as well as White Papers often represent the interests and approaches of the government of the day to which the colleges are ultimately subject. The development of further education colleges has therefore been associated with the needs and wants of society, as interpreted by interest groups and government. Where any fuzziness around boundaries of operation exists, targeting policy is at best tricky.

Supply Assessment Process

The evaluation of supply needs for further education in the economy takes place at three levels: national needs, normally developed through central committees; regional needs, normally developed through the Regional Advisory Councils; and local needs, previously LEA or local demand. Despite the potential for further education colleges to be subjected to the whim of the government of the day, as the system of education developed and became more complex, further education colleges were largely left to their own devices. These colleges thus developed a tradition of responding to local demands.

As the system of education developed post 1944, a complex power net of influencing agents grew around the further education colleges. This power net included parents and learners; a plethora of bureaucratic agencies within the educational field; employers; and examination bodies with statutory control over courses and curricula (FEU, 1985). Facing different and often opposing objectives on policy and practice, the colleges became responsive, and chameleonic, actors.

There has been significant growth in further education and training over the last 50 years. Indeed, by 1996 the DFEE had categorised further education colleges as the most common location for off-the-job training (DFEE, 1996d). In 1998 the Further Education Funding Council, a government quango, identified the colleges as providing courses for 82 per cent of post-compulsory full-time students and 96 per cent of part-time students attending college (DFEE, 1998). Despite, rather than because of, government pressure, further education colleges have become significant players within their industry.

However, 1979 marked the beginning of radical changes to these colleges brought about by government, significantly altering the way they carried out their business. In order to tell the story about what influenced the development of further education colleges over the last 50 years, and to test the government's right to bring about those changes, we need to look back through the drivers and levers that helped determine those colleges.

Influencing Agents

A Philosophical Inheritance

The culture and style of further education colleges, and their poor position in the hierarchy of the system, has much to do with the way in which popular education developed in the UK. The system of education developed within a social context dominated by Christian faith, a doctrine that has a promise of equal opportunity encapsulated in the belief of the brotherhood of man.[2]

Paradoxically, despite the fact that the Romans were persecutors of the Christians, the embryonic Christian system of education emulated the Roman system of language and literature study. After the collapse of the Roman Empire existing schools were adapted to serve Christian faith. The Romans taught in Latin, celebrated ancient texts and tested understanding by measuring rote learning of those texts. Without a reconstruction programme to bring about radical change, Jarman suggests that the old and new merged into one – demonstration of an individual's competence to function on a higher academic plane was linked to the Christian notion, a greater depth of spiritual understanding. Academic competence included critique of the pagan Roman gods.[3] Paganism and Christianity thus became caught in an uncomfortable relationship.

In the Christian context, authoritarian control was seen as the only way to ensure that the ignorant would make attempts to reach the deeper spiritual depths of Christian faith. Civil government became depicted as a divine institution, seen as acting as God's servant.[4] Therefore, right from its early beginnings the state was seen as defending justice – paradoxically perhaps, it also limited individual liberty by setting rules that the population had to obey.

In the ancient world, culture and high birth were positively related. In the medieval world the system of education now needed better to serve two distinct classes, the clerks and the knights. Therefore, despite the notion of Christian brotherhood and the need to civilise the barbarian, education for the peasant became commonly accepted as unnecessary. Indeed, Jarman (1963, p. 56) suggests that any attempt to change one's social stratum was resisted.

Two distinct kinds of education, delivered and controlled by the Christian Church Jarman suggests, emerged to reflect the needs of the two dominant groups namely, book learning, for the clerk, and training, for the knight. The study of grammar and rhetoric had become matched to the emerging Christian theological writing. Nevertheless, it was education designed for the knights that widened the remit of education beyond the celebration of book learning. Knights needed to be competent in athletics, so that they could fight, trained in good manners and loyal to their codes of honour. These codes of behaviour, although now thought of as elements of civilising society, only suggested notions of caring within the same class: the masses were considered as not worthy of such care. Education matched to class and task needs became a dominant narrative in the development of the education system in the UK. These educational processes included socialisation, a process of moulding individual character to ideal types.

The twelfth and thirteenth century witnessed the first signs of a system of education. The differentiated church schools, which had grown haphazardly, became codified to serve different functions, Universities were introduced. Also around this time, education began its slow journey away from Church control. Public schools such as Winchester and Eton have their roots in this period. By the end of the Middle Ages a decentralised and differentiated system of education had emerged. Academic content, however, remained non-progressive and delineated along class lines.

It was not until the Renaissance that a shift in this culture occurred. The rise of humanism, which celebrated individual talent, forced a shift away from a class-based and church-dominated culture. The Reformation, Jarman suggests, shifted power from the Church to the sovereign: this created an identity crisis for Church schools. Freeing learning from the Christian doctrine, the Renaissance brought a revival of the Greek classics and contributed to the concentration on scientific discovery. Inductive reasoning was the centrepiece of scientific enquiry, whereas Christian doctrine favoured deductive reasoning: each locked in their expressions of knowledge adopted diametrically opposed positions. Tradition ruled – the study of classical texts dominated curricula and examinations remained based on rote learning (Leach, 1970, p. 161).

The end of the fifteenth and the beginning of the sixteenth century marked the growth of the notion of a nation state. Perhaps because Christianity highlights communication between an individual's soul and God, a cult of individualism significantly influenced Western Europe. There was much made at the time of the ability of an individual to alter social relationships.

By the 1600s England had a centralised monarchy and a system of public education was beginning to be seen as a public obligation. However, the system of education remained dominated by class needs. Mirroring class, academic content remained distanced from the needs of the general population. By now, however, dissent was openly expressed, Francis Bacon (1966, p. 180) a renowned thinker of the time expressed his frustration, as follows:

> These four causes concurring, the admiration of ancient authors, the hate of schoolmen, the exact study of languages, and the efficacy of preaching, did bring in an affectionate study of eloquence and copy of speech, which then began to flourish ... men began to hunt more after words than matter; and more after the choiceness of the phrase, and the round and clean composition of the sentence ... than after the weight of the matter, worth of subject, soundness of argument, life of invention, or depth of judgement ... Then grew the learning of the schoolmen to be utterly despised as barbarous. But the excess of this is so justly contemptible ... For the wit and mind of man, if it work upon matter, which is the contemplation of the creatures of God, worketh according to the stuff, and is limited thereby; but if it work upon itself, as the spider worketh its web, then it is endless, and brings forth indeed cobwebs of learning, admirable for the fineness of thread and work, but of no substance or profit.

As we can see from the above, the educational needs of the gentleman still dominated. Mirroring training for mediaeval knights, we can see that such education included athletic competence, adherence to codes of honour and training in good manners. Despite the rise of humanism, the belief that everything worth knowing came from the past ensured that the measurement of successful learning remained concentrated on deductive reasoning. Despite significant revolutions in thought, the status quo thus continued to dominate curricula choice. In practical terms these learning outcomes were useless to the working man whoe participation they had not been intended to attract. Nor was there an attempt to educate the masses, except for a small widening of the elite groups. Nevertheless, accprdomg to Jarman, the notion that education should be more than book-centred was growing.

The Church's values continued to dominate through the ecclesiastical syllabus and the language of study, Latin. Despite the increasing popularity of traditional schools brought about by the Restoration, nonconformist academies began, in response to demand, to be a significant force in the education field. These schools were progressive and the fact that they taught science and commerce widened the student population.

While it became common to hear academics extolling the virtues of a broader education traditional modes of learning remained powerful. By the late eighteenth century a network of Christian charity schools providing education for the poor appeared but these emulated that of the schools for gentleman. Not surprisingly, becoming 'educated' remained an unpopular notion for the majority of the working population. The curriculum remained based on a study of classical authors. The acquisition of knowledge continued to be tested in writing and speech. Significant thinkers of the time, such as Milton (1932, pp. 67–73), expressed the view that education failed to contribute to the pursuit of knowledge, yet the tradition of classical learning remained slow to change.

By the middle of the eighteenth century feudal social order was still powerful. The Church and the landowners now functioned hand-in-hand, reinforcing existing class relations. The Industrial Revolution, however, saw off feudal social order at the same time as it generated unheard of social policy needs. Despite the efforts of idealists, mostly churchgoers, who had continued to pursue the notion of popular education, its slow growth was by no means sufficient to feed the needs now generated by industry. Demand for skilled working men exceeded supply. For the first time, education of the masses had an economic justification.

From the eighteenth century onwards, the rights of the individual, expressed by government, had replaced the ultimate power of the monarch. Rousseau,[5] Locke[6] and later Bentham,[7] great thinkers of the times, emphasised raising the level of education of the masses as central to economic advancement. The notion of social improvement thus became part of the growth agenda. Many voluntary societies of the time espoused a doctrine of progress through spiritual enlightenment. Given Christian philosophy, the need for a national system of popular education became expressed as a social motive: raising awareness of the masses to their opportunities, it was believed, would serve ultimately to reduce injustice and corruption.

The development of the notion of popular education was also significantly influenced by its antithesis, the doctrine of laissez-faire: within this paradigm the working man's ignorance was identified as a consequence of natural laws, thus any alteration to this 'natural' state was deemed dangerous. Although the notion of inherited rights and abilities remained significant to the antithesis, it was weakened by the notion of progress.[8] Nevertheless, the doctrine of laissez-faire served to condition the expression of the notion of social motive, ultimately restricting its progress.

Despite, and because of, these juxtaposed positions, growth in the emerging system of public education remained dependent on volunteers. With part-time provision for the poor mainly provided by Sunday Schools, the Church maintained a significant influence. Patronage also retained significant power, its contribution clustered around the provision of evening classes and factory schools (Blaug, 1975, p. 595).

Compulsory attendance and its enforcement underpinned the Elementary Education Act of 1876. Investment increasingly came from indirect taxation. In 1880 the age of compulsory attendance was raised to 12 years of age. In 1888, radical changes to the curriculum brought a wider variation of subjects, which included sports (Cross Report, 1888).

By 1895 the system of organisation included a central Board of Education. Local authorities were responsible for providing secondary education (Byrce Report, 1895). To meet the demands of the Industrial Revolution the old public schools expanded: they remain able to exert great influence today. Alongside this grew the demand for a national system of education to fulfil the needs of the industrial class. Still trying to combat the general reluctance for mass participation, the Education Act 1921 made parents' involvement in their child's education a legal obligation. Some interest groups also supported popular education: one such was the Workers' Educational Association, created in 1903, which provided non-vocational learning.

The system of education as we see it today was never subjected to a radical reconstruction programme, it simply evolved. Its historical development is much criticised for its concentration on the needs of the upper classes and its reinforcement of the status quo and class bias (Harris, 1993). The structure of the system is biased towards high achievers, its curricula and assessment methods are designed for them, while the needs of the general working population remain unmet. With a system biased towards the classics, technical education was slow to develop and in any case was perceived as an also-ran.

The Hierarchy of Occupation

Throughout the 1900s growing industrialisation fuelled an increase in professions. Qualifications quickly became the norm for entry into the elite professions. Gentlemen, educated via traditional curricula, taught to abstract from reality, did not favour industrial careers. Filling the gap, the middle class took up the opportunity. Nevertheless, as industrialisation gained momentum the number of publicly-educated industrialists increased (Weiner, 1992).

A hierarchy of professions now matched task to class; status was encapsulated by the distance of the profession from practical tasks. As accountants did not get their hands dirty, accountancy held high status. By the same notion, engineering became low status, simply because it implied a hands-on approach, seen as less gentleman-like. Similarly, technical engineering, with fewer hand-on demands, gained a slightly higher status. Selling and marketing were perceived as low status occupations because of their closeness to commercialism and profit, which were considered vulgar by the middle and upper classes (ibid.).

Class-consciousness was now expressed through a hierarchy of occupation. This context demanded from the education system a hierarchy of specialisation – thus the system of education placed liberal, classical studies above the study of science, because of its practical implications. The division of the educational system and its occupation selection along ability lines was legitimated by the scientific revolution, which suggested that intelligence could be measured. In 1945, reflecting the social context of the times, in schools were divided into intellectual capabilities that matched occupational choice.

Given the scale of intervention, government focused on the development of a compulsory education system, to bring about social change. Those successful within it, independent of class, had a path to higher education institutions. This meritocracy – a focus on a young bright elite who could match traditional measures of academic achievement – hampered egalitarianism. It seriously biased the development of the post-compulsory sector. Government interest focused on widening the elite student group: other students with other intellectual strengths fared less well. Paradoxically, increasing industrialisation continued to create demands for other occupations, middle and low status occupations. Filling this gap was largely left to the marketplace, in reality individual firms or workers. The gap in educational provision that began to emerge echoed the social division expressed between 'good' professions and trade.

The evident division between education and training in the UK was not common across the industrialised world. Indeed, in the 1850s a massive growth in technical knowledge caused the Germans to create technical schools to meet those changing demands. In the UK an ad hoc system of apprenticeships had continued to grow alongside the needs of manufacturing, but this tended to be job-specific training. It was 1889 before the Technical Instruction Act was enacted to empower local authorities to impose a levy, which could be used to establish technical education.

The government made no attempt to control the voluntary system of technical education. The City and Guilds Institute, a growing number of independent universities, evening institutes and day release programmes providing practical and commercial education expanded without regulation.

Although the government finally created a Board of Education in 1899, and made one of its members president, it was a halfhearted effort not followed up with any legislative changes. The Education Act 1902 ensured that secondary education became part of the political agenda, but even then responsibility fell to local education authorities. LEAs took over the evening institutes. Because of its haphazard development, the LEA and voluntary organisations provided secondary education jointly. Even so, the opportunity was created for a child, independent of income, to climb the intellectual ladder; social class and income continued, however, to limit and condition that opportunity.

It was 1922 before certificated awards in advanced technical expertise were available. This delay did little to change its growing second-rate image. The market and government continued to be uninterested in nonspecific technical qualifications, fuelling a popular bias against technical education. In reality, without government intervention no cohesive pattern existed to attract intelligent users to this sector.

Despite an evident gap between opportunities for the educationally successful and the failures, educational reform rhetoric continued to espouse the notion that popular education and injustice were negatively related. Knowledge was power, but power remained with an elite. Driven by public demand other social reforms were also gaining momentum – in the 1930s Sir William Beveridge proposed a programme of social security. With rising unemployment and public dislike of the old Poor Laws, which blamed individuals for being unemployed, unemployment support became part of the political agenda.[9] Each individual was given the right to a basic income independent of the scale of need, financed by a flat rate imposed on the insured (Beveridge Report, 1942).

These were radical changes, which eroded the social stigma of benefit. A Ministry of Social Security was born to administer such benefits. A public health service was established in 1948. The vision of revolutionary change in society was a welfare package. It was in this altered context that the challenge to an elite's right to educational advantage finally became part of the political and social agenda. These altered perceptions were reflected in the 1944 Education Act.

The Reconstruction Programme

It was during 1943 that plans to reframe the system of education were first mooted; because of the war, a national government was in power, with Winston Churchill, a Conservative minister, responsible for education. The intention was that following full-time compulsory schooling, all young people would continue under 'educational influences' until the age of 18 (MoE, 1943).

The White Paper 'Education Reconstruction' in 1943 encapsulated the revived notion that more students could attain greater levels of achievement than currently did (ibid.). This paper also made it clear that existing provision failed to meet the needs of the majority of young people. Not surprisingly, the provision of technical education was highlighted as particularly poor.

The intention of the reconstruction programme was that all young people would attend secondary education. Those from the age of 15 to 18 not in full-time education were to attend a college part-time, for one day a week. The already-established youth service was seen as playing an important part in this expansion. There was also to be increased opportunities for adult education, where further education colleges looked the likely candidates to fulfil that need.[10]

Couched in egalitarian terms recasting the system was intended to be revolutionary:

> the Government's purpose ... is to ensure a fuller measure of education and opportunity for young people and to provide means for all of developing the various talents with which they are endowed and so enriching the inheritance of the country whose citizens they are ... It is just as important to achieve diversity as it is to ensure equality of educational opportunity (MoE, 1943, p. 3).

The intention of the reconstruction programme was thus to alter Britain's existing class relationships.

Alongside the changes in the national education service, a system of inspection and registration of schools and new financial and administrative arrangements for the voluntary schools were also put in place.

The 1944 Act considerably increased the responsibilities and power of central government where the education service was concerned. In retrospect, it is difficult to be sure what finally brought about these radical changes. It is clear that the post-war climate contained a popular demand for radical reform, which would go some way to provide equal opportunity. On the other hand, as early as 1918 the Labour Party pledge had included developing educational opportunities. Indeed, working class pioneers had long demanded access to educational provision as a main instrument of social change (Webb, 1918).

It is also a matter of record that the growth in support for the Labour Party had effectively driven voting powers to become redistributed amongst a wider population. This drove the Conservative Party to make some attempts to pacify the broader electorate. The Labour Party also had to rethink how to retain their disillusioned voters after the failure of the 1930s General Strike and they began a campaign on individuals' rights at work. Policy popularity became a significant player in vote-catching the post-war electorate. Indeed, Beer (1965, p. 113) states that such was the degree of political convergence during this time that: 'General elections consisted less of pitched battles between opposing groups. As class and ideological contours faded, groups appeared as more prominent features of the political scene.'

Interest groups began to have a significant impact on the formation of the education system. Perhaps because of interest group pressure, private education provision was not abandoned, despite the rhetoric of equal educational opportunity as a vehicle of change. Certainly private provision continued to thrive alongside the growing development of public provision.

While popular education could be justified by all political ideologies, the wide-scale government intervention programme, which developed in the minds of policy-makers in the 1940s, fitted more comfortably with Labour Party ideology than with Conservative.[11] Indeed, the monetarists were against state intervention, believing it to crowd out private investment. In July 1945 a Labour government took office, with Clement Atlee as Prime Minister.

The outstanding feature of the Education Act 1944 was that all children passed on to some form of secondary education. The Hadow Report (Board of Education, 1927), the Spens Report (Board of Education, 1938) and the Norwood Report (1943) were significant to the direction that reforms took. Together they established an education system consisting of two stages, elementary and secondary.

The Hadow Report suggested the system of secondary education should be designed to fit several different student types. The system of reform in 1944 thus consisted of testing students at the end of the first stage to evaluate their suitability for the next stage. The existing grammar schools offered an academic curriculum; the secondary modern schools offered a general education; the technical schools also provided a general education but with an industrial bias. The Spens Report particularly refers to the need for a generous provision of technical schools because of demand outstripping supply.

Perhaps more importantly, the Spens Report highlighted the need for parity of status between each of the sectors to ensure participation. Paradoxically, public schools remained – indeed the Fleming Report (1944) was crucial to the development of free places within those schools legitimising its retention.

A statutory system was put in place that had three progressive stages, primary, secondary and further education. The period of compulsory education, financed by indirect taxes, was raised to 15: provisions were made to increase it to 16. All fee-paying ceased in the local authority schools and provision became the duty of the local authority. The intention of the Act was that those who chose to leave school aged 15 were to have free compulsory part-time education in 'young people's' colleges. Part-time education was to consist of, or be equivalent to, one day in the working week.

Of course, the size and complexity of the expansion programme had major financial implications for government and it needed a huge bureaucratic system to manage it. In the event, local authorities were given considerable discretion to act, particularly where further education was concerned, so that progression towards the vision of the 1944 Act began to reflect local needs.

As the further education sector grew, so did the recognition that there were two distinct categories of level in further education and government became more concerned with the advanced sector than the non-advanced, despite all the rhetoric of equal opportunity. Without clear direction, the development of the non-advanced sector began to be affected by the power plays of stakeholders other than the government.

Post-1944

With a change from a National Government to a Labour administration in 1945, the speed of growth in further education was staggering – by 1947 there were 680 establishments, double those in 1938. The number of full-time students increased by 130 per cent and the number of part-time day students trebled (MoE, 1946). Some of this growth was attributable to employers' willingness to release young people for study during working hours. Women returning from national service increased the demand for what was called 'the domestic front' instruction. Reflecting the social climate, courses in drama, music and public affairs continued to be provided by the voluntary sector for women.[12] This increased demand for post-compulsory education put pressure on accommodation provision and supply of teaching staff. The need for increased technical and commercial capability continued to be stated as key to increased economic performance – to attain that increase in participation in technical professions proved to be a very difficult task.

Social Definitions of 'Cleverness' – their Impact on the Development of Further Education Colleges

Even given the demands made by the Industrial Revolution, an anti-industrial bias continued to permeate the educational system (Weiner, 1992). The aim of the 1944 Act was to change historical culture radically, to provide equal opportunity and parity of talent difference. But to achieve this the social context, which was biased towards upper class values, had to be challenged. But that very social context had influenced knowledge in such a way that terms such as 'bright' and 'clever' were no longer value-free; they had become metaphors to describe someone who was 'academically' strong, not practical.

Grammar school education offered a route to social privilege and material wealth: there was increasing competition for places. Secondary schools and technical schools were seen as less prestigious than grammar schools. Parity between the schools was further limited by the selection procedure, which was biased towards the purely academic learner. Despite the early warnings of Bacon and Milton, and against the spirit of the 1944 Act, the educational system continues to benefit those who fit the class-biased metaphor 'clever'. All other learners simply become different levels of failures.

This process of alienation has had a particular impact on those 'other' learners. Assessment techniques developed for classical learning test the understanding of principles, rules and exceptions. Functional context theorists suggest that these traditional measurements of cognitive development ignore the intelligences acquired by learners who learn by doing. These other learners with other intelligences, when tested on their knowledge of abstract principles, are likely to fail. These 'failures' reinforce the legitimacy of the 'clever' to better life styles. The system of education reinforces social division, which in turn isolates and disillusions potential functional context learners. It is interesting to note that middle and upper working classes have used the meritocratic educational route, a central tenet of welfare state provision (Harris, 1993).

Developing curriculum content to enable cognitive development with these 'other' learners implies the need for a different educational system. It would involve keying the learning process into their individual experience, because these learners learn at the point of application (Sticht, 1996/7).[13] There are also many other reasons why individuals may reject school or become apathetic to the traditional authoritarian classroom-learning mechanism. Indeed, from 1944 a growing number of references suggest that provision for these types of learners has been unsatisfactory (MoE, 1959a).

In the event, parity between different types of achievement, a vision of the 1944 Act, remains a dream. A large proportion of further education colleges' clients is made up of those who have previously failed/rejected the compulsory system and those who learn differently.

The Department of Education and Science[14]

It was the Bryce Report (1895) that highlighted the poor coherence of the secondary school system. This was made worse as the system developed by the power plays between three significant agencies namely, the Education Department, the Science and Art Department and the Charity Commissions (Royal Commission on Secondary Education, 1894–85). The reforms in 1899 amalgamated these agencies under one roof, the Board of Education. The 1902 Education Act ensured that county councils and county borough councils administered the system of national education.

The Education Act 1944 replaced the Board of Education with a Ministry of Education responsible for policy and practice – the reforms thus brought about increased centralisation. In 1964 the Ministry of Education amalgamated with the Ministry of Science forming the Department of Education and Science (DES). It also created a Secretary of State for Education, appointed by the government of the day.

The DES's remit was to allocate resources, establish policy and evaluate the quality of provision in schools, further and higher education. Three branches dealt specifically with further education. One division influenced the formation of the local education authorities' policy on higher education in liaison with the Council for National Academic Awards (CNAA),[15] in consultation with the National Advisory Body for Public Sector Higher Education (NAB).[16] The second branch dealt with non-advanced further education: it was responsible for education and industry links, particularly engineering training for 16–19 year olds, and the development and policy of the youth service. Later it worked with the Manpower Services Commission (MSC). The third division was responsible for the examining and validating of awarding bodies, it thus maintained close contact with the British Education Council (BEC).[17] In liaison with the Further Education Unit (FEU)[18] and the Further Education Staff College (FESC) it influenced curricula matters.[19] Dealing with advanced and non-advanced further education, it created policy for adult and continuing education, general student advisory services and financial support.

The development of the further education sector, particularly that associated with non-advanced education, was thus subject to a variety of tensions. Most importantly these tensions included those brought about by the needs as seen by the DES, essentially educationalists, and by the MSC, which had a practical work based learning bias.

In theory the DES and the LEA operated in partnership. Indeed, O'Hara (1980, p. 33) describes it as: 'Whereby the (local) authorities do not enjoy total freedom of action but are more than the agents of the Secretary of State.' During the 1980s the speed of legislative changes brought in by a Conservative administration altered the partnership arrangement. The DES became less influential than the MSC as far as further non-advanced education was concerned. Added to the colleges' field of tensions, therefore, were changing power relationships within central government institutions.

The Local Education Authority

From 1944 the Secretary of State had a duty to encourage participation in popular education. To do this the Ministry had a duty to ensure that the LEA complied with national policy[20] and, although rarely exerted, power over it should it fail its duty.[21] The LEA can only act when parliament legislates but if that legislation is not specific it can interpret the law as it sees it. It thus has the potential to create a gap between policy and its implementation.[22] Case law has established that the decisions of the Secretary of State as final arbitrator can be challenged in the courts.[23] Similarly, so can LEA discretion.[24]

While the LEA had a duty to make adequate provision for the education service from 1944 and had to submit a development scheme to the Secretary of State, there were many variations of the service.[25] Although the Act indicated county colleges as part of the expansion plan, such was the level of discretion given to the LEAs that none were in fact established.[26]

Nevertheless, from 1944 the LEA had a duty to provide full- and part-time education and leisure activities for those over the school-leaving age. Such schemes had to include 'full-time vocational courses, for those wishing to take up employment or to advance their career, part-time courses day and evening for those in work and courses of all kinds to meet leisure needs' (MoE, 1944, p. 2). Priority for further education was given to those whose training had been interrupted by the war: full-time participation by mature students became common in further education colleges (MoE, 1948).

In 1946 coordination of further education provision was organised through Regional Advisory Councils. These reported directly to the Secretary of State: their task was to monitor the service and reduce repetition. However, their powers have been consistently eroded.

The structure of local government in England and Wales until 1985 derived from the 1972 Local Government Act, which replaced the legislation from the 1944 Act. The 1972 Act reorganised local government and the education function. The counties became subdivided into district councils, mostly subdivided into parish councils. The tiers of responsibility at the local government level were fuzzy, particularly those between county and district councils, who jointly funded some services; tension thus began to emerge between the needs at local level and the needs at regional level. Sadly, the Regional Advisory Councils and the Local Education Authorities were often caught in power bargaining because of their different geographical boundaries. There were some 105 local educational authorities committees, each committee now including two-thirds elected council members and a third education specialists.[27] Decision-making thus had a political context.

Although local authorities were required to appoint a Chief Education Officer no job specification existed; thus each Chief Education Officer's role differed. In general, s/he managed the Education Department and delegated power to Deputy Education Officers or Senior Assistant Education Officers. Often it was a Senior Assistant Education Officer who was responsible for further education.

Some of the power to influence the provision of education was further delegated from the LEA to education committees; indeed, the 1973 Act stated that LEAs had to consider reports from these education committees before decisions were made. These committees tended to have teacher representatives and representatives from business as co-opted members.[28] The education committee often delegated to subcommittees: there was no consistency in the level of delegation, which varied from one LEA to another. Central government had no control over the number or composition of these subcommittees.

Although the exact arrangement varied at the local level, the process of decision-making now involved the subcommittees, who reported to the committee, who in turn reported to the local education authority. Policy tended to emerge from incremental changes made at the subcommittees; these decisions had to be approved by the full committee, which in turn looked for approval from the full council. Approval was often assumed. In this way the decision-making process was consultative and driven bottom-up, although it was often disjointed. As a result, power to alter policy tended to be at the subcommittee level, which in effect was free from central government control.

By 1958 the LEA had become the controlling agency over educational provision (MoE, 1959d). It was in its interest to resist any division of education provision at the national level, otherwise power would be redirected to regional colleges and the status of local colleges reduced.

In 1972 the Bains Report suggested a management structure was needed to direct strategy, set objectives and monitor progress. Most local authorities instigated a corporate planning process and employed inspectors and advisors to monitor quality. Tensions soon emerged between administrators operating at the strategic level and the subcommittees managing operations. Consultation was commonly used as a way of reducing these tensions. The further education service was also affected by policy decisions made by the local authority with respect to 16–19 year olds, community programmes and adult education provision as well as the finance department.[29]

The Local Government Act 1985 abolished the Greater London Council and the metropolitan counties. It was clear that the power of the LEA was to be further reduced.

Manpower Services Commission

The Employment and Training Act 1973 established the Manpower Services Commission to run a public employment and training service. The committee comprised nine members, three from the Trade Union Congress (TUC), three from the Confederation of British Industry (CBI), two from local associations and one representing the interests of those professionals in education. Fifty-eight area offices' boundaries coincided with those of the Area Manpower Boards to provide the upward consultative process.

After the election of a Conservative government led by Mrs Thatcher in 1979, there was a distinct shift of power in education matters away from the DES to the DoE (Department of Employment), and more particularly the MSC. In line with government thinking, the MSC focused on education as work-related. With two main tasks – namely, vocational education and training and employment and enterprise – its remit embraced the young learner, life-long learning and programmes to help the unemployed. The subsequent Youth Training Scheme (YTS),[30] the Technical and Vocational Education Initiative (TVEI)[31] and the Skills Training Agency[32] not only challenged the power of LEAs to influence educational practice, it also affected the custom and practice of further education colleges.

With a paucity of educationalists in the decision-making process, the MSC became responsible for funding short-term non-advanced education. In response, colleges created short-term programmes which increasingly relied on part-time staff with short-term contracts – the colleges could not risk long-term investment in staff. It also created competition for the colleges by introducing of work-based schemes and skills centres. The long-term financial security of the colleges became more subject to risk and to the whims of the market.

In 1985 the MSC launched the Responsive College Project, an attempt to stimulate changed behaviour in colleges by indirect funding. The Replan

Initiative increased the development of the adult guidance service.[33] Empowering the student within the education market, individual learning plans were developed.[34]

The late 1980s witnessed increased youth unemployment, thus the MSC became a significant influencing agent of the further education colleges, dampening down LEAs' influence. The work-related bias towards educational advancement in a system formerly driven by educationalists created growing concern and controversy.

HM Inspectorate (HMI)

The 1944 Act empowered the Secretary of State to require that inspections of the education system took place (Education Act 1944, Section 77). Once again, the Act did not define the remit of the inspectorate, so no national pattern emerged. The relationship between the colleges and the HMI tended to be a partnership towards improving service rather than a judgement on the service provided. In 1983 the Conservative government's policy altered HMI's remit to monitoring quality at the organisational level and reporting on provision at the local authority level (DES, 1983c). Inspection increased in importance, mainly because its reports now culminated in publicly-available grades. Recently, further education colleges' principals have begun to respond to the grades given by the HMI. Indeed, several principals have referred to negotiation over recent grades.

Government Financing

After the reconstruction programme in 1944 central government had considerable power to influence further education; most of the funding derives directly or indirectly from three departments: the Treasury, the DES and the DoE. Non-advanced further education was the statutory duty of the LEA and was funded locally; the LEA's income for the provision of education was reliant upon central government grants, rates being the only large independent source of income.

From 1974, the Manpower Services Commission partly financed work-related non-advanced further education.[35] A national pooling system established in 1959 financed advanced further education.[36] Responsibility for maintaining all institutions remained with the LEA, which had considerable discretion in providing non-advanced further education. The different ways of funding advanced and non-advanced further education led to confusion for the institutions providing both services and for the local and national authorities, who could not easily differentiate these services and allocate resources appropriately.

Prior to 1988, the normal procedure for financing was informal and based on trust. Funding was often a simple matter of making the claims made equate with the sum supplied. Negotiation between central and local government was a common part of the decision-making process (FEU, 1988). Because the LEA had considerable autonomy over spending grants, central government had no ultimate power to target an area. Along the same informal lines, the local authority did not have a statutory duty to check spending incurred by the further education college; for this reason, prior to 1988 financial regulations were based on the concepts of trust and stewardship. Custom and practice provided the college principals with considerable autonomy.

In 1987, the Conservative government fundamentally changed the funding of higher education (DES, 1987a). All polytechnics and those colleges offering a high proportion of advanced education were taken away from LEA control and funded through the Polytechnics and Colleges Funding Council (PCFC); these institutions also became independent corporate bodies. Buildings and assets were taken away from the LEA and given to the newly-formed Polytechnics and Colleges Assets Board.

As already indicated, some of those colleges now funded under the new system provided non-advanced education. Similarly, some of those colleges not covered by the new legislation offered advanced education. Agreements had to be reached between the LEA and the supplier organisations and between the PCFC and the further education colleges. In line with Conservative ideology, these agreements were funded by contract, implying the possibility of competition for the work. An increasing bid for central control was apparent at the same as the competitive arena for further education colleges was increased.

From the 1990s the PCFC conducted its own statistical surveys. In 1993, the classification by funding changed again and the incorporated colleges in the further education sector became funded by the Further Education Funding Council (FEFC), a government quango; further education colleges now had to bid for funding. The university sector came under the funding regime of the University Funding Council (UFC) and the PCFC transferred to the Higher Education Funding Council (HEFC).

During the late 1980s and early 1990s there was a significant shift of financing agents towards the centre, away from the LEA. At the same time, government funding responsibility was out-sourced to quangos, over which professional educators and the public voice had no control; the government thus had an effective mouthpiece not associated with government interventionism.

Teachers in Further Education

Many teachers in further education belong to trade unions which represent their members' interests through collective bargaining, normally conducted through consultation and negotiation. NATFHE (National Association of Teachers in Further and Higher Education) is the largest union, representing lecturers; they also act as a professional body representing members' views on educational policy.

As professionals, lecturers had been able to exert considerable discretion over what and how they taught. The needs of local industry had demanded a technical approach; this resulted in teachers in further education colleges often being technically competent but not teacher-trained (MoE, 1959a). Indeed at one point, the introduction of a training requirement in this sector was seen as undesirable since it would reduce applicants (DES, 1966d) when demand was growing (ibid.).

The arrangements for negotiating pay and conditions for teachers were established in The Remuneration of Teachers Act 1965. Initially, decisions were made jointly by the LEA and the teachers' associations; there were no statutory arrangements, the relationship being that of a 'gentleman's agreement' based on trust and collective responsibility. By 1974 representatives from the Council of Local Education Authorities, which included seats determined by the Secretary of State, met with the teachers' associations for decision-making; they jointly issued recommendations based on mutual consent which ultimately became national agreements.

The Remuneration of Teachers Act 1965 placed the determination of salaries and allowances as a statutory duty of the Burnham Further Education Committee, which also held the rights and responsibility for bargaining. The Grading of Courses Committee produced the Burnham Further Education Document (BFED).[37] This document linked salaries and promotion opportunities to the level of work taught, creating a system of pay levels and a hierarchy of courses. The BFED document reduced LEA autonomy where salary and conditions were concerned. In 1975, regulations placed responsibility on LEAs to provide 'suitable' provision where further education was concerned (Education (Further Education) Regulations, 1975) – the LEAs exerted considerable discretion in interpreting the regulations. In 1979, by joint agreement orchestrated by the DES, the National Joint Committee (NJC) replaced the Burnham Education Committee.[38] In 1981, the NJC published a 'Silver Book', which codified custom and practice (*The Scheme of Conditions of Service*, 1981). While remuneration remained the statutory duty of the Burnham Committee, the NJC increased its scope of control.

In 1982, new regulations placed a duty on the LEA to ensure that the size and the composition of the teaching body reflected the needs of the courses (Education (Teachers) Regulations, 1982); it further stipulated that teachers' qualifications should reflect the needs of the courses.

In 1987, the Conservative government repealed the 1965 Act and replaced it with the Teachers Pay and Conditions Act, 1987: this separated lecturers from teachers, whose bargaining rights were abolished. Essentially, by establishing free bargaining it placed the bargaining process for further education lecturers outside statutory regulation, thus effectively reducing the union role from that of negotiation to that of consultation. This transition has not been smooth and some colleges have been involved in considerable disagreement. At the same time, the government set in motion teaching quality monitoring (DES, 1987a).

The Burnham Further Education Document continued to influence this sector because its power resulted from statutory instruments endorsed by parliament. However, considerable pressure to convert to alternatives began to emerge. Linked to the work of the MSC, the National Vocational Qualification (NVQ) framework, introduced in 1986, operated on a different codification of courses.[39] This in turn put pressure on the categorisation of teachers' pay and despite rising local disagreement, pay scales began to merge.

When the further education colleges' became incorporated in 1993 the authority previously held by the LEAs was given to the governing bodies of the incorporated colleges. This transition of power was met differently by different colleges. Coupled with this was a move towards fixed-term contracts alongside the increasing use of short-term self-employed agency staff; for many colleges there was a bitter battle over pay and conditions. At the same time, the need for the union and its workers to modernise has become part of the agenda.[40]

The Audit Commission

Previously, the student:staff ratio was used to measure efficiency. In 1972 target bands were established and efficiency became evaluated as meeting those bands.[41] In 1985 the Audit Commission Report (1985) focused on the management of further and higher education colleges and resource use. The audit included 165 centres from 550 polytechnics and colleges of further education.

In line with government market thinking, the findings from the audit focused on: improved marketing, image; the need for additional demand generated by improving links with local schools; monitoring of attendance, retention, non-retention. It pointed to the need to: increase availability of colleges to 48 weeks a year; a student/staff ratio of 12:1; the avoidance of overgrading of staff; the control of lecturers out of class time, in particular the limit of remission to 4 per cent; avoiding over-teaching; tight controls over non-teaching costs. Finally, it suggested that current working practices had to become more conducive to giving value for money. The findings of the audit implied that there was considerable wastage in the further education system; growth in the sector could thus be achieved without the use of additional resources. This implied that significant changes were about to occur in the policy and practice of further education colleges.

The 1985 audit failed to make any distinction between higher and further educational needs and objectives despite the fact that the two institutions have little in common, do not have the same teaching practices nor do they cater for the same clients.

The Further Education Colleges

Without a clear remit, these colleges evolved to provide a very wide portfolio of activities containing both academic and leisure courses. A significant part of a college's course portfolio offers participants an alternative to the traditional academic route, often training courses. These colleges also offer participants a second chance to attain academic qualifications. Management are guided by health, safety and employment law, the Sex Discrimination Act 1975 and the Race Relations Act 1976.

The Burnham Further Education Committee provided a formula for measuring the size of a college based on the number of students, separated into courses. The course grading system thus determined the proportion of staffing ranges, which in turn created a staffing structure. Perhaps more importantly, the staffing structure could be influenced by dictates from the LEA, which was not obliged to follow the recommendations of the Burnham Committee, with the result that the internal structure of each college tended to be decided locally. The principal's negotiating skills were thus very important to the staffing of the college. The number of staff and their classification also affected the salaries of the principal, vice principal and heads of department.

The 1980s marked a period in which the framework and principles of the established system of further education, based on trust, stewardship and discretion, came under fire. This gained momentum with the re-election of the Conservative government in 1979. The then Secretary of State, Kenneth Baker, introduced radical changes to further education in the public sector (DES, 1987a). Regulations were enacted to clarify the roles of the participating parties and laws introduced to change the policy and practice towards further education colleges.

A plethora of changes to the colleges of further education began to emerge, each targeted at different products in the colleges' portfolios. In 1982, the DES created the Industrial and Commercial Updating Programme for those clients in work. In 1984, the MSC increased its responsibility in vocational education, non-advanced education provision focused on the need to meet industrial need more effectively.[42] The MSC began to target skill updating, adult unemployment, long-term unemployment and unemployment for the under-25s. Each MSC-targeted area pulled the colleges in different directions. The influence of the DES and the LEAs began to decline.

Further Education Colleges' Clients

Clearly there is a relationship between a learner's experience in the primary and secondary education sector and the ability to benefit from further education. To some extent, a learner's participation in further education is dependent on the education policies and practices that have taken place in the backwardly-integrated education sectors, namely, infant, junior and secondary schools.

Further education colleges are distinct from schools and universities in that their customers have significantly different requirements. Filling the gap of provision between school and university, further education takes most of its clients from the 'failures' and low achievers of the academic system and low status occupations. The rejects of the traditional educational system thus become these colleges' bread and butter.

There are three major categories of potential customers for further education colleges: the traditional academic; the rejecter/returnee; and the apathetic/returnee (European Community Working Document, 1985). The rejecter/returnee and apathetic/returnee became increasingly become important to the colleges as the demand for qualifications, and unemployment, increased. These colleges increasingly cater for a mature student intake, often on a part-time basis, mainly focused on training, who often have a history of poor academic success. At the same time, these colleges provide courses for the 16 year old who has failed, or rejected, the traditional route to academic qualifications, namely school and university. So strong is the ethos of providing a second chance that participation in leisure courses is identified not simply as the development of a skill in itself, but also as a key to breaking down fears about education and failure created in the past.

Further education colleges also provided adult education. These courses are more about a learning society than education; this effectively served to reduce its status in any list of central or local government priority. As financial imperatives gained power, pressure increased for adult education courses to become self-financing: some argued that charging for these services was eroding the principle of equal opportunity.

In the new context of the 1990s and beyond, further education colleges now have to compete for clients nationally and will in the further have to compete internationally.

Global Competition

Since the 1970s there has been a trend for a significant proportion of the worlds' skilled and unskilled people to come from developing economies, with the highest paid jobs to be found within the developed economies. While in most countries the population is ageing, this is less so in the developing economies where Korea, Argentina and the Philippines enrol a growing population in colleges. As it is, the UK provides the lowest proportion of further-educated individuals in the developed economies (Johnson, 1991) and continues to fall behind its competitors in acquiring skills/qualifications ('The Twenty-First Report 1990', *The Independent*, 2 June 1991), with only 30 per cent participating in advanced education (European Community, 1990). In contrast, South Korea and France set higher university participation targets for the end of the century. Alongside this, a trend towards small families in developed economies will drive the demand for skills to become globally competitive, increasing demographic mobility.

Britain is destined to be a poor player in this global picture unless radical changes take place. It is likely that demographic mobility will lead to training standardisation: currently Britain would not be able to be a key player, in part is due to the attitude in this country to training.

The UK and Training

Since 1943, the need for increased participation in further education has been recognised as significant to economic success. Yet in 1979 40 per cent of working school leavers had no training at all, while another 20 per cent who were receiving training had eight weeks or less (MSC, 1981). In 1980 a Training in Britain Survey found that while 80 per cent of employees were involved in training, only 30 per cent of organisations had a training budget and only 24 per cent a training plan (CBI, 1980).

References can still be found about the need to end the second-class status of vocational qualifications, which has been a repeated victim of spending cuts (DES, 1984c). Indeed, the Kennedy Report in 1997 concludes that the case for widening participation continues; funding must be forthcoming for those under-represented learners of 18 and over, coupled with a government strategy to correct the failures of the market to provide (FEFC, 1997a).

Major Competitors and Alternative Systems

When formulating an education and training programme in a climate of financial limitation, choices have to be made. A report commissioned by the National Economic Council in 1984 to analyse vocational and training policies in Germany, Japan and the USA is said to have influenced the Conservative government's policy initiatives in this area (NEC, 1984). The findings of that report highlighted the culturally specific links between national competitiveness and a country's education and training policies; the main variable was identified as the relationship between the state, the enterprises and the individual (ibid.).

In Germany in 1980, the report states, employers met about 80 per cent of vocational training expenses.[43] In contrast, in the United States, where the culture is result-oriented, individuals pay for training because they recognise the potential for increased earnings.[44] The Japanese culture is differentiated from the other two on the grounds that education in Japan combines academic expertise and socialisation to the work ethic. It adopts a long-term dimension, searches for consensus solutions, has a preference for group activities and aims for perfection in employment.[45] However, the state only provides for gaps that occur in the training programmes of companies.

Clearly, the role of the government, and who pays for training, in each of the cultures is seen differently. Germany and Japan clearly link school and work, therefore the individual and society; at the time of writing, these two economies were doing well. The influence of the American system on Conservative government policy can be seen in the repeated use of 'agencies' and the evident link with individualism through the emphasis placed on the reduction of the welfare state. This preference seems much more to do with a match of political ideology than with training and education achievement.

The European Community

If the UK participates fully in the European Community it will have a major impact on policy achievement for the future. The Community's action programme for the development of continuing vocational training states that every European Community worker must have access to vocational training through his or her working life and that public authorities, firms or industry must set up training systems (FORCE, 1990). The member states were expected to implement a common framework of general principles by 1992 (European Community, 1990).

The Universal Declaration of Human Rights and the International Covenant on Economic and Social Rights already includes the UK in international legal obligations referring to a right to vocational training not established in UK law and avoided because of its implications for cost.

Clearly any government in power will to some extent be bound by the member states' common framework in vocational training. The principles of the European Community programme for the development of vocational training are: to encourage greater investment in continuing vocational training; to support innovation in training management, methods and facilities; to promote the strategic planning and design of schemes which take explicit account of the consequences of the completion of the internal market; and to contribute to the greater effectiveness of training mechanisms and their capacity to respond to changes in the Community labour market (ibid., p. 1). The report highlights a skills gap in the United Kingdom.

The CBI task force in 1990 found the UK's workforce:

> under educated, under-trained and under qualified. Nearly half of Britain's employees have no qualification to GCE O level. In France 35 per cent of school leavers reach university entrance standard, as do 30 per cent of school leavers in Germany, compared with 15 per cent in the United Kingdom (ibid., para. 30).

To achieve economic growth the UK needs policies that target the 'under educated, under-trained and under qualified'. The obligation for the UK government to develop such policies can be seen in the following: 'The right to vocational training is recognised in the Universal Declaration of Human Rights, the International Covenant on Economic and Social Rights' (ibid., para. 40) and the European Social Charter (1961). The last two of these impose binding international legal obligations on contracting parties, including the United Kingdom. The European Social Charter requires signatories to 'provide or promote as necessary technical and vocational training for all persons'. The Community Social Charter declared that 'every worker of the European Community must be able to have access to vocational training and to receive such training throughout his working life' (European Community, 1990).

Alone among Community member states the United Kingdom did not sign this charter. It is clear that a level of acrimony exists between the other member states and the UK because of the Conservative government's decision to opt out of the Social Charter ('The Re-organisation of Further Education', *Hansard*, 1988). It is made quite clear in the Community Council document that an increase in participation rates in education and training in the UK requires radical policies: 'Many witnesses indicated that exhortation alone was unlikely to be adequate to achieve the major change in cultural attitude towards training which was needed in the United Kingdom' (European Community, 1990, para. 32). In 1990 the Conservative government launched a vocational training initiative.

National Council Vocational Qualifications

The National Council for Vocational Qualifications (NCVQ), a Conservative government quango, was appointed to undertake reforms in the field of vocational qualifications in order to replace a 'hotchpotch' of examining bodies (DFEE, 1991a). Its remit was to create standards to improve monitoring; its task included reorganising the approved independent bodies that made accredited awards in the occupational sector.

The NCVQ does not have statuary powers, but funding can be withheld if the college's course portfolio excludes NVQs. An NVQ is a competence-based qualification; a completed NVQ thus consists of many small task achievements. In this model of learning didactic teaching becomes less important than work-based learning. An NVQ system can be conducted in-house; it does not have to take place in an educational institution. General National Vocational Qualifications (GNVQ), which includes broad occupational areas, was added in September 1994.

Controlled by a central body, the curriculum became more centralised and thus more controllable; power shifted away from academics as delivery of course and curricula altered to meet the requirement of the process of NVQ, and professional bodies had less input into the included criteria.

While the funding associated with NVQ courses has been instrumental in their introduction in further education colleges, employers have been slow to embrace the new changes; indeed in 1991, Alistaire Graham, director of the Industrial Society, said that they have failed to make their mark on industry (Dean, 1991). This view was reinforced by the HMI Report in 1991, which found that employers continued to be apathetic and ignorant about NVQs (DfEE, 1991b). Professional concerns were raised that quality had been sacrificed for quick implementation and the NCVQ reinforced procedures for maintaining quality in the delivery and assessment of qualifications *(Times Education Supplement,* 1991). So far NVQs have failed to bring about attitudinal change to training and education, thus training remains a problem in the UK.

All the levers and drivers presented have contributed to the field of tensions within which further education colleges function. Each of the levers and drivers has helped constitute the colleges and influenced their ad hoc development. A recurring narrative in this story is that of the class relations within society, which ultimately, despite all the rhetoric, government policy has failed to change. The system of education is thus structured to reinforce those values; thus further education colleges hold a poor position in the hierarchy of the education system. Despite this, further education colleges have survived and, although differently constituted, continue to offer a route to equal educational opportunity, one might conclude against the odds. Their survival has been determined largely by being peripheral to government concerns.

Notes

1 Statutory instruments describe an Act in detail and are enforceable by law.
2 In Galatians Paul states 'There can be neither Jew nor Greek, there can be neither bond nor free, there can be no male and female: for all ye are one man in Christ Jesus'; Galatians, ch. 3, v. 28.
3 Augustine (*De Doctrina Christiana,* IV) writes 'Two great roads lead to wisdom, authority and reason. One is for the ignorant, the other for the educated. Although reason is the greater authority comes first for ignorance precedes education.' It was not enough to know what was right, it was important to have the right habits.
4 Often quoted as the first important words of political thought: St Paul wrote in the Epistle to the Romans: 'Let every soul be subject unto the higher powers for there is no power but of God: the powers that be are ordained by God'; Romans, ch. 13, v. 1. The magistrate thus became identified as God's servant.
5 Rousseau (1966) thought an individual should be free in a free state. He was against instruction preferring learning by experience, which he thought should precede reason to enable true understanding.

6   Locke (1966) thought the human mind was blank until subjected to experience; thus for him knowledge was an outcome of experience and reflection.
7   Bentham founded the doctrine of utilitarianism. According to this view, training could increase intellectual capability, thus a corrupt government could not have power over an enlightened people. Educating the masses would thus diminish injustice.
8   Adam Smith suggested that basic education of the masses was a necessary consequence of economic improvement.
9   The French Revolution and the Napoleonic Wars were given as justification by government to keep workers under control. The emergent system relied on isolating the eligible in a social context that espoused the belief that there was a natural tendency for the lazy to be poor. The system thus became penal.
10 The Youth Service was brought in just after the war started. Its remit was to extend recreational training so that young people would use their leisure wisely.
11 While popular education was a central tenet of social revolution, it also provided the growth in skills needed to meet market demand.
12 The National Federation of Women's Institutes and the National Union of Townswomen's Guilds.
13 Functional context theory maintains that the biological make-up of human beings, combined with the context in which they function, determines what will be learned, how it will be learned and how the learning will be used (transfer).
14 The description of the DES and its role relies heavily on the College Administration Handbook, 1980.
15 Established in 1964, its purpose was to validate higher education courses and to award degrees and diplomas. It operated through a system of subject boards, which included teacher representation. In 1984 the Conservative government commissioned an inquiry to evaluate its effectiveness and efficiency. The committee recommended that some public sector institutions be able to award their own degrees.
16 The National Advisory Board was introduced in 1981 by the Conservative government to oversee the advanced further education finance pool. In 1985 fundamental changes to the distribution of funding led NAB to advocate a reduction in unit costs to ensure increased access.
17 The Business and Technical Education Council (BTEC) was formed in 1983 by the amalgamation of the Business Education Council and the Technician Education Council. The chair of the Council and up to 25 members are appointed by the Secretary of State. Its remit is to establish qualifications and validate the process and outcome of courses.
18 The Further Education Curriculum review was set up by the DES in 1977. In 1983 it became a limited company and was renamed the Further Education Unit; in 1986 it finally became independent. Much of its work reviews and evaluates curricula and is research based.
19 The Staff College is funded by local authorities and provides courses, conferences and constancy services.
20 Education Act 1944, Section 1: to promote the education of the people of England and Wales and the progressive development of institutions devoted to that purpose, and to secure the effective execution by local authorities, under his control and direction, of the national policy for providing a varied and comprehensive education service in every area.
21 Section 77 of the 1944 Act enabled the Secretary of State to ask Her Majesty's Inspectorate to inspect premises. Section 93 enabled the Secretary of State to commission enquiries.

Section 99 enabled the Secretary of State to declare an LEA or governing body remiss in their statutory duty.

22   The Education Act 1976, which required LEAs to commence comprehensive education, was simply delayed by some LEAs until the next election in the hopes that it would then be repealed.

23   In the Metropolitan Borough of Thameside in 1976 a Conservative council refused to introduce comprehensive education. The Labour Secretary of State directed the council to proceed; they challenged this directive and won. The House of Lords rejected the Secretary of State's appeal. While it was upheld that the Secretary was given discretion under Section 68 of the 1944 Act to judge what was reasonable action in the field of education, this did not exclude judicial review of the Secretary of State's view of unreasonable action (O'Hara, 1980).

24   In Meade v. London Borough of Haringay 1979 the LEA closed schools because of industrial action by school caretakers and ancillary staff on the grounds that to keep them open would exacerbate industrial action. A group of parents asked the Secretary of State to challenge this decision, a right given to them under Section 99 of the Act. The Secretary of State concluded that no breach of duty had occurred. A judicial review of this decision held that by using the complaints procedure available to them the parents did not preclude their right to challenge the decision in the courts (ibid.).

25   Section 41: to secure the provision for their area of adequate facilities for further education. Further education encompassed full and part-time education for persons over compulsory school age and leisure-time occupations (organised training and recreational activities).

26   Section 43 identified the creation and maintenance of county colleges to ensure compliance with Section 42 of the Act.

27   The 1944 Education Act had specified that the LEA had to include people with experience in education. Circular 8/73 further specified this as two-thirds elected members and one-quarter to one-third of co-opted members.

28   The Local Government Act 1972 allowed those teaching in educational institutions to have the status of co-opted membership.

29   The provision of these services was left to the discretion of the local authority. Some services became the responsibility of the Recreation and Leisure Department rather than the Education Department. As adult education became differentiated further education colleges – previous providers of these services – became more financially vulnerable.

30   The Youth Training Scheme provided education and training with work experience for 16–18 year olds whether employed or unemployed. There are four outcomes: competence in a job or range of occupational skills; competence in a range of transferable schemes aimed to provide broad vocational core skills; ability to transfer skills and knowledge to new situations; and personal effectiveness. Essentially the employers bear some costs as do training providers and the government.

31   The Technical and Vocational Educational Initiative focused on 14–18 year olds. Its aim was to bring about change toward a more practical curriculum and widen access to technology.

32   The Skills Training Agency provides full cost recovery training courses.

33   'The process of enabling individuals to evaluate their own development, identify learning needs, and choose the most appropriate ways to meet them in light of their personal circumstances; then to pursue and complete a learning programme, review their achievement, and identify their future goals' (Cooper, 1990).

34 The learning outcomes of guidance are: self-awareness – what an individual is like and what they want; opportunity awareness – what options are open to them; decision-making skills – how to go about making sensible decisions; transition skill – be aware and prepare for changes that need to be made (ibid.).

35 Established under the Employment and Training Act 1973, its remit was to run the public employment and training service. By 1986 it funded 25 per cent of work-related non-advanced further education.

36 The General Grants Regulations (Pooling Arrangements) established the advanced further education pool which merged with the Teacher Training pool in 1975.

37 By 1979 this had become classified into four major areas: taught courses or research programmes, or both, leading to a degree; courses leading to a postgraduate level requiring a first degree; courses above Ordinary National Certificate leading to degrees; courses above the Ordinary Level of the General Certificate of Education leading to the Ordinary National Certificate and courses other than those described above (Locke et al., 1980, p. 179).

38 The Association of County Councils, The Association of Metropolitan Authorities, The Welsh Joint Education Committee, National Association of Further and Higher Teachers Education, the Association of Agricultural Education Staffs and the Association of Principals of Colleges all contributed to a joint agreement to set up the National Joint Council, established in 1979.

39 The findings of this report recommended the introduction of a new vocational council. The new framework had four levels: basic, standard, advanced and higher (DES/DoE/DTI, 1985).

40 'My priorities will be ... to modernise NATFHE without jettisoning the principles on which it was built' (Mackney, 1998b).

41 In 1972 the DES established norms of student:staff ratios given certain conditions. They instituted an Annual Monitoring Survey to monitor the move towards the achievement of the bands.

42 After the White Paper 'Training for Jobs', 1984 the Commission began to purchase more work-related non-advanced education from LEAs. It thus began to have increased influence over the colleges' product portfolios.

43 In the German system a Chamber of Industry and Commerce and a Chamber of Craft are responsible for the supervision and promotion of training while the *Länder* have the responsibility for educational content. At the age of 16 students enter either the dual system or full-time vocational schools. The dual system comprises on-the-job training and day release.

44 In 1981 73 per cent of young people between the age of 16–24 were involved in a course of education. Private accrediting agencies and associations oversees the training system. Trade schools attract 9 per cent of post-16 year olds. Trade schools are often organised by particular industries as part of the internal labour market and this is used as a mechanism to ensure retention. In 1982 the Job Training Act was introduced to provide training for the economically disadvantaged.

45 In Japan the training system has two frameworks. The Ministry of Education directs vocational education and the Ministry of Labour develops the vocational training plan. The main aim of the plan is 'the propagation and promotion of vocational training on the basis of the fundamental idea of lifetime training' (Johnson, 1991, p. 14). In 1984 94 per cent of students continued education post leaving age. One in four go to university.

Chapter Four

Vision or Mission?

The implementation of policy is rarely dependent on cost alone: it also tends to be bound up with society and its values. The task of this chapter is to discover which factors influenced the debate about further education such that the political consensus portrayed in the 1944 Education Act failed to maintain its momentum.

There is no doubt that the late 1940s became a period marked by social revolution. In a climate of reform, alongside the rethink about the system of education, Aneurin Bevan proposed a National Health Service, finally established in 1948 (Foot, 1970). With a shortage of steel limiting economic development, the steel industry became nationalised. Post-war, the need to demonstrate some alteration to existing social relations became part of the policy agenda. Equal opportunity for all became significant as sociologists began to link life experience with an individual's capability to take advantage of opportunities presented. The discourse about education in 1944 raised many issues, one of which was the poor interest and participation in education and training, especially those associated with technical skills. The Percy Report on advanced technical education in 1945 led to the development of Regional Advisory Councils whose task was to improve the profile of technical education so as to increase voluntary participation training (MoE, 1945).

With rising demands on the public purse the establishment of compulsory education took precedence, by default shifting further education needs to the periphery. Indeed, as early as 1949 we find the first reference of many to the need to temper the reforms in order to reduce costs (MoE, 1949a). Paradoxically, the need for other types of education, training and skills development grew. Largely free of government intervention, the further education sector continued its growth by meeting demand in an ad hoc way.

The 1950s was a period of economic boom and the system of education expanded. Clement Attlee, Prime Minister since 1945, was replaced by Winston Churchill, now leader of the Conservative Party. Participation rates in post-compulsory education were still low: a broader curriculum was suggested as a way to increase those participation rates (MoE, 1954). A post-war baby boom increased demands on the public purse as the trend towards staying on after compulsory education increased; this in turn created a shortage of teachers particularly in science subjects. At the same time, the university sector was growing and the selection criteria for entry to university rose to stave off demand.

Demand for new skills expanded dramatically. In 1955 a MoE report states: 'the pace at which the new discoveries of science could be turned into account depended largely on whether this country succeeded in creating a sufficient supply of young men with the necessary qualification' (MoE, 1955, p. 6). The report expressed concerns that even if participation in the 'time-honoured route' – traditional academic qualifications – increased, it would leave a shortfall as far as the needs of the economy were concerned. The need to develop an 'alternative and much broader route' to attain qualifications arrived once again on the agenda. The report states 'very bold plans are called for ... these changes needed to be radical' (ibid., p. 9). Academic discourse suggested that economic and social factors were limiting the ability of working class children to reach their potential (Floud et al., 1973).

The Conservative Party again took office in 1955, Anthony Eden replacing Winston Churchill as Prime Minister. A central premise of the welfare movement had been to transform some privately-owned institutions into public services; indeed Bevan believed the community should own the institutions that drove the economy. This election marked a significant shift away from interventionism. So deep was this shift that it was suggested by some that the National Health Service would never had been established had it been subjected to the mood of the late 1950s (Maclure, 1988a).

The global economic climate was dynamic. Nasser suddenly nationalised the Suez Canal; Britain, hostile, led a discourse on the internationalisation of the waterways. Technological advance was fast-moving, sputniks were launched in space. The interdependency of nations was becoming part of the business agenda but Britain's poor competitive position remained.

By 1958, rather than altering a system based on an educated and administrative elite the educational reforms 1944 seem to have been limited by it (Cotgrove, 1958). Technical and commercial education became victims of the social context in which they were placed: the battle for industrial competence was lost as plans for technical training to be on a par with universities was circumvented (MoE, 1945).[1] Indeed in 1955, the National Council of Education, industry and commerce's vision for a Royal College for technologists, became reinvented as a request for a central awarding body (MoE, 1950).

Nevertheless, popular demand for full-time and day-release courses increased and a plethora of establishments supplied the needs of some

2,152,868 students (MoE, 1955, Table 54a). There was growth in part-time student participation and policy plans for technical education in association with industry (ibid., para. 1.3). Yet the participation rates in education and training still had not reached an appropriate level and failure rates were high.

The economy continued to be dependent on manufacturing and demands for such skills grew. The National Council for Technological Awards, suggested initially in the Percy Report, was created to raise its profile – in 1964 this became the National Council for Academic Awards. A review of secondary and technical colleges in 1956 culminated in a five-year plan for its future development, which in turn led to an expansion in further education colleges (MoE, 1956c). Despite firms being able to write off training costs to expenses, it was said participation rates in advanced courses needed to increase by 50 per cent and day-release needed to double to meet demand. LEAs were asked by government to be more generous in their grants to technical students and to make technical scholarships more available to the unemployed.

Non-advanced education and training needs were now divided into three types, each having different educational and learning needs, namely, technologists, technicians and craftsmen. There was an increase in demand for technicians and craftsman: however, supply was poor. This was in some measure due to a general lack of employer support, unsociable shift-working patterns and poor home conditions. Having been encouraged back to the home after the war, women were now seen as a potential pool of technical labour. Alongside the demand for manufacturing skills grew a demand for business skills. Local and regional colleges now included business studies in their course portfolio.

In 1956, a rationalisation programme segmented further education provision into local colleges, area colleges, regional colleges and colleges of advanced technology. Each segment provided for a specific learning capability that ranged from non-advanced to advanced work (MoE, 1956a). A pattern of provision was now emerging in further education; regional colleges tended to deliver advanced full-time and sandwich courses, area colleges offered some advanced courses on a part-time basis and local colleges tended to offer non-advanced part-time courses. However, because Circular 305/56 failed to distinguish advanced and non-advanced courses, a clear product focus was absent (ibid.).

Area colleges also provided non-advanced full-time and block-release courses. Regional colleges were also given a remit to provide diplomas in technology. Some of the regional colleges became Colleges of Advanced Technology specifically introduced to raise the profile of science and technology professions; their focus was full-time and block-release advanced work (MoE, 1956c). Sadly, these colleges did not come up to expectations and in 1961 they became independent bodies, funded by direct grant in 1961 and converted to university status in 1967.

Other training organisations continued to develop plans for a broader education that would meet the needs of 'other' learners; regulations began to be drawn up. By 1959, the legislative process for further education colleges began to emerge and governing bodies had to be representative of professional, commercial as well as local government (MoE, 1959b).

The number of teachers being trained expanded to meet demand; teacher training courses increased from two to three years. However, it was not until the 1970s that it became compulsory for graduates to be professionally trained teachers. The Carr Report in 1958 once again raised the the issue of paucity of training and recommended that industrial training remain the remit of industry (Ministry of Labour and National Service, 1958). An Industrial Training Council was created: the Crowther Report suggested that its remit should include providing an alternative route for young people to gain qualifications and training (MoE, 1959a).

In response to the findings of the Crowther Report, debate focused on the average and less than average child's achievement because it was argued that there were dormant reserves of ability. The Crowther Report was significant to the re-emergence of equal educational opportunity on the government's agenda. The report findings suggested that only one in eight of 16–18 year olds participated in further education and argued that this wasted talent was of crucial importance to economic development. Unveiling sociological factors, the report suggested that the home environment was fundamental to participation in further education. It suggested that students left study when and if it was above the needs of the job and that boys were influenced by the number of evenings a course involved. Another contributing factor, the report suggested, was the loss of bonus when attending college; similar problems were also identified in apprenticeship schemes (MoE, 1959a). It was clear that the system and policy for non-advanced education and training was not working.

The report, emulating the needs as expressed in the reconstruction programme of 1943, suggested that a network of county colleges should provide compulsory education one day a week for young learners at work. Making needs clear, it states: 'If we were confined to one comment and one recommendation about English further education it would be this. At every stage, and on every level, the need is for more time, for less pressure on both staff and students' (MoE, 1963e, p. 22). The Conservative government, with

Harold Macmillan as Prime Minister, took no action: thus it became a lost cause.

In the 1960s government interventionism once again became part of the political agenda. In a context that acknowledged the existence of underprivilege and that there was a gap in national manpower needs, it was a period of considerable growth in further education. The 'baby boom' had become adolescents; more young people were staying on at school; juvenile delinquency was increasing; and young people in work were becoming much more affluent.

The Albemarle Report was commissioned to review the youth service and evaluate its contribution in helping young people to become part of the community. Reflecting the changing financial imperatives and political context, they were also asked to address the best value for money spent (Youth Service, 1960). The report suggested that more grants were needed to train these young people. Once again, the need for an alternative route for young people who wanted to continue education, but not in the traditional academic arena, was on the agenda. The late 1960s and early 1970s thus became a watershed for the youth service, which was criticised for failing to meet the needs of young people. The Youth Service Development Council was set up to advise the government on a 10-year development programme and a building programme was initiated.

The Crowther Report had recommended that more places be made available in higher education to accommodate the baby boom; Harold Macmillan had been asked to set up a committee of enquiry (MoE, 1963c). Growth in education institutions and students' participation dominated the 1960s. Paradoxically, student unrest, in response to a general lack of resources, drove the public to question the benefits of education. Government increasingly focused on primary schools and resources were redirected to reduce class size to help solve the problems of underachievement; social circumstances remained a major contributor.

In 1961 a White Paper again focused on non-advanced education and training and a new classification of worker was added, one who could operate machinery and plant – the operative (MoE, 1961). Lack of time was again seen as a key to low participation rates in further education for the 16–18 age group and early leaving was again associated with poor home conditions (MoE, 1963f). The low status of technical qualifications was also seen as causal (Oxford Department of Education, 1963). Again, a grand plan was envisaged to reverse this trend; its aim was to increase participation in technical non-advanced further education from 12 per cent in 1959, to 50 per cent by 1979.

The term 'technician' became acknowledged as a separate category in engineering; there was a desperate need for courses to meet the needs of this type of career (MoE, 1961). Most local colleges began to develop recreational and non-advanced courses in line with these requests. Taking on board the Crowther Report, these courses were based on breadth rather than subject depth, with a practical orientation.

Despite student participation problems the 1960s was witness to a broader spectrum of society benefiting from further education. Bottomore (1971) suggests that economic growth increased disposable income, which served to alter class relations. In response to the Robbins Report, student involvement in policy-making within the colleges increased and greater academic and financial autonomy was given to the colleges (MoE, 1963d). In October 1964, after 12 years of Conservative administration, Harold Wilson became Prime Minister. In December 1964 the then Secretary of State for Education and Science, Michael Stewart, announced a review of the internal government of colleges of education.

During this period public schools flourished with 25 per cent of all sixth forms increasing participation in science or mathematics (Williams, 1957). University places continued to grow.

In response to the 1963 Robbins Report on higher education, regional colleges that had not become colleges of advanced technology became polytechnics (MoE, 1963d). Carrying on the work of the previous administration in higher education, the Labour government of 1964 created the binary system; more polytechnics emerged (DES, 1966a). Once again rhetoric spoke of parity between technical and academic qualifications and polytechnics were seen as the vehicle to provide advanced further education with a vocational orientation thus widen access. Supplying unconventional courses, they did alter the conventional hierarchy of university popularity (Gosden, 1983).

Regional colleges now supplied advanced work and local colleges elementary work. Funding further education colleges thus increased in its complexity; they became identified by the proportion of advanced work they undertook. The problem of low level achievement and participation in technology and at the lower levels of attainment remained. Much of the growth of further education in the 1960s, however, resulted from the five-year plan for technical education developed in 1956 (Argles, 1964).

Demand for business studies students increased, with supply provided largely by local and regional colleges.[2] Management courses became popular.[3] Universities, preferring specialist disciplines, remained reluctant to embrace the generalist approach needed for management teaching, thus this gap in the market was met by polytechnics and further education colleges. Day-release and block-release courses flourished, but the shortfall in participation in industry and commerce courses as a whole continued. The government asked the industrial training boards to pay greater attention to release from employment for training.

In 1963 the Newson Report again pointed to the failure of policy to reach the average and less than average student (MoE, 1963b). It highlighted the resource disadvantages of over half the young population completing their education in secondary schools. The report reinforced social factors as causal to poor children's having less educational opportunities. It suggested a shift of resources to meet the needs of these students and a major reorganisation of the curriculum. The process of selection was seen to disguise wastage of human talent. The report suggested that: 'a fundamental change in the whole educational situation ... If [the schools] do their job well the colleges of further education will have to meet rapidly increasing demands for courses by older school leavers' (MoE, 1963b).

The Hennicker-Heaton Report ensured that LEAs developed targets for growth in participation rates and completed a building programme to meet those needs (MoE, 1964a). This report had a familiar theme – that twice as many employees should attend day classes. Despite clear signals that something radical had to happen to change training trends, to this day participation remains voluntary. The Industrial Training Act, 1964, was a recognition that training could not be left to industry. The Act created the Industrial Training Boards, which were financed by a levy on industry. Its remit was to address the failure of student and employer participation.

Although the mood of the 1960s was affected by the notion of human potential wasted, the Crowther Report's recommendation of a phased programme of development supplied government with a rationale for placing the needs of secondary provision before that of further education (MoE, 1959a, pp. 188–9, paras 242–94). The outcome was a staged programme, which in turn created a new set of problems (MoE, 1963a). Downes and Flower (1965, p. 2) wrote:

> This does not simply mean that we are abandoning virtually half a generation to the present inadequacies of the post-secondary modern school system: it means the strong probability that the 'head of steam' generated by Newsom will fizzle out, since the demand for further education which it stimulates will not be met.

The Robbins Report had begun a discourse about upgrading teacher training colleges and leading technical colleges being upgraded to university status. It had also begun a process of devolving policy-making to the institutional level; the report thus recommended that governors should have detailed control of colleges' finances (MoE, 1963d).

By 1964, uptake in day-release courses was affected by a reputation for poor success rates, excluding those with low ability and only 28 per cent of 15–17 year olds participated (MoE, 1964a). The Henniker-Heaton Report, endorsing many of the findings of the Crowther Report, suggested that day-release should double, but no real expansion took place (MoE, 1947). In the report it states that the general view of the minister was that the right to day-release could not be granted without affecting more urgent educational developments; further education colleges and their clients drifted further away from government's mind. The pressure on resources was beginning to be stretched to the limit.

The introduction of the Industrial Training Act 1964 – later followed by The Employment and Training Act 1973, which in turn led to the development of the Manpower Services Commission – shifted training responsibility away from employers. Pressure on the public purse continued to grow. The Labour government made plans to end selective education, replacing it with a comprehensive system that removed the barriers between grammar and secondary schools (MoE, 1962).

By 1966 further education provision had grown dramatically. It included: establishments maintained by the LEA paid by local rates and by general grants from the Ministry of Housing and local government; direct grant establishments assisted by departmental grants; and independent establishments. Some colleges were financed jointly with industry to provide technical studies. Regional colleges provided a substantial amount of advanced full-time and sandwich courses. Agricultural colleges had been transferred to the Ministry of Employment from the Ministry of Fisheries and Food in 1964. Colleges of art and farm institutes provided non-advanced courses. Technical colleges, colleges of commerce and evening institutes provided a wide range of evening courses, including leisure activities.

The UK's competitors continued to improve at an increased rate. Population growth rates slowed, the UK remained dependent on exports and higher productivity per person was thus needed to increase standards of living. Government concerns focused on the need to increase technical and managerial skills to achieve that increased productivity. The failure to raise the profile of technology and commercial training, combined with early leaving trends, continued to affect the take-up of lower status careers. Indeed, one report suggested that sixth form boys intended to enter higher technological education only when they were rejected for pure science (Oxford Department of Education, 1963).

Despite this, by 1996 there were 8,398 grant maintained or assisted further education establishments, with 3,091,022 students involved in courses, 53 per cent of which were female. Ninety-four per cent attended part-time courses, including day-release, block -release and evening modes (DES, 1966e, Table 1). Of the total number of students, 46 per cent were over 21 years of age and 22 per cent were 15–17 year olds (ibid., Table 3). Further education now included: national colleges jointly financed by the Department of Industry; regional colleges; colleges of art; agricultural colleges; farm institutes; evening institutes and others.

In the independent sector, 89 establishments catered for .5 per cent of the total number of students; of these 46 per cent were women. Only 19 per cent of courses in the independent sector were part-time (ibid., Table 1).

The Weaver Report, moving away from the Robbins Report's suggestion that college governors should be responsible for control of the finances, recommended that colleges manage themselves: this was fundamental to codification of the relationship between the LEA, the governing body, the principal and the academic board within colleges (DES, 1966b). Initial focus was on colleges of education.[4] In February 1967, the Secretary of State promised to introduce a Bill to codify the instruments of government for the governing bodies of further education colleges (DES, 1967). The Education Act (No. 2) 1968 provided codification and its statutory force.

1969 began with a three-year building programme and many LEAs programmes included comprehensive education. The Haslegrove Committee Report pointed to the need to develop a system and validation process for technical and business course awards, a familiar story (Haslegrove, 1969). This led not only to the development of the Technical Education Council in 1973 but also to the establishment of the Business Education Council in 1974. The Open University began provided part-time courses by distance learning, which became a significant option for working students.

The government's hands-off approach left a vacuum. Responding to demand, further education colleges saw a significant growth in part-time courses. Their growth from 1956, however, had been haphazard, not helped by the balance of decision-making power constantly shifting between central and local government (MoE, 1956c). Government continued simply to monitor the process.

In 1969 the first of a series of Black Papers was published. These set out to destroy the common consensus about progressive education and halt further development of a comprehensive education system. The bipartite system of education had been increasingly criticised for alienating 11+ failures and making them second class citizens. Mr Short, Secretary of State, described the publication of the first Black Paper as one of the blackest days for education in over a 100 years. The Black Papers provided a forum for expression of concerns about progressive education – the papers argued that new trends in education were harmful to working class children. The first paper suggested that militant students evolved from progressive teaching: the assumption that learning was a natural inclination involving discovery rather than a response to reward, it argued, was unfounded and caused anarchy in the classroom (Cox and Dyson, 1971, pp. 9–12). The debate attracted considerable media interest.

In October 1969 the second Black Paper was published. This criticised the empirical research on which the growth in progressive education had been based and the rationale for a comprehensive system of education had been founded. The paper supported a return to systematic instruction, based on testing, in order to measure student needs (ibid., pp. 24–5). Again the response from the media was considerable. The third Black Paper continued the derision of progressive approaches to learning. It attacked the comprehensive principle of equal opportunity as a utopian political ideal. It argued that selection was essential to competition between comprehensive schools and grammar schools to maintain a levelling-up philosophy (ibid., pp. 27–33).

The three black papers provided the basis for a counter-revolution that rejected equality in favour of quality of education. The egalitarians were criticised for lowering standards by introducing a system in which no one failed. The system thus introduced was accused of being based on the sentimentality of social justice and fairness (Maude, 1971, pp. 37–40). The purpose and process of education became a matter for debate in the 1970s.

The quality of courses provided in the non-advanced arena had continued to improve but the numbers participating in these courses continued to decline. Indeed, during the period 1971–77 there was a 20 per cent decrease in those participating in day release and block release courses.

In June 1970 the labour administration was dissolved and Edward Heath became Prime Minister. By this time the educational system had become large and bureaucratic. In further education colleges there were 351,217 students on full-time courses, 46,734 on sandwich course and 743,343 on part-time day courses (National Statistics Summary Tables, 1975, pp. 10–14). Participation in adult education establishments was also rising. Concern about the pressure on resources began to rise (DES, 1972b).

The 1970s saw a period of decline similar to that of 1939, with rising prices, inflation and high levels of unemployment and redundancy. These were coupled with a rapid growth in skills mismatch, not helped by poor school exit performances. The number of immigrant children with English as their second language doubled; with regional deprivation already a problem, some schools were stretched to the limit and their inability to resolve the problems increased.

The education system now comprised three dominant power players, namely, the Department of Education and Science, the local education authorities, the National Union of Teachers (NUT), as the largest union. Each of the players' muscle, however, was limited by the need to ensure that public opinion remained favourable. As rising unemployment began to bite the Manpower Services Commission began to increase its impact on the further education colleges.

The system had now become very bureaucratic. The DES had considerable influence and began to dominate education debate; the previous comfortable partnership arrangement began to alter (Ball, 1990). The Industrial Relations Act of 1971 made clear that changes, particularly where the TUC was concerned, were on the government's agenda. Indeed, the Weaver Report had laid the foundations for devolution reforms and recommended institutional autonomy. The potential for a battle for power began to emerge.

In an attempt to simplify roles and relationships with the colleges Circular 7/70 made clear that the LEA had financial responsibility for the colleges, but that it was the governors' responsibility to determine the character of the college. The principal of the college would prepare financial estimates for submission by the governors to the LEA.

At this point the county council plans for development included further education, but once again implementation was impeded by financial imperatives. This period witnessed the onset of a recession (Town and Country Planning Act, 1971). Colleges were now divided into three categories determined by the character of their advanced work, namely A, B and C.[5] Category C included a large proportion of further education colleges. Category A's Academic Board was clearly defined, but the Academic Boards of category C colleges had simply to 'have appropriate consultative procedures'.[6] Left with considerable autonomy, all colleges had an Academic Board but its constitution was unique to each organisation (DES, 1970a). Such was the implementation gap that even though the Weaver reform had stipulated that each college's chief administrative officer must be clerk to the governing body, only 40 per cent achieved this, the post generally being held by the chief educational officer (Parkes, 1983).

By 1972 such was the strength of a now-entrenched system that the White Paper on integrating technology into learning stated that it was 'unrealistic' to make recommendations that implied replacement of all the various institutions with a monolithic organisation (DES, 1972a). Restructuring of the system had become unthinkable. Nevertheless, the paper's recommendations for the introduction of technology relied on a central organisation having loose control over the contributing agents. Perhaps this is why radical change in the way technology has been used in the education field has been slow.

In 1972 cost rather than educational content became a significant part of the policy agenda. The White Paper 'Education a Framework for Expansion', having identified five growing aspects of the service. states: ' this poses difficult decisions about the allocation of resources ... within those available'; thus despite justifications for spending on all five areas, choices would had to be made. Nevertheless, 'the further education system has a vital contribution to make in ensuring that the country has a work force capable of meeting ... the changing demands of industry and commerce' suggested they might not be completely disadvantaged (DES, 1972b).

As the student numbers were now falling in infant and junior schools the report suggested a 10-year development plan. In order to cope with the growing number of post-compulsory students the report suggested that further education colleges expand the scope and number of courses they provided, particularly those associated with part-time study. The intended expansion suggested in the 1972 White Paper was again conditioned by cuts in public expenditure caused by an economic crisis. Small colleges began to amalgamate or be absorbed by larger ones.

In the compulsory sector teacher training had expanded to meet the need for academically and professionally trained personnel. Low qualifying forecasts for 'A' levels in the mid-1960s meant that the excess of qualified students had to be fed into the technical and education colleges, fuelling an increased demand for teachers. This was to some extent offset by the increase in mature students entering the teaching profession.[7] The James Report suggested in-service teacher training for non-graduate further education teachers, so as to be commensurate with the compulsory sector (DES, 1972c). It suggested that further education colleges were well placed to deliver teacher training courses and that existing colleges of education should develop better working relationships with them. In the event, teacher training colleges amalgamated, merged or joined higher education colleges.

Once again the idea that further education colleges should have greater powers in their own financial decision-making was raised. There was by this time some dissatisfaction with the quality, and indeed the status, of teacher training. The Conservative government justified spending cuts because the birth rate was falling. It began to suggest the amalgamation of colleges: expansionist policies were no longer on the agenda (DES, 1972b). The UK's poor competitive position remained.

Manufacturing industries began to decline; indeed, the number of employees in those industries fell by three million during the period 1971–88. On the other hand, service industries grew and participation rates increased by three and a half million. There was a decline in semi- and unskilled manual jobs and a shift towards technical, professional and managerial jobs (Brown and Scase, 1991, p. 6).

During the academic year 1972–73 the statutory school leaving age was raised to 16. The social value of education continued to be high: indeed, a White Paper in 1972 defined a teacher's task as including ensuring social and moral awareness. Teachers were gatekeepers of the moral domain (DES, 1972b). At the same time, it was now accepted that the rise in the school leaving age to 16 meant that teachers now had to teach the disinterested and the hostile learner. The introduction of the CSE examinations enabled schools to develop courses for these children more in line with their needs and abilities. The uptake in CSE increased by 83 per cent during the period 1973–76.

The Employment and Training Act 1973 amended the 1964 Act to enable some companies to be exempt from paying the levy imposed by the Industrial Training Boards. This marked the trend towards the erosion of the ITB's power. The recommendations of the Halsegrave Committee Report – that bodies be established to validate the development of technical courses – was finally implemented and the Technical Education Council was established in 1973. In 1974 the Business Education Council, which concentrated on business courses, was founded. These two bodies together accredited a growing number of vocational courses. The Manpower Services Commission was established and ultimately became responsible for the employment and training service, effectively replacing the Department of Employment.

The Russell Committee report raised awareness of the large number of people who benefited from adult education, particularly the illiterate and innumerate. It proposed expansion of adult education as an alternative system that could recoup wasted talent (DES, 1973a). Adult education courses tended to be delivered in adult education colleges, although some were delivered in local colleges, and they tended to be recreational and non-advanced. The LEA financially supported them because it was commonly believed anything undertaken by the individual that was mildly educational was a good thing for society in general. The report expressed concerns that increasing fees, a consequence of the LEAs' reduced budgets, could reduce participation.

Despite controversy, the youth service programme had undergone fundamental change, supported by the incoming 1974 Labour government led by Harold Wilson and later James Callaghan. Nevertheless, the youth development plan recommended in the Albermarle Report was coming to an end. Harold Wilson inherited from Edward Heath's administration a three-day working week, widespread industrial unrest and the UK as a poor competitor in an increasingly competitive international arena. The Labour government tried to resolve these problems by introducing social contracts, thus substituting wage bargaining for political 'wellie'. The world recession deepened; youth unemployment began to rise.

The MSC asked The Training Services Agency to produce a discussion paper on 16 and 18 year olds. This found that, although the number of young people available for work had fallen considerably during the period of 1961–71, so had the number of jobs available, despite more young people staying on at school. Apprenticeships were popular for boys but the number on offer had fallen during the recession. Gender bias meant that the apprenticeships available to girls was restricted to, for example, hairdressing. The report made clear that the trend was towards a decline in the number of 16–17 year olds entering the work force in the 1990s. Participation in day-release or block-release courses had increased by only 2.5 per cent since 1961. The prospects of training for the majority of young people had not been significantly changed. Poor literacy and numeracy remained a problem amongst the low achievers. There was a need to measure underachievement in schools, to increase learners' awareness of possible careers and to develop second opportunities for young adults (MSC, 1975). During this period one lecturer commented that it was common for any course suggested by them to run if it got young people off the street.

The Russell Committee had ensured the addition of the Advisory Council for Adult and Continuing Education, which now became the Unit for Development of Adult Continuing Education (UDACE). Adult education, however, was consistently the poor relation when the LEA had to make choices between educational needs because of their reduced budgets. Nevertheless, the Adult Literacy Resource Agency was formed in 1975: it became the Adult Literacy Resource Agency in 1978. In a climate of resource cuts adult education fared badly.

The economic crisis continued to worsen in 1976 and deficits accumulated – the Prime Minister was now James Callaghan. The International Monetary

Fund (IMF) took control of public spending and cuts in education spending resulted. Within this context a new approach to reform emerged, epitomised in what has become known as the Great Debate.[8] The education system had failed and not delivered the vision described in the 1944 Act: the system was in crisis. Rhetoric was focused on the right to work rather than the right to equality of opportunity. James Callaghan's speech in particular drew attention to the poor relevance of education to industrial needs; he criticised teachers for their lack of industrial experience and their failure to understand how to promote it, which resulted in students being unable to relate their learning to work. Furthermore, he criticised industry for demanding high academic attainments over and above what was required for the job. The change in emphasis can be seen clearly in the following: 'The goals of our education from nursery school through to adult education are clear enough. They are to equip children to the best of their ability for a lively, constructive place in society and also to do a job of work. Not one or the other but both.'[9]

The DES, in a memorandum to the Prime Minister, criticised the Schools Councils for not addressing these problems ('Extracts from the Yellow Book', *Times Educational Supplement*, 15 October 1976). The late 1970s became a watershed period for the established education system; its central tenet that education was more the skills for the job was under fire. Many course development initiatives post 1976 included experiential learning, cross-curricula work, new teaching styles, new approaches to assessment and, of course, more links with industry (Hitchcock, 1988).

The political Left argued that, rather than altering inequality and class relations, the system of education reinforced it. The symbolic order within the process reinforced traditional social controls, continuing to alienate and limit the social mobility of the very students it espoused to educate (Bernstein, 1974). Ball (1990) suggests the Right's Black Papers created a discourse of derision against comprehensive education. From both political perspectives the system of education was deemed to have failed to change the UK's poor industrial competitiveness (McCullock, 1944). This attracted public attention and divided the professionals. The Plowden Report, instrumental to the development of progressive education, was now exposed for basing its measures of reading improvement on 1948, when standards affected by the war were uncharacteristically low. Indeed, it was argued the report had disguised very low levels of achievement (Gardner, 1968).

The Education Act 1976 enforced the Labour administration's policy on comprehensive education; rhetoric suggested it was a tool for social mobility. The Act reinforced egalitarian beliefs, not surprisingly challenged by the opposition. Some resistance on behalf of the LEAs altered their previously cosy relationship with central government.

Development of further education colleges was in limbo. There was no national forum for debate about its future and a process of negotiation now permeated central and local government spending. The Parliamentary Select Committee recommended an open, informal, public discussion about changes to the education system (DES, 1976b); it also recommended the establishment of an independent body to provide an unbiased overview of education policy. The MSC continued to flex its muscle through youth employment; with rising unemployment amongst young people it became key to non-advanced further education development.

In 1977 the government unified training and further education. The Training Services Agency and the Industrial Training Boards were now expected jointly to advise the LEAs on development plans. But the Training Services Agency became 'the central point through which developments in the training world' and the Industrial Training Boards subordinate to it (DES, 1977e, p. 116). Unemployed young people could now study for three days a week without losing benefit (DES, 1977d, p. 84).

The MSC increased its influence on further education colleges when it introduced the compulsory Youth Opportunities Programme (YOP) for the unemployed school leaver. Young unemployed people from the age of 16–18 had to attend a one year learning programme of work experience and vocational training.[10]

The disabled worker had become increasingly excluded from the work force as factory work increased (Oliver, 1991). Margaret Thatcher, then Secretary of State for Education, commissioned the Warnock Report in 1973 to consider physically and mentally challenged children's needs: its findings were published in May 1978. The report recommended the number of 16 year olds with special needs attending full-time courses in further education colleges should be increased. Furthermore, it suggested development of a variety of courses more closely linked to the world of work, to meet the needs of those with low educational and social competence (DES, 1972c, para. 10.33).

The colleges began to increase day and block release courses available to special needs students alongside courses designed to help school-leavers achieve basic skills. Against an onslaught of financial cuts, which had in turn increased fees, participation in adult education began to fall.

A national survey published in 1979 highlighted the dominance of examination assessments in secondary education system, claiming that the curriculum for able students remained narrow, while at the same time the less able had even less choice (DES, 1979b). The Labour government's Secretary of State remarked:

> The disappointment about non-advanced further education [is that] a systematic nationwide scheme of part-time attendance at college for all those under eighteen who are not in school is the only major objective of the 1944 Act that has proved unattainable. Any compulsory system was, and in the new period of restraint is likely to remain, too costly (DES, 1979a, p. 231).

Indeed, the vision of a separate college for these learners never materialised and they remain caught in a system that has ultimately failed to represent their needs.

It was now argued that the corparatist approach that had typified the 1970s – collaborative agreements between capital, labour and the state – destroyed individual freedom, not ensured it (Crozier, 1979). The rhetoric of the welfare state in crisis became a discourse of derision following the election of Mrs Thatcher in 1979. There was increasing unemployment and poverty. Mrs Thatcher removed the pressure on LEAs to submit plans for comprehensive education and set out to repeal the Comprehensive Act – she began to shift resources away from comprehensive schools towards preschool and primary education. Not surprisingly, comprehensive education legislation was repealed in 1979. Derision aimed at progressive education gained momentum.

By now it was clear that central government had to have power over the LEAs if it wanted to achieve its policy aims; the relationship between local and central government appeared to be in crisis. The development of further education remained caught in this power net. Further education colleges evolved as conglomerates with wide course portfolios and thus no clear identity or focus of provision.

Mrs Thatcher's government led a radical rethink about the welfare system, attacking the educational institutions and their values with rhetoric focused on their inadequacy. Government rhetoric focused on the pursuit of accountability as a measure of quality and derision of the LEA increased.[11] In the pursuit of accountability, government began to put in place the means to evaluate and monitor the delivery of traceable outcomes. Further education colleges now had to be able to demonstrate efficient use of the public purse and fulfil economic goals (DES, 1977b). During the 1980s, radical education reforms focused on schools; a National Curriculum was implemented and schools were removed from LEA control. Government began to change the legislative framework for further and higher education.

At this time Britain had one of the lowest growth rates among the developed economies. New problems included adolescent unemployment and increasing numbers of young people alienated from school (Davies, 1978). Further education colleges faced severe financial restraint, government made it clear that expansion was to be modest and legislation now entitled the Secretary of State to limit the amount of funding paid into the advanced further education pool (Local Government Planning and Land Act 1980, Section 63).

International competition drove the traditional industries, such as textiles, footwear, shipbuilding, steel and metal manufacturing, into decline. Labour costs became the major focus of attention as management tried to emulate the success of flexible Japanese firms (Aston and Maguire, 1991, p. 41).

The Advisory Council for Adult and Continuing Education recommended that further, adult and higher education be combined so that class and status divisions could be neutralised (ACACE, 1979, pp. 21–8). They criticised the government for failing to stimulate demand and only using intervention as crisis management. They recommended that the DES create a strategic plan for the development of basic adult education and suggested the creatio of a national development board. Concerns on all sides pointed to the need for a plan of action for non-advanced and adult education – the forgotten sectors.

The Adult Literacy Unit, which became the Adult Literacy and Basic Skills Unit, remained unable to gain any real position in the hierarchy of needs. Higher education funding also began to be driven by efficiency, now a central tenet of the Conservative government's mandate for change. In further education colleges the government began to bring about changes in college governance, the curriculum, the nature of the college and the way in which curricula were defined (FESC, 1983).

In response to the Warnock Report a new legislative framework was planned and a White Paper ('Special Needs in Education') was published in 1981. The intention was that further education colleges should focus on technical and vocational provision. Paradoxically, the Schools and Further Education Regulations 1981 encouraged convergence of further education colleges' provision with schools (Education Act, 1980). Separating general education from vocational education became increasingly difficult as both contained elements of basic education. In March 1981 the government issued official guidance to establish a core curriculum in schools, which altered GCE work in further education colleges (DES, 1981a).

The MSC continued to develop its work on training, although it was criticised for the poor level of training provided on the Youth Opportunities Programme. Once again a familiar story emerged from the White Paper, 'A

New Training Initiative', which suggested three main objectives: training or employment experience for all up to the age of 18; a skills training programme; and the establishment of an adult training programme (MSC, 1981). With the government's mind set on public spending cutback, the response was to suggest that an alternative route to achieving the objectives be found (DES, 1981b).

The Holland Report in 1977 had recommended a more coherent programme of training and work experience for low achievers deficient in literacy and numeracy skills (DES, 1977a). Re-emphasised in a DES circular, it was suggested these young learners responded better if their courses were related to the world of work (DES, 1977g). However, this report recommended that existing schemes be extended to meet these needs. There were to be no new experiments; the Youth Opportunities Programme re-emerged as the Youth Training Scheme (YTS) (DES, 1982d). MSC activity increased in the 16–18 year old market; with a qualification that could be achieved through an accumulation of credits, a new broad approach to vocational education and training was created for young people.[12]

Once again a familiar story emerged. The new initiatives were to provide young people with transferable skills that would enable them to deal with the dynamic nature of the business world. Similarly, the Labour Party had begun to consider education provision for 16–19 year olds. Indeed, Shirley Williams issued two consultative papers in 1979. Within a context of reducing public spending, the 1980s scheme was employer-based and only partly financed by government . Encouraging other training providers increased the competitive forum for the colleges. The MSC reduced the colleges' autonomy and eroded the position of the examining bodies by introducing a Training Standards Advisory Service, which was to approve and monitor the quality standards of training centres.

The MSC and the DES lacked strategic fit and the relationship was tense. The MSC focused on education for work while the DES regarded education as an alternative to work. The MSC had a flat management structure and so could make decisions quickly, whereas the LEA had a tall hierarchical management structure and could not. The LEA thought the MSC acted carelessly; the MSC thought the LEA sluggish.

The social benefit system did not encourage the unemployed to re-skill themselves, particularly those who received supplementary benefits. Yet the size and variation of courses taken up by post-16 non-advanced learners continued to grow against all odds. College systems became altered by the introduction of rolling contracts for courses, which increased their financial risk.

School-leavers were now finding it almost impossible to find work. So were many highly-skilled workers. Those jobs available tended to be part-time and more suitable for women (Aston and Maguire, 1991, p. 46). In response, the '21 hour rule' was actioned, whereby young unemployed people could at last take up to 21 hours of further education (DES, 1982c, para. 1). This was not such good news for the colleges because provision had to be accommodated through a rationalisation programme (DES, 1982d, para. 8).

The Employment and Training Act in 1981 decreased the number of Industrial Training Boards, favouring other non-statutory training organisations. The government, through the MSC, continued to move curricula in line with business needs. Several reports added to the growing belief that vocational courses would be more appropriate for some students (FEU, 1978). The government, with the MSC, commenced plans to deliver more vocationally relevant courses in full-time education and a new youth training scheme to succeed the Youth Opportunities Programme (DES, 1981b). It was clear to the colleges that the MSC would be responsible for these programmes.

By now it was obvious to government that youth unemployment was not a blip and it began planning a national approach to encourage young people and unemployed adults towards full-time education or a combination of work experience and college. Many young people seemed alienated from the work ethic and its aspirations, particularly in the north of England. As the rich and poor divide widened, civil unrest became an increasing threat. To make the poverty trap worse, it was found that children of unemployed parents achieved lower educational standards (Aston and Maguire, 1986) and were likely to be unemployed themselves (Payne, 1987).

Qualifications based on the accumulation of credits now segmented the learning experience and college processes began to change. The shift away from centrally-organised curricula threatened professionals' autonomy. The introduction of modular courses altered the delivery pattern and teaching practices within the colleges. Teaching terms and academic years no longer marked study completion. Sadly, once again without central organisation, modular systems reflected local school and college needs. The evident lack of cohesion in the curriculum attracted the critics, as did the poor in-depth knowledge achieved within a modular system of learning (Hitchcock, 1988). Nevertheless, modular systems are now common across the educational system.

The Conservative government, less than supportive of the youth service reviewed it in 1982. The Thompson Report (1982), a review of the youth service requested by government, recommended that LEAs retain responsibility and that it should continue to be funded by a combination of voluntary and statutory provision. However, it recommended that the DES coordinate the process (DES, 1982b).

The LEA and DES remit now overlapped, as did that colleges' governing body and the LEA. College governors found themselves caught between the power of the LEA, who were unhappy with the colleges autonomy, expressed through financing, and the power of the college's Academic Board. The relationship between the LEA and DES, who had dual funding responsibility, was further complicated by an increasing trend towards centralising higher education funding. The power of the LEAs were threatened and they began to fight back.

The LEAs remained responsible for planning and providing further education colleges, employing academic and administrative staff and providing in-service training. The principals of the colleges were responsible for developing curriculum and determining materials and equipment needs; Principals began to manage large budgets and resources. The Academic Board of a college, the principal and heads of departments now determined policy. As the Academic Board held hierarchical power, the governing body became the monitor of the college process. Purchasers now drove the institution and the complex structure of the colleges reflected the needs of those demands, thus the incrementalist approach to change that had now become central to the way the further education colleges' development continued unharmed.

In 1982 the MSC launched the Technical and Vocational Education Initiative (TVEI) for 14–18 year olds. Radically, this gave power not to the DES as normal but to the MSC to directly influence the education of young people. The aims of TVEI, which was funded by the MSC and LEAs, were familiar; to attract more 14–18 year olds into studying for qualifications or skills development to better equip them for employment. The LEAs now had to submit programmes to the MSC for approval and its control over local schemes thus diminished. Accommodation pressures in the colleges grew, but the LEAs were reminded that there were spare resources resulting from a general fall in student numbers: rationalisation was the game (DES, 1982d). Some attempt was made to increase industry's confidence in the changed curriculum (MSC, 1985).

A DES policy statement expressed concerns that courses currently available for post-16 qualifications did not meet those students' needs. Coupled with this, the hotchpotch of examining bodies served to confuse the consumer; clearly this situation had to be remedied (DES, 1982a).

Unemployment was growing, alongside the number of disillusioned young people whose needs had not been met by the compulsory education sector.

The debate in the UK focused on whether unemployment was caused by market forces, structural or cyclical events. Whatever the reason, with a tough economic climate, voluntary training collapsed. The government had to expand state run training programmes rapidly to fill the gap. Some saw the introduction of TVEI as a total reversal of the comprehensive ideal and expressed their fears that, once again, young people would be divided along the old lines, vocational and academic. Still of concern was whether the curriculum for non-advanced learners should simply be about training for the labour market, because it lacked the revolutionary approach required to change aspirations of these young people. Others argued that at least it stopped these young people taking a purely academic curriculum, which they would fail. It was clear the MSC spoke for the government on these matters.

A report that highlighted UK's poor levels of maths, over the whole range of ability, compared to Germany fuelled growing dissatisfaction with the welfare state.[13] Prais (1981) suggested that poor achievement levels in mathematics occurred because the UK system was a hotchpotch, which lacked central control and the narrow curriculum that existed in Germany. Germany's young people's training and socialisation to work programme was linked with their business success. One-sixth of the population in the UK now lived in poverty; supplementary benefit claims rose. Equal opportunity seemed merely to be some form of tokenism.

In 1983 the TEC and BEC were replaced by the Business and Tehnical Education Council (BTEC), a limited company and a registered educational charity. BTEC's remit was a familiar story: 'to advance the quality and availability of a wide range of employment related education, to the mutual benefit of the students, their current and future employers, and the national interests' (BTEC, 1983, p. 8). Government introduced a voucher system to enable students to purchase courses, creating the potential for power to move from the providers to the consumers. However, with a general election looming, this controversial approach disappeared from the overt political agenda.[14]

The Adult Literacy and Basic Skills Unit (1983) tried to establish a case for adult education, but lost the battle. The MSC made a bid to lead the continuing education service. In 1984, in retaliation, the DES introduced the REPLAN initiative for those involved in mid-career updating.[15] The DES then published 'Records of Achievement: A Statement of Policy', setting out the plan that by 1990, all 16 year olds would create records of their achievements, emphasising progress, personal achievement and increased social skills, not acquisition of knowledge (DES, 1984). Aping government, this moved power away from the professionals and the examination boards, towards the customer, allowing them a voice in decision-making. Student profiling became a central feature of the Certificate of Pre-Vocational Education (CPVE) and TVEI schemes. The Hargreaves Report highlighted the advantage of modular systems as short-term targeting tools (Hargreaves, 1984).

Following the Mansell Report (1978), in 1983 the DES invited BTEC to set up a joint board. CPVE was launched in 1985; this scheme offered post-16 full-time students an integrated training and education programme by joint attendance at school and college for one year. Now there was CPVE launched by the DES and TVEI by the MSC. Caught in the battle, colleges and schools had to deliver on both and inevitably they pulled the organisations in different directions. The two initiatives altered curricula and teaching styles within the colleges. Increasing the onslaught on professional autonomy, experiential, negotiated learning and student profiling drove courses away from specialist lines.[16] Government's introduction of compulsory work experience caused schools and colleges to be involved in finding work experience placements; with employers largely disinterested, one lecturer described many students as 'spending their work experience photocopying and making tea'.

In 1984 the government began to look seriously at 'A' levels. Government rhetoric highlighted the welfare state as producer-dominated.[17] Extreme Left wing local authorities refused to cut expenditure, which seemed to influence public opinion out of all proportion and provided legitimacy to the assertion that the producers did indeed have power as the government suggested. It also legitimised the Secretary of State for Education's taking a leading role (Maclure, 1988a).

In 1985 there were 64,096 full-time equivalent students attending courses. Small colleges had merged into 489 large maintained colleges, of which 31 were voluntary and direct grant colleges (DES, 1986b, Table G1). Further education became reclassified into seven categories, namely: polytechnics and major colleges, with 50 per cent of students in advanced work or over 500 full-time equivalent students involved in advanced work; intermediate colleges, comprising 10 per cent or more advanced students; minor colleges; art and design colleges; agricultural colleges; monotechnic colleges, which were classified differently, by specialist subject area. Type of work was now categorised as laboratory/workshop, art and design, or classroom-based (DES, 1985d).

The government commissioned an audit of further and higher education (1985). Reflecting the government's derision of the welfare state, the Audit Commission's (1985) findings pointed to slack and wastage in the system.

Seemingly unaware, the Commission combined the two differentiated sectors, further and higher education, in their report despite the fact that they had very little in common. Nevertheless, accountability, efficiency and effectiveness became part of the further education colleges' new agenda (DES, 1991). The report intimated that monitoring of professionals' tasks would increase. The radical move to erode professional autonomy was at last made explicit.

The Further Education Act (1985) received Royal Assent. In this Act the government increased the competitive forum for the colleges. They were now able to engage in commercial activities; LEAs were also able to lend money to companies to facilitate teaching activities (DES, 1985c, para. 7.1). The government made it clear that colleges should look to other forms of funding and should not rely on the public purse. Entrepreneurial behaviour thus became part of a further education college's agenda. In 1986 colleges were further reclassified as polytechnics and large, small or tertiary colleges (DES, 1986b).

The MSC was now well established as the vehicle for government policy, neutering the LEAs. The MSC had the resources to influence the direction of educational developments and the LEA began to suffer from lack of resources. Some shared the views of Shirley Williams (1986):

> the DES is powerless ... the Cabinet, impatient to get things done, has used the one weapon to hand, the centrally funded MSC, in consequence the MSC has invaded or taken over very large areas of education and training. It is not accountable to local authorities or even education ministers, and is resented by them.

Resolving the need for a single system of examining at 16-plus, GCE and CSE qualifications were replaced by the General Certificate of Secondary Education (GCSE). Some saw this as a victory for the comprehensive system, others saw it as an opportunity to improve standards; it thus gained support from political Left and Right.

The increasing emphasis on independent learning began to throw up problems; it relied on a mature approach to learning not evident in low ability students for whom the initiative was introduced, thus failure rates continued to be a problem. With no policy to change it, the low status of training programmes remained. The changing economic context created the need for a flexible workforce. To reduce delays in training, the 21-hour rule was amended to allow MSC training to contribute towards the qualifying period for benefit (DES, 1984a).

1987 involved all LEAs in TVEI because the government, through the MSC, was investing cash to ensure its development. In the battle for power the MSC was winning. Critics argued that curricula for these young people should not be driven simply by training for the labour market, but by now it was clear that government was pursuing education as job training. The economic climate was now in downturn; there were few jobs for these young people (Hitchcock, 1988). Falling student numbers continued to legitimise a rationalisation programme (DES, 1987b).

The Education Act 1986 was focused on the government of schools; pursuing the Conservative government's stance on accountability, it increased the public's right to see minutes of colleges' governors' meetings (Section 62). Paradoxically, student representatives on governing bodies had to leave any meetings where staffing was discussed, effectively reducing customer awareness (Section 61). A code of practice for meetings was also introduced (Section 43).[18] Yet another White Paper on training and education saw the pilot scheme of TVEI launched into a national initiative, but with reduced funding (DES, 1986a). Once again, the need for an improved programme for technical and vocational education was seen as vital to ensuring an increase in participation rates. However, following the government's focus on reducing the welfare state, responsibility was placed on the individual and the employers.

The MSC and the DES completed a review of vocational training, this led to the introduction of a National Council for Vocational Qualifications, replacing the plethora of examining bodies (MSC/DES, 1986). By 1987, NVQs had four levels: basic, standard, advanced and higher. The plan was that NVQs would replace degrees in the university sector. Continuing developments of education based on standards of competence, as defined by industry-led boards, profession autonomy became increasingly subject to threat. The competitive forums for further education colleges continued to increase – they now competed with each other and with schools, which were better resourced.

By now, the legitimacy of the MSC was questionable; it had not properly investigated the skills base of the 14–24 year olds for whom it was responsible. The MSC accused the further education colleges of not meeting market needs: provision for technology and robotics was identified as particularly poor. Some of the LEAs were angry because the rate support grant, their most important form of independent funding, was falling. To make matters worse, money was being redirected by the government to the MSC, thus LEA power was being deliberately eroded even though they were a publicly-elected local voice. The MSC argued that further education colleges had to become more market-oriented; in reality it meant as dictated by them.

Radically different methods of government financial responsibility emerged in 1987. The Conservative government announced that education establishments providing a high proportion of advanced further education would become independent corporate bodies funded by a newly-established Polytechnics and Colleges Funding Council (PCFC). The era of democratic teacher participation and control of curriculum and examinations ended. The School Curriculum Development Committee and the Secondary Examinations Council, neither of which included teacher representatives, replaced the old Schools Council. At the same time, the cut in the rate support grant from 60 per cent in 1979 to 47 per cent in 1987 further eroded the financial muscle of the LEAs.

The 1988 Education Reform Act finally neutered the power of the LEAs. Quickly followed by the 1992 Further and Higher Education Act, further education colleges were moved to the private sector. Further education colleges became a casualty of New Right political ideology, which challenged the perceived wisdom of educationalists and tested public perceptions about the purpose of education. Conservative rhetoric during the 1980s had claimed diseconomies of scale and empire within state enterprises; a central tenet of the debate in the early 1990s was decentralisation and reduced government interventionism. Paradoxically, the Secretary of State increased central powers over local discretion. The MSC had become hierarchical and directive, with wide-ranging activities in politically sensitive territory. The LEAs, having responded to government changes, found that they had less funding under the YTS scheme than the YOP schemes (FESC, 1983).

Continuing the Conservative government's attempt to control the education sector the 1988 Education Reform Act increased the intervention powers of the Secretary of State, whilst at the same time it altered the basic power structure of the education system; as a result the duties of the LEAs became more specific and less autonomous whilst schools and governing bodies had greater autonomy. Central government now had powers over the curriculum, combined with a formal system to enforce it. At the same time, Part 3 of the Education Reform Act 1988 restructured former inner London councils. The LEA retained responsibility for the further education development plan.

All was far from plain sailing in the further education colleges and tensions between the principals and the government began to develop. Some college principals argued that the data used as the basis for the development of government policy documents – for example, 'Obtaining Better Value from Further Education' (Audit Commission, 1985) – did not fairly represent the issues.[19] They began to put pressure on the government to represent their interests more fairly.

Quality assurance, established through competition, was at the core of the Act; it was argued that the 1944 Act had failed to deliver the homogeneous service needed and so equal opportunity had not been achieved. Diversity and choice replaced equal opportunity as a central tenet of educational provision. An enterprise culture replaced collectivism; as a result public faith in any level of education as inherently a good thing continued to be challenged. Now education had to be measured by its output and the relationship that output had to economic development. The New Right thus made a previous illegitimate discourse legitimate.

The aim of the government's revision programme was to provide standard measures so that customers could compare services.[20] In 1988 standard divisors used by the colleges to calculate their income changed and they became based on a national average of full-time students per week. This caused local differences and local needs to be excluded.[21] Colleges were not being treated fairly; inconsistencies, particularly around the funding of high resource use courses, and the changes in the statistics added to the growing general mêlée. Finally, the Joint Efficiency Study, a combination of DES and local authority, recommended that the Annual Monitoring Survey be revised in the 1988/9 survey.

In response to the 1988 Act and the Further and Higher Education Act 1992, a new independent further education sector was established, comprising semi-autonomous institutions operating in a quasi market. The stated aim of the 1992 Act had a familiar ring – to ensure equal status between academic and vocational qualifications. The then Secretary of State, Kenneth Clark, pointed to further education as having: 'a vital role in providing education and training ... have never been given the attention that their importance in educational policy should justify' (*Hansard*, 1991a, p. 432). Further education colleges now became a main focus for the implementation of the government's education and training policies.

Part 2 of the 1992 Act increased the competitive forum in which further education colleges functioned; they now found themselves funded by an annual budget together with a sum calculated on the student numbers enrolled. Coupled with this, the new statistical methodology for funding was focused on performance indicators.[22] College budgets, efficiency and the college's course portfolio were linked. Perhaps more importantly, a process had been put into place where one college could now be compared to another. Indeed, the Act stated that as corporate entities, the colleges could go out of business – they could be sued and governors could be removed if affairs were 'mismanaged' (Further and Higher Education Act 1992, Sections 15–16). In

1991 the government introduced a charter for further education, which drove the colleges to create their own performance targets (DES, 1993a). The professionals, however, no longer determined these targets to measure performance. Measuring achievement became standard practice and comparability of college performance was heralded as benefiting consumer sovereignty by providing tools for choice (FEFC, 1994).

In 1993/4 the now-incorporated colleges became funded by the Further Education Funding Council (FEFC), a government quango; further education thus became distanced from government grant-financing and had to bid for funding. The further education sector became reclassified into geographical categories: Greater London; metropolitan boroughs; and English counties. The university sector now came under the funding regime of the Higher Education Funding Council (HEFCE). Survival had become the dominant aim of the colleges.

Following the Conservatives' stance on accountability, national targets for education and training were introduced for the year 2000. Sixty per cent of young people by the age of 21 were to achieve two 'A' levels, GNVQ or NVQ level three, 85 per cent of 19 year olds' were to achieve five GCSEs at grade C or above, intermediate GNVQ or NVQ level two and 75 per cent of those aged 19 were to achieve NVQ level two competence in core skills communication, numeracy and information technology; 35 per cent of young people were expected to achieve NVQ level three by the age of 21. As the further education colleges provided most of the courses at these levels, they were destined to become embroiled in achieving these targets. The government merged the Departments for Education and Employment, further reinforcing the link between the two in the public mind, and value for money became part of the discourse of public accountability.

In 1995 the government asked Sir Ron Dearing to conduct a review of 16–19 year olds' qualifications. The Conservative government's targets for education and training for the year 2000 demanded a familiar outcome; increased participation rates, reduced failure and wastage rates and an increase in achievement without compromising standards. It was a predetermined context that bounded future choices, to which the incoming Labour government had promised to pay particular regard (DfEE, 1995c, para. 4.4).

The Dearing Report suggested that achievement of the national targets for the year 2000 implied a substantial increase in take-up and pass rates; furthermore, it suggested that, since participation in 'A' levels had increased from 11 per cent in 1964 to one-third in 1994, participation could be close to its maximum and thus further increases would have to come from vocational qualifications. At the same time, the report suggested that there was an implied time lag of 10 years before the NVQ qualifications would be understood and trusted by society at large. Once again there were no clear market signals suggesting that these targets would be met

The report states that 'a new approach to youth training with a re-launch with a new national identity'; hardly new, it focused on a national framework for qualifications with three main pathways developing further the NVQ framework.[23] The report also suggested that an increase in apprenticeships based on NVQ qualifications could be delivered in partnership with further education colleges. Again a familiar story – those of lower attainment were to be offered education that would make them employable. National records of achievement, it suggested, should be relaunched and 'A' levels maintained with some changes to develop the broad remit of the AS level

Under the heading of 'removing barriers to achievement', where one might expect a discourse about ensuring equal opportunity, the report refers to the paucity of high quality updated information and recommends that present arrangements be reviewed (ibid., p. 151). Furthermore, the report refers to the need for career guidance, reducing the discourse about equal opportunity to one of market information, aping the Conservatives' stance on market needs.

With growing public concern about accountability in public life, the Nolan Committee published its second report, the second chapter of which concentrated on higher and further education (Nolan Report, 1996). The report made it clear that resources for students in both higher and further education colleges had not kept pace with increased numbers and that in consequence further education colleges were now under considerable financial and administrative pressure.[24]

Accepting the view of the Holland Report that further education colleges' governance should be rooted in local governance, the Nolan Report states that freedom from the LEA had produced clear lines of accountability, namely, the FEFC to the Secretary of State to Parliament, through the National Audit Office to the Public Accounts Committee. Even so, more consistency across national provision was needed.[25] Paradoxically, the report that states the views of the local authority, as the only elected body, must remain significant. Furthermore, national lines of accountability were identified as causal to policy being distanced from the community, even though colleges published more information about themselves in the spirit of more openness.

Interestingly. the report continues: 'One of the weaknesses of central finance for local bodies is their tendency to be driven into wholly centralised control by the important need to safeguard public money', which weakens local responsibility and accountability whilst giving local bodies autonomy (Nolan Report, 1996, para. 374). Consequently, the report states, strong frameworks, rules and procedures have to be in place to protect local accountability. The report also suggests establishing a Public Affairs Forum as a possible way of resolving the new relationship between local agents.[26]

That colleges should have an independent review process was seen as essential: 'as normal good practice that the procedure has to be combined with a statement, made publicly available, of the service standards which the user can expect from the body concerned, and against which failure to perform can be measured' (ibid., para. 384). In 1996 the DES set up a Further Education Staff Development Forum; its remit was to act as a lead body for the further education sector and it began work to develop a national standard.

In 1997 the Kennedy Report on widening participation, in line with the Dearing Report, suggested the colleges as subjects for the development of national targets (FEFC, 1997c). In contrast to the Conservative government's stance, perhaps in anticipation of a Labour administration, market principles alone, it stated, would not widen participation quickly enough for society's needs; the report therefore suggested a funded and combined national and local framework to stimulate demand. However, aping market-speak, the system was to comprise strategic partnerships between contributing agencies, again reinforcing the shift away from government interventionism.

The White Paper 'Learning to Compete' in 1996 had, the report states, to some extent alleviated concerns about widening participation. Modern apprenticeships had now been introduced to attract 16–17 year olds into work-based training, to achieve an NVQ level three – the intention was to expand this to the 18–19 age group. The report thus focused on post-18 and suggested a new learning pathway for those who were eligible for full fee remission, the unemployed and those on state benefits, and those who had not achieved academically. Within a context of no free lunch, colleges wishing to provide this service had to demonstrate their capability to the FEFC, which had outlined key elements of success.[27]

In May 1997 New Labour took power, with high employment compared to other leading economies and total social security budget at 13 per cent of GDP.[28] Britain had the highest number of people living in poverty and high labour market participation and poverty could no longer be only associated to unemployment (Hutton, 1997). There was growing evidence of a divide between young people who entered jobs which demanded an extended period of education and the rest, who remained subject to semiskilled jobs, 'blind alley' jobs or no jobs (Brown and Scase, 1991, p. 91). In effect the only thing that had changed was the increasing number of young people caught in this trap.

Very quickly it became clear that New Labour, hugging the political centre, intended to restructure the welfare state. In line with much of old Labour policy, there was to be a windfall-profits tax to finance work and training for unemployed young people. Disincentives to work were to be reviewed and the social security system updated to remove gender bias. The government's economic and social strategy, however, was unclear.

In June 1997 the Secretary of State for Education and Employment established the National Advisory Group for Continuing Education and Lifelong Learning: its first task was to publish a report on lifelong learning by November 1997 (Fryer, 1997). This report, identifying cultural obstacles to change as common, suggests the government must plan and lead the changes with 'enthusiasm, vision and with commitment' to win over all the stakeholders. It suggested government should conduct a widespread publicity campaign (ibid., p. 90). The report refers to the need of a culture of lifelong learning to permeate society because such a culture is a resource in a dynamic world where global forces exert increasing influence.[29]

> Achieving this will entail profound changes in our culture and our approach to the world of work ... It will mean a switch of emphasis in our assumptions, in people's aspirations, in funding and provision. We need to change our whole approach to achievement and its measurement and even the very language and vocabularies used to describe learning opportunities (ibid., p. 13, para. 2.11).

A New Deal initiative is identified in the report as crucial to enabling a reversal of rising social inequalities which had culminated in alienation and hostility to education institutions by those very people who needed lifelong learning experiences. The report points to many research findings suggesting that social class determines whether individuals can take advantage of opportunities and attainment. New national targets were suggested as a way to reflect wider participation and achievements.

The report also suggested that educational institutions become providers, the learners managing their own learning with support. Some lecturers managing learning at the chalkface began to express concerns that non-advanced learners were again suffering from a general lack of consideration for their learning needs.

Aping Conservative ideology, New Labour spoke of the need to alter the dependency culture, replacing it with a philosophy based on 'help them to help themselves'. The Prime Minister, Tony Blair, along with the Chancellor, Gordon Brown, and the Social Security Secretary, Harriet Harman, depicted social security as a failing system (Macaskil, 1997). Leaked documents made public a Cabinet split on welfare reforms. David Blunkett, the Education Secretary, spoke against cuts in Disability Allowance. Nevertheless, a Welfare to Work Programme was launched on 5 January 1998.

The New Deal, focused on 18–24 year olds, attracted more students than expected on the education strand; this also included participation in employment, environmental or voluntary work. In the academic year 1996/97 the FEFC estimated that some 280,00 students in colleges were on courses while unemployed, against the government estimation of 80,000 (FEFC Annual Statistics, 1996/97). The colleges expressed concerns that these candidates might have to leave their courses to find work and therefore began to press for New Dealers to be able to choose between full-time college or work. The government announced that £700 million would be available for the development of this initiative; the further education colleges could bid to provide the education and training strands of the New Deal. The New Deal went nationwide on 1 April and it was mooted this would be extended over the age of 25 from June ('First Students Enrol in £700 million New Deal', *FE Now*, 1998, p. 1).

The FEFC indicated that in 1999/2000 London colleges would receive a one-off payment to help to keep them financially afloat. Other colleges expressed their concerns that these colleges should be singled out. The FEFC agreed to hold a national review of institutional and geographical differences. It promised to put up more money to provide more courses for 16–19 year olds, some from the 'Kennedy money' targeted to broaden participation in deprived areas ('FEFC to Bail Out London – For Now', *FE Now*, 1998). By now, however, colleges had become cautious of short-term funding.

The skills mismatch worsened but the required changes in skills did not take place. Employment sectors with hard to fill vacancies were: manufacturing; mining, utilities and construction; distribution and consumer services; finance and business services, transport public and other (Hancock, 1998). The National Skills Agenda promised by the Education and Employment Secretary David Blunkett in November 1998, is still awaited at the time of writing and, in any case, colleges are unlikely to be able to provide state-of-the-art equipment to fulfil the changing needs.

As further education colleges begin to move even more centre stage NATFHE's General Secretary, Paul Mackney (1998b), suggested the trend towards short-term staff contracts, created by Conservative legislation, should be reversed and efforts made to reinstall respect for lecturers in order to maintain quality. It was rumoured the Select Committee on Further Education would focus on teaching quality and increase in standards, perhaps leading to a national training organisation for further education as well as providing opportunities to update industrial experience (Dutton, 1998).

Reflection

The diversity of provision that further education colleges supply, along with the number of their influencing agents, has made tracking the historical data very difficult, which in turn has created difficulties in telling the story about the development of further education colleges. Telling the story through a retrospective thematic approach tends to make changes and decisions appear rational, since the emotions of the moment often tend not to be recorded and the rich text is thus lost.

The need for increased attainment in education and training, in order to increase the UK's competitive edge, has featured as a central story line. It has long been recognised that there is a need for an educational route other than the academic one to foster greater participation in education and training. It is clear that the interaction between employees and employers has been insufficient to generate the level of participation in education and training required to meet national needs; in any case skills mismatch has become a permanent feature of industrialised economies. In 1944, those involved in reconstructing the education system had a vision of equal opportunity; this was to be achieved through the establishment of parity of difference between different systems of achievement. I have been able to identify the consistent failure of government to achieve that parity of difference; indeed it never emerged as a central concern of government. Because the attainment of equality in the education system was dependent on a wider social reconstruction programme, it did not materialise.

The kinds of controversy exposed in this story, such as selection procedures to preserve high standards (Cox and Dyson, 1971), were legitimised because they provide options for different aptitudes (Norwood, 1965) while at the same time being identified as divisive, restricting opportunity (Donnison, 1965) and wasting some of the nation's ability (Robbins, 1965). Taylor-Goody (1994) suggests that such controversy will emerge where the ideal of equal opportunity is matched with the reality of a working world that includes unequal labour markets, class and gender inequalities.

The vision of parity of difference was eroded by society's attitude to selection procedures, which reflected old upper class values, ultimately benefitting a minority of learners. Further, the story reveals that the average worker rejects these traditional learning mechanisms very early on in the history of education. Significant changes to the participation rates in education and training have thus been hindered by an education system based on a hierarchy that values pure academic achievement above any other. Although the growth of professionalisation has to some extent altered the balance, training still has a low status in society at large. Indeed, there is no evidence to suggest that any serious attempt has been made to achieve parity over the study period. The story is one of crisis management by government despite many reports that justify something much better. With no real challenge made by government to change traditional prejudices, further education colleges have emerged as second class systems exemplifying those inequalities.

The story reveals further education colleges being consistently left out of mainstream legislation and driven by the growing power of the influencing agents around them. They have continued to operate in an amoebic and chameleonic way, changing with demand. Acting autonomously, they have developed a complex course portfolio that meets both local and national needs. Despite the lack of cohesive central government support, further education colleges have played an important role in providing a route for social mobility; the further education colleges have continued to provide a service and some people have continued to better themselves, one might say despite everything.

Prior to the 1985 Act, further education colleges operated in a difficult and diverse power net of complex relationships and it became difficult for the government to alter policy and control implementation (Parkes, 1982). With successive governments managing crisis and adopting a short-term perspective, the need to target funding became paramount. Harris (1993) suggests that the professional politician gains credibility by action. She argues that changes to the education system, both in 1944 and in 1988, were simply tools of action used by the politicians to raise their profile; the coalition government in 1944 needed to demonstrate social changes were in the pipeline and in 1988 Mrs Thatcher needed to regain public interest after a long period of Conservative rule (Glennerster, 1995). Although this may present a gloomy picture of reality, it has to be conceded that the need for increased participation in further education was not new and this would explain why further education colleges suddenly leapt into the limelight in the 1980s.

Nevertheless, the social reforms in the 1940s had their roots in socialism, which was deemed to have failed in the 1970s. Perhaps the Conservative government felt that the time was right for it to express its political ideology, which had been effectively watered down since the 1900s. Whilst socialism appeared to work, the Conservative government could not attempt to alter the public mind, but when socialist ideas appeared to be going wrong it was able to launch a legitimate alternative discourse.

Although we cannot be sure of the reasons behind the changes in the system of education, change was inevitable from the 1970s when the Conservatives began a discourse of derision based on the failure of the welfare state, which ultimately legitimised their stance on the reduction and rationalisation of the welfare state, and Labour introduced the discourse of inadequacy. Morris and Greggs have dubbed the 1970s and 1980s as wasted years. Certainly the 1970s were a watershed for the ideals of equal opportunity: a battle could have taken place and did not. However, this story has revealed that the reasons lie further back in time and seem to be associated with the failure to win workers' rights during the General Strike, which caused radical change to be swapped for incremental change in order to have popular appeal. This allowed tradition, and in particular traditional attitudes to education, to continue to play a significant part in the changes that followed, serving in some way to prevent equal opportunity becoming a government mission.

The incrementalist approach to change also served to justify the failure to implement the 1944 Act on the grounds of increasing financial strain; slowly but surely social justice became deemed unaffordable. How we can justify this to future generations I do not know; these other learners' needs have been neglected even by those institutions set up to serve them. Attracting functional context learners and those who have priorities other than academic and career oriented implied turning the world upside-down. Bennett et al. (1995) suggest that since employers do not reward low-level vocational qualifications, young people behaved rationally in not participating in training; indeed they suggest that vocational study will only achieve parity with academic qualifications when employers reward them to the same extent. It is clear that competitive advantage, so much needed for global competition, is reliant on the skill levels of the younger generation, which the market has been unable to provide.

Through this investigation of documentation, a trend towards a more organised compact system of further education provision gained momentum post-1988. Lee (1991) suggests that a 'workfare' principle – the substitution of wage for security benefits in return for work – was introduced to youth employment. He contends that surrogate work began under a Labour administration with the introduction of the YOP schemes. Although the principle may be the same, the new initiatives post 1988 have significantly changed the administrative practices and relationships between central and local government, which in turn have significantly altered the way further education colleges do business both internally and externally and have brought them more in line with market orientations.

In order to legitimise the process of making a serious bid for change, particularly at the national level, the Conservative government had to be able to express its ideology in a way that was capable of challenging the dominant set of beliefs. This new ideological perspective had also to render illegitimate the decentralised autonomy of the professional operating in that sector. To do this they used the simple language of the market, competition coupled with financial muscle. Commensurate with this, Conservative policies increased consumer sovereignty, altering value to value for money. To date New Labour appears to endorse rather than challenge these tools of change. Hugging the political centre, New Labour appears to be more in tune with incremental change than with revolution. As a result the social revolution needed to ensure parity of difference is in danger of remaining a vision rather than a mission.

Notes

1 Set up to look at ways of increasing prestige of scientific and technical training.
2 This report highlighted the need for a national approach to ensure provision and suggested a hierarchy of qualifications, block release and sandwich courses (MoE, 1959c).
3 This report suggested that professional organisations should include some management courses and that management qualifications should have credibility in their own right (MoE, 1947).
4 The instrument of government established the governing body and its composition. The articles of government outlined the conduct of the college, the function of the LEA, the governing body, the principal and the Academic Board.
5 Category A colleges had substantial levels of advanced work, Category B colleges only a certain amount of advanced work whereas category C colleges were without any significant amount of advanced work.
6 The Academic Board was to consist of a principal, vice-principal, heads of department, the chief administrative officer, the librarian and not less than six staff and student members. The governors had overall responsibility, although the Board was responsible for planning, coordination and development of the academic work of the college. In this sense it was legislative.
7 The Robbins Report suggested that estimates for growth in higher education might be low. Robbins had estimated 8.6 per cent growth by 1968; this was already 9.6 per cent. The planning paper published by the DES based its work on the Robbins projections (ACACE, 1979).
8 Speech by the Rt Hon James Callaghan, MP at a foundation stone-laying ceremony at Ruskin College, Oxford, 18 October 1976.

9   Ibid.
10 This scheme was based on the recommendations of the White Paper 'Young People and Work', published in 1977. It comprised a year-long course with a combined system of work experience and vocational education
11 The 1944 Education Act (Section 41) stated the LEAs had a duty to provide for further education for full- and part-time courses for persons over school-leaving age. The provision for 16–19 year olds had become mandatory in secondary schools, but provision was decided locally for further education. See DES 1978. The LEAs were identified as being remiss in their duty to secure mandatory provision in the further education sector.
12 The programme was delivered either as a one year for 17 year olds or two year for 16 year olds. Individual training agreements were made in a context of nationally-agreed standards of training.
13 Prof. Sig Prais (Prais and Wagner, 1983) concluded that German pupils in the bottom range of ability achieved levels of performance comparable with the whole range of ability in England and Wales. The bottom 40 per cent of pupils were thus well below that of one of Britain's major competitors.
14 Writers in free market economics had made it clear there was a need for government to separate funding from provision. It was assumed that choice was better in the hands of the consumer rather than the producer.
15 REPLAN was part of the DES Professional Industrial and Commercial Updating programme designed to expand the student's skills for work.
16 Secretary of State for Education Sir Keith Joseph called for an education system to take into account the principles of breadth, relevance, differentiation and balance (Nottingham, January 1984).
17 They took on the government and lost; new contracts followed with the introduction of the Teachers' Pay and Conditions Act 1987.
18 This placed a duty on those participating in the government of colleges to secure freedom of speech as given in law for members, students, employees and visiting speakers. Education Act (No. 2) Section 43, 1986.
19 Principals complained that the national average sample size of 29 per cent in 1980/81 was too small. The number of surveyed colleges was subsequently increased to 99 per cent of advanced and 70 per cent of non-advanced work during the period 1984/85.
20 The standard divisors are now used to convert part-time students to full-time equivalents (FTEs). Standard divisors vary according to course group, level of education and type of establishment.
21 In previous years the convergence of part-time students to FTEs had been based on the average weekly hours of each college's full-time students (DES, 1988/89).
22 The Annual Monitoring Survey, 1992/93, p. iv, defines the terms as follows:

average class size: the year's total of student timetable hours divided by the year's total of staff timetable hours;
average lecturer timetable hours: the year's total of staff timetable hours divided by staff FTEs numbers multiplied by the standard number of weeks in the academic year;
average student timetable hours: the year's total of student timetable hours divided by student FTEs numbers multiplied by the standard number of weeks in the academic year;
student:staff ratios (SSRs): student FTEs numbers divided by staff FTEs numbers. Gross and net SSRs exclude academic staff not working in direct support of teaching (exclusions and abatements).

23 'A' level and GCSE focused on subject and discipline. GNVQ was designed to develop knowledge, understanding and skills associated to broad areas of employment. Vocational training focused on the qualification necessary for a trade or profession (DfEE, 1995c, Section 16, p. 137).
24 By this time 70 per cent of further education colleges' income was derived from the FEFC and 14 per cent from other funds, including the European Union.
25 Along with the principles of openness and transparency, further education colleges were now required by regulation to make agendas, minutes and papers available to the public.
26 The Nolan Report refers to Kirklees Metropolitan District: a forum may discuss a topic which affects the Council and one other agency involved in public service in a public meeting culminating in a report (Nolan Report, 1996, para. 376).
27 'Identify and reach under-represented groups in the area without them needing to enter the institution, help the learner to make informed choices, provide opportunities to enter at a basic level, and monitor progress' (FEFC, 1997a, p 8).
28 USA, Japan, Canada, Germany, France, Italy.
29 Lifelong learning implies the implementation of a system that is guided by the same core principles across all stages, elements and levels of learning. The vision is built on equity, variety and diversity.

Chapter Five

The Archaeological System of Knowledge and its Discursive Roots

This chapter compares and contrasts the language themes used in government circulars, administrative memoranda, White Papers and reports related to further education during 1944–97 to reveal whether those themes have altered over time. The documents are analysed using a retrospective thematic analysis.

Circulars, administrative memoranda, White Papers and reports interpret government intention in accessible language; a selection of these is thus used to represent the attitudes and approaches of government to further education over time. While circulars and administrative memoranda are not enforceable by law, they are part of a government's administrative and communication process for the further education sector. These include reference to policy implementation and operating procedures; in addition they sometimes advise or invite discussion. Circulars and memoranda comprise the formal communication channels between the Secretary of State, on behalf of the government, and local authorities and further education colleges. The selection of documents has been dictated by the need to represent the study period.

The language themes used in the documentation are assessed using both qualitative and quantitative approaches. It is hoped that through this process any differences between messages and communication over the study period will be identified. This chapter adopts a qualitative approach to content analysis; the general tone and content of the documents are evaluated against sequential history. This approach provides the opportunity for comparison, over the study period, of the general educational themes. In the next chapter, quantitative analysis will be further used to isolate any trends in the use of particular words and themes.

My starting assumption is that a language for the market paradigm exists. Nevertheless, I recognise that communication through language is far from simple as it involves a complex combination of linked assumptions, symbols and myth. Hence, the possibility of finding objective or absolute truth by this process is rejected.

From 1979 onwards, the Conservative government reduced the complexity of human interaction by looking at the functioning of our economy as if it were a market. Black (1962) suggests that such metaphors are used in communication as a shorthand route to knowledge because they simply present conceptual archetypes. Metaphors thus provide a way for us to understand reality by extrapolating one experience in terms of another.[1]

In a free market prices are determined purely by supply and demand, thus government intervention is at a minimum. The metaphor of the market suggests the existence of a common understanding of value, which is expressed in price: exchange is thus easy and without cost. In reality, value is often very hard to determine, particularly where a service is concerned. Indeed, welfare state development was justified just because market failure occurred. Economic development became dependent on some goods and services being paid out of direct taxation or provided at a socially acceptable level and price. The re-emergence of the market metaphor in the 1980s contained, therefore, a direct challenge to the continued development of the welfare state and government intervention.

Metaphor is used as shorthand for communication, circumventing the need to articulate beliefs encapsulated within it. When a root metaphor is strong it acts as a sentence substitute and communicates generally-accepted norms of knowledge and understanding (Turner, 1974). Metaphors can thus become insulated from disproof because the assumptions on which the metaphor is based are not open to investigation. Consequently, with the use of metaphor in language comes the risk that current thought and knowledge can be bounded. The ability to alter a root metaphor can be a powerful tool of change as it can mark the beginning of a self-fulfilling prophecy. Making explicit any changes that take place is thus worthy of study.

To bring further education colleges more in line with its ideology, the Conservative government had to alter the drivers of those colleges. Its ability to do this was dependent on the power of the root metaphor market to effect decision-making within those colleges. The market metaphor encapsulates all the assumptions of a materialistic system; it is the commercialisation of human interaction.[2] If market language became dominant further education colleges would organise to supply the market and meet the demand, they would internalise the central tenet of materialism, namely profit, which would become its major driver. It could thus affect the measurement of educational value.

The rhetoric of the Conservative government post-1980s suggested that its policy was revolutionary. I thought it important to confront this claim and discover whether the changes made by this government were indeed revolutionary. If so, then it will be possible to identify a new set of ideas and assumptions emerging from analysis of the documentation. If, on the other hand, the changes represent a re-emergence of the Victorian values of economic liberation, individualism, self-help and private paternalism, these values will be evident.

The Changing Face of Government Intervention

Prior to the 1943 White Paper on Educational Reconstruction the system of education and training available to the general population was unregulated and of poor quality (Maclure, 1965). By 1997, in stark contrast, there was an established system of compulsory full-time education up to the age of 16: also provision for post-16 full- and part-time education. It is fair to say that changes had been dramatic. I set out to discover what language themes caused these changes to take place.

In order to promote growth in educational advancement the Education Act 1921 increased a parent's legal obligations to include a child's educational achievement. It states: 'It shall be the duty of the parent of every child between the age of 5 and 14 ... to cause that child to receive efficient elementary instruction in reading, writing and arithmetic' (MoE, 1943, para. 11). However, by the 1940s we find: 'this looks back to the times when all that was demanded or provided was a strictly "elementary" education in the three Rs designed to secure a minimum of literacy' (ibid.).

Indeed, by 1948 compulsory education up to the age of 14 was inadequate to bring about the needed increase in the masses' abilities required to support the growth in industrialisation: 'It is now generally accepted that fourteen is too early, in the conditions of modern life, for full time schooling to cease, as it does at present for some ninety per cent of the population' (ibid.). A central theme that runs through much of the education legislation for further education is thus based on the assumption that there is a correlation between an individual's educational advancement and a country's economic growth. This assumption can be found clearly expressed in 1943:

> upon the education of the people of this country the fate of this country depends (ibid., para. 1).

> Its place of pre-eminence in world manufacture and world markets has long been fading. More and more in the future will it be necessary to rely on the capacity, adaptability and the quality, of our industrial and commercial personnel ... (ibid., para. 68).

The 1943 White Paper encapsulated the general feeling of the times, that government had to intervene to create and control an educational system because the free market had failed to deliver the required increase in trained personnel (Cross Report, 1888; Bryce Report, 1895).[3] The need for revolutionary changes in the approach to education and training for the masses coupled with a centralised, controlled system to provide them became part of the social agenda. This can be seen in the 1943 White Paper: 'Education for the majority of children offers at present an example of underexposure, underdevelopment and insufficient fixing.' Human potential was being wasted (MoE, 1943, para. 66).

The early 1940s marked a distinctive period for education policy, where government intervention in an individual's education up to the age of 18 was seen as crucial to achieving the much-needed increased participation rates in education and training nationally.

> When the period of full-time compulsory schooling ends the young person will continue under educational influences up to the age of 18 either by remaining in full-time attendance at a secondary school, or by part-time day attendance at a young people's college ... the benefit of medical inspection and treatment will be available without charge. Opportunities for technical and adult education will be increased (ibid., para. 3).

The coalition government thus took responsibility for changing the social context, to bring it more in line with the needs of the economy. The attitude adopted was paternalistic; it acted as a super-parent, caring for the physical as well as mental development of the individual:

> The continued supervision of the health of young people after their full-time schooling has ceased, and the encouragement and the provision of opportunity to develop their capacities and their interests, are alike essential if the best is to be made of the nation's youth. There is a common agreement that had the provisions for day continuation schools of the Act of 1918 been operated, many of the problems of the adolescent would largely have been solved (ibid., para. 65).

This demonstrates education as a mechanism for altering the socialisation process, and post-compulsory education as a way to control or socialise young people. While the compulsory sector up to the age of 16 continued to develop in structure and style, training for the average student post-16 remained a problem. Indeed, in 1991 we find reference to the difficulties with which government has to deal today: 'Vocational qualifications in this country have been undervalued and underused. Young people and adults need a clear framework of qualifications to measure their success in education and training' (DfEE, 1993b, p. 3).

This reveals that, while much had been achieved since the 1944 Act, a hierarchy within the system had emerged by 1991 that influenced participation in vocational qualifications. In order to reverse this process the vision of the 1944 Act included this statement: 'The new system must not start under the handicap of poor and inconvenient premises, which are dispiriting to the staff, command little respect from the students, and carry no prestige with the public' (ibid., para. 75). The development of further education for the non-advanced sector relied on changing social understanding of its role and purpose.

In the 1944 reconstruction much was made of the importance of creating 'a continuous process conducted in successive stages' (ibid., para. 2). The intention was to provide a system that enabled individuals to continue education throughout their lifetime.[4] Added to this was the intention for provision for compulsory part-time education: 'All young persons from 15–18 will be required to attend an appropriate centre part-time, unless they are in full-time attendance at school, or otherwise under suitable part-time instruction' (ibid., para. 68). 'Suitable instruction' referred to the small, established apprentice programmes. Despite the grand plan, a learner's rights to part-time education was never secured, a fact that can be seen from the following in the 1990s: 'Full-time students are entitled to a place in a school or college [and] are entitled to free tuition. [If you are] 16–18 and want to study part-time, or 19 or over ... you can apply for a college place but you may have to pay fees' (DfEE, 1993a, Pt 1, p. 9).

Indeed, responsibility to pay shifted from government to the individual in this client group. At first glance, this looks like the re-emergence of a key aspect of Victorian values, but a greater in-depth analysis needs to take place before such an assertion can be made.

By the 1940s government intervention was seen as key to securing growth in participation in education and training. A structured bureaucratic system developed to blend the meeting and competing needs of industry, commerce and colleges. Criticism of the old system can be seen in the following:

> The provision of facilities for vocational training will by itself not be enough. The country cannot afford to rest content with a system under which the technical education of its potential skilled workers, industrial leaders, or commercial executives is left so largely to the initiative of the young employees. The vocational training that has come into being has not come in response to any

demand from industry or commerce, but has depended upon the enterprise and tenacity of individual students anxious to equip themselves more fully to advance in life (ibid., para. 81).

No doubt this system, if it can be called a system, has brought forward many young men and women of high intelligence and sturdy character. But a much closer collaboration between industry and commerce and the education service is essential if the country is to develop a national system and to secure ... the needs of the future ... The subdivision of labour ... tend[s] to diminish the value of training afforded by the normal course of employment ... It will be a combination of experience in the factory, farm or office and attendance ... at the institute that it will be possible to establish the belief that it is quality, and not cheapness, of labour that is sought (ibid., para. 82).

The market mechanism thus stands accused of creating a division of labour, causal to poor participation rates and quality in vocational education and training.[5] These market legacies are clearly identified as unhelpful to economic growth. 'To establish the belief that it is quality, and not cheapness, of labour that is sought' implied changed social practices. 'Cheap' labour at the cost of 'quality' labour suggested radical social reconstruction. 'Quality' labour implied more than on-the-job skills, it included a standard of general education, hence the plan was that: 'it will be a combination of experience in the factory, farm or office and attendance ... at the institute' (ibid.). The approach to education and training adopted a long-term perspective. The vision was that education and training be re-identified as a merit good.[6]

An approach to education and training was therefore embedded in the 1943 reconstruction programme which identified participation in it as desirable, not simply because it increased the productivity of labour but because it was inherently a good thing. Furthermore, employees and employers could not be left to determine consumption of education and training – they needed to be encouraged to participate, with the result that government adopted a paternalistic theme in its action.

Given, firstly, the competitive position of the UK in relation to its major competitors and, secondly, the paucity of the existing system, further education also became identified as a public good.[7] It thus became part of a discourse of the vision of growing welfare state provision. Clearly, the aim of the 1944 Act was to provide the foundations for an education system that was planned, controlled and bureaucratic, with equal opportunity established through fair rules for all.[8] The envisaged system linked with social development as can be seen in the following: 'It shall be the duty of the LEA for every area to contribute towards the spiritual, moral, mental and physical development of the community' (Education Act 1944, p. 157). This determined, at least in principle, cooperation between the suppliers of education and training; institutional interdependency was part of the educational agenda.

The government did not start afresh, they had to make some attempts to ensure that those whose education had been disrupted by the war had priority: 'The government expects that in admission to courses priority over men born in 1929 or later will be given to older students who have been prevented from completing their training by the war' (MoE, 1948). The Minister of Education and the LEAs worked together to develop the system of education, but by 1949 government already had some concerns about 'the strictest economy being exercised in the administration of education' (MoE, 1949b, p. 1). Implementation of the vision was fraught with financial difficulties.

By the late 1950s the LEAs were the controlling agencies:

> In general the Minister hopes that local education authorities will do all in their power to achieve the closest relationship between the colleges, the schools and local industry and commerce ... co-operation is necessary for the development of further education (MoE, 1958, para. 8).

The LEAs' remit thus included a liaison role. Continuing the theme of cooperation and interdependency, the governing bodies of further education colleges were 'to have a governing body containing substantial representation of industry, commerce and other appropriate interests' (MoE, 1959d, para. 3). This trend has continued.[9]

In 1959 we find reference to the composition of the governing body:

> In the Minister's view, the governing body ... should largely consist of people ... who have current experience of problems of industry and commerce relevant to the work in the establishment and have an interest in further education. To this end, substantial direct representation of employers and unions in industry and commerce is normally essential and the Minister suggests that such representations should account for not less than one third of the total (MoE, 1959b, para. 6).

Further education was thus linked to local needs and the needs of industry and commerce. The intention was a closer relationship between economic imperatives at the local level and the portfolio of college courses would emerge. With increased demand for technical competence the government supported growth in technical education:

> ... the additional cost will be greater if, as the Government hope, ... publication ... will lead to a greater appreciation on the part of pupils, parents and industry of the value of continued education ... It is already, however, the policy of Government and local education authorities that every encouragement should be given to boys and girls to stay at school and to avail themselves of the opportunities for further education (MoE, 1964c, para. 18).

Once again we find reference to social resistors preventing growth in education and training beyond compulsory education; 'greater appreciation' in the public mind towards 'value of continued education' needed encouragement. Paradoxically, this is linked to poor informing, 'publication' rather than social revolution.

Government support tended to favour compulsory and full-time education: 'The general view ... was that the right to day release could not be granted without holding back the prospects for other urgent educational developments' (MoE, 1964a, p. 7). Education needs now had a preferential order: interest in further education, particularly part-time and non-advanced, cooled. The Newsom Committee, however, spoke a different language: it included 'national targets' and spoke of 'roughly doubling the current numbers [of students undertaking day release courses]'. Highlighting need, alongside economic imperatives, it suggested the allocation of resources needed to change to reflect equal opportunity:

> The point is, could many people, with the right educational help, achieve still more? If they could, then in human justice and in economic self-interest we ought, as a country, to provide that help. Any substantial recommendations affecting provision for half the population are bound to cost money. Are we prepared to foot the bill? We are conscious that, although there is a strong body of public opinion urging public expenditure on education as a vital investment, the emphasis at present is almost invariably on the higher education of the most gifted. And with the prospect of a steady, long-term increase in the child population, the cost even of maintaining the existing services is mounting so rapidly that the competition for educational priorities is acute. We therefore think it essential to state at the outset the economic argument for investment in our pupils (MoE, 1963b, para 9).

> Briefly, it is that the future pattern of employment in this country will require a much larger pool of talent than is at present available; and that at least a substantial proportion of 'average and 'below average' pupils are sufficiently educable to supply that additional talent. The need is not only for more skilled workers to fill existing jobs, but also for a generally better educated and intelligently adaptable labour force to meet new demands (ibid., para. 10).

The system developed by the 1960s is criticised for not providing the equal opportunity or diversity and parity of talent, envisaged in the 1944 Act. The system still reflected the needs of an elite despite legislation to change it. The language of equal opportunity is clear in the use of the term 'human justice', the economic imperative in 'economic self-interest', 'competition' and 'new demands'. Social revolution had ceased to be a main thrust of the argument for post-compulsory provision: it was now tempered with, and supported by, economic validation. With resources skewed towards compulsory and full-time attendance at higher education institutions, so was the language:

> We had difficulty with our terms of reference. 'Average' and 'below average' are full of pitfalls. The words themselves are useful enough, as ways of trying to identify in broad terms two large groups of pupils; but unluckily they often carry emotional overtones: the idea of 'below average ability' easily suggests below average people, as though the boys and girls described are being regarded as generally inferior and in some ways less worth educating than their 'above average' brothers and sisters (MoE, 1963b, p. 5).

The government ceased to pursue educational diversity, envisaged, non-advanced further education began to slip from the government's mind. Indeed, by 1972 government's concerns about further non-advanced education began to focus on efficient use of resources rather than effectiveness:

> In particular [the Government] have examined five of its [education service] aspects which require close attention at the present time ... Each of these poses difficult decisions about the allocation of resources ... It is therefore on matters of scale, organisation and cost rather than educational content that attention is mainly focused in this White Paper. In the 1960s the major determinant of rising educational expenditure was the increasing number of young people using the education system ... In the 1970s these pressures will not be so intense ... Choices of a new kind can therefore be made (DES, 1972b, p. 1).

The inference that the vision of the 1944 Act needed to reflect changing imperatives and choice, even where need is apparent, was thought appropriate. Government swapped paternalism for realism; this signalled the end of the expansionist period and replaced government responsibility with target selection:

> The total resources available will always be limited. Everything cannot be done in full at once. Each programme is in a very real sense in competition for its

> share of resources with other programmes, both within and outside the education service (ibid., p. 2).

Alongside selecting from competing needs, the government introduced public utilities as competing agents. The phrase 'competition for its share' suggests that government should be distanced from the way in which funds are allocated – each agent thus becomes responsible for fighting for their allocations.

> [Given that higher education establishments must achieve economies of scale] this will set a limit to the number of further education colleges that can expect to provide advanced full-time sandwich courses, but leaves room for expansion of such provision for those colleges that already make it. The same factor makes it extremely difficult to see how a small or isolated college of education can hope to make on its own the wider contribution to higher education it would like to make (ibid., p. 42).

The plan was about amalgamation.

Expansion remained on the government's agenda:

> The substantial expansion of higher education ... to meet the Government's plans the other colleges of further education ... will also need to expand ... Alongside the expansion of full-time and sandwich courses, the Government will expect to see provision also of the widest possible range of opportunities for part-time study (ibid., p. 41).

Amalgamation of colleges was to be a reality. In the same year the James Report suggested a growth in teacher training. However:

> A large number of further education teachers enter the profession after a number of years of further education, training and experience in industry and commerce ... There is no formal requirement that further education teachers should be trained or hold qualified teacher status (DES, 1972c, p. 70).

The report recommended that 'teachers who work in further education should have opportunities to take suitable part-time courses of education and training' (ibid., p. 13). Pressure on government expenditure continued to grow, alongside rising public expectations, to improve quality across the whole system of education. The reconstruction programme put in place in 1944 now had a momentum of its own; the needs snowballed. There was a growth in the number of young unemployed people and a new issue emerged: a need to provide re-skilling and education for those receiving state benefit:

> Ministers have publicly expressed the hope that young people reaching school leaving age who cannot find employment should seriously consider continuing their education, where the resources are available for them to do so ... young people may attend further education courses for up to three days a week, or the equivalent in half days, without losing their entitlement to supplementary benefits, so long as they remain available for employment (DES, 1977d, para. 1).

The intention was further education was only to keep these people busy 'so long as they remain available for employment'. Participation in further education for this client group was not to be seen as an alternative to work.

The power to decide began to shift away from the DES:

> The Training Services Agency and the Industrial Training Boards will give the Local Education Authorities as much notice as possible of relevant plans for local developments. Where there may be resource and staffing implications for Authorities, they will be consulted before any decisions are reached with colleges. The aim will be to strengthen links at this level as much as possible. The Agency and Industrial Training Boards will also keep Regional Advisory Councils informed of their operational requirements and consult them as necessary, in accordance with agreed regional procedures (DES, 1977e, para. 6).

The Agency, which reported to the MSC, need only give the LEA, 'as much notice as possible'. Consultation with the LEA should take place only on the 'implications' for 'resource and staffing implications'. The right to choose development direction thus becomes skewed towards the Agency. Although acting 'in accordance with agreed procedures' the relationship was now altered.

Indeed, a discussion paper prepared by the Agency refers to a five-year plan involving:

> The training of young entrants to the workforce as a priority area of special national importance. It pointed to the large number of young people who receive little or no training and argued the case for improving training for young people on four grounds: an increasing need for skill and adaptability for employment; the inequity of opportunities being missed by young people because of where they live or the state of the economy when they start work; the importance of initial training and job experience in shaping attitudes to work; and the present imbalance of public funds devoted to young people entering work and those who continue in full-time education (MSC, 1975, p. 19).

Using the language of equality the solution is divisive: these students are to receive training – skills for the task in hand – not education, which provides the opportunity of job switch. Socialisation to the work ethic continues as a theme and purpose for the development of the system of education and training:

> We hold that education has certain long-term goals, that it has a general point or purpose, which can be definitely, though generally stated. The goals are twofold, different from each other, but by no means incompatible. They are first, to enlarge a child's knowledge, experience and imaginative understanding, and thus his awareness of moral values and capacity for enjoyment; and secondly, to enable him to enter the world after formal education is over as an active participant in society and a responsible contributor to it, capable of achieving as much independence as possible ... The criterion by which to judge the quality of educational provision is the extent to which it leads a pupil towards the twin goals which we have described (DES, 1978, paras 1.4–1.6).

The advantages of education now applied only to some types of client, namely those in compulsory or advanced education, while for the rest the economic imperative began to dominate and government discourse began to concentrate on education for work.

The education service became dominated by new training initiatives, driven by the MSC. It argued that this service 'needed to assess the nature and scale of the new demands made upon it [which needed to focus on full-time programmes] integrated training, education and work experience' (DES, 1982d, p. 18). In other words, it had failed in its task.

Government continued to focus on further education for unemployed young people as a stopgap:

> Successive Secretaries of State have sought to encourage the making available of such opportunities [which allow unemployed young people to undertake part-time education up to 21 hours a week] without loss of benefit (DES, 1982c, para. 1).

These young people's educational needs now lay at the bottom of the pile of competing needs; socialisation and training, rather than education, became the focus of government for these clients.

In 1982 the Youth Training Scheme was launched to attract unemployed young people into training. The intention of this initiative was to attain 'a large increase in the places made available within the education system' (DES, 1982d, para. 8). Funding for these initiatives was to be limited:

> The Secretary of State recognises that there is pressure on FE accommodation in some areas, and that LEAs will need to examine carefully the accommodation

available to them, having regard to the Government's advice on falling rolls and surplus places (ibid.).

Increased participation was to be achieved through restructuring the existing system. The theme of rationalisation, rather than expansion, became the common discourse. The government's desire for growth did not imply financial backing as in the earlier period. A focus on efficiency begins to emerge.

In the late 1980s, further education colleges became exposed to:

> commercial activities ... The central purpose of the Act [The Further Education Act 1985] is to encourage the profitable application of the resources of FE establishments to a wide range of commercial activities (DES, 1985c, para. 7.1).

The market process disassociated government not only from financial but also social responsibility. The language of the market, namely 'profit', was now included as a rationale for activity in educational institutions. The language of the market became very overt, colleges were to pay attention to 'apply[ing] the open-market value rule', which:

> requires that all suppliers ... must not be less than their open-market value [and] is intended to ensure that authorities compete on equal terms with providers of similar goods and services in the private sector (DES, 1985c, para. 8.1).

Demand for further education began to grow because jobs, particularly for young people, remained in short supply. With its remit focused on education and training, the MSC began to be a dominant player as far as the further education colleges were concerned:

> An increasing amount of places in further education is taken up by various MSC courses, which are outside the direct control of the college and the LEA concerned. The impact of the Youth Training Scheme on further education locally is difficult to determine ... most recently, part of the further education element within the rate support grant to LEAs is being passed directly to the MSC, inevitably increasing the Commission's influence over local establishments (Audit Commission, 1985, p. 5).

The government, through its quango the MSC, began to adopt central control over the further education sector, effectively eroding local influence. In the 1990s the government developed a tight financial control style with a market theme.[10]

> With effect from 1 April 1993, a new further education sector will be established [which] will consist mostly of institutions currently maintained by local authorities which have been incorporated as further education corporations (Further and Higher Education Act 1992, para. 16).

The FEFC, another government quango, took over the financing of the further education sector and power thus shifted away from the LEA: 'LEAs will also have the power to secure the provision of further education the FEFC has the duty to secure provision' (ibid., para. 5). Developing its market theme, government continued to distance itself from direct intervention in the non-advanced further education sector; privatisation of public utilities became a dominant aim.

Policy focus shifted from a critique of the market that placed interventionism as key to the abandonment of intervention in favour of provision dictated by the market. Equal opportunity, a focus of government in the 1940s, remained a good thing but only for some – in the case of further education the theme of the 1990s became institutional liberation and efficiency. To reduce government intervention, however, power had to be shifted away from traditional influencing agents. Government adopted a tight financial control style, delivered through a quango, thus increasing central government control at arm's length. To implement their policies the government focused on centralisation, while the rhetoric, paradoxically, focused on liberalisation. Coupled with this, government attitude shifted from paternalism to individualism.

Production Orientation: The Conservative Government's Management Perspective

The vision of the reconstruction programme in 1944 included a very wide definition of a college's role in society:

> The hours of compulsory attendance would by no means represent the sum total of the contribution which the college would make to the life and training of young people. It should offer all the facilities necessary to promote, outside the actual hours of instruction, all kinds of activities, recreative and cultural. The college would be in itself a youth centre taking its place in the extended Youth Service. It will thus perform what is the real function of an education service – to provide a live environment in which, by the pursuit of a variety of interests and activities, both boys and girls alike may bring to fruition the

character and capacities with which they are severally endowed (MoE, 1943, para. 76).

The vision included a wide interpretation of education, inclusive of the development of each individual's 'character and capacities' and of academic as well as recreational abilities. The role of the college was perceived as one with a close relationship with the local community, particularly its youth and their needs. Pursuance of diversity of talent in young people is also very clear in the phrase 'variety of interests and activities'. 'It should offer all the facilities to promote all kinds of activities' suggests that government identified its social responsibility. Compulsory education, independent of the level of skill for which it was designed was indicated in this statement:

> For all alike some basic elements should be included in their training. Provision must be made for their physical well-being through physical training and remedial exercises and instruction in health and hygiene ... Other essential elements will be training in clarity of expression and in the understanding of the written and of the spoken word, together with some education in the broad meaning of citizenship – to give some understanding of the working of the government and the responsibilities of citizens and some interest of the world around them ... The remaining hours may well be devoted to a variety of subjects according to an individuals needs and capacities (ibid., para. 73).

The intention was that training should comprise only a small part of the vision of education for these young people – a general education, vital for transferable skills, was a significant part. A vision of social improvement was included. Parity of difference was evidenced by the phrase 'according to an individual's needs and capacities'. The adoption of a paternalistic approach is clear: 'some education in the broad meaning of citizenship' implies an attempt to establish equal opportunity through an individual's understanding of his or her democratic rights.

What actually emerged was a system that progressively distanced itself from the component of general and recreational education, in favour of the simple model of training. Parity of difference failed to develop – indeed the Crowther Report states that:

> it could hardly be claimed that there is country-wide provision for each level. Even if a boy has been fortunate enough to find an employer who will give him day-release, he still needs to find, within reasonable travelling distance, a course exactly suited to his requirements (MoE, 1959a, para. 487).

This report refers to lack of participation in non-advanced education arising from the fact that:

> further education has grown up as the hand-maiden of employment. For the overwhelming majority of boys and girls in further education, the choice of job (or at least the choice of type of employment) comes first, and the entry into further education courses follows as a consequence, either as a condition of employment (as with most part-time day release) or as a means of obtaining the qualifications for specific employment (as with the girl's full-time commercial courses) or as a means of obtaining promotion in employment ... virtually everything that exists in it has come into existence as the conscious answer to a demand rising from industry or from the individual workers (ibid., para. 488).

The vision of general education for day-release students simply became work task-oriented, the student became the supply to meet demand; the development of an individual's 'character' was reduced to the development of skills. A college's role became reactive, rather than proactive as intended in the vision of the 1944 Act. A salient feature of the system became:

> the structure of industry and the attitude of employers determine the issue ... The college can invite and advise; it cannot compel. The individual worker may desire release but he cannot demand it (ibid., para. 489).

Employers had the power where day-release was concerned. As a result the colleges failed to become the leaders of intellectual and social development and the mechanism by which equal opportunity and parity of difference would be established.

Indeed, by the mid-1960s we find:

> there is a general agreement on the need for more time for study in part-time further education courses ... There is not, however, any single way of achieving this objective; several different approaches are possible, and the needs will vary with different types of student (MoE, 1963a, para. 5).

The provision for these students, who did not have the right to further education, was bounded by government's prioritisation process, which effectively entitled this type of student to less.

With the colleges' portfolios beginning to be dominated by the needs of industry, education began to become an input-output model; production models and further education were linked. In 1977 the Conservative government moved to attain central control over decision-making by using industrial performance measures for targeting:

> to measure, in terms of selected aspects of performance, the effectiveness of the education system as a whole ... Better information on standards should improve the quality of rationally-based discussions of educational issues. Its provision should assist those making policy decisions at central and local government level and also teachers ... At the local level it could help to indicate ... particular needs for extra measures (DES, 1977b, p. 3).

In 1983 the inspectorate recommended that local government auditors use the following guidelines for measuring efficiency in further education colleges:

> Efficiency is measured by the relation of inputs to outputs. The approach assumes that college inputs are represented by: lecturers; contact hours with students, widely interpreted; attendance hours of all academic staff, technicians, professional, administrative and clerical staff; and that college outputs are indicated by; student hours (registered and taught). Effectiveness concerns the achievement of policy aims and objectives and the outcomes of further education in terms of: successful completion of studies and/or examination; successful application of skills and knowledge in employment; individual self-fulfilment; meeting local and national education and training needs (DES, 1983a, paras 1.3 and 1.4).

The new language themes were effective use of public money and internal control as vital to quality provision. The model of social, institutional and individual influencing agents in educational achievement was swapped for management control – simply monitoring actual events against estimated outcomes.

> Though the maintenance of adequate and reliable records is subordinate to the main objectives of further and higher education, proper management control and accountability is not possible without them (DES, 1983a, para. 1.13).

Educational effectiveness became performance to specification, making it government's task to design a system that measured education institutions' performance. The language themes in the audit of the further and higher education sector (1985) refers specifically to 'the use of resources', rather than educational effectiveness, the Commission's key discourse being efficiency: its handbook was aptly entitled 'Economy, Efficiency and Effectiveness'. Effectiveness no longer implied social revolution (Audit Commission, 1985, p. 40).

> Effectiveness concerns the achievement of policy aims and objectives and the outcomes of further education in terms of: successful completion of studies and/or examinations; successful application of skills and knowledge in employment; individual self-fulfilment; meeting local and national educational and training needs (ibid., p. 7).

The legitimating discourse of public accountability was reinforced by the Conservatives' management model, where efficiency was measured by the relation of inputs to outputs. The language themes included in the 1985 audit represent much of the political rhetoric of the times: the institutions were not managed properly; there was slack in the system; they were not efficient. The report refers to the need to 'tailor teaching resources more closely to demand', suggesting a wastage, further confirmed by: 'aiming for an overall student/staff ratio of at least 11:1 eventually 12:1, ensuring that actual class contact hours for lecturers are within nationally agreed ranges' (ibid., pp. 3–5). Measures of efficiency became policy targets:

> Avoiding over-grading of staff; controlling lecturers out of class time; negotiations over lecturers' terms and conditions should provide the opportunity for agreeing changes in current working practices which are not conducive to value for money (ibid., p. 5).

The implication was that professionals, along with the traditional institutions, had exercised illegitimate power. The language in the audit was production orientated: it was a vision based on an input/output industrial model (ibid.). It is interesting to note the following statement from the report:

> The commission and its auditors have been concerned to avoid making educational or policy judgements, for example about the value of one course rather than another or the trade-off between costs incurred and levels of service. Value for money is not synonymous with economy ... (ibid., p. 6).

Yet educational judgements were clearly transmitted through the language: 'avoiding over-teaching' implied that there is existing waste. 'Change in current working practices' suggested existing systems were not effective; increased student/staff ratio suggested large group teaching. The non-discourse embedded in the audit increased pressure on the colleges to be more efficient in the market and set the foundations for the changing of working practices within the institutions. Teaching methods are referred to as the 'remit of the HMI' but the preferred approach to internal monitoring was based on a production method. Academic staff became inputs to create outputs; hence the focus on attendance hours, challenging their right to professional autonomy. Student attendance hours linked to outcomes epitomised the notion that the inputs to the outputs are known, implying that it is not the system that is wrong but the process. Clearly the assumptions behind the audit findings were destined to affect the teaching approaches in the colleges.

Significantly, 'BS5750 and Total Quality Management' was included in 'Education and Training for the 21st Century', named as appropriate models for quality enhancement (DfEE, 1991a, p. 3). The impact of these changes within colleges came from the language used. This highlighted an approach to effectiveness and efficiency measures applied to the education product that was far from value free. The definition of quality provided by the British Standards Institution defines quality as 'fitness for purpose' – a product's conformance to a predetermined specification. Conformance to specification has a requirement, i.e. that a pre-specified set of procedures for making the product exists; achievement of quality is evidenced by an audit trail. The BSI approach presupposes that it is possible to ensure the outputs by controlling the inputs. It assumes that inputs to the education service are known and the outcomes can be predetermined: only then does it become possible to define the process through which quality can be achieved.

Total quality management (TQM), however, is slightly different. TQM is a notion of improvement based on the principle that quality achievement is dependent on the shared commitment and participation of individual workers. In TQM quality management is one part of the process. The application of BS5750 and TQM to further education colleges implied that a comparison could be made between products and educational achievement. However, effective educational outcomes are individually determined. Learning is a multidimensional process in which the determinants vary and where the complete science is unknown. What we do know is that the learning process is individual, reflective, change-oriented and flexible (FEU, 1991). Indeed, success may not be related to how it is delivered as it is to the way in which the student receives it. It was inappropriate to use measurements for success in colleges that relied on knowing the determinants.

Furthermore, the use of production-oriented approaches to the management of the education service assumes a shared understanding of the form of commitment, action and approach that should be used to ensure success in learning by learners. Despite the problem of isolating cause and effect in the education industry, the government chose to use a rational approach for measurement of quality and to apply it to an emotionally governed good.

Whether TQM or QM, professional judgement became subordinated to administration because their control mechanisms rely on administrative procedures – a paper chase.

In 1993, aping industrial models, government introduced performance measures in 'The Charter for Further Education', which:

> sets targets which the colleges have to achieve ... I therefore expect colleges to develop their own detailed charter ... monitor the colleges' performance against the commitments in this charter and their own. Colleges can apply for a Charter Mark for excellence in delivering public services (DfEEa, 1993, p. 1).

The production-oriented resource utilisation approach is most clearly seen in colleges' performance indicators adopted in 1994:

> Achievement of funding target, an indicator of college effectiveness: student enrolment trends, an indicator of college responsiveness; student continuation, an indicator of programme effectiveness; learning goals and qualifications, an indicator of student achievements; attainment of or equivalent, an indicator of contribution to national targets; average level of funding, an indicator of value for money (FEFC, 1994, p. 3).

Further education colleges became involved in an enormous re-evaluation of their administrative process to comply with a production-oriented quality audit process. A college's effectiveness became measured by conformance to standard, judged by performance indicators. From 1994 onwards performance indicators were published to enable the public to compare one college against another. However, there are clear indications that the government felt these changes were not enough: 'Internal reorganisation will not be enough to prevent a decline in educational effectiveness and disproportionate increases in cost' (DES, 1987b, para. 2). An association between 'educational effectiveness' and 'cost' was stated as unquestionable. While it can be argued that fewer children in a class may not be cost-effective but could be more educationally effective, quality of education in the 1987 White Paper is defined within the market paradigm only. The emerging discourse clearly defines success as: 'value for money' (ibid., para. 17).

In 1988 the LEAs' role becomes further redefined to include 'effectively, efficiently and economically' to meet student demand. The Education Grants and Awards Act 1988 states:

> The aim of the grant is to encourage LEAs to re-deploy a limited amount of expenditure into activities which appear to the Secretary of State to be of

particular importance. The programmes are subject to statutory consultation with the local authority associations ... Councils ... will be invited to bid for such grants (DES, 1988a, p. 69).

Consultation became simply a statutory duty, minimum government involvement in consultation rather than maximum support being quite clear. The introduction of 'bidding' for grants was consistent with competition, the language of the market. The LEAs' power was further eroded in the Further and Higher Education Act 1992:

> The previous arrangements for inspection of further and higher education establishments ... are repealed as from April 1993 ... responsibility for securing quality assessment for colleges ... will rest with the Further Education Funding Council (Further and Higher Education Act 1992, p. 19).

> Co-operation in inspection arrangements and securing consistency of standards across the sectors will be important. To this end the Secretary of State has asked the FEFC to liaise with the local authority associations and with the OFSTED ... [who will make] suitable arrangements for assessments and securing of consistency of standards (ibid., p. 20).

The shift of power towards the FEFC was another example of government's distance from provision in this sector.

Discourse which makes use of production orientation appears in the supposedly independent interim report of the committee led by Sir Ron Dearing concerning 16–19 year olds, which also considers lifelong learners. Referring to the increase in target numbers for achievement 16–19 year olds, the parameters are as follows: 'the central issue in post-16 education and training will be to develop the fitness for purpose, excellence, and cost-effectiveness of these qualifications' (DfEE, 1996c, Section 4.4). The language of the market and the production industry conditioned the discourse for change. The report further refers to 'a consensus for change' but this is defined within the conditioned parameters (ibid., Section 5.1). 'Cost-effectiveness' becomes the defining parameter. Controlled by the values inherent in the Conservative government's policy for change, it was a limited discourse. The term 'educational effectiveness' was redefined in commercial terms.

Aping the market paradigm, the quality of the educational good became measured as conformance to standards, a factual description which is both value- and judgement-free. The 1940s model envisaged quality for the individual, including the establishment of human and democratic rights through increased equal opportunity where the education system was identified as the tool to bring about those changes. The education system was built on a socially-integrated view of value – within this model it was possible for education to lack commercial value but serve a social purpose. The language of the current education debate, based on commercial language, assumed simple and narrow measures of success within colleges, so that the value of education could only be identified within a commercial context. Value as fitness for purpose is completely distanced from ethical values and purposes. Reacting to demand, colleges became servants of the commercial world.

Learners Differently Labelled: From Students to Customers

To gain legitimacy it was necessary for government to apply the language theme of the market to more than simply the traditional state-controlled system, it also had to impact on those the participants in the service, the learners. In 1991 John Major, the then Prime Minister, launched the Citizen's Charter Initiative: a Student Charter followed. A charter is a formal document granting, or demanding from the state, certain rights or liberties. The language theme of rights and power emerged:

> The Citizen's Charter is about giving more power to the citizen. It is a testament to our belief in people's right to be informed and to choose for themselves. I want the Citizen's Charter to be one of the central themes of public life in the 1990s. Then we will have services in which the citizen can have confidence, and in which all those who work in them can have pride ('The Citizen's Charter', 1991, p. 1).

Paternalism of the 1940s changed to individualism in the 1990s. 'Power' was given to the 'citizen' so that he or she be better 'informed' and thus able 'to choose for themselves'.

The four aims of the charter initiative were to:

> work for a better quality in every public service; give people more choice; make sure that everyone is told what kind of service they can expect to receive; make sure that people know what to do if something goes wrong (ibid., p. 2).

Responsibility for quality shifted from the government to consumer sovereignty. Quality service became a matter of matching output to the stated objectives; in other words the level of quality became determined by the price paid. Success became a matter of achieving the stated objectives rather than social improvement.

The new Charter for Further Education 1993 provided a stronger link to the market with its focus on consumer sovereignty:

> In some areas – for example, the time taken to respond to enquiries, or to pay grants – the Charter sets targets which all colleges, local authorities and others involved in further education are expected to meet. But achieving high standards is, above all, a responsibility of the colleges themselves, because they know their customers best (DfEE, 1993a, p. 1).

Standards in educational achievement were about dealing with 'customers' in reasonable response times. Government was distanced from direct intervention; thus high standards became the 'responsibility of the colleges'.

The language themes were about expectation not obligation:

> If you want to become a full-time or part-time student you have the right to expect: reliable and impartial advice about the choices available, given at the right time; clear and accurate information about – courses, qualifications, facilities, and entry requirements – how courses will be taught and assessed, and how your learning will be managed colleges' policies and arrangements for students with learning difficulties or disabilities – accommodation if you have to live away from home – how well colleges are doing, including published reports on the quality of what they provide. You can also expect: to have your application for a place handled fairly and efficiently – to be shown where you would be taught and the facilities available for students – to be told about the fees and other charges a college makes, and any financial help that is available. Once you are accepted as a student you have the right to expect; prompt payments of grants and access fund payments if you are eligible – high quality teaching and effective management of your learning, subject to independent inspection – regular information on your progress and achievements – access to reliable and unbiased careers advice and other guidance on counselling (ibid., p. 2).

Individual 'rights' expressed what must occur – the efficient functioning of the internal organisation. These citizens' rights were more about informing customers of the boundaries than about changing social relations. The greater issue of equal opportunity drifted from the agenda. The charter provided the criteria on which customers could make a legitimate complaint; in the same way as buying any other product, a learner could complain about the service outlined in the college charter, if the service was not fit for the purpose (ibid., p. 3).

For students to become re-identified as customers depended on their being able to purchase the relevant good. In 1991 the government introduced training credits: 'Every 16 and 17 year old leaving full-time education to be offered a training credit' (DES, 1991). The intention was that, by 1996, training credits would act as cash, so that the students could take their money to the college of their choice. The student became a purchaser, the re-identification of a student as a customer was complete. In real terms students are not customers because they cannot purchase a qualification, they purchase the opportunity to achieve the qualification. As a purchaser without the right to own the good they were unique. College charters now defined the level of service it aimed to provide to its customers. Students – now informed consumers – were able to identify routes for complaint, based on fitness for purpose. The underpinning discourse was a certain type of public accountability, consumer sovereignty: government's common approach to public utilities recommended by the Nolan Committee:

> We consider that the provision of independent adjudication of customer complaints is now fully established as normal good practice, and that the procedure has to be combined with a statement, publicly available, of the service standards which the user can expect from the body concerned, and against which failure to perform can be measured (Nolan Report, 1996, para. 384).

Marketisation of further education colleges relied on students becoming customers. They could then exercise their choice and thus promote competition between colleges; it was a part of a scheme to reduce government intervention to that of governance.

A Continuing Discourse: Further Education – Who Pays?

One of the significant recurring issues in the documentation is emphasis on who pays for further education. Later discourses contrast starkly with the intentions expressed in the 1943 White Paper, that reconstruction should be financed collectively for part-time as well as full-time provision up to the age of 18. The vision included 'enabling poor students to proceed to the Universities'. After 1988 choice is based on the central tenets of commercialism, resource allocation is organised in response to demand and supply by price.

A cost focus, however, was not new. The Educational Reconstruction Programme 1944 was neutralised at its inception by the caveat: 'the rates at which it will be possible to proceed will depend ... on the financial resources available...' (MoE, 1943, para. 6). As early as 1949 the influence of economic performance on the development of further education can be found:

> The economic difficulties of the country have called for a close review of government expenditure ... schemes for further education, including plans for County Colleges, not yet completed should be proceeded with and submitted in due course. [Efficiencies were expected] in the administration of education (MoE, 1949a, para. 1).

Very quickly further education became re-identified as a quasi-public good; schemes for further education continued to be dogged by the availability of financial resources. Government expenditure on further education has been constantly reviewed.

In 1952 the first of many memoranda refers to 'the possibility of increasing the income from students' fees as a means of achieving a reduction of expenditure from public funds for the provision of further education' (MoE. 1952, para. 1). The earlier approach to payment is, however, quite distinct from the approach taken from 1979 onwards. Charges were initially evaluated on an individual's ability to pay, 'whilst still ensuring that no one is debarred from a course of further education by reason of ability to pay [remissions are only to be given to those] where there is real hardship' (ibid., para. 2). Reference is also made to the need for a division between vocational and recreational courses; the latter were to be self-supporting. College portfolios were differentiated by government support or lack of it. Over time, recreational courses become re-identified as a luxury good.

1956 witnessed the trend away from increasing government support:

> Some fees are outstandingly low ... The Minister thinks that many students, particularly older students attending part-time courses or classes in non-vocational courses, can reasonably expect to make a bigger contribution than they do at present. This applies especially to the majority – the 1,000,000 students aged 21 or over who attend evening classes (MoE, 1956b, para. 2).

Further education provision as a drain on financial resources begins to emerge as a constant theme. Those in work, independent of the level of income, were expected to pay their way, the trend towards part-time students being full fee-payers gained momentum. Further education has evolved as an 'also ran' product: because it was not central to the welfare agenda, it became the poor relation. It had to respond to increasing pressure on funding – indeed in 1956 we find:

> The maintenance of this policy depends, however, on the strictest economy being exercised in the administration of education ... expenditure can be reduced without the imposition of restrictions which would prejudice educational effectiveness or impair, save by some slowing down in some directions, the progress and development that are in hand (MoE, 1949a, para. 3).

> The Minister called the attention of local education authorities to the possibility of increasing the income from students' fees as a means of achieving a reduction from public funds for the provision of further education (MoE, 1952, p. 4).

LEAs were asked to limit provision and the trend towards self-sufficiency for the colleges continued:

> The Minister has recently reviewed the fees charges for further education by authorities ... The authorities estimate that in the financial year 1956/57 their expenditure on further education will be £32.6(m) ... The estimated income from further education, most of which comes from fees, will be about £2.5(m). At present, therefore, income from fees represents only one-fifteenth of what the authorities spend on further education (MoE. 1956b, para. 1).

In 1969/70 the gross expenditure by local authorities on further education was re-evaluated (DES, 1970b):

> From September 1971 fees from non-vocational and vocational courses for those already in employment [to be charged] so as to achieve an additional £5m of income from this source in a full year (DES, 1971, p. 12).

Government continued to rely on student contributions from these client groups. Responsibility for training based on a learner's ability to pay became an essential part of the established system, progressively limiting equal opportunity by the ability to pay.

By 1972 there was increasing evidence of pressure on resources.

> The Government has been reviewing the directions in which the services are growing: its objectives and priorities. In particular they have examined five of its aspects that need close attention at the present time: nursery education, school buildings, staffing standards in schools, teacher training and higher education. Each of these poses difficult decisions about the allocation of resources if, within those available, a balanced programme of advance across all five is to be achieved (DES, 1972b, para. 2).

It is interesting to note that further education was not mentioned as a separate category. 'Resources' were now allocated using the rationale of 'balance', not need; 'difficult decisions' suggested inadequate funds for the tasks. By 1984 the responsibility to pay shifted away from government to employers:

> ... investment in training needs to be attractive financially. That means keeping training costs down ... providing that industry and commerce play their part ... It is for them [the employers] to make the investment in training people to do the work that they require ... central and local government, at the expense of the taxpayer to ensure that general and vocational education are provided ... exercised largely through the Manpower Services Commission ... trainees themselves need to accept that the total costs of training must be taken into account in determining their pay (DES, 1984c, para. 2).

Government's role became that of ensuring provision but not supplying the investment. The Conservative government's political agenda became an important part of the context of educational reform. Employers were isolated as the key driving force: 'investment in training needs to be attractive financially', pay had to be kept down so that employers participated whereas trainees were simply expected to accept the status-quo: 'trainees themselves need to accept ... costs of training ... determining their pay'. Employees, it was intimated, had higher expectations than was reasonable; clearly this was not an economic discourse, it was political dogma.

In 1981 the number of unemployed young people rose. A 21-hour rule was introduced to attract non-working young people into education, which they could do without losing their unemployment benefit.

> First it is made clear that it is necessary to count towards the 21 hours only time spent receiving instruction or tuition. No account should be taken of time spent on meal breaks or unsupervised study, whether at the establishment or elsewhere (DES, 1982c, para. 1).

The suggestion of time-wasting by both the learners and the institution is clear. In 1984 this attitude is restated:

> The 21 hour rule is not designed to enable those committed to an education course to claim benefit and those who take advantage of it must satisfy appropriate conditions, including the need to be available for work (DES, 1984a, para. 1).

An important part of the discourse of derision of the welfare state became the inference of benefit abuse. The 1985 Further Education Act simply continued the trend towards enabling colleges to further supplement their income: 'The central aim of the Act is to encourage the profitable application of the resources of further education establishments to a wide range of commercial activities' (DES, 1985b, para. 71). 'Profitable' outcomes now drove the colleges' decision-making processes and the environment became competitive: 'The Act enabled LEAs to lend money at competitive rates to companies involved in college and work links [therefore] ... supplies ... must be made at not less than their open market value' (ibid., para. 8.1).

Market price became significant and the relationship between colleges and industry changed – partnerships between colleges and industry became contracts:

> permits LEAs through their further education establishments to sell goods and services which arise as by-products of educational activities ... requires LEAs to keep a separate revenue account of their FE establishments' activities ... to be maintained as far as possible along commercial lines, with full attributable costs ... and best endeavours used to secure a surplus on each year's trading (Education Reform Act 1988, para. 8.1).

Profit calculated on 'full attributable costs' defined the boundaries of the contracts. 'Trading' further reinforced the market metaphor.

In a circular in 1985 competitive pricing was introduced as the main driver for increased funding. 'The central purpose of the Act is to encourage the profitable application of the resources of FE establishments to a wide range of commercial activities' (DES. 1985b, para. 7.1) which will be priced on 'the open-market value rule' (ibid., para. 8.5). Accordingly, the value of further education was reinterpreted and presented in commercial terms as market price. More importantly, the new context opened the colleges to the whims of demand and supply:

> The whole effect is to put the LEA as nearly as possible into the same position as a private-sector business; able to respond flexibly to changing market conditions, but subject to the overall test of profitability of the business as a whole (ibid., para. 8.2).

With increasing pressure to allocate resources carefully, the commercial discourse post-1979 had a significant impact on the discourse within colleges. The product portfolios of the colleges were differentiated, containing quasi-public goods, merit goods, normal goods and luxury goods. The discourse of further education provision altered from fulfilling a wide remit of need to that about a differentiated product portfolio. The value of the colleges' portfolios altered to a discourse about risk management. Forced to operate in a quasi market, they became subjected to the language of the market as if they were providing a normal good. They also became subjected to the central theme of the market, price and profit.

Significantly controlled by central government they held an unenviable operating position:

> There has been little change from previous years in the factors which colleges and external institutions perceive as potential risks to the achievement of their strategic plans. The main factors identified by colleges are competition from schools and other colleges and changes in local authority policies on discretionary awards and transport. Over 40% of colleges indicated that restrictions in the availability of Council funding would limit their ability to achieve their plans (FEFC, 1997b, para. 15).

The development of further education provision continued to be held back by funding, which, sadly for this sector, became business as usual.

The Changing Value of Further Education

There are some interesting insights into a college's role in society in 1943 that are distinct from the 1980s' commercial emphasis. In contrast to the latter, the stated intention of the reconstruction programme 1944 was to establish a system of equal opportunity to provide 'a truly democratic system of public education'. Reflecting the paternalistic social context of the time, the culture of further education was to focus on the 'aptitude' of the candidate, 'not on the results of competitive tests' (MoE, 1943, para. 3).

> The continued supervision of the health of young people, after their full time schooling has ceased, and the encouragement and provision of opportunity to develop their capabilities and their interests are alike essential if the best is to be made of the nation's youth. There is common agreement that had the provisions for day continuation schools of the 1918 Act been operated, many of the problems of the adolescent would largely have been solved (ibid., para. 65).

Government involvement in education provision was seen as crucial to solving society's wider problem. Participation in education was perceived as a means of socialisation, educating the individual as part of a society:

> The young persons concerned will be involved in a wide variety of occupations – some training for one of the skilled crafts or employment for which definite training is necessary: some in employment in which no higher degree of skill or training is required, and some others in non- progressive occupations, commonly called 'blind alley', which do not lead to adult employment (ibid., para. 72).
>
> When basic requirements have been met, the remaining hours may well be devoted to a variety of subjects according to the individual's needs and capacities. ... In appropriate cases the time may be used for technical or vocational education related to their employment. For others there will be a variety of courses including handicrafts and the domestic arts, designed to stimulate their interests, keep their minds alert and create within themselves resources of satisfaction and self-development. In the case of those whose early employment is of the 'blind alley' type, attention would be given to the further training that will assist them to transfer to more permanent work (ibid., para. 74).

Education was anything that 'keeps their minds alert' and creates 'satisfaction and self development'. Education was very clearly identified as a route to self-actualisation, a much wider remit than a purely academic one.[11] There was recognition that some client groups have a wide diversity of requirements, even those of the 'blind alley' type – underachievers – were to be encouraged to advance themselves. The solution to the problem was very much in keeping with the paternalistic approach of the times. It included 'handicrafts' and 'domestic arts', to ensure that individuals, particularly women, could serve society by contributing to an increase in the health of the nation.

In contrast, in the 1980s reference to the UK's poor competitive position talks more about resource efficiency than the educational process:

> Resource utilisation ... Though the maintenance of adequate and reliable records is subordinate to the main objectives of further and higher education, proper management control and accountability is not possible without them (DES, 1983b, p. 4).

Quality of delivery is paramount:

> We are determined to achieve better standards throughout the education service ... but we still lag behind our competitors in the participation of our school leavers in further education and training and their achievement of useful qualifications (DES, 1985b, para. 8.5).

'Useful' qualifications were now those that serve work. Education and training became more directly linked to job specification, because this reduces the opportunity to develop transferable skills. Self-actualisation, the central tenet of a wider education, was reduced to a discourse about that which is occupationally useful. Quality of further education became reinterpreted to mean that which matches the needs of the market. The standard of measurement reinforced educational value to a narrow interpretation; narrowing of the term 'education and training' became part of the political agenda. Discourse was couched in terms of 'educational effectiveness' and 'value for money in 16–19 provision' (DES, 1987b, para. 17).

In 1988, legislation for further education tried to narrow the gap between education and work:

> I believe that further education colleges have a vital role in providing education and training for both school leavers and adults ... Through links with business they are well placed to provide the knowledge and skills needed in the work place (*Hansard*, 1988).

The 1959 vision was about students 'find[ing] their way about the adult world'; understanding 'a standard of moral values'; 'continue[ing] to develop their leisure activities'; and lastly appreciating 'an educational task in the narrower sense' (MoE, 1959a, para. 274). Work orientation was one small part of an individual's total learning activity; more important was an individual's understanding of, and contribution to, society. Information assimilation was seen as an important part of self-actualisation, so the process of education had a dual role. On the one hand, it was a process of informing a learner about his or her role in society; paradoxically, it was also about providing the route towards the breaking down of those very traditions.

Education was thus seen as a way of bringing about common behaviour in adolescence, of getting them to 'to fall into line', at the same time as 'there is the chance that it may take the socially desirable form of non-conformity' – the recognition of anarchistic behaviour and free thinking as a benefit to society. There is also recognition of the need to set the tone of behaviour: 'they need a code of both morals and of behaviour, indeed of etiquette' to bring about change, but within parameters (ibid., para. 268). In 1959 colleges were seen as a vehicle for reinforcing tradition, the role of the state as a 'super caring' parent:

> It remains true to say that, in the normal course, hundreds of thousands of boys and girls are left without the supervision and help that they need during the

most critical years in the formation of character and the training of body and mind (ibid., para. 64).

Caring by the state involved moral as well as educational responsibility, social reconstruction could not be brought about without supporting those for whom the change was intended; further education could therefore provide a 'youth service' as well as adult education which also includes '... cultural ... liberal ... vocational ... creative provision' (ibid., paras 83–5). The development of the whole person was perceived as socially desirable. This in some way explains how further education colleges came to deliver such wide course portfolios.

The perception of an educational system based on the concept of community can be traced to the 1940s:

> It is only when the pupil or student reaches mature years that he will have served an apprenticeship in the affairs of life sufficient to enable him fully to fit himself for service to the community. It is thus within the wider sphere of adult education that an ultimate training in democratic citizenship must be sought (MoE, 1943, para. 85).

The language of commercialism, in contrast, suggests the market is the best method by which to allocate resources; it heralds individualism as more important than collectivism. Thus another language theme emerges in the 1980s, that which denigrates the concepts of community and society. In contrast, in 1959 we can identify the education process as containing two interrelated purposes, which link human rights to national investment:

> It is now considered to be the right of every boy and girl to be educated; and the right exists regardless of whether, in each individual case, there will be any return. From this point of view education is one of the social services of the welfare state. The 'service of God in church and state' has also been expanded ... into the need of the community to provide adequate brains and skill to sustain economic productivity. From this point of view, education is a national investment (MoE, 1959a, para. 83).

Investment implies delayed gratification, it was a long-term perspective that was adopted. Education without direct commercial validity was seen as an attainment in its own right. Yet the commercial value of education and the establishment of human rights were identified as interdependent:

Primacy must be given to the individual human rights of the individual boy or girl. But we do not believe that the pursuit of national efficiency can be ranked much lower – not least because without it the human rights themselves will not be secure (ibid., para. 86).

In 1959 we therefore see that human rights were seen as secure only when national efficiency is being pursued; herein lies the conundrum. Human rights, in particular equal opportunity, can best be pursued when the economy can provide the resources for ensuring them. Which, then, should drive education provision – commercial needs or government on behalf of learner choice?

In spite of the vision of the 1943 Reconstruction Programme, by the 1960s further education colleges had developed as the 'handmaidens' of industry:

For the overwhelming majority of boys and girls in further education, the choice of job ... comes first, and entry into further education follows as a consequence ... English further education cannot be understood without realising that virtually everything that exists in it has come into existence as the conscious answer to a demand rising from industry or from individual workers. Where something does not exist it is because there has been no effective demand for it (ibid., para. 88).

Despite the focus on human rights and meritocracy, the courses provided in further education had developed as a response to major employer needs (ibid., para. 486).

The colleges now catered for a wide set of intellectual capabilities (ibid., para. 487), but there had been no 'cohesive plan or mechanism' (ibid., para. 492) for those who did not follow the traditional academic route – these learners remained a disadvantaged group. Participation in further education was determined by the employer, not the individual (ibid., para. 489) and reflected the 1950s' social context of gender discrimination (ibid., para. 496). The gender-biased social context can be seen here: 'It must be remembered that girls largely look to leaving factory, shop or office to get married and set up homes of their own' (ibid., para. 72). Gender bias clearly had an impact on the type of education supplied for the majority of girls, demonstrating the strong influence on decision-making of acceptable social constructs. Equal opportunity was only for some. It is worthy of note that 'he, him, himself, his' is used 139 times in the Crowther Report; 'her, she, she'll' 10 times.

By the 1960s, a gap emerged between the intention of the 1944 Act and the outcome. The lack of equal opportunity for post-16 further education had become institutionalised. The language theme of further education as a quasi public good became the dominant discourse. Expressions such as 'direction must be gradual', 'as soon as practicable' and 'important contribution to industrial efficiency' encapsulated the growing trend towards commercial considerations as dominant in this sector. The actual development of further education was driven from the supply. The social welfare context was still evident:

> ... that though employment may perhaps from time to time be somewhat less than it has been in recent years, there will be no relapse into the conditions twenty years before the wars (ibid., para. 69).

The state still had a duty to change economic trends. This duty was built on the new doctrine, the notion that:

> the nation can control its own economic development ... cost of education is seen as a burden on the state but also as a method of creating economic development (ibid., para. 85).

Cost of education arrived on the policy agenda as a consideration. The new emerging discourse for long-term investment became based on a cost and benefit analysis. Yet it is still possible to identify a reluctance to judge educational performance solely in commercial terms.

> Children are not the 'supply' that meets any 'demand' ... they are individual human beings ... concern of the schools should not be with the living that they will earn but the life they will lead (ibid., para. 85).

The theme of community was still evident. So too was the theme of self-actualisation: 'There are indeed parts of everybody's education which have no economic value, and there is nobody whose education is entirely without it' (ibid., para. 86). Further education became seen as a quasi public good:

> Until recently education has been statistically, and one may guess, generally regarded, as one of the social services – that is one of the burdens that the state lays on its taxpayers for the benefits of its citizens (ibid., para. 84).

In 1963, however:

> the National Advisory Council are in sympathy with the proposal in The Crowther Report for the development of sandwich courses for technicians, but consider that progress in this direction must be gradual ... The Minister shares the view of the National Advisory Council about the desirability of increasing the normal

hours of study ... as soon as practicable ... This will make an important contribution to industrial efficiency as well as being of benefit to the students (MoE, 1963a, para. 6).

Coupled with cautionary government spending, the development of a theme of provision inadequacy began to emerge:

Despite some splendid achievements in the schools, there is much unrealised talent especially among boys and girls whose potential is masked by inadequate powers of speech and the limitations of a home background. Unsuitable programmes and teaching methods may aggravate their difficulties, and frustration express itself in apathy or rebellion. The country cannot afford this wastage, humanely or economically speaking (MoE, 1963b, p. 3).

A democratic theme is also apparent in:

The point is, could many people, with the right educational help, achieve still more? If they could then in human justice and in economic self-interest, we ought, as a country to provide that help (ibid., p. 9).

The theme of equal opportunity within the context of democracy and paternalism can be seen clearly in the use of the terms 'human justice' and 'provide that help'. This became combined with a commercial context, 'economic self-interest'. The link between human rights and national investment made in the 1940s still remains. However, education products are now clearly differentiated: 'The practical subjects have special value for the less able.' A close association is thus made between having practical interests and low ability:

Vocational is a dangerous but indispensable word. It rightly means all that belongs to a man's calling. That itself is no doubt an old fashioned word, but at least it suggests that there is more to a job than money (ibid., p. 319).

A preference for the academic route, which distances reality, can still be found in the expressions 'at least it suggests' and 'more to a job than money'. 'Calling' is refereed to as an 'old fashioned word', suggesting changing values. However, the use of the phrase 'more to a job than money' is a direct challenge to materialism, this suggests the trend towards materialism was already part of the social context.

Vocational education became separated into different levels of achievement

For historical reasons a distinction has come to be accepted between training and further education which is reflected in the institutional arrangements. Vocationally-oriented learning is, however, essentially a single process, though for many purposes it is convenient to regard training as being more concerned with learning job skills – i.e. how to do things – while vocationally-oriented further education is more concerned with general concepts involved – i.e. why things are done. It is also convenient to distinguish vocationally oriented further education from the further education, which is primarily an extension of general education, although both contribute to the fuller development of the individual (MSC, 1975, p. 12).

Training became even more distanced from 'the fuller development of the individual'. Training was thus placed at the bottom end of the hierarchy of learning. Parity of difference, envisaged in the 1944 Act, was dropped from the political agenda in favour of:

> To improve standards of achievement on the part of the pupils and students of all abilities, the quality and range of the curriculum and the effectiveness of its delivery and to secure the best possible return from the resources found for education (DES, 1985a, para. 4.1).

Some phrases in the 1988 Act are similar to those in the report of 1959: 'To improve standards of achievement ... of all abilities ... the quality and range of curriculum' (MoE, 1959a). However, commercial language clearly differentiates the new focus from the old: '[the important factor is to ensure] the effectiveness of delivery and to secure the best possible return from the resources found for education' (DES, 1985a). Boundaries now existed around what was reasonable to consider as possible, education now has to compete with other demands for resources.

The language used in the Education Reform Act 1988 exposes the Conservative government's particular vision of acceptable organisational behaviour. Let us take the term 'good management' as an example. The government's preferences are clear: the linking of the words 'good management' with 'effective and efficient' use of resources shows they favoured a cost-driven approach (DES, 1988b). Effectiveness of education then becomes measured in terms of cost only. In one paragraph the language used transmits a set of assumptions about the measurement of success and it defines the ways in which this success can be measured; the shift away from equity is achieved not by doing battle but by using a different set of language themes.

Further education becomes not a process that the individual experiences but an outcome. Although it is stated that 'it will be premature to advocate any one quality framework,' (DfEE, 1991a, Vol. 2, p. 38), the direction this would take was clear. A new commercial focus for further education became evident: 'Young people need to be made fully aware of the importance of qualifications to their future prospects' (DES, 1988b, para. 1.15). A direct relationship between increased qualifications and individual advancement is acknowledged. Sixteen to 19 year olds become identified as the group that has a high rate of course 'wastage', suggesting that they choose not to play the game. While wastage is term used in the Crowther Report, here the word is used as in manufacturing production lines, suggesting a completely different connotation. All that is required is to get the production line performing to quality measures and the wastage will be removed; social reconstruction is not required. In the Crowther Report the inference is of the waste of human potential not that of wasted resources:

> A proper programme of careers education and guidance ... as part of a wider programme of personal and social education as a preparation for adult working life ... so [they] have a clear picture of the responsibilities and obligations of adult life (DES, 1987b, para. 21).

Having differentiated the education market, government began to target training so that 'a more comprehensive and largely employment-based approach to the education and training needs of minimum-age school leavers could be developed' (DES, 1982d, para. 2). This targeting approach can be found in the Dearing Report:

> As a nation, we must raise our levels of expectation for all and increase achievement at a faster rate than our competitors. The new national targets for education and training represent essential national needs. But at the same time we must ensure that these achievements are genuine improvements, and that standards are rigorously safeguarded (DfEE, 1996c, para. 2.2).

The use of the term 'fair competition' implies an ethical stance driven by different values, this can also be seen in Sir Ron Dearing's report of 1996:

> Education about the world cannot avoid moral and spiritual issues and discussion of personal qualities such as honesty, integrity and consideration for others (DfEE, 1996c, para. 13.1).

> Life entails a continuous series of moral judgements and decisions. In work, the need to face ethical issues arises constantly. It is increasingly recognised that companies as well as professions need to have a code of ethics. History is much

> concerned with human action, codes of values and the inter-play between those codes and actual behaviour. Literature is replete with ethical dilemmas and spiritual issues. Any researcher has to ensure that advocacy of a point of view not only does not compromise the dispassionate accumulation and presentation of evidence, but preferably grows from that evidence. Those on medicine and genetics are increasingly confronted with complex moral issues. New scientific developments do not simply give humans new powers, but pose new ethical problems (ibid., para. 13.2).

The phrase 'it is increasingly recognised' suggests that ethical issues had not been dominant in decision-making but were now reappearing on the agenda. Science, 'posing new ethical problems', suggests there is a different view of action than previously. There also appears to be a re-emergence of the concept of society. Industrial growth was now thought of in terms of containment, to be tempered by ethical value.

> An active policy [in schools] of awareness of responsibilities and rights can do much. Schools and colleges can and do transmit a common culture and common standards of citizenship. But the times we live in suggest there is merit in re-emphasising the need to address moral and spiritual issues and to build on the public and private virtues of citizenship and community (ibid., para. 13.5).

While the term 'responsibilities' suggests that the old language theme is being used, linking it with 'rights' suggests a new dimension. The new theme appeared to be one built on individualism tempered by citizenship, thus it may be an indication of a drift away from individualism.

The value of education, for those involved in non-advanced further education, has changed from self-actualisation to education and training as a means to increase national competitiveness. While educational ideals and economic realities are not mutually exclusive, and indeed have always been part of the further education agenda, the model chosen to measure effectiveness changed the focus of achievement. The model of efficiency dictated the approach taken to change and quality within the further education colleges. Consequently, government's choice affected the students' and colleges' experience by driving them to achieve particular outcomes.

Linking education to employment removes power from the individual and places it with the employers; the achievement of equal opportunity, a central tenet of the 1944 Act, is thus circumvented and the status quo remains unchanged. Given the Conservative government's political preference for the market paradigm, it is not surprising to find that the efficiency study undertaken in 1987 (DES, 1987c) drove the majority of performance indicators within the colleges 'to include efficiency and effectiveness but for equity to be only a minority interest'.[12] The central tenet of the 1944 Act, equal educational opportunity, was rendered impotent because of the use of the language of commercialism. 'Those who need support in the critical years of late adolescence get least' (MoE, 1959a, para. 263).

The Breaking Down of the Established System: A Theme of Inadequacy

The change to the statutory system introduced in 1944 altered local education administration. Two separate local authorities, elementary and higher, were reviewed:

> That all local authorities should be charged with all educational functions; that the population should not now be regarded as relevant to the question whether its council should be a Local Education Authority; [and lastly that] however Local Education Authorities may be constituted, there should be arrangement for preserving and stimulating local interest in education (MoE, 1943, para. 114).

The organisation of the system of education was thus placed in the hands of one provider but a central tenet of local democracy was maintained; central power and local power were expected to work together. By the late 1950s the LEA had developed such that it determined the nature of supply:

> It is for the [local] authority to determine the general educational character of the establishment and its place in the local education system. Subject to this, however, the Minister considers that the general oversight of the conduct of the establishment and its curriculum should be entrusted to the governors, the principal being responsible for day-to-day management and discipline (MoE, 1959b, para. 17).

There was a division of responsibility at the local level between elected representatives and college representatives. The governors' task, in 1959, was to take an overview of their college's strategic direction, the principal having full responsibility for the management of operations of the college. By 1977 the governors' task of 'general oversight' had changed to responsibility for day to day activity but again, following the theme of local democracy, there was a coalition between 'industry, the trade unions and commerce [who] should be involved in curriculum planning processes' (DES, 1977f).

A trend towards increased commercial intervention and a decrease in academic intervention in a college's decision-making process emerged. This trend is exemplified by the increase from one-third of commercial representatives on the committee to 50 per cent in the 1988 Education Act where these governors were 'to be, or to have been, engaged or employed in business, industry or any profession or in any other field relevant to the activities of the institution' (DES, 1988b, Section 152). Government intention was clear. Discourse within further education institutions increasingly became biased towards commercial activity; local democracy was thus hijacked by commercial interest.

This trend towards the market paradigm culminated in the radical removal of further education from the public sector to the private sector. The LEAs were now thought to limit local needs:

> [Further education colleges] are still subject to bureaucratic controls from local authorities. They lack the full freedom which we gave the polytechnics and higher education colleges in 1989 to respond to the demands of students and the labour market (*Hansard*, 1991b, p. 432).

The use of the term 'freedom' implied the removal of state intervention; 'respond to demand' is an example of market discourse. Furthermore, proposing that a college be free to respond to demand suggests a short-term focus. In the 1990s there is evidence of a changed discourse from the interdependency and cooperative nature of the education system to one which identifies the system as a barrier to local needs. Indeed, an assault on the local education authorities and their power to control supply locally began. The statement that colleges were 'still subject to bureaucratic controls' carried a strong message about bureaucracy inhibiting the community and local democracy. Colleges were perceived by the government to be caged, needing to be released from bureaucratic control; the underlying message was that bureaucratic control was bad.

A changed attitude towards the LEAs can be seen clearly in the following:

> It is the Government's firm view, not only that these councils are capable of becoming effective LEAs, responsible in their own right for the full range of service, but above all that this restructuring will provide a stable framework within which urgently needed improvements in the performance and accountability of the education service in inner London (DES, 1988b, Section 1.1).

An attack on the established system was in motion. The phrase 'capable of becoming effective' implied that the LEAs were inadequate. The expression 'need improvements in the performance and accountability' suggested lack of accountability and poor performance. The cure – 'restructuring' of the system to make LEAs 'responsible' for its actions. The government's new policy discourse included measuring of performance, effectiveness and accountability.

Government set out to break down the cooperative relationship between the Inner London Education Authority ILEA and central government:

> The Secretary of State fully recognises the important role of ILEA throughout the transitional period and welcomes the constructive approach being taken to the transfer of responsibility, in particular, the Authority employees, most of whom will have a continuing role within the further education service in inner London ... (ibid., Section 1.4).

The tone implies that a 'constructive approach' was surprising, suggesting a battle was taking place. If the discourse was one of war, the government was winning; power was delegated from one ILEA to several councils;[13] the transfer of responsibilities coincided with the Local Government Finance Act 1988 (DES, 1988a, p. 69) with its instruction to spend 'at the level of their needs assessment ...' (ibid.) to supply local needs.

The system based on cooperation and interdependency began to be eroded. This can be seen in the 1988 Act:

> Under delegation college governing bodies will be responsible for the general direction of colleges (Education Act 1988, Section 2.1. 7)

> Each governing body to submit to the LEA annual proposals. It will be for each college to determine its internal arrangements ... to submit views and proposals ... [to take on board] the importance of effective consultation between LEAs and colleges (ibid., Section 2.1.8).

Government pursued its theme of increasing governors' power, now skewed towards commercial interests, to decide. Governors became 'responsible for the general direction of the colleges'. The LEAs' role shifted from controller to that of monitor.

The Further and Higher Education Act 1992 then continued to diminish LEA control:

> The new Further Education Funding Council will take over from the LEAs

with effect from 1993 statutory duties in respect of the provision of full-time education for those aged 16–18. The Council will also take over duties in respect of part-time education for those over compulsory school age and full-time aged 19 and over ... (DfEE, 1993b, para. 2).

Removing the LEAs as the direct funding agencies was further evidence of the battle to reduce LEAs influence over the development of education provision, its duty to provide it remained: 'The duty placed on LEAs by the Education Act 1944 is changed in its scope, not in its substance' (ibid., para. 64). In 1943 LEAs were thought to have the potential the potential to 'preserve [and] stimulate local interest in educational affairs' (MoE, 1943, para. 118). Now they had responsibility but little power. Local democracy was being eroded.

Similarly, an attack on the DES began. The emerging discourse implied illegitimate power was entrenched in the traditional system of provision. In 1971 we find the state education system described by the Central Office of Information as follows:

> To secure for all children a happier childhood and a better start in life; to ensure a further measure of educational opportunity for young people and to provide means for all to develop the various talents with which they are endowed and so enriching the inheritance of the country whose citizens they are (COI, 1971).

A social motive within the system of education is evident. There is also reference to the need for a wide definition of educational provision to provide for the diverse talents of the population. In the 1970s, against a background of unemployment, particularly for the 16–19 year old, a different perspective dominates: 'a consequence of the cyclical nature of recruitment for long-term training is that in periods of economic downturn places are not available to some young people who would get them in a better year' (MSC, 1975, Pt 3, p. 9). Government was concerned about the rising number of disaffected young people, the theme of further education as a process for an individual to develop his or her potential for an industrial niche became central to the new debate; education-industry links began to dominate curriculum initiatives.

There were concerns that:

> wastage among long-term trainees is heavy in some industries ... Wastage is also affected in ways not directly related to the quality or method of training. For example, the combination of two factors – that the length of apprenticeship is often greater than the time needed for adequate training and that higher wages

may be paid to less skilled workers – prompts some to abandon their training prematurely ... The attitude of both employees and young people to day release depends significantly on the kind of courses provided. Some employees ... accept the value of release for general education and make good use of the facilities available; others are more doubtful and some indeed are critical of it. In general, employers' attitudes towards release for further education become more favourable the more the courses offered are vocationally-oriented (ibid., p. 10).

While there were clear signals that government intervention was needed, government concerns focused on the disaffected youth rather than the employers:

If young people are to choose jobs for which they are suited and to settle successfully into employment they need to be given adequate information and guidance about the possibilities open to them and to have acquired some understanding of what life at work will be like ... It is becoming increasingly important to help young people to develop an awareness of the world of work and of the way wealth is produced and used by society. In recent years the social environment in a number of schools, with more emphasis on personal development and less on formal instruction, has been diverging from that encountered in most work situations, where the need to achieve results in conformity with desired standards and to do so within fixed time-limits calls for different patterns of behaviour (ibid., Part 4, p. 15).

Despite the fact that there were very few jobs to go to, government discourse focused on the attitude of young people to work, which was then associated with failure in schools.

The DES became accused of poor democratic decision-making:

The DES does not encourage interest groups, or indeed the wide public, to participate in discussion of long-range planning of the overall purposes and shape of the education service ... DES planning ... resource oriented, being concerned with primarily with options of scale, organisation and cost rather than educational content (DES, 1976b, p. 4).

The inference was that DES monopoly power was being used illegitimately in order to pursue its own aims at the cost of fulfilling changing educational needs in the economy. The dominance of the economic imperative and the attitude of the government is typified in 1977, where industrial objectives are 'to be given priority over other policy aims, and that policy in other areas, including education, will need to be influenced by our industrial need' (DES, 1977c, p. 3).

On 18 October 1976 the Prime Minister, James Callaghan, gave a speech at Ruskin College, Oxford, which ultimately led to discourse about the inadequacy of the welfare state. He stated: 'there is no virtue in [education] providing socially well-adjusted members of society, who are unemployed because they do not have the skills'. Consequently, a learners' education linked to commercial considerations became part of the agenda: 'nor at the other extreme must they be technically effective robots'. Despite this caveat, the emergence of a new approach to the success of education institutions became based on the ability to contribute to industry, a trend continued by the Conservative government, for example in the White Paper 'Working Together: Education and Training' in 1986:

> The main purpose of the initiative [TVEI] has been to test methods of organising and managing the education of 14–18 year olds across the ability range to improve the provision of technical and vocational education in a way which will widen and enrich the curriculum and prepare young people for adult and working life ... has reinforced moves towards the development of a broader and more relevant curriculum and closer collaboration between education and industry ... (DES, 1986a, p. 9).

and in 'Working Together for a Better Future', published in 1987:

> The broad and balanced curriculum, designed to allow each pupil to achieve his or her maximum potential in every area, is not only desirable in itself. More than that, it is the best preparation for a future in which the pace of economic and technological change will demand adaptability and versatility from all (ibid., p. 3).

'Broad and balanced' curriculum and 'maximum potential' are terms reminiscent of the 1944 Act; 'will demand adaptability and versatility from all', however, reinforces the link with work. In common with much of the earlier initiatives, overseas competition is used as justification for education to be more closely linked with industry, causing education to shift from pure to applied knowledge.

The comprehensive school system, brought in by the Labour government in 1976 became caught up in the inadequacy debate (Education Act 1976). Progressive education was also attacked:

> In the name of 'equality of opportunity' the egalitarian seeks to destroy or transmogrify those schools which make special efforts to bring out the best in

talented children ... in his impatience the egalitarian takes the alternative course of levelling down the higher standards towards a uniform mediocrity ... This leads him to decry the importance of academic standards and discipline ... and indeed learning itself (Maude, 1971, p. 37).

Individualism, expressed as inherited ability, formed the basis of the attack. It implied that new teaching methods were 'levelling down' standards, rather than enabling more to pass.

Discourse in the 1970s contained two themes: firstly, the failure of the system to alter the economic situation; and secondly, the failure of the system dramatically to change the educational achievement of the masses in society. The value of education thus became unclear to the masses and the importance of economic imperatives gained ground. The theme of rationalisation of the system began to emerge and a short-termism became vogue:

> To make schools and colleges as cost-effective as possible: this entails reducing the already large surplus capacity, which will be further increased by falling rolls (DES, 1987b, p. 3).

Yet the same need as that articulated in 1943 can be found in 1987:

> One of the main aims ... is to raise the attainment of young people (16–19), and their confidence in their own abilities, and thus to encourage more positive attitudes to continuing education and training post-16 (ibid., p. 6).

The need to create 'confidence' to enable the process of self-actualisation is still seen as vital to increasing participation in further education. In contrast to the earlier period, however, the 1988 Act uses the language of competition. At the same time as meeting the needs of the students, colleges now had to balance those needs with 'the question of viability and survival' (FEU, 1990, p. 1). 'Viability' implies sustained demand. Student needs thus became re-identified as student demand, conditioned by price. The purpose of further education colleges was thus transformed from educational effectiveness to institutional efficiency and a competitive price became essential to college survival.

The welfare state discourse shifted from expansion to rationalisation:

> For the 16–19 age group there is a significant overlap between the type of course ... and in further education colleges ... much remains to be done ... to improve educational quality in the most cost-effective manner. Educational, financial, social and practical considerations should all play a part ... promoters should draw up rationalisation plans (DES, 1987b, p. 4).

Restructuring thus became part of the rationalisation discourse 'to improve educational quality in the most cost-effective manner'. The battle against existing practice began. This is significantly different from the approach taken to rationalisation in 1966.

In the Pilkington Report 1964, with reference to class sizes, we find that:

> the Committee's conclusion is that there is very considerable reserve of resources which could be more fully used without any educational disadvantage, and that the effective utilisation of this reserve would be invaluable in helping the colleges meet the heavy demands in the next few years (DES, 1966c, para. 3).

A conciliatory tone is expressed: 'could be more fully used' and 'would be invaluable' suggest a democratic approach. That there was cooperation between government, bureaucratic institutions and a shared vision of society is very evident in the following:

> The Secretary of State welcomes in particular its positive approach and the emphasis which it places upon the importance of consultation and co-operation in achieving its objectives. He wishes to commend it warmly to all concerned as a major contribution to the problem of using the resources at their disposal to maximum advantage in the common interest (ibid., para. 10).

The term 'commend it warmly' contained no threat – rather it implied a good working relationship.

By 1987, however, the theme has changed to that of inadequacy:

> New arrangements should offer an education better suited to the needs of the pupils and students of all abilities than would be offered taking account of the probable effects on existing arrangements of expected fall in student numbers (DES, 1987b, para. 4).

> The prime challenge ... is to improve standards of achievement on the part of the pupils and students of all abilities, the quality and range of the curriculum and the effectiveness of its delivery and to secure the best possible return from the resources found for education (ibid., para. 1).

> [the new framework of courses is focused on] The need for educational effectiveness and value for money (ibid., para. 17).

> The Secretary of State expects to see a further improvement ... of NAFE efficiency (ibid., para. 28).

The rationale for change is given as 'falling numbers', but the statement 'education better suited to the needs of the student' suggests inadequacy, the inference being that professionals can be blamed for misuse. The benefit that learners could accrue as a direct result of the reduction in class size is not part of the discourse. Such is the power of the metaphor 'commercialisation' that other reasons for failure of the system to provide increased participation rates fail to arrive on the agenda as part of the discourse for change. The driver for restructuring changed from student need to 'return from resources'. 'Value for money' became a key indicator of educational effectiveness. The language of efficiency is apparent; resources are now 'found' for education, funding was no longer an established right.

The theme of efficiency as a measure of value in the 1980s is in stark contrast to the value of education in the 1960s and 1970s. Value in the earlier period included the notion of social responsibility, implying the existence of a society. Educating the masses thus had a wider remit, that of enabling the masses to contribute to society. The notion that increased participation in education and economic success are interdependent became central to discourse: 'Conservatives believe that high standards in education and training are the key to personal opportunity and national success' (Conservative Party, 1992). The Labour Party states: 'Good education is the best investment for Britain's future. All girls and boys, from every background must be able to discover their talents and fulfil their potential' (Labour Party, 1992). The Liberals comment: 'British citizens are our best asset. Liberal Democrats will invest in people to enable every individual to fulfil their potential and in doing so build the nation's economic and social strength' (Liberal Democrat Party, 1992).

The 1990s looked like a period of political convergence. Nevertheless, Labour and the Liberal Party use 'fulfil their potential' to describe the central driver to the educational system. In contrast, the Conservatives use 'personal opportunity'. The latter creates images of survival of the fittest, an opportunity if you are good enough, whereas the terminology used by Labour and the Liberals suggests opportunity based on merit. There were different solutions to solve the same problem. It is in this context that Sir Ron Dearing was commissioned to conduct a review of 16-19 year olds' qualifications framework. The National Commission on Education proposed radical reorganisation; that 'A' levels, GNVQ and NVQ qualifications be merged into a single framework. While these findings were accepted by Scotland, Sir Ron Dearing gives his rationale for rejection as follows:

> Acceptance of these proposals would mean a fundamental recasting of the present structure of qualifications. This is the course to be developed in Scotland. It has attractions in bringing coherence to the framework of qualifications and in removing the divide between the vocational and academic. A potential disadvantage lies in the risk that it may reduce the value that comes from having distinctive characteristics of the GNVQ being subordinated to the proven A-level approach. That would be to the detriment of students who have not responded well to academic learning and who are stimulated by a different approach. There might also be a risk that by integration of the NVQs, they would be distanced from employers and the Industry Training Organisations, Lead Bodies and Occupational Standards Council which have devised them (DfEE, 1996c, para. 5.7).

Risk aversion is evident in the phrases 'fundamental recasting', 'danger', 'distancing,' and 'risk.' The fear was that these radical proposals might be 'distanced from employers'. At best, therefore, the approach to change could only be incremental, it could not be revolutionary. This is further confirmed in the statement:

> Developments in Scotland could have a long-term bearing on policy elsewhere. For the immediate future, I set out ways of securing greater coherence, from which it would be possible to develop, if that seemed appropriate (ibid., para. 1.4).

The discourse contained the language of caution and a context of non-radicalism, hardly a good recipe for change.

This theme of compromise can be seen further in the following:

> There are strongly held and contrasting views on the purposes of education and training post 16; on what it should consist of; on the best method of assessment; and on what a qualification means (ibid., para. 5.10).

> There are also major differences in assessment. Achievement in A levels is largely measured by examinations ... GNVQ is based primarily on course work (ibid., para. 5.11).

> There are differences in the way A level and GNVQ describe what the candidate is expected to know (ibid., para. 5.12).

> However, there is enough common ground on which to build greater coherence without losing the distinctiveness of each of the individual qualifications ... Both qualifications include knowledge, understanding and skills, though the balance and emphasis varies (ibid., para. 5.13).

The debate about the breadth as against the depth of education became re-identified as product 'distinctiveness'. The discourse thus became one about focus, rather than fundamental differences about the value of education.

This theme is repeated in the discourse about participation:

> In the consultation leading to the Interim Report, the need to motivate and lift achievement amongst the least successful has been recognised, but so has the difficulty of finding ways to do this. By the time a young person is 16 the difficulties are compounded. This points to initiatives before 16–19. A key element in any solution is engaging the learner's interest in some activity and thereby providing motivation and the prospect of achievement. What that 'breakthrough' area of activity may be is less important than securing involvement and building progressively on it (ibid., para. 9.1).

'Engaging the learner's interest' simply implied poor professionalism; lack of aspiration caused by social and economic factors was not part of the discourse. The problem was reduced to one of technique rather one that demanded social revolution.

Further Education: A Managed Market

In the 1940s government intervention was thought essential to ensuring an increase in participation rates in education and training. From the mid-1980s, the Conservative government, with Mrs Thatcher as Prime Minister, introduced radical changes to the further education sector. The language of the market dominated the rationale for development:

> For the nation and all who work in its businesses – both large and small – survival and success will depend on designing, making and selling goods and services that the customer wants at the time he wants and at a price he is prepared to pay; innovating to improve quality and efficiency; and maintaining an edge over all competition (DES, 1986a, p. 1).

Markets are controlled by protecting individual's rights hence inspectorates began to play a more significant role: 'The sector's performance is revealed by the inspection grades awarded during college inspections' (FEFC Annual Report 1995, para. 7). Government controlled by a punishment system: 'The funding penalty attaching to areas of work graded 4 or 5 by inspectors has encouraged colleges to address such deficiencies with speed' (FEFC Annual

Report 1995, para. 16). Clearly it was a financial paradigm, delivered by a government quango, but controlled by central government. It was not a free market but a managed market.

By 1995 market themes of efficiency and (the newly-defined) educational effectiveness were entrenched in policy. This can be seen in the terms and purposes of the review of 16–19 qualifications requested by the Secretary of State for education and employment and conducted by Sir Ron Dearing: '[I was asked] to have particular regard to the need to ... increase participation and achievement in education and training and minimise wastage ... [and to] secure maximum value for money' (DfEE, 1996b, p. 2).

In addition to this remit, the Secretary of State for Education asked a number of questions:

> Is there scope for measures to achieve greater coherence and breadth of study post-16 without compromising standards; and how can we strengthen our qualifications still further? Why is it that many students do not complete their courses? Can school and college resources be better used to enable young people to take full advantage of the ability to mix and match qualifications to suit their needs and abilities? Should we make sure that most able students are stretched and suitably rewards for excellence? And should we encourage core skills, which are already an essential part of GNVQs, as part of the programme of study for more 16–19 year olds? (ibid., p. 1).

However, if answers to these questions are bounded by a market mind-frame then only one avenue of answers is open to discourse; thus it is a managed discourse which means that free speech has become a nebulous notion. Such was the power of commercial language that in 1996 Gillian Shepherd referred, not to ensuring competition, but to fair competition:

> We have achieved a great deal over the last decade to create a climate of competition in the delivery of education and training in this country. However, if this growth is to be sustained then the competition on which it is based must be fair (DfEE, 1996a, p. 1).

It is as if the battle to shift the public mind towards a commercial orientation has been won. Reiterating the finding of the White Paper 1996 'Competitiveness: Creating the Enterprise Eentre of Europe' (DfEE, 1996c) the Conservative government indicated its intention to: 'secure greater convergence of funding arrangements' (DfEE, 1996a, para. 4) in order to provide 'fair and effective competition between providers' (ibid., para. 3). Competition between the providers was orchestrated by government intervention and favoured its mental models. Government was saying one thing and doing another.

Further Education: The Need for a Public Relations Exercise

Over the period of investigation, further education evolved as second class. This sector needed promotion to alter participation rates (MoE, 1959d; MoE, 1959a). In 1959 we find:

> The work of the further education service is handicapped by the ignorance and misunderstanding which are still too common despite all that has been done in the last few years to make it better known (MoE, 1964b, para. 2).

The message was clear – much work still needed to be done to change society's attitude to the value of further education and its position in the hierarchy of knowledge. But in the 1985 audit, the need for a radical change is reduced to the need for 'better marketing' (Audit Commission, 1985). The discourse became one of compromise, the speed of change incremental.

In 1995 reference to the social context favouring the academic route is still evident:

> The prestige of A levels influences choice. Unless the standing of vocational qualifications can be strongly established, too many students are likely to disregard professional guidance and choose a pathway which may serve them poorly (DfEE, 1996b, Section 9.1).

Despite the evidence of low uptake and low achievement, the solution was identified as one of informing: 'It is essential that parents, students and employers understand the framework of qualifications' (ibid., para. 13.1). Social revolution was swapped for a discourse about information dissemination – the problem was presented as more to do with understanding the role of vocational qualifications, which in turn leads to low uptake. Yet in 1990 the report from the European Communities Committee includes the following statement: 'The existence of a skills gap in the United Kingdom is well documented. The CBI task force found that the United Kingdoms workforce is 'under educated, under trained and underqualified'. Nearly half of Britain's employees have no qualification to GCE 'O' level. In France 35 per cent of school leavers reached university entrance standard, as did 30 per cent of school leavers in Germany, compared with 15 per cent in the United Kingdom

(European Community, 1990, para. 30). It seems that other countries now understood what policies were required even if our own government did not.

The UK's obligation to develop such policies can be seen in the following:

> The right to vocational training is recognised in the Universal Declaration of Human Rights, the International Covenant on Economic and Social Rights [ibid., para. 40] and in the European Social Charter [1961]. The latter two of these impose binding international legal obligations on contracting parties, including the United Kingdom. The European Social Charter requires state parties to provide or promote as necessary technical and vocational training for all persons ... The Community Social Charter declared that 'every worker of the European Community must be able to have access to vocational training and to receive such training throughout his working life.' This Charter was not signed by the United Kingdom, alone among Community Member States (ibid., para. 40).

The UK's relationship with the EC was clearly acrimonious because the Conservative government had decided to opt out of the Social Charter. Nevertheless the issues still needed to be resolved. The Committee continues: 'Many witnesses indicated that exhortation alone was unlikely to be adequate to achieve the major change in cultural attitude towards training, which was needed in the United Kingdom' (ibid., para. 31).

The suggestion from our European colleagues was the need for radical policies to change 'cultural attitudes' towards education and training. In 1997 we find:

> It will be essential for further education to develop a concerted approach at national and local levels to stimulate demand for learning. This means some visionary planning directed towards the better dissemination of information and the creation of positive images of further education' (FEFC, 1997, p. 7).

These are the objectives stated in 1944, expressed differently. It would seem that 'positive images', or rather the lack of them, had been what government over the period of time has failed to achieve. A policy based on incremental change had not yet been able to break free from the status quo: given the evidence it looked unlikely that it ever would.

In conclusion, much has been achieved in the provision of compulsory education up to the age of 16 and similarly in full-time further and higher education. However, post-19, retraining, second chance and continuous vocational advancement has failed to achieve the status of a merit good, although to be fair, some provision has been made and financed. Failure of the compulsory sector to turn around the achievements of the rejecter/returnee and the average or below average student, has presented this sector with the problem. A large part of the further education colleges' course portfolio serves the greater number of post-compulsory education students in the population. With or without a policy, therefore, this sector has a considerable impact on a large sector of the population who lie outside the privileged category, university students. Several themes have been key to the discourse, namely: vision; inadequacy; rationalisation; the market; and compromise.

A Theme of Vision

This gained momentum alongside the opportunity for radical social reconstruction that developed towards the end of the war. The theme of vision contained two themes. First, the assumption that increased educational achievement of the masses would contribute directly or indirectly to economic development; this in turn led to a language theme about the economic imperative of educating the population. The desire for increased intellectual advancement also had a political motive, namely social improvement. Improvement was to be achieved by providing routes for an individual to achieve equal opportunity; consumption of education creating increased intellectual capability was identified as crucial to ensuring that an individual could embrace opportunity. In 1944 the coalition government simply increased its commitment to the social motive because the market had failed to deliver. Evidence of both language themes have been used to justify government intervention. The state adopted the role of parent, to ensure that opportunity would be available to all. Over time, however, an incremental approach to change ensured that the emerging system was about intellectually and morally training individuals to know their rights and carry out their duties – the language theme of compromise, rather than that of social revolution, thus began to dominate. In the 1880s the theme of equality was dropped in favour of the theme of quality. By the late 1990s the discourse had become dominated by the economic motive, delivered through the metaphor of the market, and the vision became reduced to a discourse about cost. The market metaphor altered the meaning of words like 'value', 'quality' and 'need' and thus rendered impotent the vision of social improvement. In the late 1990s some elements of the theme of social improvement seem to be fighting back.

A Theme of Inadequacy

What initially began as a theme of inadequacy in the 1970s – the failure of the educational system to change the lot of half the young population – provided the basis for the theme of derision. This theme attacked the professionals' right to decide as well as the usefulness of the established bureaucratic system and the role of government. With high public expenditure and low growth the economic climate added credence to the theme of inadequacy and provided the context that enabled the credibility and legitimisation of the democratic system to be challenged.[14] From the late 1970s onwards, therefore, this theme provided legitimacy for government to become involved in restructuring the domain of social welfare that continued into the late 1990s.[15]

A Theme of Rationalisation

This initially began as careful spending in the context of growth – efficiency was important because the increasing demands of the welfare state increased the demand on public finances. This seems to be a dilemma embedded in public policy-making.[16] With rising consumer expectations, government has to balance increasing demands for welfare at the same time as it responds to pressure to reduce the tax burden, which becomes particularly acute when the economy is in downturn. In the final analysis, the vision of 1944 could not be realised and ultimately choices had to be made. Further education provision thus became peripheral to the main debate. In the 1980s, with a Conservative government in power, and in a context of a decreasing young population, the discourse became that of cutback and a rationalisation programme became one of the tools with which to achieve it. The theme of rationalisation encompassed decisions about the right way to ensure efficiencies, based on a production industry, and this impacted on how educational effectiveness could be measured. The discourse about educational value thus became conditioned by the discourse about efficiency and resource utilisation, or rationalisation.

A Theme of the Market

The theme of inadequacy contributed to the derision of government intervention. Furthermore, the theme of rationalisation, with its focus on efficiency, provided some legitimacy for the idea that bureaucratic systems were sluggish. The domination of the market metaphor as an explanation for action changed the discourse from government intervention to institutional survival – as the competitive environment increased the drivers within the colleges changed. At the same time, and in line with market freedom, the language theme of need was altered to that of consumer rights delivered through a system based on production orientation. These discourse themes legitimised a reduction in direct government intervention and reinforced a drift towards a context of individualism.

A Theme of Compromise

Throughout the period studied, a theme of compromise is central, although the reasons for this differ. The radical reforms of 1944 were fuelled by the need and desires of the population at large for social reconstruction but were always conditioned by an incremental approach to change. There was always a rationale based on finance, which tempered that radical vision. In the 1970s, the discourse of inadequacy gave way to the market metaphor and economic imperatives. As a result, the discourse on educational effectiveness became subordinated to a discourse about institutional effectiveness and the theme of compromise changed to that of domination. By 1996 the theme of social improvement had become a non-discourse. As a result, consultation on restructuring the system culminated in the rejection of a system that merged disparate qualifications in favour of continuing the established system, a system that reinforced traditional classifications of difference. The theme of compromise thus provided the path for radicalism to be legitimately rejected.

In drawing some conclusion from the themes outlined, we must, of course, be very cautious. The findings rely on the selection of documents used and the writer's interpretation of the information. It has also to be borne in mind that documentation tends to be written with an audience in mind – thus the language is biased. Given these limitations, a thematic analysis has enabled the identification of a shift in educational value from educational effectiveness in 1944 to organisational efficiency post-1980s. This changed language theme also reflects the changing role of the government, which has changed from one of parent and guardian responsible for the development of society in 1944, to one of monitor.

Finally we need to answer the question posed at the beginning: are post-1980s Conservative government policies radical? Put differently, have the essential principles of meritocracy, and the central theme of equality, on which the educational system was based in 1944, been subjected to a paradigm shift?

There is some evidence to suggest that the development of the education system, particularly for further education, is described by social continuity. The derision of the welfare state, freedom from bureaucratic control and the changed governmental role from mentor to monitor are consistent with the Victorian values of economic liberation, individualism, self-help and private paternalism and represent some degree of social continuity. However, to ignore the evidence of incremental change would be a folly since this process can also lead to revolution – it simply takes a less obtrusive route. Incremental change kills a paradigm softly.

The discourse centred on the rights of the individual fits less comfortably with the theme of social continuity. The learner's changed role from student to purchaser, the Student Charter and the introduction of credits, coupled with the rejection of markets epitomised in the new ethical stance, suggest changed power relationships. It has been possible to demonstrate, as Taylor-Goody (2000) suggests, that the Conservative model has moved power into the centre and that this is popular under the banner of accountability. There does, however, appear to be a growing ethical stance, which rejects the market as a perfect method of allocation for all resources. Consumers do have the potential to be sovereign and use their power to decide, but these rights are distinctly different from democratic rights. There is something here that cannot just be categorised into two simple dimensions, old and new.

Dunn, in his work on old and new paradigms in industrial relations (1991), building on the work of Khun (1981),[17] Black (1962),[18] King (1980)[19] and Nisbet (1969),[20] suggests that change may not be simply divided into old and new. Root metaphors may be evolutionary, serving to stimulate new and creative activity. A biological metaphor is created by the death of an old set of beliefs; thus it represents revolutionary change in ideas. A journey metaphor describes leaving a safe place and returning; thus it represents social continuity (Dunn, 1991, p. 18). In the journey, the exit and entry points are static, an individual may break with tradition but then conform, thus reinforcing society's belief in the value of the archetype. Where a journey metaphor describes reality, traditional sets of beliefs condition and control learning, enlightened experience will be denied at re-entry.

Dunn, building on Campbell's (1988) work, suggests a third option, a new type of journey metaphor. When this metaphor is used there is no return to the past or revolution. Ideas and past assumptions become adapted to suit the emerging reality; change is conditioned to a certain extent by the past but exit becomes a pioneering journey (Dunn, 1991, p. 20).[21] In the new journey metaphor, return to a stable set of beliefs is irrelevant because change, rather than stability, is accepted as the natural state.

Adopting Dunn's proposition, the possibility exists for the growth in commercialisation through the archetype root metaphor 'market' to be part of a process of pioneering, the continued development of a new journey metaphor. Evaluation of the documentation has shown traditional rites of passage, class relations, being consistently challenged by the Left and Right. More recently, this has been under the banner of consumer rights, but now seems to include ethics, which suggests that discourse on consumer rights may lack a certain something. These factors suggest a journey metaphor, as described by Dunn; new knowledge created by a failed experiment. Finding a journey metaphor would be conversant with Giddens (1999), who suggests that today's society needs a different democratic dialogue.[22] Maybe modernising democracy has become a natural consequence of the dynamic world in which we function and indeed crucial to the continuance of legitimisation of government and its agencies. The policies of the Thatcher era did not create a paradigm shift but are a recent part of a consistent incremental trend towards the abolition of class relations. Let us hope, as Dunn suggests, that a new journey metaphor is distinctive, in that there is no 'going back'. Indeed, Jones suggests that postmodern times are distinct, in that grand designs have become obsolete in favour of image, which serves to distance any meaning.[23] In postmodern times, explanation is at best impermanent and is quickly replaced, causing democracy to become fluid.

In order to examine the more subjective approach taken in this chapter the next task is to subject the documentation gathered to quantitative techniques. This will test further the proposition that there is a change in the language theme over the period 1944–96. We conclude that there is a paradigm shift in governmental discourse during this period from educational effectiveness to institutional efficiency.

Notes

1 Black defines root metaphors as systematic collections of ideas that enable description, by analytical extension, of ideas, which do not literally apply.
2 Interest in and desire for money rather than spiritual or ethical value.
3 The Cross Report led to radical modification of the curriculum. As a result, a wider variety of subjects were included in the curriculum; physical exercise and sports also became part of school life. The Bryce Report led to the formation of a Board of Education. Furthermore, it was suggested that local authorities should provide secondary education where the market did not.
4 It is interesting to note that the popular advertising slogan for the 1990s in colleges and universities has a familiar ring: 'lifelong learning'. Curiously this approach is also reminiscent of the basis of the training programme in Japan.
5 In a free market, labour is treated as any other input to create an output; thus the price of labour changes with demand for it. Employers' need to protect profit suggests a downward pressure on the price of inputs. Employers who are focused on profit are therefore unlikely

to invest in training programmes as these will eat in to their short-term profit; thus the free market leads the employers to focus on low wages, few training programmes and a short-term management perspective. In terms of the individual, participation in training programmes relies on delayed gratification, paying now for increased prospects in the future; it was evident that the market signals were such that few were prepared to participate in delayed gratification.
6   A commodity which society identifies as intrinsically good or bad and adopts methods to stimulate or discourage.
7   An important property of a public good is that consumption of it by one individual does not reduce the amount available for consumption of it by others. Consumption of the public good cannot be restricted – individual suppliers are not attracted to supply, therefore communal supply is the preferred option. Quasi-public goods are supplied by the state out of taxation because their quality or quantity of supply would be inadequate if left to the private sector.
8   Bureaucratic procedures are used to ensure that, where transactions take place, the rules for participation are both fair and clear to the participants.
9   In Circular 351, 7/1959, 7/1970.
10 A tight financial control style is one where the centre sets tight financial targets which the business units have to reach. The centre also takes responsibility for making the decisions which are then imposed on the business units (Goold and Campbell, 1987).
11 Self-actualisation is seen as a key driver for individual motivation when basic needs have been met. Individuals' motivation is key to organisations achieving quality outputs, because it can increase the level of good will. Work motivation strategies are advocated by human resource managers as solutions to worker alienation.
12 The equity indicators are age/sex/race, entitlements and disability.
13 In Part III of the Education Reform Act provision was made for the councils of the Inner London Boroughs and the common council of the City of London to become the LEA from April 1990.
14 Britain had one of the highest rates of public expenditure among OECD countries, against a background of low economic growth.
15 Ball uses the term 'discourse of derision' to describe the discourse in the 1970s. A right wing discourse, it criticised the social imperative as a means to bring about change.
16 The welfare circle is public service provision, the welfare square public service finance. The authors argue that governments in all industrial societies face an increasing struggle to meet the increasing demand for better quality welfare while at the same time meeting the demand for limiting taxation. The 1980s was a decade in which policy reflected an ideological commitment different from that of the early post-war period. The role of social welfare politics, policy and institutions became part of a new discourse. Squaring the welfare circle, George and Miller (1994) argue, describes the emergence of a new paradigm – affordable welfare.
17 Thomas Kuhn suggests that the distinguishing mark of science is to be found in the normal puzzle-solving stages rather than revolutionary phases.
18 Developing the concept of metaphors as dynamic Black argues that not only do metaphors allow comparison of one against another but that this interactive process has the potential to generate new thought.
19 King, building on Kuhn's puzzle-solving stage, suggests that the shift from an old way of thinking to a new involves non-rational decision-making. This occurs because proof in

social science is illusive; thus, he argues acceptance of the new paradigm is in some part driven by belief.

20   Nisbet warns that a 'becoming' metaphor, and the theories it implies for describing social change, risks saying nothing about the here and now. There is a danger, he argues, where incremental change is pursued as a description of reality, that the natural state of institutions and social behaviour 'fixity' can be ignored. Fixities survive failed experiments. Thus the more cognitive distance the metaphor has from today's reality the more useful it is as a tool of analysis. Dunn, developing Nisbet's point, argues that if concentrating on a 'becoming' metaphor can distort today's analysis, by emphasising change over fixity, it can also be blamed for distorting the past. 'Thus trade unions behaved as if they had a vested interest in laissez-faire rather than a sword of justice' (Dunn. 1991, p. 25).

21   Campbell argues that science and technology have served to reduce the occurrence of the journey metaphor because of their link with tradition, which can now be proved wrong. Individualism has superseded associations with group or society. Dunn (1991) argues that even if tradition no longer has a hold on knowledge, other symbols now take its place – thus journey metaphors are not extinct.

22   In Western societies, Giddens argues, the recreation of society through traditional symbols and behaviour was crucial to its authority and legitimisation. The failed experiment – what Giddens calls the shortcomings of liberal democracy – coupled with the shifting role of the state and its agencies, alongside that of the polity in the new globalised world, produce new political dilemmas the resolution of which demands a different democratic dialogue. The welfare state, he argues, has become stale, inflexible and impersonal at the same time as the public has become more informed. Thus he suggests that greater government transparency could enable the new democracy.

23   In postmodern theorising the fluidity of socialisation constructs and redefines explanation, constantly causing meaning to become lost to competing current trends (Jones, 1992).

Chapter Six

The Archaeological System of Knowledge: A Broad Panoramic Sweep

This chapter seeks to check and balance the thematic analysis presented in the previous chapter.

The Context and Content

It is well known that in 1943, the coalition government in the UK set out to deliberately alter tradition by introducing a radical social reconstruction programme. The stage for a change agenda developed from dissatisfaction with traditional values and norms, which seems to have evolved from wider inclusion practices during the war. This watershed period thus provided me with a benchmark against which I could relate political trends over a 50-year period to recent changes brought to bear. The sheer amount of documentation, however, was so overwhelming I had to be content with a narrowed field of study and a sampling method.

    I selected content analysis as the research instrument. An important assumption of content analysis is that, by a process of deconstructing the discursive content into language streams, inferences about the sender, the message and the audience can be drawn. I narrowed the field of study to government's discourse with further education colleges from 1944 to 1997. A sample of government Circulars, Administrative Memoranda, White Papers and reports was used to encapsulate government discourse. The account of government discourse with the colleges is thus impoverished by exclusion but, it is hoped, not more so than in other work of this kind.

    Developing the analysis of language themes as instruments of power relies heavily on the work of Bernstein and Foucault. Building on Durkheim's work, Bernstien (1973) presented the thesis that social actors are a function of the language they use.[1] Important to the development of Bernstein's work was Durkheim's conclusion that the process of social order created belief systems that influenced social and psychological consciousness.

Using a process of deconstructing message systems, Bernstein was able to show that themes in language had the power to affect knowing. He suggested that such power was dependent upon two factors, namely, the content selection within the message and the limiting boundaries of the message. Limiting the boundaries of content within the message served, he suggested, to exclude some knowledge thus conditioned what was in the public arena to know. He demonstrated that message systems expressed both explicit and implicit meaning – he was able to show that as an individual decoded a message, explicit meaning affected their task direction and implicit meaning altered their conduct in line with social behavioural rules. Embodied within language themes, he argued, was an exercise of power; thus studies of communication had to include an understanding of its semiology.

Bernstein's work contributed to the study of language as a complex network of linked assumptions, symbols and myth. Sentence substitutes were understood to express conceptual archetypes, associating one experience in terms of another, they were thought to be built on commonly-believed patterns of behaviour and understanding (Black, 1964). It was postulated that such shorthand communication circumvented the need to articulate the beliefs and associations encapsulated: through a process of disproof, avoidance such beliefs gained a self-certifying right (Turner, 1974). Metaphors were thought to blur the distinction between subjectivity and objectivity (Morgan, 1996). Free thought thus became considered by some as a nebulous notion.

Similar to Bernstein, Foucault's (1990) work addressed symbolism in speech. In particular he was interested in what caused accepted language themes, or root metaphors, to change (Dreyfus and Rabinow, 1982). Arguing that all knowledge is embedded in power, Foucault's work suggests that the process of regulation within industrial organisation limits its knowledge assimilation.[2] In particular, he thought the taxonomic naming aspect of language had the potential to manipulate man's consciousness because it became a material force of its own causing subjects and agents thought to be constituted by those codes.[3] Further, he thought such regulation created an acquiescent, task-focused consciousness amongst the polity. Metaphor, he thought, was particularly powerful because it influenced knowledge by transmitting conceptual understandings of linked events.[4]

More recently it has become more significant to understand what causes people to be interested in movement rather than how people get locked into inherited paradigms (Holland, 1999). The danger with investigations based on personal histories is that they tend to be packed with ideological *a priori*, because such taxonomy is powerful, epistemology becomes conditioned by it

(Macey, 1993). To reveal the expression of power through language themes, Foucault thus suggested that researchera needed to distance themselves from personal histories because discourse is comprised of a discontinuous dialectic, which contains juxtaposed descriptions of reality. Foucault suggested that revealing the panorama of this narrative would help identify the profusion of powers at play which helped to determine the knowing expressed through personal histories.[5]

This new epistemology of practice suggests the possibility that new knowledge and contexts can be a process of development (Schon, 1983). Carrying out the tasks of everyday life, and reflecting upon them with others, can alter an individual's understanding of events and thus provide escape from cognitive bonds. To learn, however, individuals have to be aware of the conflicting paradigm positions, the underlying assumptions of the construct systems at play and their limitations to create an interactive process of knowing. The notion that how change takes place is more important than why tradition is maintained has become part of discovering the evolving story of human interaction, knowledge and learning.

Lichtenstein (1997) postulates two characteristic triggers in such dynamic learning processes, namely discontent and conflict at the mature stage of a theory because resources are fully utilised and the emergence of a new dialectic as a consequence of the increased momentum of an alternative discourse. Further, it is postulated, new contexts develop to address the limitations of old ways of doing things which thus fit the environment better (Gersick, 1998).

This movement of ideas can be tracked in language themes using metaphor analysis (Dunn, 1991). There are three types of metaphor: biological, journey and pioneering. The death of an old set of beliefs and the emergence of a new way of imagining – revolutionary change – is captured by a biological metaphor. A journey metaphor represents the continuance of tradition. A pioneering metaphor is distinguished from both these states and captures a nonlinear creative process from which new imaginings emerge.

In Foucauldian terms I adopted a panoramic approach to examining the discursive routes that have contributed to the development of the further education sector, in order to isolate the levers and drivers that have led to its constitution, and applied the principle of externality to discover the conditions of possibility. Adopting some important components of reflexive analysis, I set out to expose the threads of argument and so to expose the underlying paradigm positions and the social and ethical values embodied within each position. My assumption was that any contradictory paradigm positions in government discourse would be exposed in the collective symbolism of its vocabulary.

Measuring and Evaluating Communication

The first step in this work was thus to test the hypothesis that there had been a significant change in the value system within which further education policy has been expressed. In order to identify the discourse themes involved, the first task was to identify keywords that encapsulated the semantics at play as far as those working within further education colleges were concerned.

A randomly-selected group of employees was asked to compile a list of words they used to describe the current attributes of the further education sector as they saw them. Surprisingly, this revealed that at the orientation stage of the verbal planning procedure, these employees functioned with two unique notions. Indeed, while some respondents included these two notions in one list, others went so far as to present them in two separate lists. The words that encapsulated these two notions were thus used as a starting point for the development of the key language themes. The historians thematic approach in the previous chapter revealed that these two notions were key players in the government discourse over the period of study.

Frequency tables and relative frequency tables were compiled for each of the selected documents, to isolate the most common words appearing in the documentation. Testing these against the themes presented by those working in further education colleges, the data text was grouped into coding themes namely, caring and commercial coding. Each of the coding themes describes a different view of reality.[6]

Account, budget and *fees* highlight a strong financial aspect to the commercial coding theme. *Demand, market* and *efficiency* with *profit* seen as the measure of success decided by *competition* between the players describes the market paradigm. A hierarchical power structure in day to day *business* is implied by the use of *management*, legitimate power and authority given to *managers*. In this scenario the individual is a *client* or a *consumer*, a purchaser.

In contrast, the caring coding system transmits the pursuit of a social ideal, namely that of *equality of opportunity*. The need to control *inequalities* in society suggests some social responsibility, combined with a **duty**, to reduce unfair *hardship* caused by the uneven distribution of resources available. The approach is *consultative* and paternal; a *student* studies under a *committed* professional who *enables* his or her learning; the context is one of a *caring* community.

The two distinct language themes thus imply contrasting imaginings about the world in which we function and its organisation. The recognition of inequality, and the pursuit of equality, implies that existing social relations are divisive and thus in need of change – this implies that the government and its institutions have a role as change agents – whereas the use of markets in the commercial coding theme implies that fair play is mediated by the price mechanism and government's role is thus limited to ensuring the infrastructure for markets to perform.

In the caring theme, educational *institutions* adopt a paternalistic, all-knowing stance enabling the student not only in academic specificity but also in the socialisation process – setting benchmarks and measuring students' distance from others isolates the components of success and thus aspiration. In the commercial theme the colleges are *educational organisations* operating in a competitive arena, where demand determines organisational survival. Indeed, rather than lead the student to a better life, the commercial theme implies that the colleges need to be reactive to their clients' demands. Similarly, *student* suggests a passive role on behalf of the individual and a paternalistic role for the institution and its employees. *Consumer* suggests a proactive purchasing power role on behalf of the individual and a servicing role on behalf of the organisation and its employees.

Using the two discursive roots – caring and commercial coding – and plotting their influence over a 50 year period revealed an interesting story about the power of these two discursive roots over time.

Figure 1 offers an analysis over 10 year periods; Figure 2, every three years. Through this process it can be seen that at its inception the so-called radical reconstruction of the state education system in 1943 was conditioned by commercial considerations. Despite the coalition government of the time, and what appeared to a political consensus, two distinct views were locked in the same virtual space dialectic. While the overt political agenda espoused equal opportunity, the attainment of equal opportunity through access to education was always conditioned by price. It is interesting the see the reduced power of commercial coding in the late 1960s as the system of equal opportunity became normalised. Indeed, the increase in the power of commercial coding commences in the 1970s, peaking in the 1980s under Mrs Thatcher. This goes some way to explain why the political consensus portrayed in the 1944 Education Act failed to maintain its momentum. It also goes some way to explain why further education colleges were catapulted from the public sector and became incorporated entities.

Despite the conditioning factor, however, the visionary theme encapsulated in the caring coding has maintained its power over the study period. It could be argued it has refused to be put to death.

The Archaeological System of Knowledge: A Broad Panoramic Sweep 157

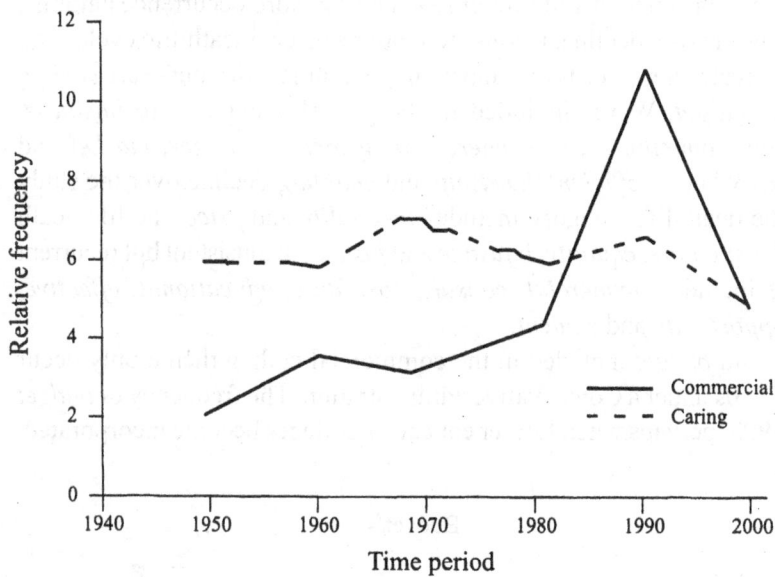

Figure 1   **Language coding themes**

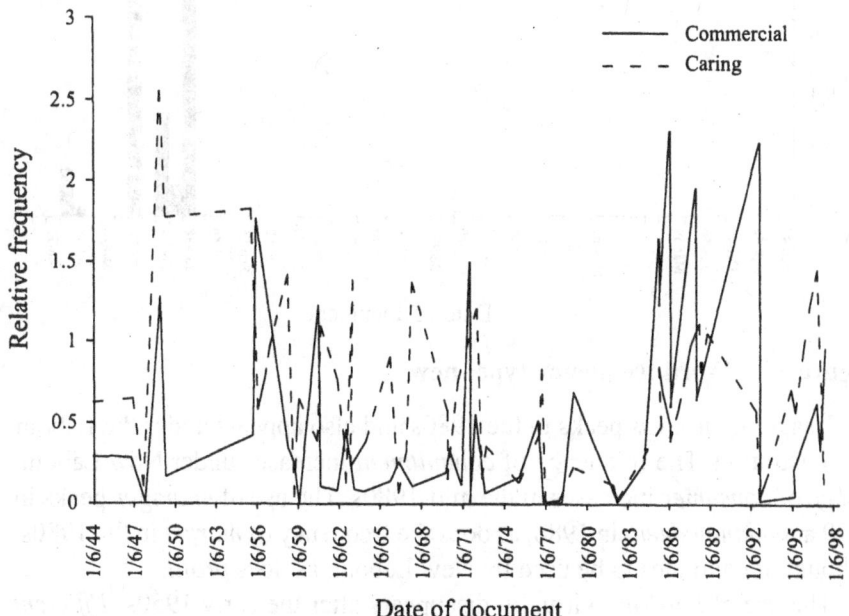

Figure 2   **Document language themes**

Analysing the content still further revealed six word occurrence patterns, namely new, growth, decline, inconsistent but recurrent, death/life cycle[7] and life/death[8] cycle. New words that appear in government discourse are *caring*, *client* and *budget*. Words included in the growth category are *business*, *competition*, *commitment*, *consumer*, *management*, *manager*, *market* and *profitability* whereas *efficient*, *hardship* and *enabling* decline over the study period. The death/life category includes *inequality* and *price*, the life/death category *competitors*, *equality*, *injustice* and *justice*. Inconsistent but recurrent categories include *commercial*, *consult*, *cost*, *duty*, *educational*, *effective*, *income*, *opportunity* and *student*.

Client and *budget* included in the commercial coding theme only occur from the 1980s under a Conservative administration. The frequency of *budget* peaks in 1993, perhaps when further education colleges become incorporated.

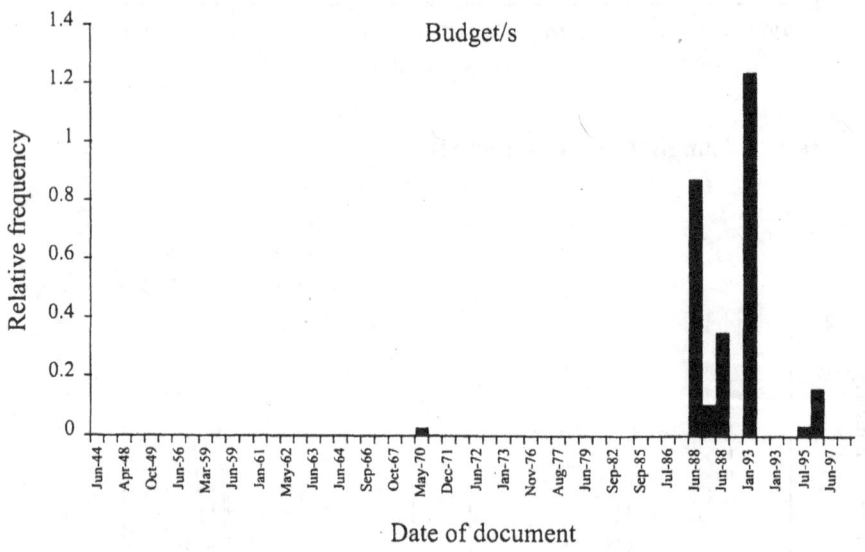

Figure 3   **Word frequency type: new**

Usage of *business* peaks in the 1980s and also appears under the Labour administration. The frequency of *commitment* increases under New Labour. Usage of *consumer* increases in the mid-1980s. The use of *manager* peaks in 1979 and *management* in 1986, as does the frequency of *market* in the 1980s, although it continues to be used by New Labour, as does *profit*.

The use of *hardship* virtually disappears after the early 1950s. *Efficient* peaks in the late 1940s, marking the increase in the theme of compromise driven by financial imperatives. *Enabling* fits with the paternal approach of the 1944 Act.

Both Labour and Conservative administrations over time use this category of words. The frequency of those included in the commercial coding, however, increases during the 1980s. The occurrence of *opportunity* peaks in the 1970s, possibly marking the arrival of the theme of inadequacy.

With the growth in the market theme it is not surprising to see *price* reappear on the agenda. The re-emergence of *inequality* is interesting since it appears under the New Labour administration.

The reduction in the use of *equality, injustice* and *justice* may well represent the exchange of radical change for incremental change.

Fifty-three per cent of words included in the commercial coding theme occur in the new and growth categories compared with 13 per cent of the caring coding.

Further analysis of the pattern of word occurrence shows 53 per cent of words in the commercial coding theme appear in the new and growth categories compared with 13 per cent in the caring coding. Both themes contribute 40 per cent to the recurrent category. Caring coding comprises 26 per cent of the decline and life/death categories, compared with 13 per cent of commercial coding. I have also been able to isolate the growth of market speak within commercial coding as influential post-1980. Matching the data to the political party in power revealed the Labour Party utilising the market theme from 1997.

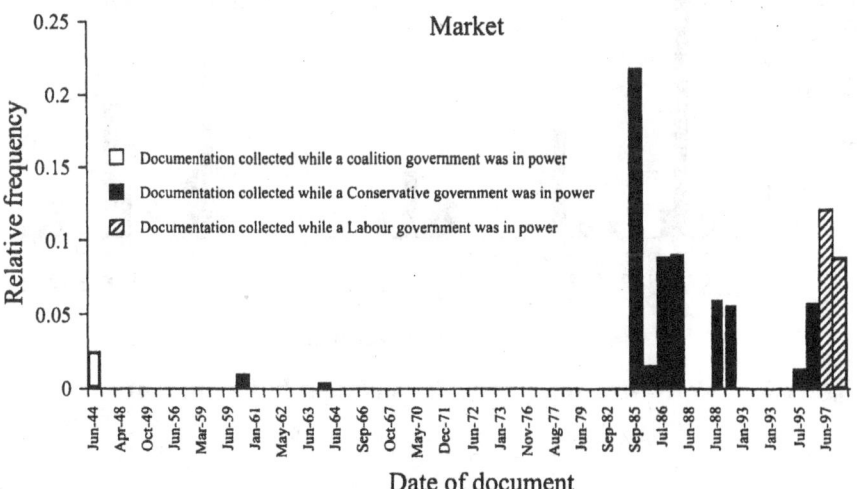

Figure 4   Word frequency type: growth

160 *Further Education, Government's Discourse Policy and Practice*

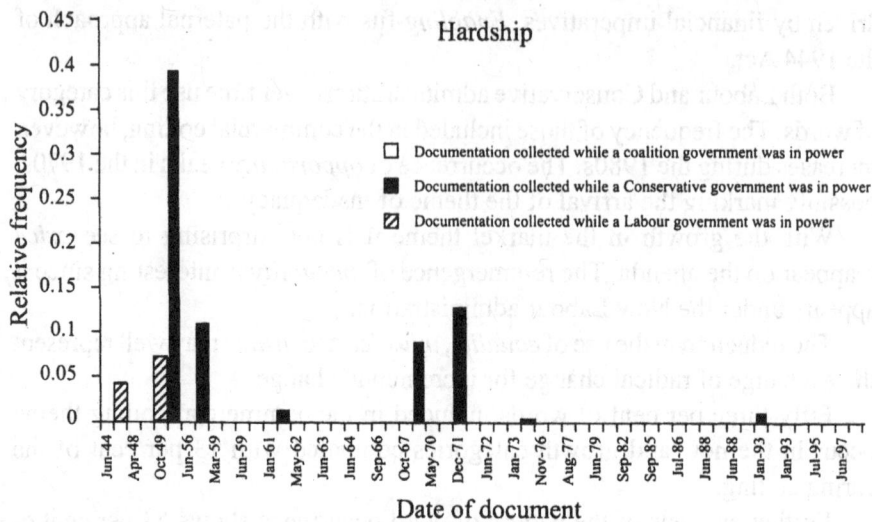

Figure 5   Word frequency type: decline

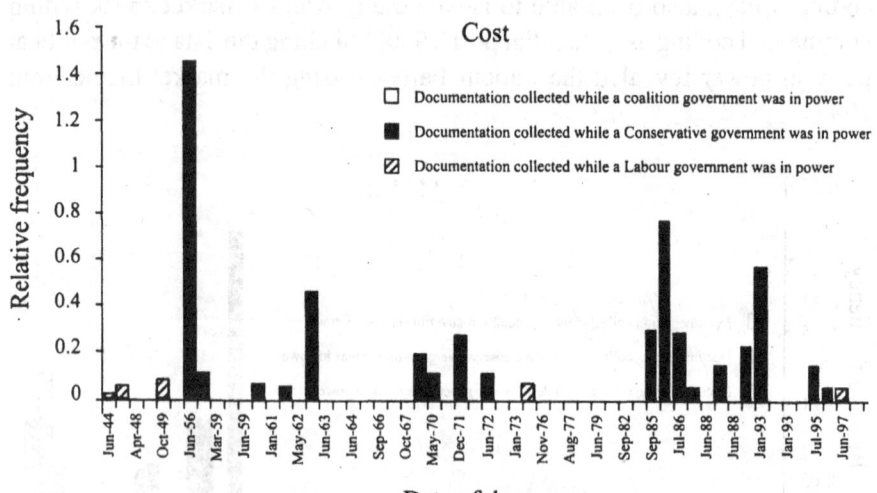

Figure 6   Word frequency type: inconsistent but recurrent

The Archaeological System of Knowledge: A Broad Panoramic Sweep   161

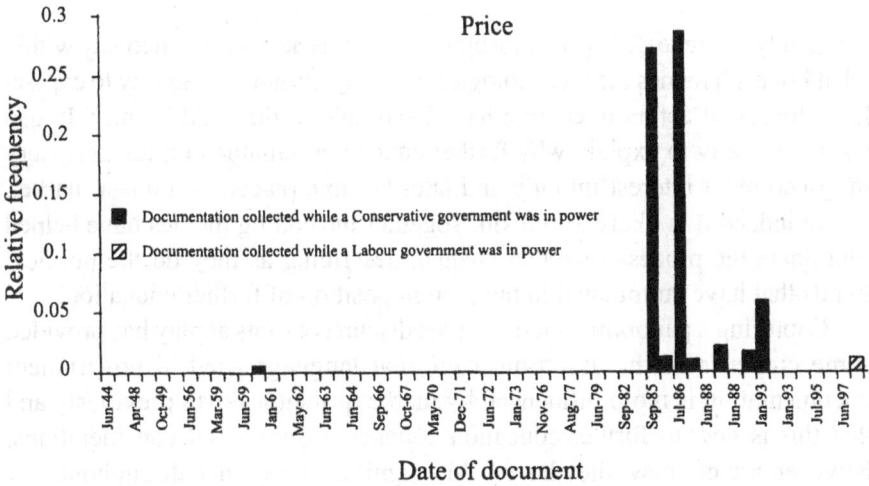

Figure 7   Word frequency type: death/life

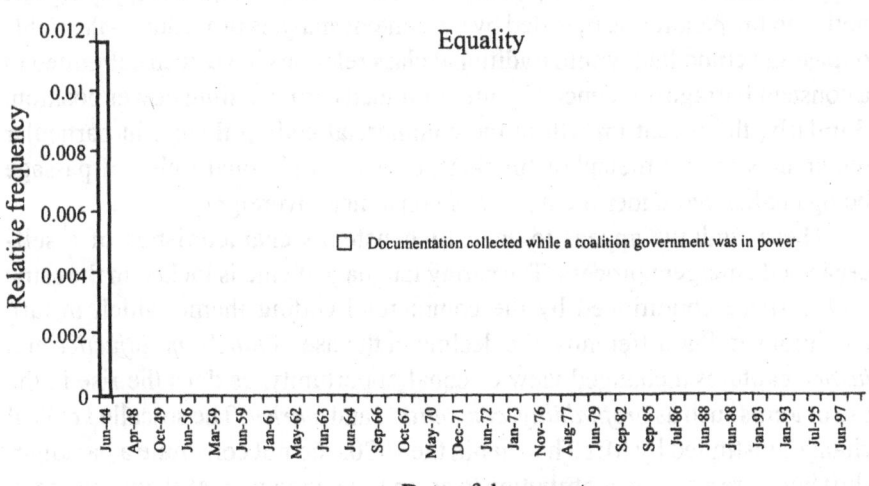

Figure 8   Word frequency type: life/death

Considerations

This study has revealed two philosophical systems held simultaneously within what Foucault names the archaeological system; this goes some way to explain how the social actors over time have been able to think differently. It also goes some way to explain why further education remained on the periphery of government interest initially and later became placed in a quasi market, where indeed it is likely to remain. Together the coding themes have helped illuminate the process of social change, describing as they do the political trends that have culminated in the current position of further education.

Capturing a panoramic picture of the discursive roots at play has provided some credence to the assertion made that language used in government documentation is more influenced by market principles than previously and that this is new to further education colleges. Commercial considerations, however, are not new: they have held a significant presence throughout.

It is important to the analysis of power to note that the analysis of the discourse in this case has not revealed any evidence that suggests the discovery of a biological metaphor. This is an important finding. There is, therefore, no evidence of revolutionary change. On the other hand, there is much here that suggests I have captured the journey of a pioneering metaphor. Applying this notion to the panoramic revealed by the content analysis procedure – the rights of passage embodied within traditional class relations have been submitted to a constant barrage, evidenced by the continued caring coding power position. Similarly, the recent growth in the commercial coding theme, in particular the archetype root metaphor 'market', exposes traditional rights of passage being challenged under the banner of consumer sovereignty.

These findings appear to echo Lichenstein's characteristics of a self-organised emergent process. The caring language theme is locked in the same reality space conditioned by the commercial coding theme which in turn conditions it. Put differently, the decline in the use of *hardship, injustice* and *justice* captures a changed view of equal opportunity, as does the rise in the use of terms such as *profitability, competition* and *market*. The so-called radical changes instituted by Mrs Thatcher in the 1980s did not constitute a paradigm shift but were a recent contribution to an ongoing incremental change process.

It remains, as always, important to be cautious and recognise the limitations of the panoramic explanatory power of discourse analysis. The deconstruction of meaning in communication brings its own problems. It remains important to recognise that inputs to social issues are multifactorial, interrelated and individually interpreted; as a consequence, any attempt to evaluate language has to be understood in its social context. A quantitative approach to content analysis has nevertheless provided a useful corrective checking device to guard against bias and has been usefully complementary. An element of subjectivity remains a basic property of the investigation of social interaction and discourse.

Clearly there is the opportunity for more work to be carried out in this area. A syntactic approach applied to content analysis does have the potential to provide a greater in-depth analysis of sociolinguistic codes. The possibility that this process could isolate the elaborated code of objective consciousness from the restricted code of subjective consciousness is clearly of interest.

In brief, the results from the quantitative content analysis have provided more credence to the assertion made in the previous chapter that the language used in government documentation is more influenced by market values than previously and that this is new in educational speak, while commercial coding is not.

Notes

1 Durkheim identified two types of organisation, namely organic and mechanistic. Socialisation created by organic solidarity, based on the interdependency of specialist division of labour, was superior, he argued, to mechanical solidarity based on authoritarian rule. He thought work enhanced social relationships because it bridged the self and communal need paradox. The interdependency of fragmented work was thus instrumental to the negation of repression. Thus social order had the potential to be the embodiment of moral behaviour expressed through rites, rituals and myth, belief systems and social and psychological consciousness. He thought bureaucracies had the potential to inhibit expression of greater good by binding the individual to the work task and that solidarity was threatened by rapid change and the specialised division of labour because these factors contributed to an individual's sense of normlessness. Durkheim's solution was to institutionalise associations with codes of ethics. Durkheim argued that specialist divisions of labour were interdependent – this created the potential for a social cohesion superior to mechanical solidarity ruled by authority.

2 Foucault argues that society's development is an expression of the struggle between the exercise of power and the fight for freedom. Ethical awareness is the diminishing of self in favour of the collective which is dynamic – it is thus the embodiment of reflexivity.

3 Developing forms of alienation and arguing from socio-anthropological grounds, his goal was the liquidation of identity, which he believed created individual referential behaviour, and thus the pursuit of anonymity. He identified industrial organisation as containing controls through methods of organisation and assimilation of knowledge, which he believed created a culture of 'docility-utility' consciousness – all knowledge, he argued, was embedded in power. Language defines identities and differences, but for Foucault classification defines discourse possibilities – its epistemology. Discourse is treated as discontinuous, separated but not exclusive, juxtaposed practices – study must therefore

begin with discourse and look for conditions of possibility; the principle of externality. Power is exerted through the boundaries of discourse possibility, which alters consciousness. Changed discourses simply reflect changed power relations.

4   Foucault saw society's development as an expression of the struggle between the exercise of power and the fight for freedom. He saw ethical awareness as the diminishing of self in favour of the collective, which is dynamic.

5   The rules of archaeology reject universalism in favour of a panoramic view, in order to explain how one epistemic approach, 'discursive practice', could change in preference to another – the principle of reversal.

6   Commercial coding: account, budget, business, client, commercial, competition consumer, cost, effective, efficient, fees, management, manager, market, price, profit. Caring Coding: caring, committment, community, consult, consultation, duty, educational, enabling, equality, hardship, inequality, injustice, justice, opportunity, student.

7   Where the word usage ceases but re-emerges later.

8   Where the word occurs then use ceases.

The Archaeological System of Knowledge: A Broad Panoramic Sweep   165

Appendix 1: Scanned Documentation

1. MoE, 1943, *Educational Reconstruction*, Cmnd 6458, ch. 5, pp. 1–5.
2. MoE, 1947, *Plans for County Colleges*, Circular 139.
3. MoE, 1948, *Technical Colleges and other Further Education Establishments Arrangements for the Deferment of Students in the Calendar Year 1948*, Administrative Memoranda No. 274.
4. MoE, 1949, *Recognition of Schools and other Educational Establishments as Efficient*, Administrative Memoranda No. 327
5. MoE, 1949, *Expenditure of Local Education Authorities*, Circular 210.
6. MoE, 1952, *Further Education: Income from Fees*, Administrative Memoranda No. 410.
7. MoE, 1956, *Local Education and Responsible Bodies for Adult Education*, Administrative Memoranda No. 526.
8. MoE, 1956, *Fees for Further Education*, Circular 307.
9. MoE, 1958, *Public Relations in Further Education*, Circular 343.
10. MoE, 1959, *The Further Education Regulations*, Circular 351.
11. MoE, 1959, Central Advisory Council (England), *The Crowther Report. 16 to 19 Year Olds*, chs 2, 3, 5, 6, 18, 28, 29, 30, 35, 37, HMSO.
12. MoE, 1959, *Governing Bodies for Major Establishments of Further Education*, Circular 7/59.
13. MoE, 1959, *Further Education for Commerce*, Circular 5/59.
14. MoE, 1961, *Regional Colleges*, Circular 6/61.
15. MoE, 1961, *Better Opportunities in Technical Education*, Cmnd 1254.
16. MoE, 1962, *Fees in Establishments of Further Education*, Administrative Memoranda No. 5/62.
17. MoE, 1963, *Half our Future: a Report for the Central Advisory Council for England and Wales*, chs 1, 2, 4, 5, 6 (p. 41), 7, 9, 11 (pp. 87–9).
18. MoE, 1963, *Organisation of Further Education Courses*, Circular 3/63.
19. DES, 1964, *The Public Relations of Further Education*, Circular 17/64.
20. DES, 1964, *Day Release*, HMSO, pp. 5–11.
21. DES, 1966, *Technical Colleges Resources*, Circular 11/66.
22. DES, 1966, *Training of Teachers for Further Education*, Circular 21/66.
23. DES, 1967, *The Government of Colleges of Education*, Circular 2/67.
24. DES, 1967, *Joint Planning of Industrial Planning and Associated Further Education*, Administrative Memorandum No. 25/67.
25. DES, 1970, *Government and Conduct of Establishments of Further Education*, Circular 7/70.
26. DES, 1971, *Tuition Fees in Further Education*, Circular 4/71.
27. DES, 1972, *Education: a Framework for Expansion*, Cmnd 5174, pp. 1, 2, 17–25, 41–5.
28. DES, 1972, *Committee of Inquiry into Teacher Training. The James Report*, chs 1, 2, 3, 5.
29. DES, 1972, *Report of the Working Party appointed by the Secretary of State for Education and Science. Central Arrangements for Promoting Educational Technology in the United Kingdom*, HMSO, chs 2, 3, 4, 5.
30. DES, 1973, *Local Government Act: Reorganisation of Local Government*, Circular 1/73.
31. MSC, 1975, *Vocational Preparation for Young People: a Discussion Paper*, Parts 2 and 3.
32. HMSO, Education Act 1976.
33. DES, 1977, *Further Education for Unemployed Young People*, Administrative Memoranda No. 4/77.

34 DES, 1977, *Links between the Training and Further Education Services*, Administrative Memoranda No. 12/77.
35 DES, 1978, *Review of Educational Provision for Children and Young People with Special Needs. The Warnock Report*, pp. 1–5, 36–9, 172–8.
36 HMSO, Education Act 1979, ch. 49.
37 DES, 1982, *The Youth Training Scheme: Implications for the Education Service*, Circular 6/82.
38 DES, 1982, *Further Education for Unemployed Young People*, Administrative Memoranda No. 2/82.
39 DES, 1984, *Further Education for Young People under the '21 hour rule'*, Administrative Memoranda No. 3/84.
40 Audit Commission, 1985, *Obtaining Better Value from Further Education*, HMSO, pp. 2, 5–40.
41 DES, 1985, *The Further Education Act 1985*, Circular 6/85.
42 DES, 1986, *Working together Education and Training*, Cmnd 9823.
43 DES, 1987, *Providing for Quality: the Pattern of Organisation to age 19*, Circular 3/87.
44 DES, 1988, *Transfer of Responsibility*, Circular 6/88, pp. 69–71, 94–6, 106,
45 Education Reform Act 1988, *Local Management of Further and Higher Education Colleges: Planning and Delegation of Schemes*, Circular 9/88, pp. 212–27.
46 Further and Higher Education Act, Part 2, *Planning of LEA Further and Higher Education*, 1992, pp. 201–11.
47 DfEE, 1993, *The Further and Higher Education Act 1992*, Circular 1/93, pp. 3–30.
48 DfEE, 1995, *Review of the 16–19 Qualifications Framework: The Dearing Report. Interim Report: the Issues for Consideration*, HMSO.
49 DfEE, 1996, *The 16–19 Qualification Framework: Final Report. The Dearing Report*, pp. 1–9, 100–50.
50 FEFC, 1997, *Widening Participation Committee: Pathways to Success. The Kennedy Report*.
51 FEFC, 1997, *Analysis of Institutions' Strategic Planning Information for the Period 1996–97 to 1998–99*, Circular 97/04.
52 FEFC, 1997, *Sector Accounting Policies and Financial Statements: Guidance on the Requirements of the Council*, Circular 97/28.

The Archaeological System of Knowledge: A Broad Panoramic Sweep   167

Appendix 2

Graph type: new

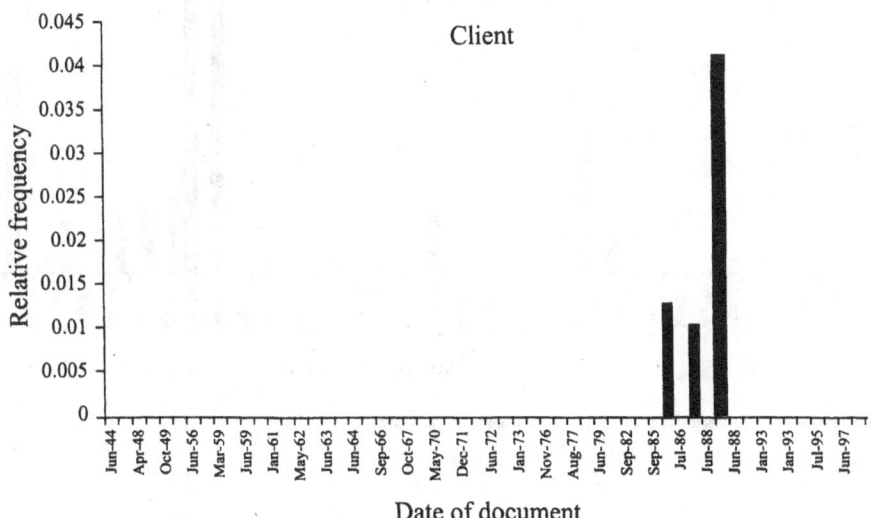

Documentation collected while a Conservative government was in power

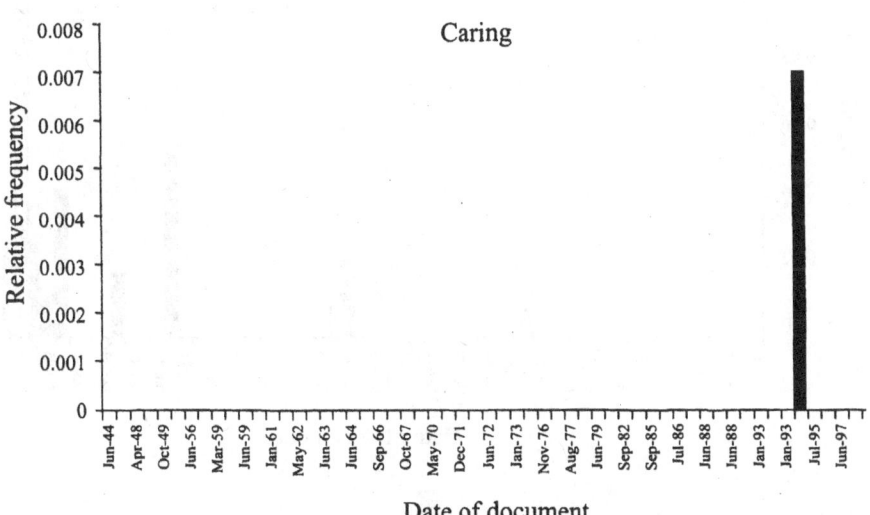

Documentation collected while a Conservative government was in power

168 *Further Education, Government's Discourse Policy and Practice*

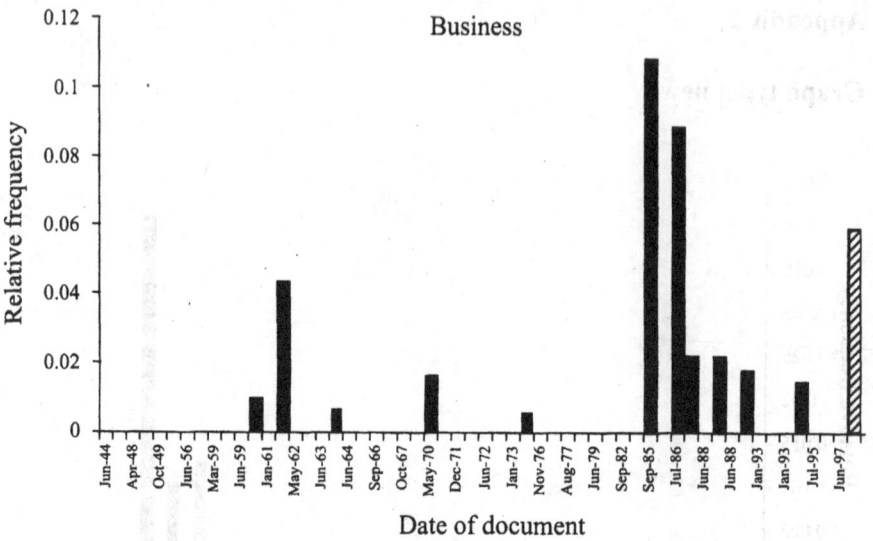

Graph type: growth

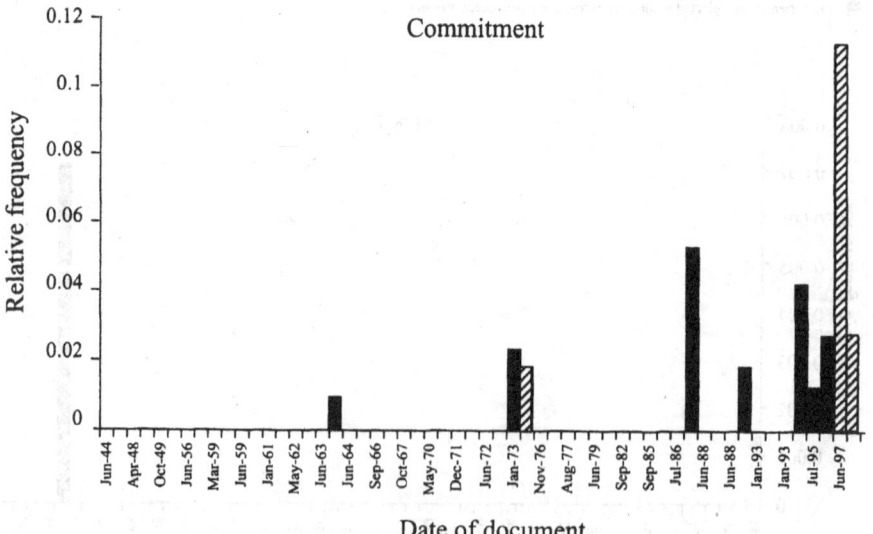

The Archaeological System of Knowledge: A Broad Panoramic Sweep   169

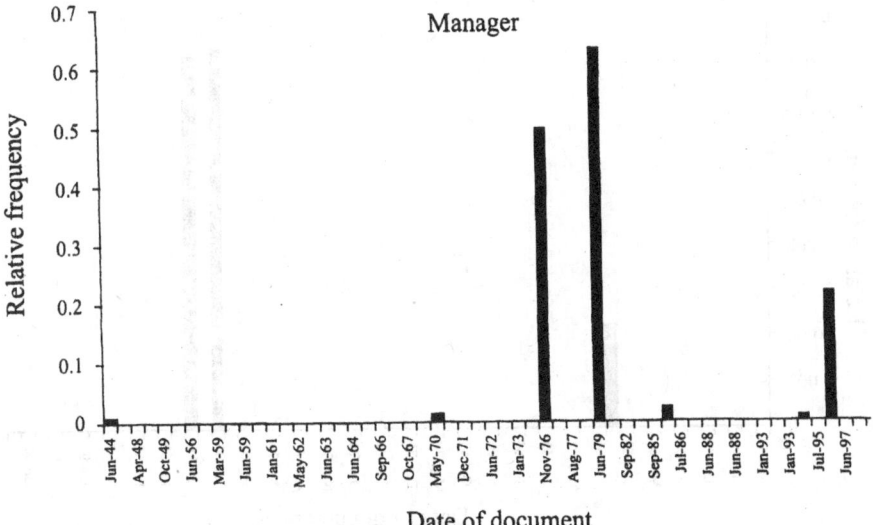

■ Documentation collected while a Conservative government was in power

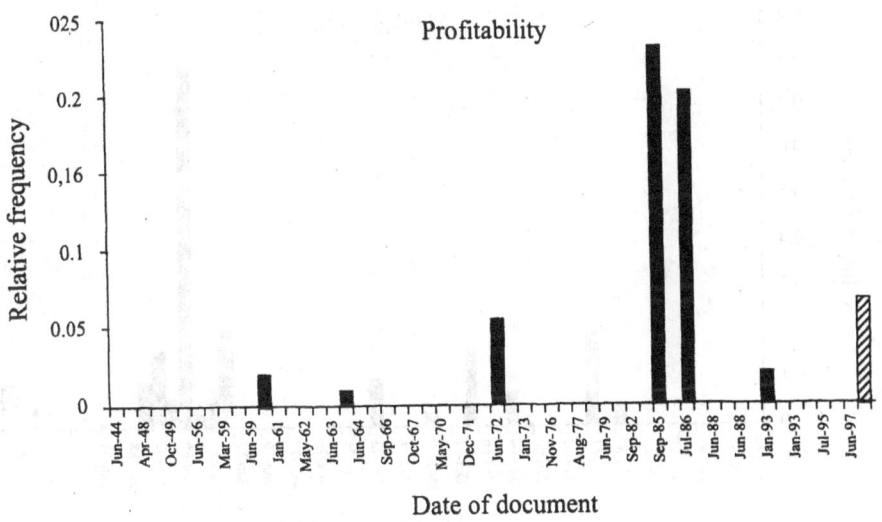

■ Documentation collected while a Conservative government was in power
▨ Documentation collected while a Labour government was in power

170 *Further Education, Government's Discourse Policy and Practice*

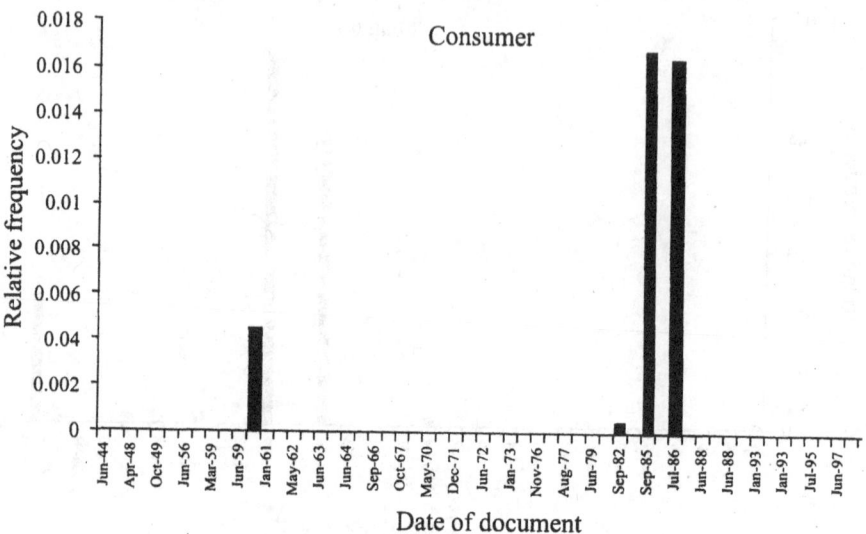

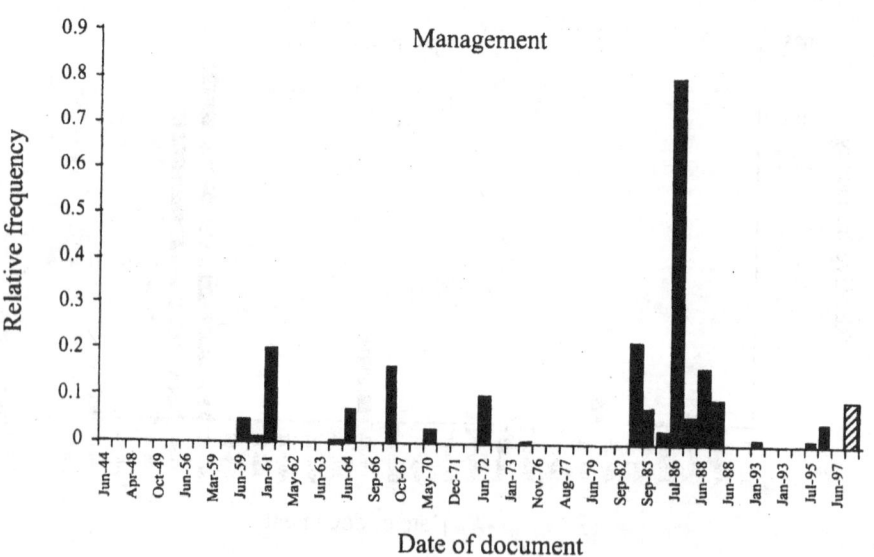

The Archaeological System of Knowledge: A Broad Panoramic Sweep 171

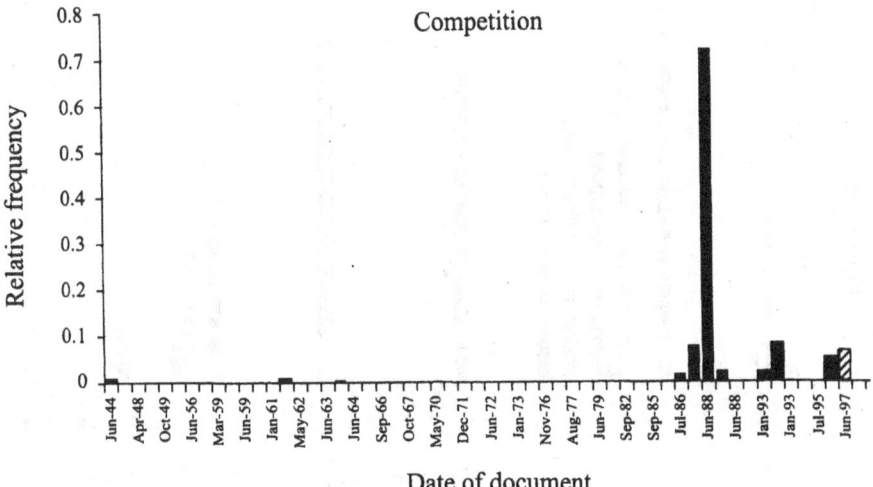

Graph type: decline

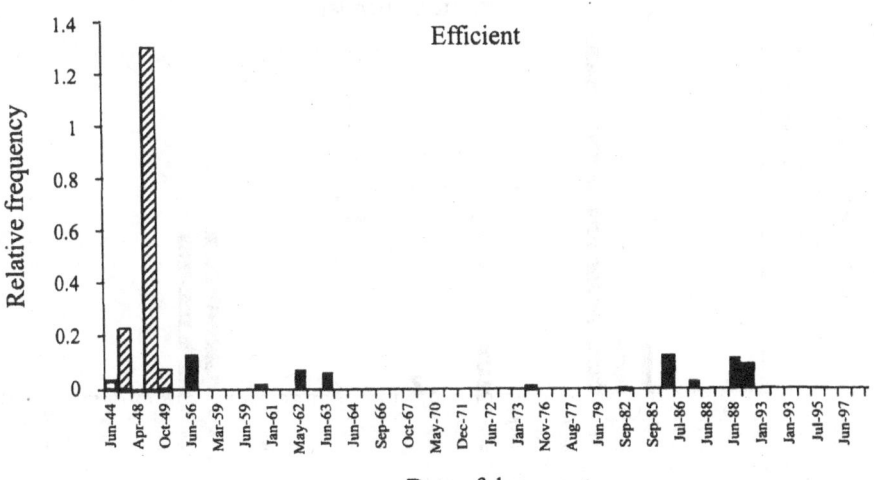

172   *Further Education, Government's Discourse Policy and Practice*

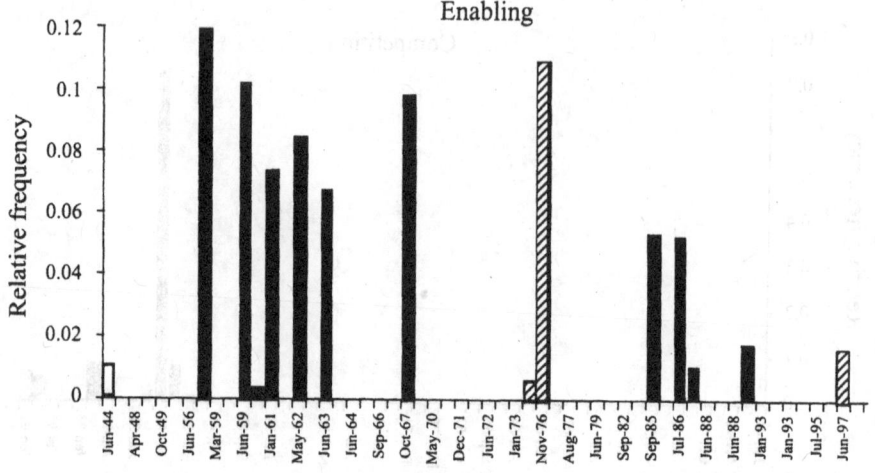

☐ Documentation collected while a coalition government was in power
■ Documentation collected while a Conservative government was in power
▨ Documentation collected while a Labour government was in power

Graph type: inconsistent but recurrent

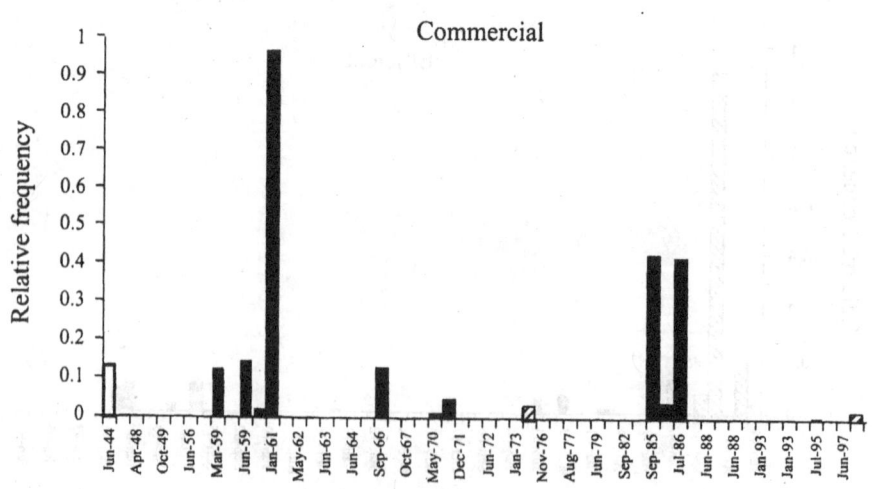

☐ Documentation collected while a coalition government was in power
■ Documentation collected while a Conservative government was in power
▨ Documentation collected while a Labour government was in power

The Archaeological System of Knowledge: A Broad Panoramic Sweep

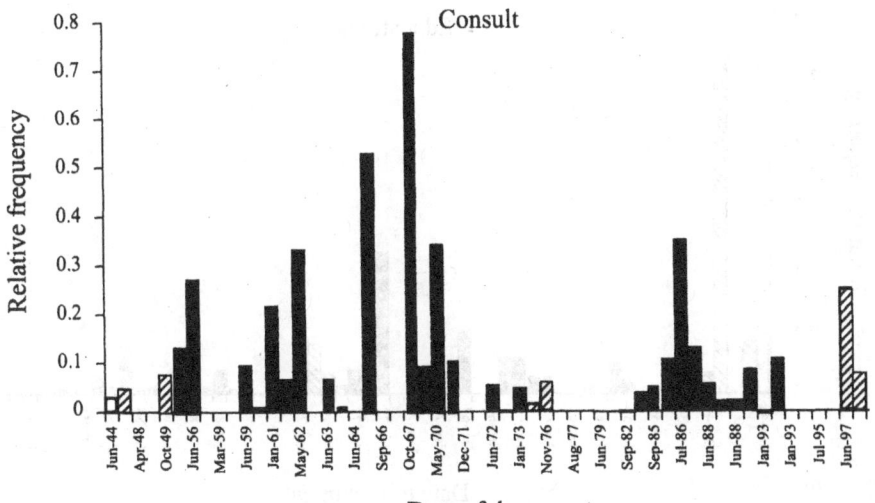

□ Documentation collected while a coalition government was in power
■ Documentation collected while a Conservative government was in power
▨ Documentation collected while a Labour government was in power

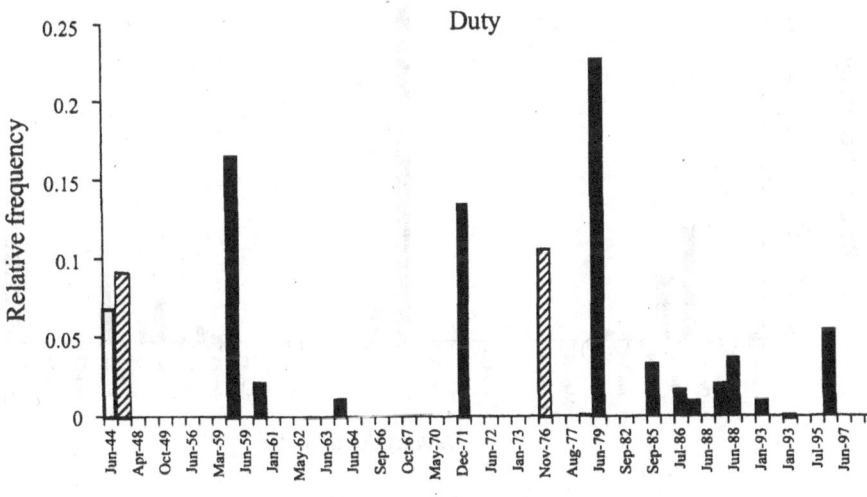

□ Documentation collected while a coalition government was in power
■ Documentation collected while a Conservative government was in power
▨ Documentation collected while a Labour government was in power

174   *Further Education, Government's Discourse Policy and Practice*

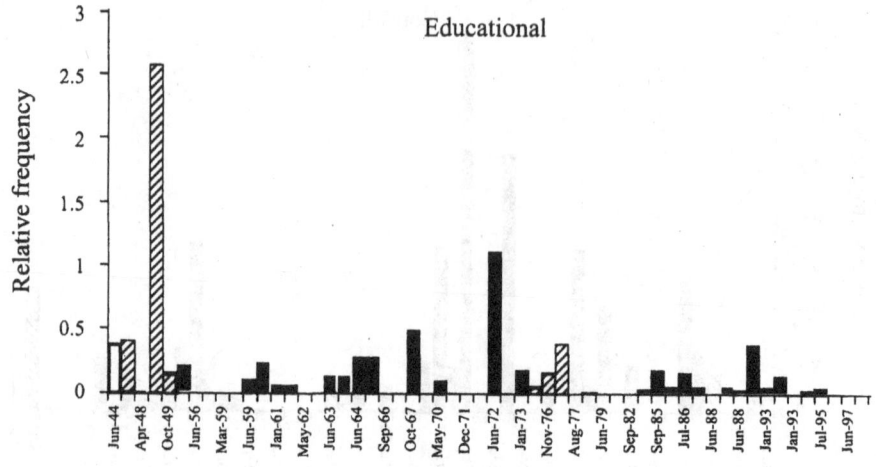

- ☐ Documentation collected while a coalition government was in power
- ■ Documentation collected while a Conservative government was in power
- ▨ Documentation collected while a Labour government was in power

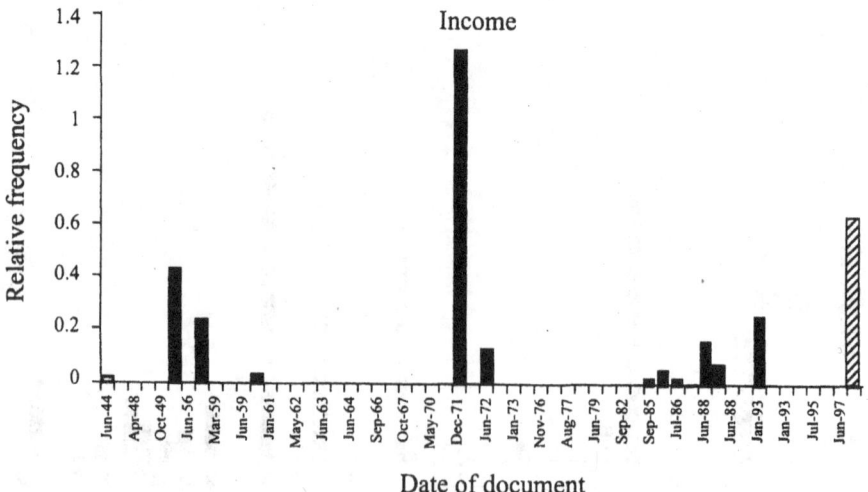

- ☐ Documentation collected while a coalition government was in power
- ■ Documentation collected while a Conservative government was in power
- ▨ Documentation collected while a Labour government was in power

The Archaeological System of Knowledge: A Broad Panoramic Sweep 175

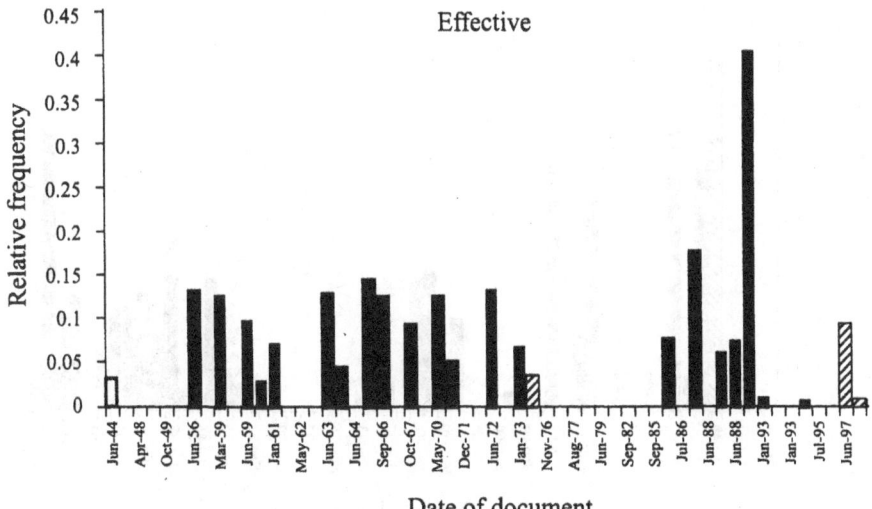

☐ Documentation collected while a coalition government was in power
■ Documentation collected while a Conservative government was in power
▨ Documentation collected while a Labour government was in power

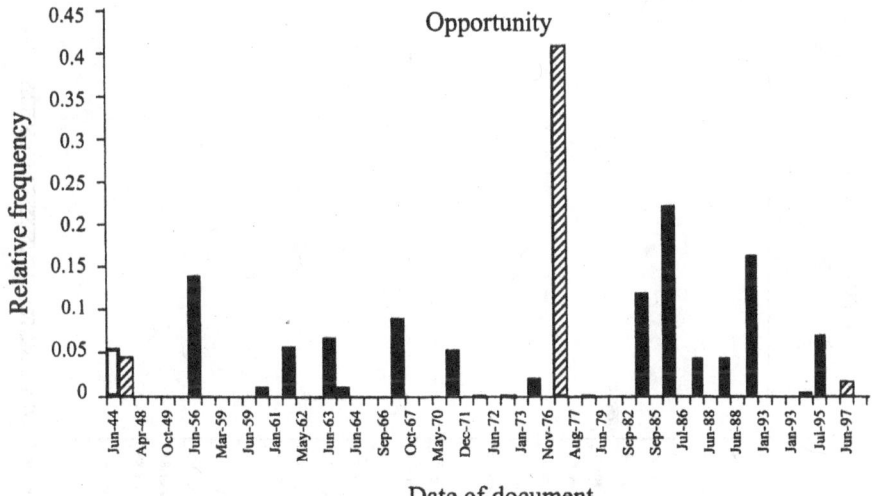

☐ Documentation collected while a coalition government was in power
■ Documentation collected while a Conservative government was in power
▨ Documentation collected while a Labour government was in power

176 *Further Education, Government's Discourse Policy and Practice*

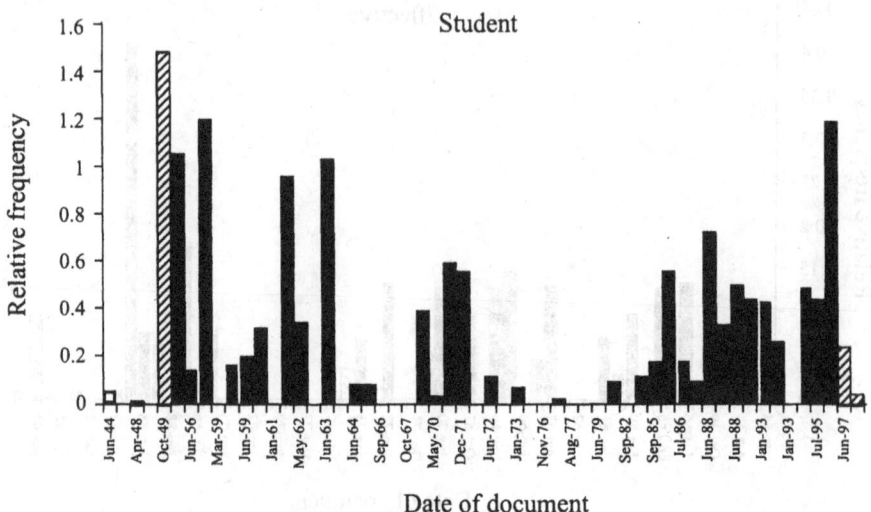

□ Documentation collected while a coalition government was in power
■ Documentation collected while a Conservative government was in power
▨ Documentation collected while a Labour government was in power

Graph type: death/life

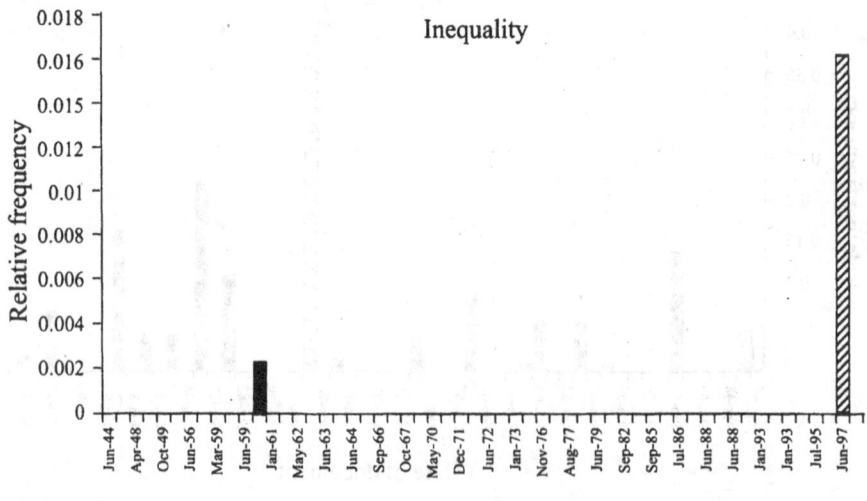

■ Documentation collected while a Conservative government was in power
▨ Documentation collected while a Labour government was in power

The Archaeological System of Knowledge: A Broad Panoramic Sweep 177

Graph type: life/death

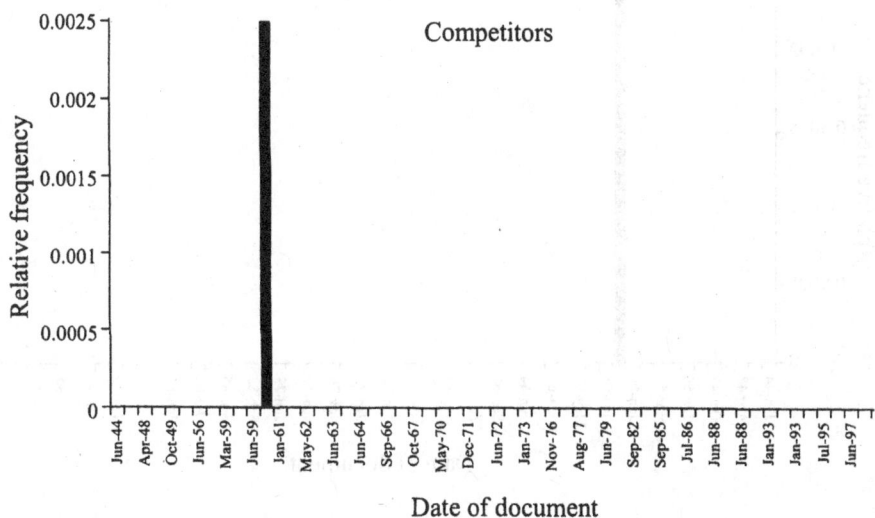

■ Documentation collected while a Conservative government was in power

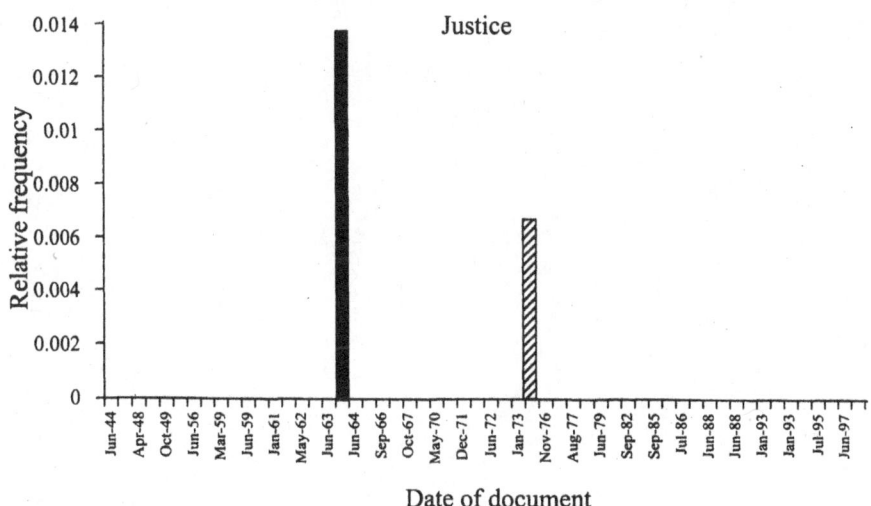

■ Documentation collected while a Conservative government was in power
▨ Documentation collected while a Labour government was in power

178 *Further Education, Government's Discourse Policy and Practice*

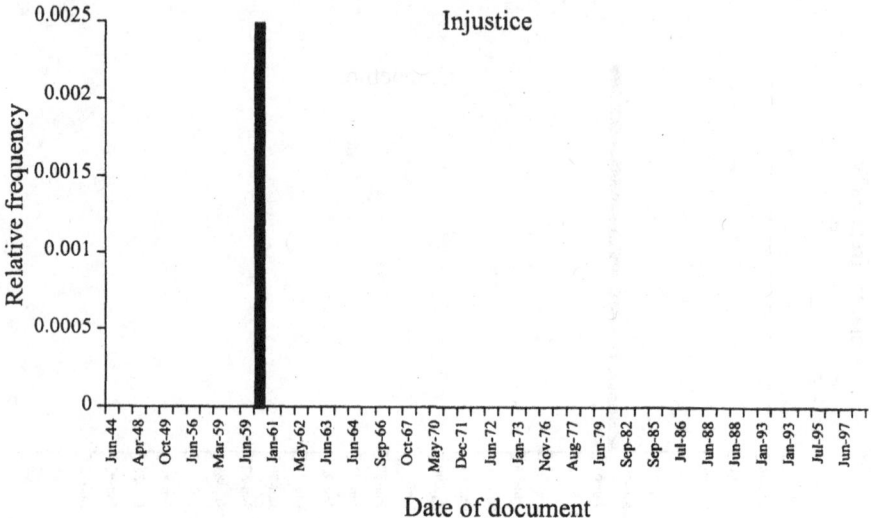

Chapter Seven

Mastering the Paradoxes: Regulation as Problematic

This chapter evaluates the second lever used by the Conservative government to bring about change in the further education sector: financial rules and procedures. Evaluation of the collective effect the financial levers have on the colleges will tell us much about the government's power to bring about change and alter institutional ideologies more in line with policy intention.

The new funding regime was initially introduced in the 1988 Education Reform Act and made specific in the Further and Higher Education Act 1992. It has three general components which affect the operations of further education colleges: core funding through a block grant; activity-related funding associated to full time equivalent student numbers; demand-led funding (which ceased in 1997); and training credits. Originally applied only to the private sector, this financial approach now permeates previously non-commercial sectors such as education. The funding regime used by the government, however, is not an objective tool; it simultaneously transmits a preference for the market paradigm and measures for success.

Trends in Accounting

It is important to recognise that accounting practice is not a science but an evolved art that encompasses a set of beliefs about how business should be managed. A balance sheet, for example, makes no attempt to value a business; the focus is on profit not on cash flow, yet cash flow is the instrument that oils an organisation's growth process and thus ensures its long-term survival.

Accounting practice has a preference for tangible assets, ignoring the intangible aspects of the business so important to the service sector for measuring quality; it thus tells us little about how a business is doing. Accounting methods affect all company transactions but include only those which can be expressed in financial terms. The high status of the accounting profession in the UK has served to ensure that traditional accounting procedure has the potential to alter organisational behaviour and strategic direction.

An accounting system comprises addition of assets and subtraction of expenses. It is a fundamental taxonomy that terms used in accounting systems must have clearly-defined necessary and sufficient conditions (Anthony, 1991, pp. 20, 36–40). In order to ensure relevance and reliability, the criteria for measurement should share the same attributes, otherwise different outcomes are measured (Wood and Townsley, 1986). It is thus surprising to find that no clear agreement exists for accounting measurement criteria.

The paucity of sufficient and necessary conditions is apparent in the debate related to defining assets. The Financial Accounting Standards Board in America (FASB) defines them as 'probable future economic benefits' and refers to 'the problem of definition', since all items that conform to the former need not be assets (FASB, 1978–85). This lack of clarity not only leads to concerns about the reliability of data, it also suggests the scientific image of accounting models is but a myth. Paradoxically, the language of accountancy leads us to believe that it is distanced from belief and therefore applied fairly. In reality, financial models include beliefs about the way factors should be measured.

The system of accounting should be understandable, reliable, complete, objective, timely and comparable. The Conservative government's accounting approach has some commonality with current trends in accounting which include unit costing as performance indicators, standardisation for comparability of service costs, planning programming budgeting systems (PPBS) to ensure efficiency throughout departments and new accounting procedures to deal with new income sources, leasing, etc. The difference between the Conservatives' financial model and the current trend in accounting practice is in the tools selected for the accounting focus. The Conservatives' model apes the traditional approach – a focus on profit and price based on financial incentives and penalties. In contrast, the new accounting techniques focus on the production process.

Commercialisation of exchange developed during the Industrial Revolution. Initially, a simple accounting method of recording expenses and revenues was used, the risk being born by the owner and regulated by the degree of his or her wealth. This was superseded by limited liability where ownership became a shared responsibility, enabling a company to increase capital resources independent of personal wealth. Concerns that this might reduce owner/manager responsibility and thus 'prudence' in financial transactions led to a focus on 'stewardship'; methods to safeguard a company's assets. This in turn led to an overemphasis on balance sheets in order to demonstrate financial soundness (Anthony, 1991). Reduction of information appeared as accountants attempted to increase shareholder confidence on the principle that the less they knew the better (Reid, 1989). At the same time this contributed to the professionalisation of accountancy.

Once a year a company must publish three accounting statements: a profit and loss account; a balance sheet showing the assets owned by the company and how they were financed; and a funds flow statement showing the sources of funds and their uses. Realised value and prudence in estimating value and profit are used as a base line. The measurement of financial performance is now controlled by legislation. The Companies Act 1985 provides the general accounting framework; it states that the accounting system must demonstrate 'a true and fair view', which has evolved to mean the consistent application of generally-accepted principles. Companies are also expected to follow guidelines set down by the Statements Standard Accounting Practice (June, 1988). This includes standardisation with the EEC (The Fourth Company Law Directive, USA).

Latterly, 'disclosure' has become important, forcing companies to reveal more about their organisation's performance. The legal responsibility for disclosure lies with the directors of a company. Large stewardship companies, where managers are not owners, are subject to heavy disclosure practices with the result that the measures of financial performance have become deeply entrenched in the system of management and control of a business (Eccles, 1993).

Indeed Sikka (1995) argues that controversial intellectual debate has become marginalised by traditional accounting principles, causing the practice to proceed largely unchallenged. There are, however, two competing systems of accounting practice, the proprietary approach and the entity approach. The traditional 'proprietary view' developed in the 1920s and focuses on the role of shareholders and accounting profit; financial performance is based on return on investment (ROI). Profit responsibility is decentralised to operating units and ROI is used to measure a unit's performance. The ROI objectives become the profit budgets to which the company operates (Dearden, 1991). Accounting profit charges interest payable on debt capital only. In contrast, entity theory utilises the 'economic profit' approach, which includes the 'opportunity cost' of goods and services consumed. Charges are made on the interest on total capital employed, including a notional interest on equity capital – thus entity theory puts the company at the centre of decision-making, managing 'stakeholders'' interests. It attempts to separate shareholder capital from capital accumulated by company action in order to define a company's worth (Reid, 1989). Clearly, the different financial measurement approaches place different claims on a business and alter the management approach.

Traditionally the focus has been variable costs, labour, materials and their relationship to volume. Fixed costs are largely ignored. A focus on flow of financial resources in and out of the company, rather than on profit, suggests a very different approach for accounting practitioners. In general, costs associated with production and supply must have a downward trend as businesses move up their experience curve (Charles Ames and Hlavacek, 1991). When a product is at the point in its life cycle where similar products enter the market, those who can produce at the lowest cost will gain competitive edge. Hence the focus on ROI and management concentration on cost minimisation. However, in some products and services price is only part of the customers' perception of value – accounting procedure should be linked to the process of production in order that these other drivers can be recognised. In the education sector these other drivers may include reputation and roots of added value.

The traditional accounting system, focused on profit, is not designed to recognise the multi-value outputs of educational products because it simplifies value to price. Furthermore, it does not attempt to measure intangible assets such as savings that are incurred as an outcome of improved staff morale. The concentration on hard rather than soft assets has a negative effect in a service industry where the intangible assets are important components of customer value. For example, in the education sector customers refer to 'a sense of belonging'.

Accounting discourse thus began to suggest that accounting systems, focused on profitability, had distracted debate away from other issues important to organisational development. Indeed, reducing cost through non-maintenance of machinery, non-investment or machine overuse can result in an increased profitability figure but adversely affects long-term organisational growth.

The New Accounting Approach

The new 'total factor productivity' (Drucker, 1995) approach to accounting suggests that organisational effectiveness has been reduced by institutionalised conceptual errors about what makes a business work, which in turn has led to faulty choices for strategic direction (Dearden, 1991). The total factor productivity method attempts to understand the factors other than profit and price that drive the business. It attempts to represent the portfolio of issues that influence the production process, including the product, the corporate strategy, market conditions and management performance. It differentiates department performance from manager performance, since he or she cannot exert control over shifts in industry volume, and includes instead the factors that a manager can influence, for example, market share and operating costs (ibid.).

Furthermore, current accounting thought suggests that companies need both an internal and an external reporting system. The external system must conform to the legal requirements and reflect shareholder/stakeholder interest. The internal cost system, Allen (1995) suggests, needs to provide information inclusive of intangible contributors to success, for three different functional levels namely: operational control; individual product cost measurement and inventory evaluation for allocation of costs.

Indeed, Dearden (1991) suggests that a focus on the short-term bottom line has limited innovation and hidden error to enable innovation to develop, which he argues requires a long-term perspective where all costs are variable. Conventional accounting costs are variable only if they change with short-term changes in output and thus ignore any changes in cost that result from diversification, product mix and range crucial to value in the service sector (Cooper, 1990). Cooper suggests that any measure of product costs should include all the value chain costs, excluding research and development, that can be considered as an investment in future production (ibid.). In the education sector this implies the ability to link the whole education process from infant school onwards.

Accountancy and its Image in Other Social Contexts: Germany and Japan

As accounting practices are culturally determined it is not surprising to find that other cultures operate in different ways. In Germany, for example, accounts are seen as only one factor in decision-making. Some Japanese techniques use a possible market price as a strategic tool. This is used to push technological development at the design stage, freeing innovation in order to produce in line with what the market demands at a target price. Production techniques become focused on reaching the market price; this de-emphasises standard costs focused on optimisation and replaces them with continual improvement achieved by concentration on the overhead burden and its causal relationship with costs to individual products. The Japanese approach thus places accounting practices as subservient to strategy formulation and places human resources as central to product innovation (Hiromoto, 1991). In contrast, the concentration in the UK on benchmarking creates a tendency towards lookalike reactive strategies, since an organisation measures itself against others and sets a target given best practice.

Unit Costing and the Service Sector

Since the educational product is specifically customised, a professional may perform many tasks in an unrelated sequence, dependent on the customer need. This product complexity renders the measurement of cost to task very difficult and thus expensive. Indeed, Sandretto (1991) suggests that where the output is made up of discrete parts, modularisation or choice of product mix for example, the process becomes technically very difficult to cost.

Unit cost control is an appropriate financial measure for organisations that have undifferentiated low-margin products. In contrast organisations that have unique high-margin products may find marketing more important than cost control through price. Accounting tools should thus be selected to reflect the needs of the product portfolio, rather than dictating what those needs should be.

Public Sector Organisations

Organisations functioning in the public sector are expected to pursue objectives other than profit as a measurement of success because the outcomes are determined by need. Indeed, the Financial Account Standard Board (FABS) in America defines the public sector as nonbusiness entities that do not have any transferable ownership interests: their purpose is something other than making a profit and they receive contributions that are seen as conceptually different from revenues arising from sales of goods or services. Public organisations are thus distinctly operationally different.

The post-1979 Conservative government, however, assumed that all organisations had shared characteristics, namely: they function within what the law prescribes: are subject to the authority of a departmental minister, who enforces national policy; there is provision for public participation on the boards; the accounts are externally audited; and effective financial control is required for accountability (Wood and Townsley, 1986, p. 150). It thus pursued a policy based on the commonality of factors between public and private sector organisations rather than on diversity.

Public Expenditure

Prioritisation, selection and allocation of public spending take place in an annual public spending round based in Whitehall. Where public funds are used, overt 'stewardship' becomes particularly important. Externally, publicly-financed institutions are subject to legal controls, stakeholder needs and political pressure, mostly from the opposition MPs. Central government departments previously operated essentially on a cost basis of receipts and payments and there was thus no distinction made between capital and revenue (ibid., p. 170).

In response to the findings from the Plowden Report (1961), the Baines Report (1967) and the Redcliffe-Maud Report (1969), the Treasury began to highlight the need for a system of monitoring and strategic planning of public expenditure. In the 1980s discourse focused on public accountability and the Nolan Committee suggested seven principals of public life namely, selflessness, integrity, objectivity, accountability, openness, honesty and leadership; in the 1990s these became central to the functioning of the colleges' funding council.

Central government, responsible for macro planning for education provision, devolved funds to the LEA through the rate support grant.[1] Spending by the LEAs was classified as either capital[2] or current[3] expenditure, total outgoing was known as revenue expenditure.[4] The LEAs had extensive discretionary powers as a result of the ambiguity in the 1944 Education Act.[5] As early as 1949, however, these discretionary powers were significantly influenced by the economic climate. The context was one of strictest economy supporting growth (MoE, 1949a).

As the further education sector was not clearly defined, further education colleges had two main targets of funding, namely advanced and non-advanced work. This presented them with problems both in isolating funding opportunities as well as in forming a strategic direction in line with government intention. Central government maintained significant control over education funding. It supported training and education services via the Manpower Services Commission; it also provided education support grants.[6] In addition, from 1959 the funding for advanced education in further education colleges came from a national funding pool, funded collectively by LEAs, as well as LEA 'top-up'.[7] The pool was essentially derived from local and national tax, with very complex lines of accountability. The DES provided a small amount of financial resources for non-advanced further education and also reimbursed the LEA for mandatory student awards. In addition, the colleges were also able to derive income from student fees, the amount of which varied from institution to institution.

In 1979 the Conservative government, with Mrs Thatcher as Prime Minister, led a discourse on public spending accountability and began a process of reducing the welfare state by removing public ownership. The Public Expenditure Survey Committee was given the responsibility for providing information on costing governmental policies and short-term expenditure planning.

In 1980 the size of the advanced further education pool was 'capped', making clear government's view of its undesirable, uncontrollable nature (Local Government Planning and Land Act, Section 63, Schedule 10). In 1983 free fee levels for students were cut for advanced further education.[8] In 1984 the Conservative government began the process of diluting LEA control (DES, 1984c). The Rates Act 1984 ensured that some authorities were subjected to punitive measures by rate capping.[9] At the same time the government increased the education support grant, further reducing LEA power (Treasury, 1986a).

Advanced further education (AFE) was also moved from LEA control when the polytechnics and other colleges became corporate bodies funded by the Polytechnics and Colleges Funding Council (PCFC). The MSC took control of work related non-advanced further education, thus marginalising the LEAs even more (DES, 1984c). An entrepreneurial context became part of a college's agenda in 1985 when the LEAs became empowered to market the goods and services of further education colleges as trading companies (Further and Higher Education Act, 1985). Alongside this, expenditure on education had fallen in real terms since 1981, so further education colleges were obliged to obtain their income from other sources. Central funding increasingly placed an emphasis on efficiency.

The DES introduced the first monitoring measures in 1972, based on norming bands of student staff ratios (DES, 1972b). In 1985 the Audit Commission pursued its work based on efficient, economic and effective use of public resources and suggested that growth in further education colleges could be achieved by the efficiency gains. Furthermore, they suggested that quality control measures would ensure that the use of resources lead to successful output.

The Working Context Prior to the 1988 Education Act

In general, the further education colleges estimated their needs and the local education authority collated the information and transmitted a request to the government, who ensured that the national budget would meet those needs. The local authority was run by elected councillors and chief officers, financial work being normally controlled through a subcommittee. This relationship tended to vary from one area to another and to reflect local needs. Indeed, there was the potential for the political bias of the LEA to affect central government's control of policy implementation.

Prior to the 1980s each LEA had a duty to provide a Chief Education Officer (CEO) and an education committee to manage the education department (Education Reform Act, 1944). The education committee had an academic ethos, with co-opted teachers as members; the work of the committee was often delegated to subcommittees. There was no common administrative structure but often there would be a Deputy Chief Education Officer and a Senior Education Officer responsible for further education.

The Further Education Committee, principally a negotiating body, came to collective agreement about the size of each college's funding allocation. Nominally the agreements were based on a relationship of Burnham Points, the nationally-agreed figure of teaching time to grade, and to student numbers. In the final analysis it was the LEA who had the duty to make decisions about the size of a college's budget.

Since there was no commonality of LEA systems, funding seems to have been allocated on an ad hoc basis. Some colleges were able to secure more money than others: indeed one principal related the story of another principal who was renowned for giving money back! Clearly lack of future funding was not perceived as problematic. College funding relied on colleges' relationship with the LEA, in particular their relationship with the education committee. Funding does not appear to have been unlimited, but reliant on student numbers per course and/or the ability to demonstrate a justifiable need. A significant level of trust existed between the transacting parties.

The public demand for increased stewardship, coupled with the Conservatives' preference for cutting costs and reducing public sector organisations, meant that further education colleges were destined for change. However, significant discretionary powers initially remained with the LEA.

The Further Education Funding Regime

The 1988 Education Act established that further education colleges were to be incorporated bodies: the 1992 Further and Higher Education Act described the process and responsibilities of incorporation due to commence in 1993. The newly-incorporated colleges began to prepare for financial control in 1990; in September 1992 colleges became eligible for financial assistance from the newly-formed Further Education Funding Council.[10] From April 1993 the FEFC had a duty to:

> secure the provision of sufficient facilities for full-time education for those over compulsory school age and under 19 (Education Act, 1988, Section 2).

> secure the provision of adequate facilities for part-time education for those over compulsory school age, and full-time education for those aged 19 and over, in relation to the types of education listed in Schedule 2 of the Act, section 3 (DfEE, 1993b, para. 5).

In 1991 it was stated that the FEFC funding would 'consist of a basic annual budget together with an element dependent on the numbers actually enrolled' (*Hansard*, 1991a). It was, at this stage, an input-related funding model. The Conservative government's attitude to public sector accountability can be seen in the remit for the Audit Commission in 1985, which was to 'promote efficiency, effectiveness and economy' (Audit Commission, 1985). The funding model, however, gives greater credence to efficiency. The Conservatives' preference for measurement of success and its indicators became clear – efficiency not effectiveness became the bottom line.

Since the 1988 Act the colleges' governing body's role has developed to include managing the college budget, monitoring the management of the college and improving its efficiency and effectiveness (DES, 1989). Its duties included: managing the budget effectively and efficiently; not incurring a deficit; complying with the financial regulations of the LEA; avoiding commitments that involve the LEA in providing extra resources; maintaining the college premises in a fit state of repair (DES, 1988b). It could incur expenditure within budget without reference to the LEA and exercise 'virement' across all current expenditure except for earmarked funds. It could also purchase supplies and equipment and services and carry forward surpluses from year to year and determine charges for services (Education Reform Act, 1988). The Academic Board retained legitimate authority, but without power.

The Education Reform Act 1988 specified that the LEAs should submit a scheme for local financial management, requiring:

> that each scheme should: give colleges as much freedom as possible to manage their own affairs and allocate their resources as they think best within the strategic

framework set by the LEA; promote responsiveness by colleges to the changing needs of students, employers and the local community; promote good management and the effective and efficient use of resources in colleges; provide for college budgets to be based on an objective and equitable allocation of available resources; in particular the formulae used for calculating budgets, should be as simple and clear as possible, so that college governors, staff and students, and the community in general, can understand how it operates; give colleges appropriate incentives to earn additional income by providing courses and other services and facilities for the local community, including in particular the business community (ibid., Section 139).

A DES circular became the blueprint for the funding scheme most of which came into effect in April 1990 (ibid.). These defined the managerial relationship between the LEA and the newly independent colleges. LEAs retained a strategic role, but delegated executive control to the further education colleges.

In order to understand the impact of these changes the actual, rather than the intended, events need to be evaluated.

The Implementation Factor

The task here is to provide a picture of what went on in the further education colleges at the policy implementation stage. The discussion concentrates on a few significant factors: the aim is to provide a feel for what was going on rather than an in-depth financial analysis.

As a reminder, the funding regime contained three general components: core funding through a block grant; activity-related funding associated with full-time equivalent student numbers; and demand-led funding through training credits. It relied on price as the competitive advantage – hence unit costs and performance indicators were being used for the measurement of quality of service. One aim was to standardise service costs across the further education sector. In line with new accounting practice, the linking of college funding to the process of education for a student, not the input or output, was a positive step forward. Unit costing, however, drove the measurement of value in the educational process, missing important service drivers.

When the change in financing the colleges was first initiated, unit resource calculations were based on historical cost; previously these had largely been discretionary and thus some colleges were able to acquire different resources independent of their size. In one case a college in direct geographical competition with another had the added advantage of money to refurbish the refectory, library and student services, all well-known drivers of student choice. This funding anomaly led to some colleges claiming that historical costing created unequal opportunity in the market. Coupled with this, in 1991 the funding model became based on full-time equivalent (FTE) student numbers. The simple conversion from enrolments to FTEs, where different weighting was applied to different programme areas, produced wide variations (Atkinson, 1993).

Coupled with this there was a lack of clear rules about what constituted unit led, enabling colleges to use different measurement models. In 1991 the most common process being used, Atkinson suggests, was the national Training Occupational Classification (TOC), based on student hour attendance. Part-time student hour conversion included average hours, standard hours, annual hours, weekly hours and various attendance mode weightings. The Further Educational Statistical Record (FESR), the Annual Monitoring Survey (AMS) and the National Advisory Body for Public Sector Higher Education (NAB) were based on a mode weighting, each mode representing a set of courses, thus Atkinson (ibid.) argues that no common understanding of what constituted a mode existed: even the number of modes varied. Budgets were thus subject to individual college interpretation and possible manipulation, despite the Conservative government's intention that weighting mode conversions to full time FTEs should be used (DES, 1988b). Furthermore, Field (1993) found the multipliers poorly defined and, indeed, not designed to reflect the actual study time taken or resources used for an individual to complete a programme of learning. Clearly, these factors presented problems of comparability on common grounds.

Activity-related funding produced a whole new set of monitoring procedures in further education colleges. Generation of the kind of information required for the appropriate division of overhead costs required an MIS system but even in 1993 principals said they were not fully on line. Other issues also appeared to be causing problems.

The Implementation Factor: Virement

The freedom for governors to 'vire' between allocations, given local changing needs, was limited only by the requirement not to 'cavalierly disregard' the LEA assessment; most colleges only notified the LEA when significant (Education Reform Act, 1988). Indeed Atkinson (1993) found that some LEAs did not require informing at all. Clearly virement is essential to enable the milking of the cash cows' products, to nurture new innovative products. The evident flexibility here supports this approach.

The Implementation Factor: Budgeting Period

The nonalignment of financial and academic years created major problems for budget setting. Atkinson (ibid.) found that most colleges were using a system of moderation calculated on the basis of five-twelfths of one academic year target and seven-twelfths of the next. Depreciation of work in progress becomes problematic where transactions are incomplete, resulting in the subjective calculation of profit (Reid, 1989).

Another key factor for comparability is whether the budget is net or gross. Atkinson (1993) found that even what appeared to be a common net budgeting group included netted income based on student fee income and netted income inclusive of other fee sources.

The Implementation Factor: Central Services

Prior to incorporation the LEA had provided central services that included further education advisors and curriculum and staff development support services. Circular 9/88 offered two new options: colleges could purchase central services from the LEA or buy from any supplier (Education Reform Act, 1988). Atkinson (1993) found national and local networking supporting central services common, though there was some evidence of college autonomy. Decentralisation of services brought with it changed relationships between the purchaser and the provider and a need for a different management competencies. There had been no process in the colleges for managers to develop these skills and they just had to do the best they could.

The Implementation Factor: Excepted Items

Excepted items are those which are outside normal assets and liabilities, but which occur on a sufficiently regular basis to be subjected to the rules. Though these rules should be applied in the same way, Atkinson (ibid.) found that responsibility for premature retirement and views on the development fund differed, whereas a common approach to contingency funds did exist, probably, he suggests, because Circular 9/88 intimated that this would be paid from the authority budget (Education Reform Act, 1988). The split between college and LEA responsibility varied from individual responsibility to a joint agreement specifying that costs could be imposed on the college budget if the authority had good reason.

The Implementation Factor: Miscellaneous Fund Issues

Whilst the LEAs retained little influence, in the event they were able to have a significant impact on a college's income through reserve funds; these are used as security for demands in the future. By 1991 Atkinson found that the majority of colleges had opted to have a central LEA development fund, though the colleges' contribution varied from 0.25 per cent to 4 per cent. The majority of colleges selected LEA control of a contingency fund, with an average of 1 per cent of the college budget.

Cost recovery lay within the control of the independent colleges, but clawback arrangements by the local authority differed in size (DES, 1988a). In 1991, when the possibility arose for individual colleges to hold bank accounts, Atkinson (1993) found that only a small number of LEAs delegated full responsibility. The claims on a college budget under the heading 'variables' were exacerbated by the treatment of planned debt, which was treated as borrowing, with the agreements negotiated locally. Atkinson (ibid.) found that some LEAs imposed interest charges and others did not.

The variability of the LEA schemes meant that college budgets were significantly affected by the relationship that each LEA had with their local colleges. Similarly, colleges were affected by the system of bidding between establishments within LEA control. Control varied from central strategic planning to decentralisation.

Demand-led Funding

In order to increase student participation and completion rates the FEFC provided funding not tied to agreed growth rates but paid on the actual achievements over and above the expected.

Output Related Funding: TEC

The government introduced another player into the funding game, the Training and Education Council (TEC), in a White Paper in 1991. Its remit was to link enterprise, skills and economic development (DES, 1991a, Vol. 2, para. 4.1).

The TECs became responsible for the allocation of some funding (ibid., Vol. 24, para. 6) with a remit to establish funding from other sources (ibid., Vol. 2, para. 4.10). The FEFC funds the TECs through a cash grant plus additional funding based on student numbers, with weighting applied for differential teaching cost (ibid., Vol. 12, para. 6.4). Funds are also associated with specified student outputs; this output component is a weighted award, which can vary between components of a particular programme. TECs also contract with many training providers.

Clearly, output-related funding had an important impact on the formation of a college's course portfolio. Indeed, courses that require high cost provision either in terms of facilities or more teaching time are likely to be under threat (FEU, 1994). A focus on price also created a bias towards a particular type of course, flexible modes of teaching being more expensive than full-time courses.

TEC Demand-led Funding

TECs have also been responsible for piloting the training credit scheme intended to be completed by 1996. Training credits establish a 'contract' between the purchaser and the provider; each student holds a number of credits to 'spend' with any provider. Credits only become money when outputs are completed.

The vast diversity of approaches to college income generation contradicted the requirement for simplicity and understandability of the system essential to ensure informed and fair customer choice; as a result the customer remains unable to compare one college fairly with another. Alongside this, the diversity in accounting methods created different competitive positions for colleges.

Funding 1993–96

Clearly, changes to the funding methodology had to be made. In 1993 each college supplied the FEFC with an estimate of its enrolments from 1992 as weighted full-time equivalent students (WFTE) so that the recurrent funding could be calculated. The WFTE at this time was divided into two broad course groupings and seven modes of study, differently weighted.

FEFC 1995: Aims and Methodology

Under the old system there was no way to adjust cost for student drop-out. There was no consensus on weighting applied to different modes of attendance and the old modes of classification were outdated. The FEFC has adopted several key factors as instruments of change based on the following working context: 'To foster an environment that will encourage institutions to be enterprising, flexible and responsive to their students, potential students, and employers' (FEFC, 1995, para. 12).

The funding agreement contains: block funding, known as recurrent funding, that is associated with student volume; agreed performance measures and funding, associated with meeting the performance criteria; demand-led funding; and a safety-net. The aim of the new funding methodology is to provide 'financial and planning stability', 'cost-efficient growth' and 'improved quality' (ibid., para. 25).

The FEFC has also altered the budget mechanism to 'converge' the unaccountable differences between colleges' funding using a two-pronged offensive – recurrent 'core and margin'. Core funding is inflation-protected but only a percentage of the previous year core is guaranteed. It is also linked to the achievement of a percentage of the agreed target, thus it should decrease unfair allocation of funds caused by historically-based costing. The margin consists of 'additional funds' as performance-related enticements as well as 'demand-led funds'. College budgets were adjusted for cost associated to geographical location and divided by WFTEs to provide the unit of funding. This varied from £1486–£4664 per student. Interestingly, for sixth form colleges it ranged from £2205–£3840, thus presenting the colleges with unfair competition (DfEE, 1993c).

In December 1992 the council published its new funding learning methodology. The funding units were: entry activities; on-programme activities; achievement; tuition fee remission; child-care support; and additional support (FEFC, 1995, Section 19). The unit was now calculated on an agreed tariff of costs per student, overseen by the Tariff Advisory Committee (TAC) funded by the FEFC (ibid., Section 21). TAC was an advisory committee which comprised senior college members and 'other' institutions.

In 1994, 95 per cent of FEFC funding went to colleges of further education;[11] further education enrolments comprised 84 per cent of total full-time equivalents.[12] The FEFC defined the range of further education as: general; vocational; training; higher education; and adult (FEFC, 1993–94, p. 20). The funding model allocated financial resources based on the level of activity in the colleges classified into 10 programme areas.[13] The common FEFC tariff was reviewed, with consultation, in 1995 and changes were made for 1996. Essentially, the tariff was based on the standard length of programme, guided learning hours, weighting for course differentials and additional support for special students. Under the new system each student, who has an individual programme of learning, generated a different sum of units. The student was protected by prior agreement between the FEFC and the college as to the number of activities for the agreed funding (ibid., Section 20).

Projected Fund Allocation

The funds made available by the Secretary of State to the FEFC for 1995–96 and projections for 1996–98 included an expected growth rate of 25 per cent. The spending plans reflected the 'crucial' role of further education to national targets for education and training (*FEFC News*, No. 19). Nevertheless they had to make efficiency gains between 4 per cent and 5 per cent and the government indicated that the year-on-year increase would be zero by 1996–97; the colleges had to increase participation with a decreasing budget based on the more risky activity funding (FEFC, 1995).

Activity-related Funding

An organisation's income is derived from two sources, namely capital and revenue. The 1988 Act changed the emphasis of revenue funding from national taxes and government grants to the sale of goods and services. Since revenue income supports revenue expenditure, the day-to-day costs of the colleges were now dependent on student intake, activity-related funding.

Capital income was provided for colleges through schemes backed by the government, or through loans; revenue income could be used to fund capital expenditure by contributions to capital outlay namely reserve funds. Since the 1988 Act, colleges can own buildings – assets – which, if sold, could increase reserves for capital expenditure. Wood and Townsley (1986) suggest that it is in government's interest to encourage reserve funds as these smooth costs over time, avoid interest paid on loans and provide a buffer through difficult times.

Unit costs will rise where student numbers fall, imposing overhead costs on fewer customers. Colleges who find their student numbers falling will also experience cash flow reduction. Colleges who can increase their numbers, on the other hand, will increase cash flow and chances of survival. This situation is influenced by clawback when students fail to complete a course of study, which in turn may alter a college's choice of course portfolio. The FEFC has a duty to ensure sufficient and adequate provision and can enter into an agreement with a college to ensure particular provision. Nevertheless, the drivers for the colleges are the numbers of units consumed per student and the participation and completion results. The funding methodology thus creates a number of policy steers in order that the colleges can respond flexibly to the market and be accountable.[14] At the same time, the structure of the methodology attempts to measure the amount of education, training and learning by a common currency.[15]

Since 1996 a higher unit value has been available, where the qualification contributes to the national targets; the units available for the on-programme elements can be enhanced where a student requires learning support or is entitled to fee remission or has a low income.[16] Government has continued to pursue convergence and public funding levels have to be justified in terms of fitness for purpose (DfEE, 1996a; FEFC, 1997e).

In 1997 the DfEE confirmed that there would be no changes to public expenditure settlements for 1997–98 and 1998–99. As promised, three years later the funding methodology was reviewed.[17] The main conclusions of the first stage of the review suggested that the system was difficult to explain to outsiders, that it needed to be tested for the next five years and that no other methodology appeared as flexible (FEFC, 1997e). In the foreword to the review, Helena Kennedy QC suggests, perhaps acknowledging the change in government, that the focus of the next 10 years needs to be on values and priorities for the further education sector rather than on market forces (ibid., p. 5).

All newly-incorporated colleges have charitable status and most are exempt charities. However, all colleges have to disclose information as set down by the Statements of Standard Accounting Practice (SSAP).[18] They also have to conform to normal procedure based on four fundamental accounting concepts: the going concern;[19] the accruals concept;[20] the consistency concept;[21] and the prudence concept.[22]

In response to increasing pressure for disclosure, any exceptional departures from a college's financial statement and their estimated financial effect have to be reported to the Urgent Issues Task Force (UITF) (FEFC, 1997e, p. 3). The Nolan Committee on Standards in Public Life (1996) recommended that colleges should have the following information made public: a list of members of the governing body; the corporate governance structure of the institution; policies on openness; a statement of objectives; and performance against key criteria. They should also set out key information to a common standard in their annual reports (FEFC, 1997e, p. 20).

The review undertaken in 1997 concluded that the funding methodology works, but requested the addition of a further list of aims.[23] In particular, the addition that the funding methodology should be able to accommodate the value-added indicators seems to hit at the very heart of the funding methodology and to render it insufficient. At the same time, responding to the evident distance between student demand and the economy's need, demand-led funding ceased. The FEFC has suggested that the reduction in demand-led funding would result in 86 per cent of colleges facing funding reductions in 1998. This shortfall, they anticipated, would be exacerbated by the reductions in competitiveness funds, the diminishing value and availability of discretionary awards, the addition of significant costs resulting from teachers' superannuation schemes, reduction in funds for capital purposes and the need to absorb the full costs of pay awards for staff. In the FEFC's view the further education colleges now faced real financial difficulties (FEFC, 1996–97, p. 3).

Implications of the Changes Post-1988

As a government quango, the FEFC is an effective mouthpiece for the government; it has pursued a strategy based on accountability, which it has interpreted to mean the efficient and effective use of resources. The Conservative government moved the operation of the further education colleges from the context of the public sector to that of the quasi-private sector; risk management and environmental scanning became part of the management function in further education colleges. This situation inevitably altered both the management task and the organisation's strategic focus.

The FEFC adopted a funding methodology based on a student's progress through a course. Other funding was available to the colleges from: fee remission; European Community; TECs; and HEFC. At the same time, the focus on accountability created a demand for quantifiable data to measure unit costs, which led to changes in the administration process and the introduction of a management information system. This in turn created a strategic focus on hard rather than soft data.

The strategic importance of environmental assessment in the private sector has long been accepted. Nevertheless, Huff and Ranney (1981) suggest that there are significant barriers to environmental scanning where education institutions are concerned. The most significant barriers, they argue, are lack of resources to carry out environmental scanning and a weak causal link between the educational input and output inhibiting targeting. This has led Crisp (1991) to conclude that assessing future demands is likely to be the most difficult task in any college's strategic planning process.

Indeed, Bennett et al. (1992, p. 1) argue that the FEFC has served to create boundaries in the market. The government vigorously promoted vocational qualifications with finite spending, skewing the colleges feasible product portfolio. It thus gave further education colleges freedom to operate in the market while at the same retaining financial and strategic planning dependency. Indeed, Hoy et al. (1987, pp. 86–107), building on work by Emerson (1962), conclude that an organisation can gain power over another where the second organisation cannot gain resources elsewhere to fulfil its strategic objectives. The FEFC as the primary, and dominant, player in financing the colleges has the potential to control the organisation and its strategic objectives. Furthermore, Glatter et al. (1989) suggest that resource dependency skews the organisation's perception of the environment in line with the controlling institution. It would seem that the shift of funding responsibility from the LEA to the FEFC is more about central government control than organisational freedom.

At the same time as fulfilling economic needs, the funding methodology provided the Conservative government with a pathway to pursue its ideological beliefs. This power was limited if the colleges could prove that they were effective; effectiveness, however, was also redefined by the increasing concentration on effectiveness measures based on unit costs which in turn denied input and output product complexity.

Garvin (1988) argues that transcendent quality, an indefinable condition of excellence and user-based quality, provides the capacity to satisfy user needs and preferences for fitness for use in the service sector. Harrison (1993, pp. 118–48) suggests that high customer interaction and customisation services will be costly, harder to administer and control and will pose problems in the management of customer intervention. Indeed, Coote and Pfeffer (1990) posit that in some service situations customers are also providers. This has led Harrison (op. cit.) to suggest that the meaning of quality in an educational context could include academic excellence, conformance to specified attributes of the curriculum as well as student demand.

The idea that a further education college should define the level of service it intends to provide and be accountable should be welcomed: increased disclosure is desirable in a democratic society. At the same time, however, the financing process raises issues about how standards are set and who decides. Apportioning a value is complex and must include all stakeholders' needs and perceptions of quality; procedures for measuring therefore need to reflect this in order to balance the tensions between the marketisation of colleges and their social role.

Where an organisation uses an inappropriate cost control method it will generate faulty information, which in turn will lead to faulty strategies. An inappropriate cost system is demonstrated where departments invent their own cost system, where managers identify problems which arise, because the cost system drives the organisation away from the 'on-the-job' needs, and where results are hard to explain. Also where financial accounting regulations change, as in the case of further education colleges, this may lead to the distorting of information simply to fit the requirements of the system (Cooper, 1990).

The ambiguous nature of the rules and procedures provided a route for local government and individual colleges to interpret that policy differently, alongside the application of an inappropriately designed cost system. Coupled with this, the current accounting discourse suggests that where the traditional profit approach is applied to a complex system, the identification of the organisation's drivers will be inadequate and as a result strategic decision-making information will be faulty.

Even given some watering-down of government policy at the implementation stage, the changes to further education colleges implied by the funding methodology for such colleges should not be underestimated. In the future these colleges face a risky, turbulent, education market where the right to professional power to decide has been altered; at the same time, the FEFC would be applying a range of policy steers using tools which favour quantifiable measures against others. Through this process, educational effectiveness can become subordinated to efficient use of resources. The power struggle is not a managerial one, though it is transmitted through a managerial paradigm; rather it is a highly political one. It is about the right of government to change society's ideological perspectives and to restructure the welfare state, which continued with the election of New Labour. The exertion of financial muscle may be the very process that provokes policy resistance.

Notes

1. The RSG has two elements: the Domestic Rate Relief Grant and the Block Grant. The DRRG depends on the number of domestic ratepayers and is used as a benchmark for judging overspend. The rate paid can vary over time but has a tendency to remain static. The BG is designed to compensate differences between authorities and is calculated through an assessment procedure.
2. Current expenditure refers to day-to-day expenses and is met out of current income.
3. Capital expenditure relates to the spending made on creating tangible assets such as buildings and is financed by borrowing.
4. Revenue expenditure is current expenditure plus the costs of borrowing.
5. The poor clarification in Sections 43 and 53 of the 1944 Education Act led to misinterpretation.
6. Education Support Grants funded target areas of educational development.
7. Essentially, contributions to the pool were retrospective and thus the LEAs could not budget for their contribution until the end of the year.
8. The DES cut these fee levels by 50 per cent. Further education colleges thus became wary about recruiting above target.
9. This means that the local authority is given an upper limit to spending by central government.
10. This was established in the 1992 Further and Higher Education Act, Section 1.
11. The remainder of the funds supported students with disabilities; further education courses provided in HE institutions; further education provided at other institutions (FEFC, 1993–94, p. 19).
12. The remaining comprised 5 per cent in sixth form colleges and 10 per cent in specialist colleges (ibid., p. 20).
13. These were: sciences; agriculture; construction; engineering; business; hotel and catering; health and community care; art and design; humanities; basic education (ibid., p. 31).
14. The aims are: to apply a range of policy steers, including those deriving from its duty to secure provision; to provide a sufficient measure of stability and continuity to afford institutions the confidence to plan strategically and to enable them to manage change; to enable the diverse institutions to operate effectively and respond flexibly in their local environment; to promote accountability and value for money; to be capable of maintaining and enhancing the quality of provision; to accommodate growth on the part of the sector as a whole and varying rates of expansion within and between individual institution (FEFC, 1997e, p. 10).
15. The basic structure measures the amount of education, training and learning rather than learner support provided to a student in a common currency instead of a measure of full-time equivalent students. Students' learning comprises three elements – entry, on-programme and achievement which includes differential rates for different kinds of provision. A core and margin approach is used to encourage growth and institutional stability. Additional funds above the core are agreed in advance, with a rationing mechanism for these funds alongside the 'you are paid for what you do principle' (ibid.).
16. All students in full-time education aged 16–19 get full fee remission.
17. This was based on the findings of the Public Expenditure Survey Settlement 1997–98 to 1999–2000, extrapolated forward one year (DfEE, 1996e).

18   The SSAP suggest: full name of corporation; indication of the nature of the governing instrument; the names of all the members including method of appointment; names and addresses of any other relevant organisations; an explanation of what the organisation is trying to achieve and how it is going about it; a review of the development, activities and achievements of the organisation; a review of the transactions and financial position of the corporation and explanation of the salient facts of the accounts; the effects of present and future account revaluation of fixed assets; the extent to which the corporations are financially dependent upon the support of any third party; the nature of important events affecting the corporation (FEFC, 1997e, p. 20, para 58).

19   The going concern concept is defined by SSAP as including the underlying presumption that the college will continue in operation in the foreseeable future (ibid., para. 64).

20   The accruals concept is defined by SSAP as that which recognises revenue and costs as they are earned (ibid.).

21   The consistency concept is defined by SSAP as a system that treats like items in the same way in each accounting period. Sector accounting policies and financial statements (ibid.).

22   The prudence concept implies that revenue and profits are not anticipated but recognised only when they are realised (ibid.).

23   These are: to accommodate a contraction in student activity and/or funding levels; to be capable of dealing with a modular or unitised curriculum; to deal with the implications of inclusive learning; to promote widening access to, and participation in, education and training; to accommodate a regionalised approach to the assessment of adequacy and sufficiency, and responsiveness to local market need; to be capable of dealing with value-added indicators; to simplify, as far as possible, the operation of the methodology (FEFC, 1997e, p. 7).

Chapter Eight

The Roots of Competitive Advantage

To carry out its policies at the institutional level and bring them into line with its policy objectives, government had also to alter the behaviour, and the power base, of the educational institutions and their teaching professionals. Professionals are a special class of social actors who are given dispensation by society to govern themselves (Barrett and Fudge, 1981). They are guided in their behaviour by their membership to a professional body, which is responsible for creating the ethical codes that bound and control the professional/client relationship. Ethical codes are heavily determined by emotional and moral values, thus it is possible for those codes to clash with the principles of bureaucratic rule (Wilding, 1982; Larson, 1982). Indeed, it is not unknown for professionals to circumvent, or break, imposed rules (Foucault, 1990). Society endorses the autonomy of professionals to act differently because of the core competencies that they hold and because their professional bodies externally monitor each individual's professional performance.

Professionals' operating tasks tend to be very complex because the decisions that need to be taken alter according to the client's needs and environment. Decentralised decision-making, where power is devolved to the professional, has thus proved to be a more practical way of managing and so a decentralised reporting has become the norm for professional organisations within state institutions (Mintzberg, 1973). In the 1980s, however, New Right rhetoric challenged the growth in the discretionary powers given to professionals and their freedom from bureaucratic constraints. Rhetoric focused on the need for increased accountability and control of professionals so that they would be forced to meet the needs of their clients better (Wilding, 1982).[1] It is clear that the potential existed for a battle for power to take place between professionals and government. In any case, the validity of government public policy-making is tested at the point where that policy becomes practice, at the organisational level (Crozier, 1964; Gouldner, 1964).

In order to be successful, the government's educational policy had to influence the internal operational process within further education colleges, creating a new strategic direction for them in line with its policies. If the government's discourse was powerful, my assumption was that any implementation deficit would be controlled (Bachrach and Baratz, 1963). A demonstration of such power would be evident if the colleges' social value systems and organisational style changed in line with the direction desired by the government. I thus set out to test whether the government's policy themes were reflected in the principals' own language in the four further education colleges, and whether they saw their tasks differently and were trying to change organisational tradition accordingly.

To evaluate the impact of government policy on organisational success, the first task was to establish a benchmark against which the government's approach could be evaluated. Since further education colleges were to become more market-oriented, it was clear that one significant need was a greater level of uncertainty tolerance in management policy and practice. I thus set out to evaluate management theory in terms of uncertainty tolerance. My aim was to develop from the discourse factors considered significant to uncertainty tolerance, against which the government's policy could then be evaluated. To reveal something about the depth, or otherwise, to which government regulation could penetrate organisational space, I set out to capture information before and after three of the colleges transformed to corporate entities using the story as told by the four principals.

The Management of Change

Sadly, management theory cannot provide a definitive answer to how organisational change should best be managed. There is a plethora of explanations, not helped, it would seem, by some confusing myth with reality. Nevertheless, the notion of a clear mission, a vision of the future, a direction for growth and a means of achieving those objectives typify strategies for better matching an organisation's objectives to the marketplace. The approaches taken to the application of control over these processes encapsulates the discourse about how change should best be managed; these vary from tight central control at one extreme to very loose at the other.

A zone of uncertainty tolerance is used to link management discourse. One extreme of the uncertainty tolerance zone assumes certainty, stability and rationality and thus reinforces traditional ways of doing things. The other extreme of the uncertainty tolerance zone accepts uncertainty, instability and irrationality and thus embraces change as endemic. Both extremes aim to create sustainable competitive advantage in the marketplace, but other factors vary.[2]

At the left-hand side of the uncertainty tolerance zone, it is assumed that change phenomena can be identified and plans created and implemented to

Uncertainty tolerance zone

Static/predictable change   Dynamic change
Rational theory   Non-rational theory

meet it, thus underlying the low uncertainty tolerance position is the assumption that the change organisations are faced with is fairly predictable. An organisation's objective, in this case, is to manoeuvre in the marketplace so as to outdo the enemy, the competitor. The aim of the organisation is to maximise profit to sustain its growth. An organisation acts as if at war with its competitor when creating its strategic plans; indeed, the language of battle is used.[3] The rules of the game, the boundaries of possibility, are set by the invisible hand of the market, thus the game and its outcomes are distanced from any moral obligation to society (Freidman, 1962). Organisations set their strategies in order to do battle with their competitors and either win or loose. It is based on a scientific approach to the analysis of the work task. It distinguishes between managers of organisations, who are responsible for systematic planning, and workers, who are simply an input to fit a predestined organisational role (Taylor, 1911).[4]

To enter combat, management creates a mechanistic operating system so that they can control through a chain of command (Burns and Stalker, 1961). Five key management tasks became important to the chain of command namely, planning, control, command, coordination and organisation (Fayol, 1916).[5] All combat moves are based on rational, unemotional decisions, thus all action is identified as impersonal and estranged from emotion. Any ambiguity or evidence of incongruent goals is denied. The manager is thus 'believed' to be capable of, and employed in, rational, systematic, reflective planning.

Moving along the change tolerance zone, Mayo (1960), critical of the scientific approach, began to develop what became known as the social psychology approach. Mayo's approach to management and control highlighted the informal communication process within the structure of an organisation as a significant contributor in determining organisational behaviour.[6] Maximising the potential of the human resources in the organisation, he argued, was the key to success. How to maximise such potential has proved to be a tricky management issue. Nevertheless, moving along the uncertainty tolerance zone, significant factors for success were now thought to include an employee's relationship with the formal and informal parts of getting the job done. Emerging management techniques now focused on maximising individual employees' growth potential in various ways (Maslow, 1959; Argyris, 1987; Mcgregor, 1960).

Research into what managers did revealed that they were involved in face-to-face communication, horizontal and lateral transfers of information, fragmentation and constant interruption (Mintzberg, 1973). Contradicting the assumptions made in the scientific model, mangers were now thought to have a preference for action rather than reflective activities; they favoured gossip, hearsay, speculation and intuition as a basis for making their decisions. This caused another shift to the right along the uncertainty tolerance zone. A reduction in innovation and flexibility was now thought to be the unintended consequence of tight management control techniques (Loabsy, 1967). Indeed, where formal planning was linked to a system of penalty and rewards, it was discovered that individuals became increasingly risk adverse because they were afraid of failure. More emphasis was now placed on understanding the qualitative issues implicit in decision-making (Quinn, 1980). Organisational decisions became viewed as emergent processes, consequences of interactive alliances (ibid.).[7]

Moving along the change tolerance zone, planning became identified as a necessary, though not sufficient, management tool. The informal subsystems within organisations began to be recognised as necessary complements to the formal analytical management process. Strategy making began to be considered as a consequence of the emergent and non-directional organisational process. Indeed, some thought that, at best, managers were simply muddling through (Lindbloom, 1968).[8] Strategic decisions could no longer be seen as part of a grand plan; strategies appeared to emerge from the implicit consequences of small decisions taken as a consequence of doing day-to-day business. Indeed, Etzioni (1961) suggested that such decisions could comprise a random walk leading nowhere.

It was now recognised that a paradox emerged from the application of the control required to do battle with the competitor and how control needed to be applied to derive maximum output from the dynamic organisational context: this paradox pulled the organisation in different directions. The pursuit of synergy, between the external environmental variables and the internal formal and informal variables, began. A cost focus enforced through tight management control was now thought by some to be damaging to internal synergy, because it increased risk averse organisational behaviour (Mintzberg, 1984). Creating an organisational culture that contained diversity tolerance thus became the management gurus' aim.

Moving further along the change tolerance zone, the organisational context, internally and externally, was now recognised as dynamic and disorderly (Peters, 1980; Moss Kanter, 1983). Indeed, chaos theorists argued that stability theorists could not account for the discontinuous and erratic side of doing business (Gleick, 1987). Espousing everything tending to disorder, chaos theorists reduced the emphasis of planning as a management tool. Investigating randomness, coupled with a belief that the tiniest changes could create dramatic organisational effects, became part of the strategist's agenda.

Adopting the chaos theory philosophy, management's task became concentrated on techniques to manage continuity and change simultaneously. This debate focused on the informal system within organisations because it was felt it dealt with the complexities the formal system could not, simply by avoiding rites and rituals (Stacey, 1993).[9] Management approaches, it was now believed, needed to deal with the resultant fields of tensions created by non-rational as well as rational phenomena. Flexibility as a management style and a love of change, instead of treating change as something unusual, typifies these approaches in management (Peters, 1991).[10] Flexibility, it was now thought, could be achieved through empowering and training the organisation's stakeholders.[11]

Production approaches based on standardisation and fitness for use became shelved in favour of those that provided customers with a wider definition of quality.[12] The team became identified as the route to added value and became the focus of efficiency and effectiveness in the value chain.[13] A total quality approach to product/service created the need for a different type of leadership style and exercise of legitimate authority. Effective decisions in dynamic markets were now thought to require lateral consideration of choice possibilities, which challenged the accepted rule – anarchistic behaviour, rather than consensus, was now seen as advantageous, and indeed necessary, to organisational survival (Sengee, 1996).[14] Leadership was dropped in favour of facilitator styles because these encouraged the exercise of individual autonomy through loose management of anarchistic groups (Brown and Scase, 1991).[15] Inductive reasoning approaches, which focused on disproof, were now criticised for endorsing *a priori* beliefs (Brown, 1991). New knowledge was now thought to emerge from contradiction, enquiry enhanced by dialectic (ibid.). Management styles now set out to reduce individual/organisational myopic thinking (Quinn, 1980).[16]

The new management task became the creation of an organisation that supported learning (Sengee, 1990).[17] Stimulus-response behaviour, learning from experience, was seen to produce a process of normalisation where difference was seen as dangerous, bad rather than good. The promotion of active learning, rather than reinforced reactive behaviour, became part of management speak.[18] Linear thinking, regularity, stability and consensus decision-making were now understood to cause managers to hide mistakes, more importantly they caused managers to coerce others to do the same. Tolerance of error was now seen as important to the pursuit of excellence because an organisation needed to learn from its mistakes.[19] Conflict had to be aired and the status quo challenged in the light of new information, in order to bring about change.

While bureaucratic structures remained useful in predictable situations, they were not now seen as the ideal organisational structure to manage all change phenomena. Indeed, the rapid change in technological and market factors had caused task specification, a central component of bureaucracy, to break down – changed management styles were needed (Burns and Stalker, 1961).[20] Employees' adherence to rules was now thought only useful where it decreased power visibility or interpersonal tensions; however, the unintended, often informal, consequences which rule-bound behaviour created were now seen as largely dysfunctional to the organisation.[21] Significantly, it was now thought that rule enforcement caused employees to lose the ability to think independently and thus innovate (Merton, 1957). Theorists began to think that bureaucratic organisation processes limited creativity and thus organisational survival.

Because investigations in social science neither prove nor disprove an earlier hypothesis, studies in social science are peppered with such coexisting, competing, explanations of reality. Nevertheless, to bring about change at the organisational level, state of the art theory thus far has suggested that government has two tools to hand, namely: changing the structure of the organisation thus changing organisational actors roles and responsibilities; and changing the way in which the organisation is controlled thus changing the power base and who decides.

Tools for Change: Leadership Styles

Beginning on the left-hand side of the uncertainty tolerance zone, leadership style developed from the belief that organisational processes should be steered by top management, who were thought better informed to do so. In hierarchical organisations leadership power is exercised through legitimate authority. It is believed that a leader only acts to improve organisational performance; the leadership task is directing employees' tasks and controlling/monitoring of performance to target (Heck, 1996). In this model leaders are responsible for setting the strategic direction of an organisation.

Some argue that the former model denies the political-conflict context of organisational processes, where power may not be dependent on authority and dispersed throughout the organisation (Ogawa and Bossert, 1995). The exercise of power in organisations can thus be seen to have many forms and to operate through the informal as well as the formal organisation (French and Raven, 1959).[22] Such approaches suggest that a leader may not be wholly responsible for organisational success. Indeed, employee empowerment is seen as a way to increase individual accountability, freeing workers to be innovative, thus creating greater opportunities for organisations to be successful. Following this theme, a managers task is to release the untapped competencies amongst employees, facilitating employee responsibility, commitment and involvement and developing greater ownership of his/her task (Keenoy, 1991). Nevertheless, even Sengee (1990), the guru of empowered organisations, suggests that such employee empowerment cannot be achieved without central support.[23]

The type of leadership competence required is contingent upon the strategic issues an organisation faces, particularly the state of change in which it operates (Fielder, 1994). More complexities follow from the individual preferences exercised by a leader, his/her perception of what works and how participators operate (Fox, 1965).[24] Assumptions that a leader makes about the best way to manage influence the power set he/she selects with which to bring about change. The power that leaders have, and the approach they adopt when exercising that power, can thus considerably affect the culture of the organisation.

While accepting that is a plethora of leadership styles, to simplify the analysis I have used McGrath's (1962) description of two main categories of style namely, the autocratic and democratic. McGrath describes autocratic leadership as directive and critical – the leader designs and dominates the decision-making process through a culture of command. This leadership style thus fits with low uncertainty tolerance. Whereas democratic leaders operate by consent, they prefer consultative processes and person-oriented approaches. They believe that employees are willing to contribute and capable of contributing to the organisational process. Democratic leaders trust their workforce to perform; any monitoring tends to be loosely applied. This leadership style thus encapsulates high uncertainty tolerance.

Leadership styles that closely resemble the democratic leadership approach are thought more appropriate styles to manage professional organisations, such as further education colleges, because they allow the professionals to act freely. Indeed, it is the perception that stakeholders have about a leader's ability to cope with uncertainty, thereby reducing his/her uncertainty, which ultimately determines a leader's power.[25] The perception of those over whom power is being exercised is of paramount importance. An organisation can maximise added value if there is a synergistic relationship between the human resource strategy and the organisational strategy. Indeed, where organisations are dependent on their operational core of professionals making the strategic and operational decisions, product/service quality is strongly linked with the level of staff retention (Mintzberg and Quinn, 1991).

What organisational leaders pay most attention to, how they react to crisis situations and what role models they display are tangible and visible ways of bringing about change (Schein, 1992). Any change to organisational culture involves altering norms of behaviour and challenging deeply entrenched beliefs. While revolt in the education sector is, in the main, rare (Innaccone, 1977; Lewellen, 1992; Bentham et al., 1994), if leadership style has power to influence, and is individually determined, each principal could implement government's policy differently. One of the tasks was thus to establish how the four principals described their own leadership style, then to evaluate whether that changed in light of government influence.

Tools for Change Management: the Role of the Centre

The centre can play its leadership role with its business units or departments as tight or loose. Tight top-down control, it is argued, will limit innovation and autonomous action by its employees and managers (Lindblom, 1968; Loabsy, 1967; Argyris, 1987). Where tight top-down control is expressed through tight financial control, managers tend to limit their activity within the boundaries of their job specification; the only changes they make are those that are small enough not to be too noticeable. Where the centre exerts tight control it thus expresses risk aversion and low uncertainty tolerance.

In contrast, central control can be loose, where responsibility and authority is devolved to personal accountability and collective responsibility. In this approach, decisions tend to be made through shared vision.[26] Management's task is thus to facilitate a decision process, where incongruent objectives and disparate needs are expressed, adopting pluralistic principles managers act as stewards enabling strategy to emerge. Where the centre applies its control loosely it demonstrates high uncertainty tolerance.

Tools for Change Management: Organisational Structure

There is a link between the structure of an organisation, its management style and its control mechanism. No one style, however, best fits all organisational types (Goold and Campbell, 1987). In the hierarchical bureaucratic structure:

> Tasks are broken down into small elements rules and procedures are applied to those elements; standard budgetary and cost variation controls are applied; technology is utilised to limit variation in pace quality and methods; routine decision making is delegated within prescribed limits (Child, 1973, p. 57).

The hierarchical bureaucratic structure supports an autocratic leadership style.

In this structure incremental change can be accommodated because job specifications, rules, and procedures can be quickly adapted. However, control expressed through the reward and punishment procedures can create behavioural conformity, encourage departmental myopia and result in the lack of corporate identity. Together, these factors decrease an organisation's ability to create added advantage through its process.

Whereas the predictable part of the business may be best organised as a hierarchy, dealing with the unknown creates the need to free innovation, which the hierarchy limits. Bringing together as many views of reality as possible is thought to help balance risk given uncertainty, it is thus suggested that departmental structures need to be abandoned and replaced with structures that create interdepartmental communication. A less radical solution comprises a combination of hierarchical structures, for day-to-day activities, and a matrix structure[27] for innovation or problem solving (Moss Kanter, 1983; Stacey, 1993). However, these hybrid structures have a tendency to continue old traditions (problems with traditional ways of doing things have already been highlighted).

Despite the need for a revolutionary approach to organisational structure, it has become common for tall hierarchical structures to be abandoned in favour of flat structures, sometimes including matrix problem-solving units, ad hoc. These structures have fewer communication channels but tend to retain traditional ways of doing things. They provide the image of changing everything while changing very little, retaining low uncertainty tolerance.

Tools for Change: An Organisation's Ability to Learn

There are two reasons why it is argued that the learning style of an organisation needs to be based on conflict resolution. The first is that organisations reflect society, which is made up of individuals who have incongruent objectives and competing needs. Adopting this approach, consensus management is more about complexity denial than an expression of reality. The second is that decision-making, given an informed, intelligent workforce, suggests that management needs to manage empowered disparate actors and bring about resolution, given a field of tensions.

Developing the notion of organisations as conflict arenas, growth in staff commitment and trust can only be achieved if the organisation's structure and style enables disparate views to be met fairly. If unfairness exists in the formal system, employees may turn to the support of informal groups, where they can deal openly with paradox, complexity and compromise (Stacey, 2000). A formal organisational process that denies different views within it can thus serve to distance an organisation from accessing the very innovative learning it needs to survive in a dynamic market.

Similarly, because emotional displays are often seen as a sign of weakness and indicative of illogical behaviour, organisations tend to deny the emotional context within communication.[28] While such denial makes it easier to assert conformance (Waldron and Krone, 1991),[29] emotion can be seen as the source of meaning, thus where an organisation ignores emotion it ignores individual's reasoning (Thurton, 1991).[30] Such denial can cause individuals to turn from their work to their leisure activities to express their choice, creativity, personal satisfaction and social integration. Organisational denial is thus strongly correlated with a reduction in employee involvement, autonomy and job satisfaction at work (Parker, 1991).[31]

The majority of people in professional organisations tend to be more individually adept at self-awareness and psychological insight.[32] Professionals tend to favour action driven by principle because their ethics are rooted in empathy (Hoffman, 1984).[33] Indeed, professionals are paid for their expertise in emotional management skills (Fineman, 1993).[34] Employee commitment, however, is not only dependent upon an individual's competence, it is also dependent on an employee's willingness. An individual's management of their emotion determines their action by balancing their emotional reaction with their reasoning powers, thus, it is argued, supporting employees' growth in emotional intelligence is important to their job satisfaction and organisational performance.[35] While self-management is a learnt competence,[36] some people learn to manage their emotions better than others. Thus variations between the levels of employee commitment are high (Ekman and Freisen, 1975).[37]

To reap the benefits of increased employee commitment, particularly in the case of professional organisations, managers must transform their task from control to one that facilitates an individual's learning process (Beer, 1990). This means accepting a field of emotional tensions and setting out to understand the part the emotional arena plays (Fineman, 1993).[38] This approach embraces high uncertainty tolerance because solutions to labour issues may not reach even semipermanent dispositions (Sui, 1980).

Conclusion Thus Far

Thus far, it has been argued, new management approaches embrace high uncertainty tolerance as a way of managing. Further, it has been argued that professional organisations operate as organised anarchies because of their particular needs for synergy. Several characteristics have been developed as key to the promotion of uncertainty tolerance: a formal decision-making process to enable the development of clear structures for the known part of the business; cross-departmental and vertically-integrated decision groups used as a way of freeing innovation; a facilitator leadership style[39] to free innovation and develop trust;[40] and an empowered workforce to enable the organisation to tolerate and learn from error. These characteristics thus form the benchmark against which government's transformation of further education colleges can be evaluated.

Notes

1   Wilding (1982) outlines professional status as based on the nature of the task, the expertise required to carry it out and manner and spirit in which the tasks are undertaken: all these aspects were subjected to criticism.
2   Competitive advantage describes a distinct advantage a firm has in the marketplace that enables it to add more value than its competitors. Roots of competitive advantage include price; product range; manufacturing quality; product differentiation; resources external and internal; and culture, to name but a few.
3   Strategies are 'indefensible', companies are 'attacked at every weak point', competitors are seen as the enemy – 'he'll wipe you out' (Lakoff and Johnson, 1980).
4   Scientific management developed from the philosophical roots of economics. It emphasises planning, standardisation and management by exception. A division of labour separates

management from the production/service task. The manager plans and manages strategic developments. Workers' rights, choice and discretion are limited by managerial control.

5 Managers' ability to carry out their tasks, Fayol argued, was dependent on the link between authority, responsibility and fair discipline. Formal rules imposed through a division of labour, monitoring of tasks and impersonal relationships of participators were essential, he believed, to the maintenance of a manager's authority to act.

6 In 1924 Mayo found that individual's behaviour responded to informal networks, group norms and standards. He suggested morale, a sense of belonging, management style and job satisfaction were important contributors to better worker participation.

7 Quinn (1980) thought that informal alliances were purposeful, effective, proactive management techniques that improved analytical and behavioural aspects of strategy formation.

8 Lindblom (1968) argued that business decision-making processes were reactive. Actors adapted to the multi-goal, rapidly changing, environment in which they found them but became risk averse because the control procedures denied such complexity. Managers thus preferred 'nibbling' at change decisions rather than taking a 'good bite'.

9 Stacey (1993) thought that an organisation's informal subsystem was a vehicle for change. Circumventing formal power, such groups could focus on plans, tasks, random action, political process and learning in ambiguous situations. These subsystems, he argues, provide social and psychological relief to individuals confronting ambiguity and uncertainty. Members of the subgroup are more motivated and able to operate more effectively because problems can be aired without the repercussions evident within the formal decision-making processes. Stacey suggests that managers need completely different skills to manage such informal and self-selecting subsystems.

10 Peters (1991) suggested that a historical management focus on narrowly specialised labour had caused untold harm.

11 Peters suggests that high labour involvement, minimal hierarchy and rewards based on quality and responsiveness is consistent with a fast-reacting organisation.

12 Product design is focused on specific target groups, consumer value is intrinsically linked to life style and aspiration.

13 Peters suggests that people need to be seen as more important, internally and externally, so that quality and responsiveness can be key.

14 Organisational learning requires that error be tolerated. Sengee (1990) suggests that individuals need to recreate themselves continually: managers need to create and sustain shared vision and team building.

15 In the total quality model the intrinsic components of customer value are recognised as significant, thus more emphasis is placed on industrial relations as significant to the achievement of organisational goals.

16 Narrow thinking is task-oriented and rule-bound: it prohibits thinking about the uncertain.

17 The skills required for organisations to learn, Senge suggests, are personal commitment, proficiency to do the task, challenging the ingrained assumptions and generalisations of understanding and the conceptual framework that makes the patterns within the system clear.

18 Argyris (1987) suggests that an individual's learning curve ranges from immaturity to maturity. He classifies professionals as mature because they express choice independently of the rules. If individuals are at the mature state of learning but are not allowed independence, Argyris argues, they will be unfulfilled and may display dysfunctional

behaviour. It is thus in an organisation's interest to move individuals along their learning curve.
19 Argyris suggests that in double loop learning actors openly discuss error and thus can correct it. The organisational environment has to be such that error is accepted and not punished.
20 Contingency theorists suggest that organisational structure, leadership and managerial style needed to be flexible. Organisational interaction should be vertical and horizontal, based on consultation and advice giving. Hierarchical control should be replaced with consultation processes, less status should be placed on knowledge and more on the informal flows of information. The management approach should be diagnostic, applying different techniques to various situations.
21 Gouldner (1964) identified the unintended consequences of intended action as vicious or virtuous to the organisation. Unintended vicious circles are where the individual minimises, rather than maximises, behaviour in response to the rule.
22 Power operates in the following forms: reward power, built on the ability to control resources; coercive power, built on the ability to punish; legitimate power, based on a common set of goals; referent power, based on an individual admiring and wishing to emulate another; and expert power, based on expert knowledge that others do not have.
23 Sengee (1990) identifies three leadership roles namely: designer, where the leader engages the employees in the vision and core values of the organisation; teacher, where the leader coaches, facilitates and helps the employees learn: and steward, where the leader demonstrates personal commitment and responsibility.
24 Fox (1965) suggests that an individual's view of the world is individually determined, formed by social conditioning and altered by experience.
25 Thurton (1991) explores this point using reward power, more pay. If the subordinate is not reliant on the employer to meet his or her material and psychological needs and can get more money by working elsewhere, then being offered more money is not a reward and thus subordinate compliance will not be the outcome.
26 The practices of shared vision are activities engaged in by groups that lead to the development of principles which are understood by the group.
27 A matrix structure is different from a departmentalised structure in that the decision-making system operates both vertically and horizontally.
28 Early investigations of psychological behaviour measured stereotypical reactions to given stimuli.
29 Waldron and Krone (1991) found that where there is a high degree of emotional control, disagreements are often suppressed and the employee voice neutralised.
30 The process of determining which rules apply in a situation involves attributing meaning to that situation, a consequence of experience, expectations and value.
31 Parker (1991) suggests three relationships between work and leisure: the extension pattern, where the actor overlaps the responsibilities of home and work; the opposition pattern, where the actor has a clear separation of home and work and indeed may transfer his/her central allegiance to leisure activities as a way of forgetting work; and the neutrality pattern, where the actor is simply neutral to it, often because of highly routine tasks. If the individual's expectations do not include satisfaction at work, he/she will exchange work for leisure if the money is attractive. Professionals are said to belong to the extension pattern of behaviour because their leisure activities are often associated to their choice of career. Given that the split between leisure and work is less obvious in professional work

it is reasonable to assume that professionals seek involvement and creativity within their professional role.

32 Goleman (1996) suggests that emotional intelligence is not just about being morally attuned to righting wrongs; it involves the competence to speak out against them. There is, he argues, no connection between specialist expertise and being seen as trustworthy. He suggests that there are three variables in organisational relationships, namely communication webs (who talks to whom), expertise networks where others turn for advice and trust networks. Trust networks are built where the individual displays the ability to understand the perspectives of others and the ability to be self-motivated and self-managed – all of these, he argues, are aspects of emotional intelligence.

33 Hoffman (1984) suggests that actions driven by impulse lack empathy and are exhibited by those who do not have self-control – they do not display will and character and cannot understand the needs of others. Empathy alters social rules using discretion – an individual assesses the believed consequences of his/her action outside the immediate context; they act on behalf of others.

34 Fineman (1993) suggests that their task is to look caring, display understanding and demonstrate benign detachment, so that they can defend against personal displays of feelings. Professionals have to create a social defence system – ritual – so that they can practise outside the moral anxieties that would otherwise overwhelm them. He argues that Taylor was able to distance emotion from production because contemporary factors needed the fix he offered.

35 Scientists have found the removal of the amygdala in animals causes them to lack fear, rage and an ability to cooperate or interact. It is thought the amygdala short-circuits the thinking brain, the neocortex. It springs into action while the thinking brain conceives a plan and triggers reactions before evidence. The neocortex brings an analytical response to the emotional response, it modulates natural emotional reaction.

36 Some emotions are biological, for example fear, where the body and the brain prepare for flight; others are culturally defined. Goleman (1996) argues each individual has two components of mind creating meaning, one that thinks and one that feels; in combination they create knowing. The important factor for individual development is the social interactive skill, understanding self and others, he argues. How that emotion is expressed is dependent on the level of personal intelligence. Goleman defines emotion as a feeling, its distinctive thoughts, psychological and biological states, and a range of propensities to act. Emotional intelligence, he argues, is the measure of self-control, zeal and persistence that individuals demonstrates. A key social competence, he argues, is the ability to express ones feelings.

37 Ekman and Friesen (1975) found that some displays of emotions can be socially controlled – they are learnt early on in the socialisation process and displayed as a form of social consensus. Outside of such control individuals display their feelings differently.

38 A fine line exists between how much emotion can be displayed to describe reality and be acceptable, and that which cannot. Risk averse individuals learn to manage expressions of emotion within social constructs dictating acceptable behaviour – linked to task and institutional goals.

39 A facilitator style is used here to describe a leadership style that is enabling, not controlling. A facilitator has no predetermined outcome in mind when problem solving, his/her task is to smooth the consultative process, keeping in mind the organisation's strategic aims and objectives.

40   Trust is used here to express the process through which professionals acquire their autonomy. The legitimate authority that professionals have to complete their task implies that society trusts them. Trust can be based on subject specificity, knowledge, or their particular task. In an educational institution, therefore, the expectation would be that the level of trust would be high.

Chapter Nine

The Cast

The ability of the government to assert its political ideology within the further education colleges is determined to a large extent by its ability to control the decision-making process at the organisational level. Indeed, Crozier (1964) and Gouldner (1964) suggest that the validity of a public policy is tested where that policy is put into practice. The way in which a policy is managed at the organisational level thus becomes an important variable in the policy action process.

In order to be successful, governments had to be able to influence the internal operational process within the further education colleges, creating a new strategic direction in line with its policies. My assumption was that implementation deficit would be controlled if the Conservative government's discourse was powerful (Bachrach and Baratz, 1963). Government power would be demonstrated if the colleges' social value systems and organisational style changed in line with the desired direction. I set out to discover whether the principals within the colleges saw their tasks differently in the 1990s, and were trying to shift their colleges towards a new perception of its role and to change organisational tradition accordingly. Only then would it be possible to evaluate whether the government's language themes were reflected in the principals' and the organisations' own language.

The four principals gave their accounts of the changes as they saw them in two stages. Firstly, prior to three of the colleges becoming incorporated and then four years after. The responses were then compared and contrasted to provide a story about the colleges in action during this period.

If government did manage to change the culture and remit of further education colleges in line with its policies it would be regarded as a major coup because areas such as education had previously been considered politically sensitive and untouchable (Maclure, 1988). Such an attempt at change was fraught with difficulties because professionals are legitimate rule breakers thus relatively free to act autonomously. It could be said that they are more difficult to control than some others (Barrett and Fudge, 1981).

The value of leadership and different approaches have been discussed previously. To simplify here, two main categories, namely the autocratic and the democratic, are used. An autocratic leadership style is directive and critical

– the leader designs and dominates the decision-making process. Autocratic styles of leadership have a tendency to focus on economic factors and create a management culture of command. In contrast, a democratic leadership approach is consultative and person oriented (McGrath, 1962). This approach to management has a consent culture as a central tenet; the decision-making process assumes intelligent employees who are capable of contributing to the decision-making process. Monitoring of the organisation tends to be loose in order that employees can be empowered to act. The democratic approach is thus a more appropriate leadership style to use in professional organisations such as further education colleges.

In spite of the dynamic context in which organisations function, Lewellen (1992), Bentham et al. (1994) and Iannaccone (1977) have concluded that revolutions in the education sector are in the main rare. Nevertheless, if leadership style has power to influence and is individually determined, each organisation could implement the government's policy in a different way. One of the tasks was thus to establish each principal's leadership style and to evaluate whether that changed in light of government influence.

Case Study: College Profiles

Of the four colleges selected for study *colleges one*, *two* and *three* were public sector further education colleges. *College four* was registered as a private school and had always operated as a sixth form private crammer college. *College four* was similar but different from the other three and selected for comparison purposes.

In response to the ad hoc way in which the further education sector has developed, *colleges one*, *two* and *three* serviced a wide course portfolio in an attempt to satisfy both national and local community needs. Portfolios included academic, craft and career-oriented courses, all offered in various forms: part-time day; block release; full-time; and evening. In contrast, *college four*'s course portfolio was narrow and focused. As a crammer college, it specialised in the retaking of GCSE and 'A' level qualifications. The average student stay was one year, attending on a daily basis.

The principals' interviews were in two separate parts. The first focused on operational questions: namely, the number of full-time equivalent students; full- and part-time staff; courses; number of departments; and areas in decline or growth. The purpose of the second part was to establish each principal's personal style and their perception of their college and the way in which it operated.[1]

For ease of analysis the principals' responses are separated are under four specific headings for diagnosing corporate culture, namely, the principal's management style and focus; college structures and the decision-making process; the manager's role in the organisation as a change agent; and the college's competitive environment (Cameron and Whetton, 1988).

The Principals' Account: Before

Prior to the changes in 1988, it was not necessary for the principals within further education colleges to be managerialist. College funding had been relatively stable, as had the market. Risk, particularly financial risk, was not a game of which they had much experience. One of the key skills of a principal had been in his/her ability to function and gain advantage in committee meetings and complex consultative processes; their expertise lay in negotiation techniques.

Part III of The Education Reform Act 1988 shifted LEAs from controller of the further education service to monitor; this transfer of responsibilities coincided with the Local Government Finance Act 1988 (DES, 1988a). Government made it clear that funding responsibility was to be shifted from the LEA to a funding council. At the same time, government indicated that colleges were to be removed from the public sector. Since little information was available about that process there was rumour as to what the responsibilities of incorporation implied and speculation about how budgets would be calculated and devolved. However, there were signals about the likely route of the impending changes. The power of the governors in further education colleges had been increased, with their responsibility shifting from a general oversight of the colleges to the responsibility for general direction of the colleges (MoE, 1959b). Principals were adjusting to the implied shift of power away from the academic board; lecturing staff were expressing concerns about their jobs and responsibilities.

From the 1980s public accountability had become the dominant discourse of central government. Internal monitoring control measures were seen as key to quality provision (Audit Commission, 1985). Within colleges, monitoring comprised: lecturers' contact hours with students; attendance hours of all staff – academic, technicians, professional, administrative and clerical; and outputs indicated by student hours (ibid.).

Staff in *colleges one*, *two* and *three* were either on long-term full-time contracts or short-term contracts. If they were on short-term contracts they were on contract but paid by the teaching hour; full-time and part-time contracts were nationally agreed with the trade union. In contrast, the staff in *college four* were mostly part-time, paid by the hour and individually contracted.

Management Style and Focus

In *college one* the principal said his style of management was proactive. He identified the major part of his new role as acting as a change catalyst. He described his management style in the following way:

> I am proactive. I am involved, maybe too involved. I would like to delegate but that is not included. The changes that are taking place are spread too wide. The principal's role is to set the stage for innovation. I am using structural change as a way of instigating change. You need to move change into the environment.

In college two the principal saw his approach to management as:

> A high profile. I am charismatic, directional and attentive. I do not spend much time out of the college. I know all the staff and all the students know me because I am always walking about.

This principal's style was very people oriented. He thought the main tool of change was information dissemination. He used 'a network of consultation' as a process for discussion and a route for information dissemination.

In *college three* the principal saw his role as being an example to others: 'I give a lot of myself – I am here early and leave late. I try to be an example of good practice so that it will encourage others. I also still teach.' The main focus of his attention was on the financial aspects of the business: 'I have employed an administrator who comes from a military background. Plans are of limited value and must be changed regularly.' He said he hoped he maintained an open style of management. However, he was aware that internal promotion had led to some jealousy. He identified information as the key tool for the management of change: 'It is important that they are informed of the right things. NATFHE resisted change in the first instance and this has affected staff attitude.'

In *college four* the principal perceived her style as 'non-confrontational, to calm the problem areas' and 'by example'. She said she hoped through this process to bring about a culture of 'optimism'. Paradoxically, she regarded meetings 'as a waste of time'. When changes were needed, she said, the approach she took was to make a suggestion and then leave it until the staff gradually came round to it: 'I know I will get my own way in the end.' Her approach to change had evolved, she purported, because:

> I have tried asking first but get negative responses. For example I suggested that full time staff might each like a room of their own. They discussed it and said they preferred open-plan.

She shrugged her shoulders as if to indicate the inappropriateness of their decision. She made no reference to their reasons for their decision and one was left with the impression that she was not interested. Staff now worked in an open-plan office. The main focus for change, she said, was the students' needs: 'Every child has potential.'

College Structure and Decision-making Process

Each of the principals was asked if they could provide an organisational structure chart. Only *college three* had an organisational chart, demonstrating the lack of a managerialist perspective in all four colleges. It would, however, be incorrect to assume they did not keep such records; it was rather the shape and form of records that was the issue.

College one had been involved in a merger with a geographically close competitor, while *colleges two* and *three* had just completed a major restructuring programme. In general the principals recognised there would be increases in some areas of their market and decreases in others. Historically, of course, changes in the product portfolios had never been market-tested; they developed in an ad hoc way, generally in response to the last few years' intake numbers and feedback from lecturers, students or employers.

The principals in *colleges one, two* and *three* spoke about their colleges being affected by the general economic decline in construction and engineering courses and anticipated changes to their product portfolios to reflect this. *College three* in particular was built mainly to feed local engineering demand – consequently a large part of its product portfolio was linked to engineering. This principal was very concerned about survival.

Similarly, all three colleges were anticipating growth in the numbers of full-time students as a result of the recession and the resulting lack of jobs for young people. Coupled with this, *colleges one* and *three* were contemplating a move into franchised courses with local higher education institutions. In *college three*, participation in higher education, already part of the course portfolio, had nevertheless been restricted by local agreements; these were still operational in 1991. The principal hoped this would change in the near future.

College four had been largely untouched by the 1988 Act and no dramatic changes had taken place in the immediate past. The principal did not anticipate that any changes would take place in this arrangement in the foreseeable future. In general she felt they were winning against their competitors because they focused on the student, which she believed would lead to sustainable growth.

In *colleges one, two* and *three* there was clear departmentalisation of responsibility because of subject specificity and academic matters. Academic matters tended to include all management decisions, since any changes affected a course, this being the main focus of decisions.

College one had two sites and 11 departments. The structure was hierarchical, with an Academic Board, heads of department and approximately 140 full-time teaching staff and 'some' part-time staff. The principal estimated that there were approximately 20,781 part- and full-time students. He identified the decision-making framework in the college in terms of the formal structure only; no reference was made to the informal links of decision-making throughout the interview. The formal decision-making structure was hierarchical; he saidthat there were several routes for decisions that differed depending upon on the level of the decision-making category. The Academic Board made academic decisions and power was devolved downwards. It is interesting to note that he stated: 'Whether staff realise that this is a strong mechanism for influencing decisions I don't know.' This appeared to indicate that, in the principal's opinion, the decision-making process might not be representative of the organisation as a whole.

There were two vice-principals who had the power to make decisions on day-to-day issues; the principal met with the vice-principals once a week for general updating purposes. College-wide decision-making was made through a senior management team comprising all heads of department.

In *college two* the structure comprised the principal, a governing body, an associate principal and a management team; the decision-making process was hierarchical. However, as in the previous college, the power in decision-making was devolved downwards. The principal shared his responsibility with the associate principal, who had responsibility for resources. The management team met weekly; this management team included heads of department, academic and administrative staff and governors. The meetings were organised by the principal, who said he controlled agenda setting for the meetings. His approach to these meetings was made clear in the following:

We have minutes but no matters arising. All papers to be discussed at the management team meeting have to be submitted four days prior to the meeting. The 'no matters arising' rule has been established because people who had not read the papers would take up a lot of time discussing unimportant issues in an effort to get themselves noticed.

Clearly the principal was trying to defuse politicking in an effort to create task orientation. Alongside the management team, policy groups also made decisions: these policy groups tended to be subject, though not necessarily departmentally, specific. The heads of department met with him every third week. Marketing responsibility was a cross college responsibility. Decisions he said should be made 'at the right level ... People should be making the decisions that they should be making.' This indicated he preferred a clear, hierarchical, division of labour. He commented:

The Academic Board meetings were not being used to discuss things that had academic depth. They have become more operational and organisational. This has to change so that they become more focused on academic matters.

Prior to the 1988 Act, the Academic Board had been the main decision-maker in the college; the proposed shift suggested that this principal was keen to move away from the Board's larger role. He said that feedback loops from the policy groups to the department were operational:

I am a great believer in the departmental system ... but we also need cross college departments for what will not be delivered. Subject specialism and departmentalisation can create narrow views. The creation of cross-college roles where managers have corporate responsibilities has improved the corporate approach.

Whilst the principal stated the organisational structure was fairly flat there was clear evidence of a hierarchical decision-making system. He said:

Decisions are devolved downwards and made at the right level. Power is devolved downwards and decision-makers given autonomy. Some decisions are made without me knowing. Policy groups that are subject specific inform the lecturers and keep them informed.

College three had two sites, three boards of study and 19 teaching sections, 240 full-time and 120 part-time staff. The number of students was estimated at 2,000 full- and 13,000 part-time. There was clear evidence of a hierarchical organisational structure. As in the other two colleges, the decision-making also involved devolution of power:

> Decision-making in this organisation tends to be separated. If it is a more important strategic decision this is made between the senior lecturers and me whilst higher level decisions are made between me and the governors. Teaching decisions are made at the team level, I hope. Anyone can suggest a change. The changes are tied to accountability.

The principal expressed his concern about the autonomy of his teaching team. He identified the following problem:

> with the team that resist change ... who have a narrow focus as a result of non-movement. I am starting to use informal subsets of chosen people to generate discussions on college issues which can then feed into the formal decision-making.

This principal was clearly making some attempt to free the bottom-up information process by using white knights to signal good practice.[2] He hoped he would inevitably challenge the old icons and was operating in both the formal and informal context of the college to bring about change.

College four had two sites. It had a flat organisational structure with two governors, two principals and six 'informal' departments. Only six of the 45 staff were full-time: these six were subject leaders. One of the principals said there were around 400 students in each year. There were no formal meetings or procedures. Part-time teaching staff were employed by the hour, for teaching contact only. Major strategic decisions tended to be made by the two principals jointly although she felt they could 'make a decision without the other' when they needed to, without confrontation.

In general, the principal said, the subject tutors chose the syllabus they wanted to teach; this occurred because she trusted her staff's abilities: 'We employ excellently qualified staff who must make their own decisions', she stated. It was not her task to interfere on academic matters. After all, she continued, it was in the lecturers' interests to make the best choice on behalf of the students. 'If the students do not like the classes they will not attend and the lecturers will not be employed.'

She used an open-door policy – innovative ideas were normally generated on an ad hoc basis by the lecturers, who simply sought her approval. This freedom to innovate was evident in her following statement: 'Directors come every three weeks but they just play games. They have to approve expenses, for example, but would not quibble if those expenses changed.'

The Manager's Role in the Organisation: Change Agents

In all four colleges the selection of managers were subject specialists. It was not unusual to find managers who did not know how the organisation as a whole functioned, or indeed what funds and customers the college attracted. The managers' decisions were largely academic ones, with practical implications. They were often appointed because they demonstrated their ability to work hard and/or their merit as teachers. Their strength lay in their specialist ability and in their ability to enable consultation processes. The managerialist approach, introduced by the government, implied a vast culture change for these managers. It also implied the need for different skills.

In *college one* the principal stated that he wanted his managers:

> to organise the strategic plan, set their own targets for development and create their own vision of where we are going. They should understand the responsibilities and ownership of those plans should be in the hands of the management team.

The targets, he said, would be within a five-year plan but would be reviewed yearly. He identified good communication as key to change but he felt that this was an area 'we fall down on'. He said that 'the senior management team are well informed but this does not seem to filter down to others in the organisation'. The implication was that the senior management team was blocking his attempts to increase communication within the organisation. In consequence, he saw his first task as altering the way the communication channels functioned; he believed he had started this process with the introduction of a newsletter.

He expressed the view a clear strategy for change was needed; if this was not in place he felt that people would feel 'unsettled'. Furthermore, he felt it was important to 'build up ... a team approach and commitment'. As the key to raising the organisation's awareness of a changing climate, he wanted to change the organisational structure. He stated he wanted to 'move change into the environment for example get staff changing rooms etc. ... it will set the pace for the future'.

The principal felt the governors' role was constitutionally powerful. However, he thought there should be a demarcation between what he termed 'governance versus management responsibilities'. The perception he had of a principal's role as managing director can be seen clearly in the following:

> Governors can play shop if they want to but they will need a better understanding of involvement. They are the employers but where will they stop in terms of human research management? Governors see themselves as responsible for everything within the college. I am just piggy in the middle. My task is to try to get the governors to see that they cannot use simplistic comparisons of their job to that of the college.

This principal regarded his expertise in further education as crucial to ensuring appropriate strategies for the future.

In *college two* the principal felt that managers of the future would need to be able to demonstrate a portfolio of skills, which included 'leadership potential be able to act as a facilitators, motivators, planners and be able to warn and advise'. He expressed the view that he wanted to 'move away from academics having managerial responsibility, they are not the right people for it'. His frustration was evident in the tone and facial expressions demonstrated when this view was expressed. On the whole he was happy for the agenda of any meeting to be set by his managers, he said. He stated he had a different relationship with each of his managers. However, his need to control the process is evident in his statement:

> I keep them all informed but do not necessarily let them have a say. I rarely instruct them. I do not believe in lots of paper, I tell them to communicate with each other and not through me. It is better that they address the problem straight out.

In terms of other managing agents the principal stated: 'both politicians and governors' had played a low profile. He stated:

> If you cannot control them they will stray into operational areas. The decision route is better, there is more accountability. If you have more confidence in one another then the principal must be accountable and therefore have to explain, consult and support. I have had an altercation over no consultation. You have to take the new on board.

Again, the task of the principal conflicts with that of the governing body.

In *college three* the principal had inherited what he described as:

> A Japanese lookalike management style which was supposed to deliver democracy and devolution of power. Sections were headed by elected representatives. There was no management control and a massive overspend. The governors were keen to increase control over human resource management

and create accountability as well as financial control ... When section heads became facilitators not managers communication collapsed ... I have tried to get [the managers] to change their roles ... I have a problem with the teaching teams who are too narrow and resist change. This has been watered down by new initiatives which has allowed new staff to be employed.

This principal identified the new management role as one based on departmental as well as individual accountability. The governors' task, he said, was 'to serve as advisors'. He wanted his colleges to be seen as 'part of the community' and he expressed concern that competition might alter this perspective. He was concerned that all the 'local good will' built up over time could be eroded by the introduction of a competitive environment.

In *college four* the flat management structure consisted of two principals, one male and one female. The principals were jointly responsible for decision-making but, the female principal said:

> Staff can come with any new ideas ... and can be instrumental in initiating changes. We have to approve expenses ... but would not quibble if those expenses changed. We employ excellently qualified staff who must make their own decisions.

Competitive Environment and the College

Competition was a newly-emerging context for *colleges one, two* and *three*. Colleges had always competed over reputation, but this had never taken an aggressive stance. Indeed, it was not unusual for one college to recommend another to a student, if it fitted the student's needs better. It is worth remembering that competition was anathema for many in educational circles; indeed, for some it still is. Educational institutions had never previously operated in a market – the professionals did what they did and the students bought into it if they wanted to. One college might have a better reputation than another, but this would be based on student perception of excellence and coincidental to a professional's behaviour. Professionals may have striven individually to achieve excellence, but rarely collectively.

The principal in *college one* thought incorporation would have a major effect on his college. He said the government had:

> An unwritten agenda. The constitutional government is going to have major responsibilities and will accept them it will institute various practices throughout the country, there will be major financial changes, focused on student-led finance.

> Colleges are inefficient, as they have never had to face space issues and are complacent. There will be much better-defined procedures, systems and accountability. There will be unit-costing, emphasis on size of classes, length of courses and premises management. There will be major changes in further education colleges and they will accept them.

The principal thus anticipated there would be increasing central control over his task; he said that competition between his college and others had already become overt and they felt that 'mutual understanding between colleges is over'. He recognised that his college needed to beat the competition: 'We need to be a market led organisation. We need to build up our student numbers.'

In contrast the principal from *college two* said that, in his case, there was no competition between colleges because there was:

> no over-provision in the area. The college was already on the road before the changes began, we have always changed incrementally. The LEA had previously had a rationalisation programme over the county and all excess capacity has been removed. Over-provision is a bad thing whereas competition is not.

The principal believed that an earlier rationalisation programme had secured the college a safe place in the local market. The government, he thought, was playing a major role in terms of:

> financial control and in terms of potential increase in bureaucracy. Politicians and governors have taken a low profile in the area as a whole. There will be funding performance indicators in the future but what form these will take I don't know.

The principal expressed the view that if the government pursued a process of accountability his task would be to communicate that. It would be his task to 'explain, consult and support' the process to ensure that the changes needed took place.

In *college three* the principal said:

> We were pioneers of the LMS and have backing as we are a Conservative area. In 1980 we were more ready than some to move forward. The 1992 Act provides opportunities of greater freedom through competition. Though our relationship with the LEA has been a good one our growth has been restricted by regional management of this sector. There is great potential for growth in this area. TEC will have an increased part to play and we will get a lot more freedom. I am concerned that further education could be perceived as a soft target for financial

cutback. The distance of the college from its immediate competitors restricts the extent of competition in the area, whilst student choice is limited by public transport problems.

Here a close alignment of policy between central and local government was evident and identified as a positive aspect by the principal. He believed this gave his college a leading edge over his competitors outside the immediate locality. Freedom from restrictive practices, he thought, would provide the college with growth potential; paradoxically, he had already indicated his college was protected from local competition. Evidently he clearly perceived competition as that with other boroughs.

The principal of *college four* said that, as a private sector organisation, the college had always operated in a competitive environment. Competition, she said:

> comes from other local private and public schools. The ethos of this school is on the students' individual needs. For example, where does the individual student need to be in the future, it is not community related.

There had been no overt government intervention in the management of the college; the principal said, 'it is not inspected even though it should be'. She anticipated they could be affected by the national curriculum changes. If the rumours were true that 'A' levels, which were their business, might change she anticipated this would make a significant difference.

Conclusion: Stage One

In *all four colleges* the principals saw themselves both as leaders and role models. In *colleges one, two* and *three* they saw themselves as having some degree of referent power and perceived their behaviour as signalling what others might emulate: 'I stay late'; 'I still teach'; 'by example'. In contrast, in *college four*, the principal felt it was much more important that 'the students know me', demonstrating a clear customer focus.

In *college one* the management style was autocratic. The principal led and directed through the formal system; he changed the structure to alter the culture. He saw himself as fully responsible for bringing about change. At the same time, he used referent power to influence the informal organisation. In *college two* the principal's leadership style is much more in line with that of the democratic approach. He personalised his role by being attentive, exerting expert power and using participation to bring about change. Similarly, in *college three* the principal used a people-oriented consultative approach and still participated in teaching. The principal's leadership style in *college four* was based on a shared vision, that of the students' attainment. Although she stated that she got her own way, inferring that her style was autocratic, her style was very decentralised; she gave staff considerable autonomy to act.

There were also differences in the composition of the organisational structure type. *Colleges one* and *three* had a tall hierarchical structure, *college two* had a fairly flat structure, while *college four* had a flat structure. All *four colleges* had consultative processes. The process of consultation, however, varied with each principal's personal style of leadership. *College one* had a 'top down' decision-making process; *colleges two and three* operated with a clear division of labour and *college four* used a 'bottom up' decision-making process.

In *college one* there seemed to be some contradiction between the principal's autocratic management style and how he wanted managers to act as change agents: he wanted his managers to be able to act autonomously while at the same time as he wanted to control. In *college two* the principal recognised that his specialist managers did not at the time have the administrative skills needed to act as change agents. In order to bring about change, his solution was to bring in managers to manage; in other words, to circumvent the consultative process. Similarly, the principal in *college three* identified his managers' lack of administrative skills: again, he had circumvented the consultative process by bringing in new people as change agents. All the principals talked about resistance to change. In *college four* managers were seen as the main change agents; innovation occurred through the autonomous action of the teaching fraternity.

In *college four* the target market was clearly identified and there was therefore a fit between what the organisation wanted to achieve and the skills to achieve it. In contrast, the course portfolios of *colleges one, two* and *three* had been largely determined by LEA action pre-1990, so their target markets were unclear. The principals were beginning to identify a skills gap, the introduction of monitoring implies the need for audit trails, hence the need for managers with administrative skills. At the same time economic and technological changes had changed the demand of students for training and education – causing different expertise requirements within the colleges. In contrast, in *college four*, experts' flexibility was part of everyday activity. This college responded to market pressures by using flexible staffing; this was combined with a 'bottom up' management style in order to use the expert knowledge of staff effectively.

In *colleges one*, *two* and *three* the principals had started to recognise their organisations' strengths and weaknesses against others. In *college two* the action of the LEA had to some extent circumvented local competition by a rationalisation programme; the survival of the colleges was thus to some extent secured. Similarly, the close political alignment between central and local government in the case of *college three* was thought to provide some competitive advantage. *College four* was used to managing operations competitively and was indeed surprised to be asked the question; the organisation's culture and success were built on incremental change. In contrast *colleges one*, *two* and *three* seemed to be adopting a re-engineering approach.

Given the evaluation of state of the art discourse about management in the previous chapter, the following organisational characteristics have been identified as those which will enable successful change management in a dynamic and complex environment namely: a formal decision-making process to enable the development of clear structures for the known part of the business; cross-departmental and vertically-integrated decision groups used as a way of freeing innovation; a facilitator management style to free innovation and develop trust; and an empowered workforce to enable the organisation to tolerate error and learn from it. These were used as a benchmark to evaluate the principals' responses.

The following conclusions were thus drawn from the principals' responses in 1991:

As these colleges were professional organisations it is not surprising to find that all the principals used a process of empowerment.[3] Each principal

College	Hierarchical decision-making	Matrix decision-making	Flat structure	Facilitator leadership style	Empowered workforce
1	Yes	Yes	No	No	Yes
2	Yes	Yes	Yes	Yes	Yes
3	Yes	Yes	No	Yes	Yes
4	Yes	Yes	Yes	Yes	Yes

demonstrated a level of trust in the professionals' autonomy.[4] There is, of course, clear evidence of this remaining in the case of *college four*, where the principal made it clear that teaching staff knew their task best. In the other three colleges the organisational structures are changing in line with the common trend towards flat bureaucratic structures. In the case of *colleges one*, *two* and *three* there was evidence that suggested that the consultative organisational styles were altering in favour of more autocratic styles. This appeared to be because quality trails were needed – hence the leaders were focusing on the administrative task. *College four* clearly performed best, given the benchmark criteria.

The next task is to compare the findings four years on, to evaluate whether any changes had actually taken place and had been driven by the government's policy.

The Context: Four Years On

I returned to the colleges to ask the principals to reflect on the previous four years. The context had changed; the Further and Higher Education Act 1992 had confirmed the process for incorporation of the colleges in the public sector. *Colleges one, two* and *three* were now incorporated colleges; the FEFC now controlled the allocation of funding for incorporated colleges, which was tied to student numbers.

Returning to the colleges after four years was an interesting experience. *Colleges one, two* and *three* gave the immediate appearance of being more managerial and less collegiate. The principals were less immediately accessible on the telephone. The principals' secretaries, in one case now a PA, played a more significant role in terms of greeting visitors. The reception areas were more businesslike and the receptionists spoke as if to customers. In *college four* there was no reception area, as before, and a small notice sent the visitor to the back of the building, in error. No one took any notice of me and when someone did notice, they peered over their glasses and asked in an autocratic tone whether I had an appointment.

Management Style and Focus

In *colleges one, two* and *three*, all three principals talked about increased caution as an effect of the removal of the LEA safety net for funding. In college one the principal said:

> Yes, my style has changed. At the college where I was before I had a reputation for being entrepreneurial. I was a lone operator, innovative and proactive. The LEA was there as a safety net. This college was very traditional – it was like entering a time warp, something had to change. I had to go down to their level. I had to appoint personnel manager, from industry, because I had to spend so much time on it. I have also appointed a director of finance for industry and I

make no decisions until it has been checked by her. I am still entrepreneurial but with a tighter remit. The governing body has taken its role seriously, but the governors have been led by a very strongly opinionated man. I have had to adapt to work with them; on balance it has worked out.

The needs of administration had created the need for specialists. The principal said:

> Understanding where you are going, a clear vision of where you are going and developing the people to achieve it. You have to get the people with you. They have to trust me. I try to create a friendly outfit.

Now, he said, he was adapting to work with others in a more businesslike format, with more meetings and a less 'hands on' approach. The process was thus not so much one of consultation as of information dissemination. His style, he thought, was still entrepreneurial but had a tighter remit of accountability. He took fewer risks, he said.

In *college two* the principal expressed his concern that the figures generated on college activity were unreliable: the information system was not working: 'They [the lecturers] do not see the importance of the data' to funding, he said. He thought the staff uninformed about the 'realities' of the market. In consequence he had commenced a programme of information dissemination:

> I am still trying to get things in order. You need planning, good information and clear responsibility. Quality is most important. At this moment I am controlling. I need to identify the people who are prepared to grow in order to liberate innovation, but I also need to control the process. Controlling is a personal tendency of mine. The need to monitor will become more important. I am more consultative than I used to be, because the Union has some benefits. I am less directive in many ways. You do need to set a tone and it is the little things that are significant. Concentration on significant details is a way of doing things.

The principal's preoccupation with qualitative data and administrative tasks is clear.

In *college three* the principal said that he was now trying to develop funding from sources other than the government, so his college had at least some control over the budget. The FEFC wanted targeted outputs but, he said, his problem was that the college had a large portfolio. He felt there was still a need for a community college that did not fit a business model. He said the consequences of changing college portfolios in response to the market mechanism had not been thought through. The FEFC still had a statutory duty for provision. He was concerned that engineering expertise, for example, could completely disappear unless the FEFC intervened. He felt his style had become more businesslike. He said he used: 'honesty, openness and clear direction' as a way of progressing and stated he had to buy in the required expertise namely, a company secretary, personnel manager and marketing manager.

His management style had become more consultative but more controlling, he said, it was more businesslike as it involved strategic planning, more responsibility for finance, more meetings.

> It's put ten years on me. It has made me more independent ... The change will continue towards that of a management ethos including strategic planning and more responsibility for finance. There is more sharing of responsibility but there is a need to control. In the old system it was unbelievable the issues on which you had to vote. Committee meetings have to be functional and procedures adhered to. Decision-making has to be sharper because of the accountability.

Again it is possible to identify the influence of the government's model on the principal's style of management: the control and monitoring role had become more significant. Again consultation is redefined as information dissemination.

In *college four* the principal said: 'There is really no change in my style. Maybe I do lunch with people a bit more often to communicate more and keep contact with people.'

College Structure and the Decision-making Process

In *colleges one*, *two* and *three* the principals now had a positive attitude to the expertise possessed by the governors and to the contribution they could make to college management. Problems with role definition, however, remained. In *college one* the principal referred to the chairperson's inability to praise staff without 'a sting in the tail'. He said his management style had had to change to adapt to this. In *college three* the principal felt a review was needed to clarify roles for the governors 'and their purposes' because they were constantly treading on his toes.

Lecturing staff had new contracts in *colleges one*, *two* and *three*. The new contracts involved staff being on the premises for 37 hours although teaching commitment varied. Each principal's individual approach did seem to have altered the process of changing contracts. In *college one* the outcome of new contracts had been negotiated, whereas in *colleges two* and *three* the approach had been more of imposition. Indeed, the principal in *college three* said that confrontation had attracted much 'adverse media attention' and some staff had still 'not signed' the new contracts.

In *colleges one*, *two* and *three* the organisations were leaner. Redundancies had been voluntary in the first stage. In *colleges two* and *three* the next stage of redundancies were in the pipeline, *college two* having increased staff with increased growth. In 1996 three colleges were able to provide structure charts; these clearly show the amalgamation of departments. Interestingly, in *college one* the chart is now called a 'College Management Organogram'. I was also given their first annual report for the period 1993/94. The principal in *college four*, sent a reply to the request for an organisational structure chart as follows:

> I am sorry to say we do not have such things as a structure chart of our college in any form. I can only suggest that since you know what a structure chart is and what you want to show, you prepare what you think is suitable ... and let me have a copy to check its accuracy.

In *colleges one*, *two* and *three* the course portfolios had changed in response to demand. Engineering was in decline, as had been expected, and so was business studies, but to a lesser extent. In *colleges one*, *two* and *three* media studies had become the most popular area for growth. *Colleges one* and *three* had increased their higher education work.

As a result of the changes in the way part-time students were measured it became difficult to evaluate whether the three newly-incorporated colleges had increased participation. I was reliant on the principals' interpretation of the figures. The Directory of Colleges provided the following data: in *college one* student numbers were now at 21,913, the largest proportion of provision being in the area of humanities, hotel and catering and business. In *college two* the number of students now totalled 20,161, the largest provision being in engineering, business and the sciences. In *college three* student numbers now totalled 3,897, the largest proportion of provision being in humanities, engineering and business.

In *college four*, despite the principal's opinion that nothing had changed, clearly something had: the influence of the national curriculum changes, in particular the monitoring systems, was in evidence. At the time of the visit staff were involved in telephoning parents to find out why students were not attending and this continued all morning. There was evidence of a more organised system.

The principal in *college three* identified innovation and quality as most important to organisational success but said that at that time his organisation had to be focused on budgets. The changes in structure and decision-making processes in *colleges one, two* and *three* were remarkably similar. College survival had become crucial and dominated decision-making; commercial language was used constantly. In *college four* the principal said a rise in student numbers had followed as a consequence of their improved reputation.

There had been two major restructuring programmes in *colleges one, two* and *three* driven by the need for efficiency savings. All three restructuring programmes involved amalgamating departments under fewer control areas with functional heads. The organisations had remained hierarchical and bureaucratic in structure, which fits with the accountability requirement of the funding methodology. In *college one* the principal stated that the structure was now:

> a more industrial model which mirrors that preferred by the government. It has functional directors. The heads of department now have a direct line to the function heads. In the next review we will be narrowing this even more. We have gone down from eight to five departments and need to merge some again.

It was now leaner, with fewer functional heads but more cross-college responsibilities.

The principal went on:

> The accountability issue from the Nolan Enquiry will have an effect. The Public Expenditure Survey suggests massive efficiencies. There are two approaches redundancies: or increased growth with no increase in staff. I have chosen the second approach. There must also be massive changes in delivery patterns, more student centred learning, more reliance on IT so that we can reduce the number of taught hours. The government is using all three approaches but God, isn't it effective?

The government's perspective had influenced the structure of the organisation and its main strategic direction, which was now focused on survival. Course content had changed in line with the government's delivery pattern. It is interesting to note that the principal supplied no educational reason for the changed delivery pattern – it was purely a financial rationale.

In *college two* the principal stated:

> We have restructured. We had seven departments but this is now down to five. The college is now flatter at the top, mean and lean. The governors now spend

more time on strategic issues. The auditors influence operational issues and I think there needs to be a review of their legal purposes ... We do have some very unreliable statistics on which to base our decisions ... The less important decisions tend to be left. There are central decisions. I tend to consult on the big decisions. You have to be autocratic until you feel comfortable.

Again the influence of administration and accountability is obvious.

In *college three* the principal said:

The structure has become more business oriented and I have brought people in who have these ethics. Now I am trying to bring it back from a business. It's not a business – it is there for the good of the community. We have restructured and all areas are now narrower. This has followed in line with our declining areas. We have set up a separate centre for media and performing arts which we were prevented from doing before ... We have to be more accountable ... The governors are more involved with decision-making and they give us lots of useful advice.

Decision-making in *colleges one, two* and *three* had become more centralised, 'autocratic' and 'top-down'. In *all three colleges* the change in the decision-making process had occurred in response to the need to control the operational process and to be accountable, the principals said. In *college three* the strength of the principal's style was still very much in evidence.

In *college four* the principal said the college had become:

more formal as we move towards a centre of excellence. We still have a flat management structure. We are influenced by a decline in physics, because the 'A' level is difficult. We have increased our standard in maths because the system is now modularised. The new governors tried to be more involved but this is discouraged as it takes too much time to explain the business to them.

There is some evidence here to suggest that the same pressures that the other three colleges had had towards more consultative styles, rather than leadership, were present here also. There were also signs of growing administrative functions.

The Manager's Role in the Organisation: Change Agents

In *college one* the principal said they were just entering a new restructuring programme. It was at the stage of information dissemination, he said. Once again he identified communication as an important tool for change and was clearly using it; he stated that information was being communicated through small groups. The Heads of Department now reported directly to the functional heads, he said, and replication of work across the college had been reduced. The number of administrative staff had increased because of the growing area of IT monitoring and human resource management. At the same time he commented that:

> The staff need to trust me. The 'no redundancy' has gone down well with the staff. I use an open door policy and I try to be user friendly. There needs to be a clear statement of what that change is going to be, a well thought out reason for change. This has to be communicated at a very low level.

Decisions were made at the top and communicated downwards, he said.

In *college two* the principal said:

> I have two types of manager, one being the initiators and developers the other the maintainers. I need to dilute the maintainers. The structure was heavily departmentalised. I would like to devolve responsibility particularly in the areas of monitoring and controlling. I can do that when information technology is well managed centrally, at the moment there is duplication ... then I can manage them through accountability and targets.

Again, the government's model could be seen to be driving the changes, significantly affecting the way operations were managed within the organisation.

In *college three* the principal suggested: 'there was a feeble management structure of devolved management. They were coordinators ... now they have more devolved budgets. Accountability of management is important.' The change of management style was clearly evident. In contrast, in *college four* the principal said:

> Teachers who do administration forget to focus on the customer. We need to keep a close focus on the student with feedback to the parents. I am buying a new building and then I will ask staff what they want to do with it. It will be subject oriented, towards the goals they are set. I would find it alien to impose changes on them. The changes in GCSE mean we have to be more rigidly supervisory ... Anyone can come and see me at any time, contact is very informal. Innovation is dealt with on the spot. Other than a change in curriculum staff have autonomy. You have to trust your professionals.

She still clearly used a system of empowerment.

In *colleges one, two* and *three* the principals expected managers to be more accountable. The management was linked to a specific area; the management task was one of monitor and controller. Budgets had been devolved and managers were now responsible for controlling and allocating budgets. The principals said that accountability had been reinforced by the FEFC inspection.[5] Decision-making was now driven by administration because of the need for an audit trail.

In *college one* the manager's role had changed from having 'a vision of where we are going' with an external focus, the principal said, to an internal monitoring one. In *college two* the principal said that he had hoped to bring in more managerial people but this had not happened; everything had largely stayed the same. In *college three* the principal said that managers had become controllers where they had previously been facilitators. In *college four*, evidence of a shift towards managers taking on more administrative tasks was also apparent, although the evidence was weaker.

The change in management styles to control orientation suggested a change in organisational culture towards reactionary, rather than proactive, management. A business that has a reactionary culture is likely to have problems with innovation. Government incentives were thus driving the colleges towards a process of managing operations that could lead them to be less successful in the market.

The government's commercial discourse had also begun to affect the meaning of words. In *college one* some managers were identified as 'innovative' by the principal. In his case, however, innovation referred to the staff's ability to accept the new teaching methods, which were imposed; these were considered 'efficient', where efficiency meant less classroom contact. New people were being identified as significant to bring about the 'necessary' changes. The old holders of these posts were seen as 'not innovative'; there was top-down direction and 'informing' rather than consultation with staff.

The principal felt that employees 'have to be able to trust me' in order for changes to be made. He had tried to develop trust through an open door policy, he said, by creating a friendly atmosphere and being open and direct with information. He believed that a clear statement of 'a well thought-out reason' for change needed to be communicated through the organisation. The principal stated that he had taken this approach and met very little resistance to change.

Innovation appeared to have become a metaphor for more efficient operation. Quality had become interpreted as meeting the objectives and innovation had become a metaphor for conformance to, and working within, the government model.

In *college two* the principal said that staff needed to be 'willing and competent to change'. Management was about changing the culture of the organisation so that everyone 'played the game', he said. The inference was that all staff had to conform to the new model. In *college three* the principal said he believed that the managers in his college had experienced a major culture shift. Previously, managers had been coordinators, whereas now they needed to be able to persuade people to understand the strategic direction in which the college was going. They needed to be more accountable and more in control. The communicator role, he said, had changed to a monitor role. Accountability referred only to a monitor process. In contrast, in *college four* the principal said her managers:

> are professionals who are trusted to make all the decisions. They need only liaise over any issues they feel important – these are usually saying what they have already done rather than asking permission.

In this case accountability was about the teaching task itself.

Competitive Environment and the College

Competition had increased in all colleges. This contrasted with the expectation of the principal in college two. The principals in *colleges one*, *two* and *three* said competition came mostly from schools. All three principals thought schools had an unfair advantage.

In *college one* the principal comment: 'The competition is massive and FEFC has not helped it. We are competing for more funding.' In *college two*, the comment was: 'The competition is coming from schools and they are playing some dirty tricks. There is some competition from other colleges but not much' and in *college three*: 'The competition is coming from schools, other colleges and higher education who want to fish in our pond.' This principal went on to say that the problem was that his prospective students were currently attending schools for their compulsory education. Schools were making it 'difficult' for the colleges to enter the schools to advertise their courses. On top of that, the principal said, schools were given a higher funding rate per student than his college was. There was also some competition from other colleges and HE institutions. One college, he said, had provided a free bus service for students; this occurred because its LEA was controlling the allocation of money for fares by distance travelled. This had led to unfair competition.

In *colleges one*, *two* and *three* the principals said that they had widened their target area for student participation as LEA control had reduced. They all said they were now more able to alter their course portfolio as a consequence of the reduction of LEA control.

In *college one* the principal expressed some dissatisfaction with the FEFC audit process. He said that as the grades awarded were made public there was pressure for them to audit properly. In one case, he said, he had asked to be re-inspected because he would not accept the grade given. At re-inspection the grade had been improved. The historical funding mechanism had helped their immediate competitors to cancel some fees. The principal felt there should be some mechanism to recognise that his college, on lower funding, was providing added value and increased student participation over and above the competitor. Although the new government-funding model was removing historical anomalies, it was not solving the immediate competitive situation. The principal saw immediate action as important for the competitive position of the college in the future. Reputation, he said, had always been identified as a driver of student choice and if the competitors had unequal power to add value, their reputation would benefit into the future long after the value had been reduced.

The government, he said, had also effected an open-management style and influenced governance. The reduction in funding and pressure for efficiency, local agreements on lecturers' pay and changes to the course delivery pattern had all opened up the competitive elements of the colleges. The principal identified the stopping of all capital investment as a major tool of change; he stated that the colleges would now need to build relationships with private investors or appeal to the Public Funding Initiative. He suspected that competition would significantly increase in this area, with the maintenance of the buildings and facilities in good condition seen as added value to the student. He stated that:

> full-time students have increased 100 per cent since incorporation. The growth rate has increased in the area. We have targeted a number of areas outside the remit of the LEA. We are targeting the North London area and Essex. We have also changed the format of our course portfolio from knowledge base to competence base in line with NVQ and GNVQ.

The principal went on to say that a changed mode of course delivery, particularly in the light of the Higgins Report (1996), was essential for efficiency savings.[6] No mention was made of these approaches as being significant to educational effectiveness, but the principal did speak of them enabling organisational efficiency.

In *college two* I was told that:

> we have both growth and decline. The statistics are unreliable. We have growth in arts, media studies and adult education. Business studies, science and technology and GCSE are all suffering from competition from schools. The decline in catering may just be a blip ... I suspect the government will just leave us to it.

In *college three* the principal indicated they had a problem with funding:

> We have had a problem with decline that has affected our funding. There have been new staff contracts and disruption. This had been public which has affected our marketing. Some areas are of course in growth – media and the performing arts and full-time HE students. Leisure and tourism are suffering from competition from schools. Business and management is static.

Interestingly, in *college four* the intake had changed from a one-year to a two-year stay. The reason given for this was that students came by 'choice' rather than because they were 'marginalised'.

> We have more minority subjects now, modern Greek or whatever the students need. The competition comes from the whole independent sector. Now one displaced student means decreased funding. Competition has therefore increased and student choice has increased to attract the students. We have to be much more flexible. We are now much more academic. We offer fewer distractions, smaller classes and increased teaching hours. We have now changed directors and they are much more involved.

The operational process of *college four* had been affected by the changes to GCSE in response to the National Curriculum; this had altered the delivery pattern. It had also changed the management of operations resulting in a lot more register-keeping and attempts made to keep the student. This had clearly changed the principal's attitude towards a more long-term view of staff: 'The majority of staff do not roll over: even part time staff like to stay and some of those will become full-time.' Clearly, the need for reliable staff had become more important because of increased administrative monitoring. The principal said that the types of course had stayed the same but the subjects had changed. First languages such as Greek and Italian were now common at 'A' level, she said, and more students were now studying 'A' level Maths. She thought that this was because it was now a modularised course. Physics had declined. The staff had introduced short courses in the holidays, she said, but personally she was concerned that this took their focus away from their main business, which in her opinion they 'could not afford to do'. These changes, she said, had been driven by the new governors.

Some distinct differences between the two types of organisation were apparent. The newly-incorporated colleges were reducing teaching hours and increasing students in classes, driven by their need to conform to budget. In contrast, the principal in *college four* was increasing teaching hours and making the classes smaller, which she believed would give them sustainable competitive advantage. The government's incentive strategies seemed to be driving the newly-incorporated colleges towards administrative effectiveness at the risk of customer orientation. *College four* was beginning to widen its customer focus in order to reduce its risk and increase its market. Paradoxically, *colleges one, two* and *three* were being driven to narrow their customer focus by reducing their product portfolio.

Outcomes of the Education Policy: Four Years On

Colleges one, two and *three* had shifted away from matrix decision-making to top-down decision-making. *Colleges one* and *three* now had a flat structure. *Colleges two* and *three* no longer had a facilitator style. *Colleges one, two* and *three* no longer used empowerment systems.

In *colleges one, two* and *three* the principal's management style had become more control oriented and increasingly focused on information dissemination. At the same time, the increased market risk factor had created a more cautionary management style. The principals did see their tasks differently as a consequence of the government's education policy – they had shifted their colleges more into line with government objectives. The principals were therefore altering the tradition of the colleges; the language of the market was much in evidence in the principals' approaches to change.

Similarly, in the case of *college four* there was evidence that government intervention, even at a low level, had had some influence. The drive for more accountability had made the teaching task more administrative. The principal's style had been forced to become more cautious, with a need to keep in touch with staff and governors. Paradoxically, all four colleges flexibility had been restricted by the government induced curriculum changes, which had created more focus on bureaucratic procedures and control.

The management styles of the principals had affected the implementation of policy, but only at the fringes. Over the period of study they shifted from change agents to instructional leaders. Hallenger and Heck (1996), suggest that school principals' roles shifted from manager to street-level bureaucrat, to change agent, to instructional leader and transformational leader. The four college principals also identified organisational transformation as a major task.

There is also much evidence to suggest that the strategic phase of change had been achieved; the discourse had been about goals, the language that of the market. The colleges were now task driven, the main task being accountability demonstrated through administrative excellence, although perhaps at the cost of educational effectiveness.

At the beginning of this chapter it was asserted that the government's power to exert its political ideology would be dependent upon its ability to control the decision-making process. The government's combination of a changed discourse reinforced with a funding regime altered the way in which the principals behave in the colleges. The budget structure was devolved and showed clear signs of continuing to influence and control the management of operations in colleges.

The introduction of competition did not lead *colleges one*, *two* and *three* to adopt a more flexible structure like that of *college four*. This was partly a matter of college size, but also because these colleges functioned in a quasi market (Glennerster and Le Grand, 1995). The incorporated colleges simply responded to central government's incentives to survive. They operated in a market orchestrated by central government. The focus on the customer appeared weak. Paradoxically, the government at the same time had empowered the customer. The colleges thus appeared to be caught with neither the advantages of a free market nor the advantages of a collegiate organisation as in the case of *college four*; to use Porter's (1979) terms they are 'stuck' in the middle, the worst of all positions.

On the other hand, the advantage of the changed organisations was they are now administratively neat. At one and the same time, central government could target funding of these organisations more accurately and control them. Responding to this, principals were fast becoming masters of administration techniques.

Bridges (1982) and Heck (1991) have looked at leadership attributes of principals in schools and concluded mastery of administrative traits are not important contributors to, or consistent with, school effectiveness. School principals appear to affect positive outcomes through mission building and social networking. This led Heck (1996) to conclude that a principal's role is crucial to emphasising a school's social and cultural context. Although these findings cannot be directly translated to further education, it is reasonable to surmise that further education principals act similarly. Indeed, this leadership style is conversant with Mintzberg's (1984) description of the professional organisation. Mission building and social networking, essential to leaders within professional organisations, is being replaced by the less useful administrative traits. Coupled with this, consultation has become a metaphor for information dissemination and empowerment a metaphor for accountability hence loose control has been replaced by tight control.

State-of-the-art management discourse suggests that top-down decision-making and information dissemination are unlikely traits for sustaining competitive advantage in the market place. This leads me to consider the possibility that the government's discourse is more about control than it is about competitiveness; there is a difference between the real and the espoused meaning of action.

The next task was to investigate the extent to which these changes were mirrored by those employees who work within the colleges. Only by understanding how these professionals reacted to the changes within their colleges can we understand whether, and if so how, the government's policy outlined in the Education Act 1988, was implemented and thus evaluate what power any government has to alter society and its values. Policy deficit can occur if a policy is not supported at the grass roots level (Halsey, 1981). In the case of professionals, role conflict can occur between the needs of the organisation and their professional ethics (Henderson and Parsons, 1947). Professionals' rejection of the standards set by the organisation in favour of their ethics can be seen as resistance to change, limiting that organisation's ability to achieve its managerial and administrative goals (Titmus, 1971).

The intention here is to evaluate the extent to which government's commercial discourse is reflected in the professionals' own language, to test whether the government had succeeded in attuning the colleges to its set of values. The interview questions were designed to evaluate whether the government had been able to commercialise further education colleges as well as to discover whether the organisational behaviour within the colleges mirrored the government's policy themes. It was anticipated that any changes to the organisation could affect different levels of employees in different ways, thus three heads of department as well as three lecturers in each college were included in the sample. The principals in the newly-incorporated colleges provided a list of names and appointment times for the interviews and the principal in the private college supervised the distribution of the questionnaire. The questions were designed to get the respondents to reflect over the last four years and thus generate a greater depth of information about the extant organisational process.[7]

The responses from the respondents in *colleges one*, *two* and *three* were so staggeringly similar that 'snapshot' statements are used to provide the common discourse expressed. This approach can be criticised for using statements out of context, but without it there would be much repetition. Where appropriate, the responses are presented in their discourse context. The responses from *college four* are distinctly different from those of the other colleges; they are therefore presented separately.

The Workers: Organisational Behaviour

In *colleges one*, *two* and *three* the heads of department and the lecturers provided a clear common picture of the drivers in the colleges: these were financial and focused on budgeting procedures and student numbers. All respondents mentioned that the need to make money, and compete for it, was new to their colleges.

The use of commercial coding to describe what was going on within the colleges was very common. 'The need for accountability' was commonly used as the main reason for change; this had caused the colleges to focus on 'audit trails', which were acknowledged as the prime drivers of change at the operational level. 'Conformance to budget', the need for 'institutional efficiency', 'cost awareness' and 'income generation' formed the common language theme of change: these were key variables in decision-making. The education market, the respondents said, had become 'competitive' and 'demand led'.

One respondent spoke of the new focus as: 'Where does the money come from and how do we use it?' In another college a respondent said that, such was the influence of the budget on decision-making, their budget was now reviewed weekly; this influenced the discourse to such an extent no other discourse was possible. All respondents spoke of the 'targets' that had to be met; this factor had led the colleges to become 'much more formal' where the 'audit trails' had a particular influence on behaviour, in as much as they increased the focus on administrative traits. 'There is more paperwork than ever before', typified the comments made.

There were new factors that drove the way in which the colleges' performed the common theme is demonstrated in the following:

> Money is what drives the institution; the government has shifted from seeing education as a public service to education as a product and we have to keep our heads above water financially.

In contrast, in *college four* everyone said there was no change: 'The main motivation is still to enable the students to achieve high grades', was a typical comment.

In *colleges one*, *two* and *three* the heads of department, as well as the lecturers, intimated that financial targets, as well as documentation in order to account for reaching those targets, had become the colleges' objective. There were some different views about the organisation's objectives from the heads of department: this occurred because of their different levels of accountability in the organisational structures. They said they now had 'much more of a controlling role', which had occurred for two reasons: firstly because they now had 'devolved budgets and responsibility for efficiency savings'; and secondly because 'we now have explicit clearly defined targets'.

The objective of setting targets was seen by one respondent as follows: 'All the targets including things like recruitment and retention are now related to the nominal target: achieving increased student numbers.'

Respondents spoke of many different financial targets, which included a focus on earnings as well as efficiencies, student success and student progression. Other targets were focused on efficient use of resources, for example effective facilities management. These targets, they said, formed the basis of the audit trails. The lecturers perceived their objectives as associated with their teaching task whereas the heads of department made associations between their objectives with the organisation's strategic objectives

The lecturers' concerns were more about the pressure on their teaching as a result of the increased administrative task: 'preparing lectures takes second place' and 'I want to maintain quality as well as achieve efficiency' typified their reaction. The difference that course and subject specificity had is clear in the following where one 'A' level teacher said:

> Our department is still laissez-faire; we have an action plan but it is never followed up. We have always monitored retention rates but this has just involved giving a reason for the student leaving.

In contrast information technology-related subjects had acted as triggers for changed practices, one respondent said; lecturers now had to focus on:

> multi-skilling, much less on specialism. Students can be working on five or six different packages at the same time. We try to get a group of students to start at the same time so we can move them through packages together. It is very difficult to answer questions on all the packages at once.

Assessment had shifted from the traditional term or annual assessment to unit assessment, he continued; these units were now preprepared so the student could gain a qualification at his or her own speed. The speed of assessment was now driven by the student's desire for completion rather than determined externally.

In *college four* the organisation's objective remained the same, to achieve the highest grades through 'the personal development of the students'. One respondent felt that competition had increased the pressure for good grades both for the student and for the organisation, which in turn had created a need to focus on mock examinations; nevertheless, the essential objectives remained the same.

In *colleges one*, *two* and *three* the task had clearly become more managerialist. Heads of department spoke of 'much more time spent on a monitoring role', being 'more concerned with strategic planning', 'more formal meetings and cross-college meetings' and 'fire fighting and crisis management'. The accountability requirement, respondents indicated, had caused 'more time at the computer' and 'verifying accounts'; they were less actively involved in the day-to-day activity of the teaching.

The lecturers said that while their involvement in administrative rather than academic tasks had increased as part of devolved responsibility they were now much more involved. The term 'more involved' was commonly used to describe a different set of tasks concerned with departmental planning; it did not imply that lecturers were empowered but actually meant they were better informed. Organisational decision-making was 'top-down', one respondent said, and 'finance driven'. Several respondents said taking a decision actually meant conforming to the objectives set.

Another common frustration for the lecturers was associated with the management information systems; these were either in place or nearly in place but either way they were not functioning in a useful way. Many of the respondents referred to the amount of time they wasted because different people asked them for the same information several times. The level of duplication varied from college to college; in *college two* several respondents said the

MIS system was operating against them, rather than for them, and because of this staff were generating handwritten information as well.

The tasks carried out every day had shifted from the academic to the administrative – 'you now have to evidence what you are doing'. Many respondents referred to the administrative task as having significant power to dictate their working day: whatever happened, they said, it had to be evidenced.

In contrast, the tasks in *college four* remained focused on ensuring students attended classes and completed their set work. There was more 'opportunity to discuss student' work with the parents', one respondent said; this had occurred because of the need to monitor the progress of GCSE and GNVQ students in line with government guidelines. The tasks of heads of department and those of the lecturers tended to be syllabus-driven, with the consequence that several respondents referred to some 'modular changes to coursework'. Several referred to some change in their tasks because of the changes to the National Curriculum; this had influenced the setting of coursework as well as the way in which it was marked. They felt 'trusted to get on with the job', 'free to make decisions within prescribed limits' and 'expected to act as what I am, a professional,'

In *colleges one, two* and *three* increased governmental influence in the colleges decision-making was obvious. The respondents said that many decisions were 'top-down', driven by the financial model, and that decisions had become 'more centralised'. Similarly, concerns about the effect the government's perspective had had on decision-making were also very obvious. This was not a criticism of the decisions in general but of the fact that the government was known for 'changing their mind', one respondent said. This inconsistency led several of heads of department to talk about 'scenario planning as a way of reducing risk'. Change, one respondent said, had become part of the 'game'.

Many heads of department said that information was now much more freely available but it tended to be linked to finance and the need for more detail 'to isolate financial implications' of change. Similarly, lecturers referred to having been able to 'have a go' when they had introduced a new course in the past, but the focus on financial accountability had made that much more difficult.

A consultation process continued to be part of the decision-making process but now, one respondent said:

> there is an urgency to achieve the strategic direction. It goes back to funding, there is more accountability and top-down monitoring decisions are linked to the level of accountability.

It was clear that the terms 'innovation' and 'risk' had been redefined. 'Innovation' was not about introducing new courses, as in the past, but about introducing courses that increased student numbers at less cost; innovation implied cost reduction. Similarly, 'risk' was not about launching a new course but about not being able to meet the budget. Indeed, several respondents indicated courses were now evaluated in terms of their overhead costs and increased risk was associated with increasing overhead cost. All heads of department said they feared subjects that attracted high overhead costs could be cut. One head of department in particular said:

> My department is said to be expensive. At the moment we are regulated by safety procedures. We have to have more staff and only a set number of students in a room.

Yet another common theme was the emerging conflict situation between administration and the academics; this was described by one respondent in the following way: 'Administration should have a servicing role but it has its own agenda and this had led to conflicts which are pulling people in different ways. The need for data is there all the time.' The pressure for administrative information had begun to alter the power relationships.

In *college four*, however, it was made quite clear that decisions at the head of department level, as well as those at the lecturer level, were not made 'in terms of the school – these are made at the appropriate level by the principals'. Decisions made by lecturers tended to be concentrated on subject- and student-specific activity: 'We make all the changes we need to make to ensure that classroom contact goes well.' In contrast, decisions made by the heads of department tended to be focused on the selection of the examination board.

The Workers: Organisational Style

In *colleges one, two* and *three*, the most dominant change, the respondents said, was the lack of trust they now had in management. One respondent explained that 'the national scene related to changed contracts has caused suspicion of management's motives'. Many respondents referred to the alteration of contracts as central to changing staff morale as well as to creating low-level trust in management. At the same time, they said, the growing pressure brought about by increased contact hours had dramatically changed their way of teaching: 'We could not continue to teach in the same way as before. Our student-centred approach had to change to fit in with the time we had spare.'

Many respondents referred to the change in the environment as one that was more 'competitive and innovative.' The colleges' decision-making processs had become 'finance-led rather than curriculum-led'. One respondent commented that the work environment of the college had always been 'a political institution but now it is competitive: people's egos and careers' were becoming a feature; 'some come out of it well', the inference being, of course, that others do not.

At the lecturer level the introduction of curriculum changes – NVQ, for example – had become 'owned', one respondent said, by the staff. Keen participation in the new initiatives was a common theme identified by many respondents as a route to promotion: 'you have to be part of it to get on here now'.

Another common theme from the lecturers is typified by 'you need to pull in the same direction'. One respondent in particular described this as 'a command type culture where the control mechanism is exerted with very little feedback'. The new contracts had brought a general feeling of being undervalued and morale had become a problem. These changes to culture are epitomised in the comments 'less staff centred and more managerial', 'less parochial' and 'more admin. focused'. One respondent described the changes in the following way: 'It has gone from a cooperative culture to a top-down command culture driven by the FEFC.'

In contrast, one respondent said 'the heads of department have autonomy but I am not sure what that means'; another remarked, 'I have more autonomy and can be more entrepreneurial'; and another commented, 'I have to be able to be an autonomous actor and aware of competition'. Autonomy seemed to imply being responsible for achieving the targets they were set rather than suggesting any power to control; decisions had become top-down. Autonomy had been redefined to mean spending, or not overspending, a budget.

The culture of the organisation was no longer controlled by the principals, yet the staff were still influenced by the principals' leadership style. Many respondents referred to their principals' statements to add clarity to their own with the words 'the principal said'. At the same time, their facial expressions were interesting in that their faces tended to light up, the reference being accompanied by a smile. Those respondents who did not agree with what their principals were saying prefaced their answers with 'it's not popular for me to say this but ...', 'I may be the only one to say this but ...' and 'the principal does not agree with me but ...'. Their facial expressions were also interesting in that they portrayed guilt and defiance.

The common theme in *college four* was that they had become, if anything, 'more professional'. One respondent said that there was a 'greater effort to engender a community', rather than 'individuals as subject specialists'. This change appeared to be a response to the need for more accountability and the need to monitor a student at the college rather than on a course.

The Influence of a Principal's Leadership Style

The number of common themes in the respondents' discourse from *colleges one*, *two* and *three* led to the conclusion that a principal's leadership style had much less influence than might be expected. This finding corresponds with the information provided by the principals themselves, who said that their leadership styles had changed in order for them to respond to the needs of the government's policy implementation tools, namely financial imperatives.[8] In consequence, their leadership styles had become more focused on control and monitoring than had previously been the case.

At the same time, they referred to the principal as a leadership figure. In *college two* the leadership style was often commented on and compared with that of the former principal who had 'adopted a more paternalistic style and informed people about outcomes'. In contrast, they saw the new principal as 'wanting people to be better informed about the decisions'. He had put in a process of information dissemination, the respondents said, throughout the organisation. This increase in openness had raised the staff's concern about whether the college would survive. They identified the new principal's style 'as more proactive and more appropriate to the circumstances'.

In contrast, the principals in *colleges one* and *three* were seen by the staff as buffers between the government and the implementation of policy. Their more secure financial position meant that staff in general were less fearful of survival. The respondents associated their secure financial position with their principal's leadership style: 'he keeps ahead of all the changes'; 'he is good at keeping the governors out of decision-making'; 'we have had to increase substantially the number of students we teach but he has kept all our jobs'.

In *college four* the principal's management style was seen as 'hands off' and 'trusting'. The following comment typifies the respondents' view of the principal: 'She recognises that we know how to do our job. If I need to change things I tend to talk to her about it to check if it is possible.'

The Workers: the Staff's Personal Feelings

Professionals in *college four* had not been involved in their organisations shift from the public to the private sector, so were not asked to talk about their feelings. The most striking commonality in the responses from *colleges one, two* and *three* was the way in which they interpreted 'feelings'. Feelings were expressed with reference to the individual's own college and its competitive position. This appeared to be related to the respondents' current fear about the future – survival was the most dominant 'feeling' they had: 'I think we're doing quite well'; 'we are doing better than ... college – we have some of their students'.

Some of the respondents described their feelings as if they had been at war, comments such as 'we came through it fairly well' being common. There was also a theme of abandonment – 'we have been left to sink or swim'. There was a sense of the inevitability of education always being used by government for its own purpose. 'Was it essential? Probably not; desirable, probably yes' typified this. Alongside this were many comments related to the desire to get on with the job without interruption. 'Let schools do what they are best at and let us do what we are best at' and 'I wish they would just go away and let us get on with the job' were typical of this theme.

The most striking factor in the responses was what the respondents did not say: there was very little criticism, and yet one could feel that it was there. Of course, one of the limitations of discourse analysis is that it can only be applied where language is used for communication, ignoring facial expressions and sighs, which emphasise unstated emotional responses to events the listener interprets. The emotional context of 'soft' communication serves to embellish that communication; it often gives meaning to what is said.

To a certain extent, it can be hypothesised that discourse omission would be a direct product of the depersonalisation process of working relationships. At the same time, discourse omission must also be a product of the rules of the society in which we live, differentiated by an individual's needs and values. Even so, discourse omission does not fit comfortably with what we expect of professionals; namely their right to use discretion and interpret the bureaucratic rule. Indeed, the expectation had been that any discourse theme would involve some level of critical evaluation by the staff working in the colleges, even if it was not personalised and focused at arm's length on the government.

Understanding the role a theme of nostalgia can play in discourse goes a little way in helping to evaluate discourse omission. Nostalgic reflection provides a way of dividing the old from the new reality – it is often sentimentalised and tends to be highly selective because it is formed from an individual's recollections; for this reason it tends to be disregarded in discourse analysis. Rationalists tend to interpret displays of emotion as a weakness and as indicative of illogical behaviour, which they denigrate; in order to explain reality their preference is to separate emotion from reason. However, emotion can be seen as the very source of meaning and idealism. Adopting this approach, to ignore emotion is to ignore reason.

To understand organisational behaviour it is important to attempt to understand that part of the organisation that is not managed, an individual's emotions (Gabriel, 1993, p. 118). There is a fine line in organisational behaviour between how much emotion can be displayed to describe reality and be acceptable, and that level which is not. Risk averse individuals have thus learnt to manage the expression of their emotions within social constructs that dictate acceptable behaviour – linked to task and institutional goals.[9] Within organisations, emotion becomes a commodity like any other, feelings are displayed as a public ritual and thus a gap emerges between those emotions that are felt and those espoused. Removing emotion from communication means, in general, that it is much easier to express conformance than it is to express opposition.

Ignoring the role emotion plays in discourse, it would be possible to conclude that the government exerted considerable power and changed the colleges' activity more in line with its policy. Adopting this conclusion, the lack of critical analysis in the professionals' discourse would be associated to the dominance of the managerial paradigm over professional ethics, brought about by the use of commercial language.

However, marginalising emotion is not simply about organisational denial – withholding emotion from day-to-day communication may simply be a way for an individual to avoid being totally managed by the organisation (Hochschild, 1983). Indeed, professionals have traditionally expressed control avoidance in their use of autonomous action, expressing their emotions and beliefs in ethical codes. Rather than ignore the role of emotion in discourse, it seemed an attempt had to be made to interpret it, in order to understand the meaning of the responses and signals provided by the professionals.

Where emotion becomes subject to control, resistance or non-conformance is transmitted through paralinguistic signs such as non-eye contact, sighs and pauses, embellishing and in some cases replacing words. These signs of communication were particularly obvious when the respondents talked about their feelings concerning the changes that had taken place; there was a highly emotional unspoken context. The former led me to suspect the lack of critical analysis in the professionals' discourse did not imply that the managerial paradigm controlled the hearts and minds of those professionals, though it had altered behaviour. This led me to look to explain discourse omission, the unstated. Understanding the role that nostalgia plays in communication has been used, therefore, as a way to explain the emotions displayed in the responses from the professionals in the colleges, to understand the meaning better.

Nostalgic reflection is communicated through organisational symbolism – it uses typical characters to describe past culture and folklore. Therefore, analysing the nostalgic symbolic reflections in the discourse of those working in the colleges could provide an understanding of both the past and the current discourse, because it is a process that is centred on comparing the past with the present.

The study of nostalgia concentrates on nostalgia as a positive emotion. Nostalgia is used as a way of coming to terms with the present in order to let go of the past. In communication it is used as a symbolic watershed (Gabriel, 1993, p. 118). It is interesting to note that respondents had to be prompted to reflect on the past. There was very little evidence of organisational nostalgia and very few reflections on any 'golden age' present in the interviews. Had nostalgic reflections been included in the responses, I could have concluded that the past was seen as over and done with. As it was, the lack of nostalgic reminiscences in the discourse suggested something quite different: the past had not been put to rest. If this was the case, what had caused the respondents to limit critical analysis to paralinguistic communication – emotional displays.

There is a counter-emotion to the theme of nostalgia – that of demonisation, where the past is identified as a problem the future has to cure (ibid., p. 120). Evidence of this theme can be seen in the following: 'It was self-indulgent with no need to be efficient because the LEA were a safety net'; 'Laissez-faire was an idea that never got off the ground. There was no plan, no structure. It was protecting crumbling empires – now staff recognise it has to change.'

The influence of demonisation on past reflection can be seen here in the response by one head of department: 'It's embarrassing really, I just used to do what I liked doing, what I was good at. I am much more accountable now.'

Another head of department remarked that she now recognised she had:

> custody of the education product [because] the governors do not understand the primary task. The product we deal with is different, it is not measurable ... equal opportunity and the rights of the individual have to be protected – we are

not dealing with a tin of cat food. We have to ensure and keep a focus on what the task is. It matters that I have the right number of the right students to ensure quality. I have to keep a clear picture of the totality of the task.

The evident difficulty in expressing this view in other contexts was clearly demonstrated when she stated that 'the Chair of Governors would say I was being an educationalist', the inference being that an educationalist approach had become unacceptable and no longer openly discussed. Reference was made to the fact that 'those who don't belong are leaving', indicating the level of control over any mismatch of individual views with the government's strategy expressed in the organisation's goals.

The power of the new discourse reinterpreted, as well as demonised, the past such that is became an embarrassment. The lack of past accountability was seen as decadent; furthermore, because commercial coding did not have a language to describe emotional contexts, autonomous action and a trust-oriented decision-making environment, it was omitted from the discourse. In other words, it became even more difficult to counter the theme of demonisation.

There was much evidence of a new 'political correctness' and debate was clearly influenced by a need to 'sing to the same tune', one respondent said. Another respondent commented that 'the context of 1996 needs to be taken into account – you are lucky to have a job now'. On the whole, the respondents found it difficult to put into words what drove the institution before the changes. Pauses, hesitation and lack of eye contact during communication transmitted the highly emotional context; the unstated discourse was powerful.

At the same time, there was evidence that features of the past were based on caring, altruism and professional ethos. These themes can be seen in the following: 'We are still trying to hold on to a service, to the fact that we help people'; 'we are driven by personal motivation to do better'; 'it didn't matter except to personal pride'; 'previously I could do what I enjoyed'; 'laissez-faire and staff-centred'; 'did monitor before but it was not written down formally'; 'didn't have objectives'; 'professional with integrity to do your job'; and 'used to be academic achievement'.

In the past, an academic and altruistic focus had been stronger: 'we strived to produce the best courses', change was 'curriculum led' and 'innovative – you could take a chance on a new course but not any more'. Now it was 'more concerned about the product'. A common theme was the mismatch between student demand and demand for skills: 'courses [were] matched to local need, which is better than now – look at media courses leaping ahead when there is no demand for jobs in this area.' Now there was, one respondent said, 'less involvement with the curriculum now that decisions are devolved downwards'.

The common theme related to decisions in all three colleges prior to the change was epitomised by 'we [the lecturers] only made minor decisions' – the inference was that decisions previously were directly related to the teaching task. The management role was said to have 'changed year on year because the LEA decided'. One head of department mentioned the burden of responsibility that accountability had brought with it, while another stated that he 'didn't like responsibility'.

The environment before the changes was seen as predictable and 'stable', 'teaching was enough, it was frowned on to have innovative ideas'. Although all appeared to think the process had previously been consultative and hierarchical, there was a common theme; 'it didn't go anywhere' because of the control power of the LEA. Another common theme was that decisions in the past were made 'with difficulty', the reason given being the consultative processes.

The 'caring coding' theme was in evidence when the respondents referred to the teaching task: 'The product is not the same for everyone – some are low to average achievers', which indicated a need to re-focus on individual student capability and the equal opportunity teach should achieve. The former view was reinforced by the concern:

> There should be more steer centrally so that the organisation matches the skill needs of the economy, or at least a closer resemblance – look at the growth in media. I dislike the fact that there is no match of course development to need.

This clearly indicated a common theme: there should be a close resemblance between the needs of the economy and course choice to ensure equal opportunity for each student in the future.

> It has been a paper exercise – the agenda is about reducing funding. How a college can be a company I don't know. The government funding has just brought more problems: I am not empowered, I am neutered. My professional role has changed so that I have no time to give what I would like to give. To a certain extent the teaching is the same, but the FEFC and the inspectors alter the way you teach. It is much more threatening than HMI. If you don't perform you are out – a professional's position has shifted.

This set of statements demonstrates a shift in professionals' power and their right to decide.

Many expressed concerns about the maintenance of quality, which was seen to be under pressure from increased numbers and reduced staffing. The lack of a national perspective was also giving some concerns in terms of quality:

> I am unhappy about the change in FE and NVQs they are set up to challenge the professional ability to choose how to teach. The lead bodies have been set up willy-nilly and have a much more serious effect. It's not been thought through and is a right mess and will give us problems in the future.

The strongest theme from the lecturers was the focus on administration and new contracts because they were 'working much harder'. The focus on a time budget meant they did not have as much time as before to help individual students, although several felt the students were better served than previously.

There was a common theme about the appropriateness of accountability which seemed to be a reflection in line with the changing role of the professional in society as a whole: 'I feel very positive about being accountable'; 'we always were, we just never wrote it down'; 'we can now prove that we do more than our contract hours'; 'retention should be monitored so that we can prove what we do'.

Accountability was contrasted with the new commercial context of the education product. One head of department commented: 'The last five years have been caught up in the dynamic pursuit of efficiency; we know the price of everything and the value of nothing', and another: 'The supermarket policy – stack them high and sell them cheap.'

Language Themes

The discourse in *colleges one*, *two* and *three* had become dominated by 'commercial coding' language themes. Budgets, organisational or departmental, became the main focus driving decisions in the organisation, leading to concentration on increasing student numbers in order to attract funds.

The demands of the market had an increasing influence on decision-making within these colleges, altering the environment to a competitive one. The government's preference for accountability increased administrative monitoring and planning which had become endemic; this added responsibility for administration to the professionals' task. Changes made to the delivery of courses were focused on the achievement of efficiency or the generation of income; driving quality to become reinterpreted to mean conformance to standards.

The 'caring coding' system was very little in evidence in *colleges one*, *two* and *three* because the discourse themes had been heavily influenced by 'commercial coding' themes and anyway had been demonised. In contrast, the 'caring coding' system is very much in evidence in *college four*; the students and their attainment were at the very heart of decision-making where the focus on student care was identified as its competitive edge. Whereas one might expect hourly pay and part-time modes to be a disadvantage to the maintenance of quality staff, the use of the 'caring coding' in discourse served as a tool to keep staff – they felt valued.

Resistance Factor: *Colleges One, Two* and *Three*

The focus on 'commercial coding' redefined the focus of the colleges from education to organisational survival. The need to survive in a competitive environment skewed decision-making and affected the professionals' right to choose. It is very difficult to have a discourse on educational value when the organisational driver has become cost and effectiveness as determinants of reasoning.

Commercial coding affected the interpretation of value: 'I am very sad about the changes, not angry, because of the focus on funding, which I accept' typifies the attitude of the professionals to the changes. The discourse was controlled at the time by the government's choice of management, control and funding tools.

The driver for change in these colleges had become budget-focused where the decisions now flowed top-down. The explicit objectives had become financial targets and the lecturer's task more administrative and involved, though not empowered. In line with the government's objectives, the colleges organisational styles were more competitive. The discourse was about institutional efficiency and not educational effectiveness.

These findings are similar to those of Waldron and Krone (1991), who found that where there is a high degree of emotional control, disagreements are often suppressed and the employee voice neutralised. Certainly, behaviour of the professional actors in the further education colleges, at the head of department and lecturer level, changed in response to changed tasks, objectives and control mechanisms.

However, the use of paralinguistic signs, coupled with the lack of nostalgic folklore, have provided glimpses of resistance in *colleges one*, *two* and *three*, which suggests that the new discourse based on efficiency was not completely accepted by the professionals. Comments like 'how can a college be a company,

I don't know', leads one to surmise that these professionals could be saying one thing and doing another; in other words the 'caring coding' system may still have dominated the minds, if not the actions, of professionals.

The power of the monitoring system used in the colleges to implement government policy served to redefine effectiveness to mean conformance to specification. While colleges struggled to come to terms with organisational survival, the discourse about educational effectiveness was controlled. Nevertheless, it is contended the government has power over discourse simply because the dialectic between it and the professionals had been avoided by the careful, or incidental, choice of the policy implementation tools; namely monitoring processes and financial muscle which, intentionally or unintentionally, introduced a different language theme into the colleges.

The principals' leadership styles in the newly-incorporated colleges also changed in order to meet the government's policy. They became much more directive. However, leadership style did have some affect on the way in which policy was implemented; in some cases enabling a smooth transition for the inevitable changes. While the principal's management style had changed, in order to carry out their changed tasks, their attitude towards their subordinates remained personalised.

College four stands out as clearly different from the rest. Since the government had not subjected it to major changes it operated much as it had always done. Those working in the college clearly felt valued by their managers, who held old-fashioned views of professional behaviour: they were expected to exert their autonomy and be committed to the cause. The language theme used in this college was rooted in 'caring coding'; it was emotionally connected This factor survived alongside, and indeed was seen as essential to, commercial awareness.

Even though caution must be applied in interpreting the results of *college four*, because the research instrument negated the opportunity to observe any paralinguistic phenomena, there is evidence to suggest that commercialisation of the further education colleges and trust in a professional and their ethics are not mutually exclusive. This provides more evidence to conclude that the change in discourse was more about political ideology, coupled with the government's desire to control, than it was about the efficiency of the further education sector. In other words, emotionality does not have to be abandoned in favour of a commercial focus but rather the simultaneous use of the two approaches, as adopted by *college four*, actually serves to create competitive advantage – added value.

Notes

1. The questions were as follows:
   How would you describe your style of leadership?;
   What role do you perceive your managers to play?;
   How will incorporation affect you?;
   Is your college in competition?;
   What role do you think governments will play in college organisation in the future?;
   Has the role of the governors changed, how will that role affect your decision-making process?;
   How are decisions made in your organisation?;
   What are the important issues for you in managing change?;
   What role does your managers /staff play in this process?
2. White knights are people who understand and support an organisation's new change agenda. They are used in organisational change to highlight what the organisation wants. They thus indicate good practice as seen at any one point in time.
3. A facilitator style is used here to describe an organisational process which is enabling, rather than controlling. A manager's aim becomes the easing of the process of consultation rather than to control. A facilitator has no predetermined outcome in mind; his/her task is to smooth the consultative process, keeping in mind the organisation's strategic aims and objectives.
4. Trust is used here to represent the process through which professionals acquire their autonomy. In Chapter Two it was established that the legitimate authority that professionals have to complete their task as best they see it implies that society trusts them. As previously discussed, this can take the form of their subject specificity, knowledge, or their particular task. In an educational institution, therefore, the expectation would be that the level of trust would be high.
5. FEFC required that there was evidence of an identified route for decision-making within the colleges, accompanied by appropriate forms to monitor the process.
6. The Higgins Report suggested that colleges would be information technology led.
7. Have the drivers of the institution changed since incorporation? What are the explicit objectives you have to meet, have they changed since incorporation? Is there any change in the tasks you carry out every day and how are they different from before? Has the culture of the organisation changed and if so in what way? How do you make decisions in the organisation and has this changed? What are your feelings about the incorporation process?
8. See previous chapter for a more in-depth discussion.
9. Emotional labour is the term used to describe the situation where organisational roles and tasks exert control over emotional displays.

Chapter Ten

Genesis of a New Theme

An important purpose of this work has been to compare the revolutionary social policy of the 1940s with that in the 1990s, using discourse analysis. In view of the complexity of the subject the span of investigation has been narrowed to policy-making and further education, particularly following the development of four further education colleges and their identity. To reveal the depth to which government policy could/could not penetrate organisational space and affect an organisation's identity, the story of the four further education colleges as they responded to the Education Acts 1988 and 1992 has been told by the principals and the professionals working within those colleges. Tracing the policy action relationship right down to the organisational level has revealed much about how policy altered the colleges' custom and practice.

The intention was not to prove conclusively that changes in local practice would not have come about merely by virtue of the colleges' changed financial incentives because the language signals were changing simultaneously. However, if the research revealed that language did change, both on the part of government and in the colleges, this would be some indication that the government had been successful in achieving at least surface acceptance of its policy at an institutional level. Moreover, the result would then at least be consistent with the thesis that language is an important tool of policy change.

As previous studies of further education had been causal and fragmentary, the first task was to place the development of further education in its historical context, to describe and analyse its identity better. Analysis of the narrative themes over time revealed the drivers, levers and constraints, in some measure explaining the process that led to its identity and reasons for its bias. Another benefit of this approach was that it provided a benchmark against which the 1990s could be compared.

Adopting Barrett and Fudge's (1981) proposition, the expectation was that any gap between policy and its implementation would occur within the organisation for whom the policy was intended. Two scenarios were postulated: the combination of changed financial incentives and discourse skewing would be a successful tool for policy implementation; or the professionals would resist those changes. Testing for the possibility of an antithesis revealed two coding systems in action within the archaeological system of knowledge, namely 'market' coding and 'caring' coding. These two language themes were used to explain how social policy rhetoric can both espouse equal opportunity and consistently fail to bring about the changes in social relations needed to achieve it.

Further Education and its Clients

Adopting a Foucauldian approach and exploring the panoramic of the narrative revealed education for the majority of the post-school population to be at odds with their needs. Surprisingly, this trend can be found creating some current parameters of social division as early as the sixteenth century. Furthermore, further education policy failure and abandonment is not uncommon. I have been able to show that curricula development was driven by old upper class ideals that valued academic achievement above any other measure of intelligence. The reconstructed system of education post 1944 emerged as reinforcing difference; it did not fulfil its vision, parity of difference.

While education became valued as one of the trappings of social privilege, training and skills development came to be seen as an alternative measurement of ability weighted less socially than academic qualifications. These social processes disenfranchised a large part of the educable community, despite evidence of some valiant efforts to bring about change. The vision of a society providing equal opportunity remains an ideal.

While government legislation made provision for further education, it left the task boundaries unclear. In uncharted territory, further education colleges simply responded to market demands, offering education and training, a second chance and an alternative route to success. These colleges have provided many with an opportunity for success, one might say despite rather than because of legislation.

Further Education – the Narrative

The study task, however, was not to devise, or advise, on a new approach for these clients – it was simply to explore the narrative through the text. Using the two language themes as the basis of analysis, revealed a visionary theme with a central tenet of equal opportunity as the main driver of change. Further analysis revealed the visionary theme consistently being conditioned by the commercial theme. In the 1970s this was combined with a powerful theme of inadequacy. It was the theme of system inadequacy that created the dialectic which provided the springboard for the growth of the market theme.

Nevertheless, analysis revealed that the market theme did not comprise a biological metaphor, thus it is not revolutionary. I have presented evidence suggesting that the two coding themes are journey metaphors. Indeed, they appear consistent with Dunn's (1991) concept of a pioneering journey metaphor, concepts that challenge traditional rites of passage. The root metaphor 'market' that became popular in the 1980s appears simply to represent a stage in a journey towards modernising democracy.

The chameleon within the narrative is the theme of compromise. Through many guises it has served consistently to temper radical change. Combined with the theme of rationalisation in the 1990s it grew in strength and influence. These themes are journey metaphors, representing convention; they pull knowledge back to the status quo. The vision of equal opportunity was conditioned by a rationale based on economic sufficiency, thus policy became an incremental rather than revolutionary process. The theme of rationalisation that initially represented careful spending in the context of growth became, in the 1980s, the need to control spending because of the unreasonable demands made by a growing welfare state.

Both Nisbet's (1969) point that fixity survives failed experiments and Dunn's (1991) proposition that today's analysis can be distorted by emphasising change led me to consider that the weighting of the two codes within the discourse could be important in explaining the power of a changed discourse. Analysis revealed that the two narrative themes within the journey metaphor bound and controlled the pioneering journey metaphors. This is not consistent with Gidden's (1996) proposition that reflexivity ensures instability and a reduction of the power of tradition. The two themes in the journey metaphor justify retaining capital and labour in an unequal balance. This goes some way to explain how bias is mobilised: society can embrace radical changes along the lines of equal opportunity but in reality nothing fundamentally changes.

In Foucauldian terms the combined metaphors form a common archaeological system. This study has revealed two opposing philosophical discourses held concurrently within the system. This helps explain how the social actors over time have been able to think differently. Together they shed light on the process of social change, describing the intellectual and political trends that have led to the current position of the welfare state. Furthermore, these findings lead to the proposition that the theme of the market and its assumptions about effectiveness and efficiency will continue their journey towards the development of a better democracy, contributing to the development of more acceptable forms of state intervention. Indeed, although at the time of writing New Labour was in its infancy, its policy discourse added credence to this assertion.

Another gain from narrative analysis is that it has helped explain why and how the further education sector was subjected to adaptive, responsive and stable policies at one and the same time. It also goes some way to explain how further education colleges came to be placed in competitive market facing efficiency drives based on production models in the 1980s.

The research has also revealed some evidence to suggest that a paradigm shift from the pursuit of educational effectiveness, based on equality and the notion of social responsibility, to the pursuit of educational efficiency did take place in government circulars and administrative memoranda. This occurred as a consequence of the vision of the welfare state being subjected to the themes of inadequacy and rationalisation. The resultant dialectic challenged the 'truth' that social benefits of the system outweighed the social costs. These two themes, operating in unison, brought about two drivers for change: the market theme highlighted the dissatisfactions of the customer in state-run enterprises; and the rationalisation theme highlighted the lack of accountability of the professional and their institutions. Furthermore, the market theme shifted state responsibility from parenting to supervisor, providing the forum for government to distance legitimately itself from moral responsibility and the need to right society's wrongs. It has also been possible to isolate New Labour discourse using the rationalisation theme within commercial coding combined with an altered caring coding, thus explaining how they can hug the political centre and pursue left wing politics at one and the same time.

The Conservative Government's Management Technique

When imposing the market theme within public sector organisations, the government assumed that all organisations shared the same characteristics. Legitimising rationalisation called for more public disclosure; it drove the government to focus its financial methodology on tight control and output measures to demonstrate improved efficiency and effectiveness. By the 1990s the rationalisation and market themes were peppered with production assumptions and methods.

Paradoxically, Drucker (1995), Dearden (1991), Allen (1995) and Cooper (1990) recommended total factor productivity measures as a more useful way of measuring business success. In any case, Garvin (1988) suggested that the customised nature of the education process made transcendent measures of quality more significant to success within the service sector. All these factors suggested unit costing was unsuitable for measuring educational outputs. The application of production orientation to education by government was thus premised on a basic misunderstanding of the business.

The government's finance methodology forced further education managers to embrace risk management for the first time. The inability of this methodology to accommodate other value-added aspects of the service, I have argued, rendered it insufficient for and indeed detrimental to the pursuit of educational effectiveness. Furthermore, the FEFC, as a primary source of finance, skewed activity in line with government desires, further preventing the much-needed dialectic. The colleges now had increasingly risky cash flows that inhibited innovation, methods of funding that drove them in different directions and costing systems that failed to represent the process of educating.

The Conservative government's chosen instruments of change shifted the colleges from a professional organisation to a more traditional bureaucratic control-oriented organisation. In consequence, the principals were less able to manage the risky environment that government had selected for them.

Alongside this, professional autonomy became weakened. My findings were conversant with Geoffe (1995) and Brown and Scase (1991): the role of support staff overlapped with that of the technostructure and administration began to control standard-setting. Indeed, client needs were increasingly determined by administrative requirements. Lecturers spent more time on administration and their problem became how to maintain their individual intellectual freedom.

Some considerable evidence has been presented suggesting that the principals did change their behaviour, their management style and the language they used to describe what they were doing. Consistent with Hallenger and Heck's (1996) findings in schools, the principals had moved to a more bureaucratic, control-oriented and cautionary style of management. Along with Hecks (1996), I am concerned that informal decision-making and trust have diminished in importance as tools of management within these colleges at the same time as current management thought suggests they are best in class attributes.

Those professionals working in the pre-public sector colleges have adopted a more commercially-oriented discourse to describe what they are doing. This leads to the conclusion that the narrative frame can affect professionals' selectors. There is some evidence to suggest that government discourse has the power to alter the strategic direction and core activity of further education colleges. Paradoxically, government's move towards central control does not fit comfortably with its espoused market theme.

In short there is much to suggest in this work that professional autonomy had been threatened. Adopting Lukes' approach (1993), the investigation focused on the inactivity of these professionals.

Emotional Decision-making

Analysis of the narrative revealed a lack of resistance by the professionals in the incorporated colleges. There was some evidence to suggest that those working in the colleges accepted the theme of rationalisation but did not accept the theme of the market – thus it was possible to postulate evidence that changed action and skewed organisational discourse did not imply changed beliefs.

The demonisation of past modes of behaviour evident in the organisational narrative led me to conclude that discourse was being controlled within the colleges. Further, the absence of nostalgic reflections in the responses contributed to the assertion that these professionals were expressing their dissatisfaction using paralinguistic signals. This led me to conclude that the journey metaphor had created a theme of political correctness bounding its denial. Nevertheless, the strength of the paralinguistic signals combined with the lack of nostalgic reflection suggested that the old professional paradigm has not been relinquished; rather, resistance may be dormant. This leads me to postulate that the observed behavioural change may be short-term. This can only be speculation, but is consistent with my findings.

The work of Argyris (1987), Sengee (1990), Parker (1991), Fineman (1993) and Goleman (1997) suggests that professionals' decision-making is grounded in emotional intelligences. In combination with Hoffman (1984) and Gardner's (1993) conclusions that empathetic people favour action driven by principle, professionals emerge as extraordinary social actors involved in high reflexivity: their knowledge would thus be affected by the pioneering journey metaphor and goes some way to account for their non-discourse.

Consistent with my findings, professionals' minds, thought and knowledge are affected by current discourse. However, it would seem that emotional thinking creates a greater level of autonomy, which may alter as knowledge changes, but remains free-floating because it is expressed in emotional responses, which transcend known truth. Emotional intelligences may be free-floating attributes that professionals have which they bring to bear at specific times to reconstruct reality. These become tangible only when they adhere to an expressed decision: their nonverbal nature makes them significant and uncharted contributors to the acquisition of professional knowledge worthy of further research.

The Private College

In stark contrast, the private college remained largely untouched by the government initiatives, although there was evidence of a small shift towards administration. The study revealed that the key to this college's commercial success was that it operated with professional autonomy: it scored the highest, given the benchmarking criteria. It would seem that professional autonomy and commercial success are not mutually exclusive. Indeed, the study confirms the assertions of Stacey (1993), Argyris (1987) and Sengee (1990), amongst others, that the key issues for holding these two needs in unison are decentralisation with a management approach based on trust. The professionals in this college were given discretion to decide; indeed, the principal linked their success to professional discretion. Despite these professionals being outsourced from the operating core, she deliberately encouraged and supported their autonomous action.

2000 and Onwards

Although the private college system may be the way forward, it has to be borne in mind that it operates in a niche market which allows the college to be very focused on its product and its customers' demands. The incorporated colleges have very wide product portfolios, reflecting government, society and local needs.

The further education college of the future needs to be able to adopt and drop courses in line with current demands at the same time as it needs to sustain society's needs for traditional training and education. However, in an unequal society the basing of opportunity on market selection, or the ability to pay in any form, will cause individual rights to decline for a certain section of the community, reinforcing class, racism and androcentric thinking, thus increasing not decreasing wasted talent. In order to fulfil national education and training needs and reduce wasted talent, further education colleges also need to set out to attract and create demand from those sections of the disadvantaged community. Yet, already, at the time of writing, government policy is forcing some employers to run very costly in-service courses because fewer colleges provide the required facilities, thus putting pressure on support that is already very weak.

The task for further education colleges, with pressures on financing in a culture that clearly differentiates between education and training, is an unenviable one, which the reconstruction of the education system 50 years ago set out to resolve. While something clearly needs to be done, placing further education colleges in a competitive market appears to serve neither the individual, the employers, nor national need. The government's training and education strategy in the 1980s and 1990s seems inappropriate to the task. Indeed, while current management thought contends that organisational success is dependent on workers increasing their cognitive ability to meet market demands of flexibility and better the global competitive position of the UK, the NVQ system limits knowledge to task specificity.

Education reconstruction in 1944 was based on a radical rethink as to how society should function – it recreated tradition and in so doing altered the role of the state to include righting society's wrongs. In order to understand the government's ability to change existing social order I needed to understand better why people might accept the authority of the state to change those existing social relations. This study has told the story of why and how the educational goals were changing and has set out to identify who had the power to do the changing.

Presenting a panoramic of the narrative has enabled identification of the political and intellectual trends that existed and thus to some extent account for, in Foucauldian terms, the archaeology that enabled Mrs Thatcher to have legitimacy to act. Furthermore, the rationalisation theme has been isolated as significant to legitimising Mrs Thatcher's right to pursue educational change based on reorganisation and redistribution.

Dunleavy (1989), Poulantzas (1993) and Bachrach and Baratz (1970) suggest it is in government's interest to massage the population as long as capitalism is protected. The discovery of a pioneering journey metaphor is not then evidence that power is dispersed; indeed, the conditioning nature of the journey metaphor adds weight to their argument. Neither can I conclude, as Foucault (1990) suggests, that individuals are constituted by discourse. Research has revealed that pioneering journey themes do challenge tradition. Whilst only the naïve would conclude that polyarchy rules in order to benefit all, the evidence of a pioneering journey metaphor leads me to conclude that in a democracy, however power is balanced, and even where there appears to be an absence of collective grounds on which to base resistance, the possibility exists for incremental change to kill a paradigm softly.

Research has revealed the story of policy implementation as a rich stream of events tumbling and jostling for position as it rushes towards the future. The wide diversity of topics and materials used have made it difficult to summarise them into a coherent whole, but the notion underpinning the rigour of these proceedings has been the story of governmental power told through its discourse. This has revealed that policy-making and implementation are part of the chameleonic flux of a dynamic society. Even so, the study has demonstrated that, at least in the short term, government discourse does have the power to affect intellectual trends; this is demonstrated in the new wisdom that the welfare state must change.

Revolutions imply a known alternative – perhaps that is why no evidence of a biological metaphor has been found. Although the possibility exists for the pioneering metaphor to kill old paradigms, if those that hold emotional intelligences do not rejuvenate the political system from the bottom up, the power to decide will rest with the government and there is no reason to assume that its interests will be representative.

Some Reflections on Method

Much research in social policy relies on quotations from policy documents and is open to the criticism that the story presented simply reflects what the author wants it to be. The sheer amount of documentation touching on this subject has been so overwhelming that, to keep the study within reasonable limits, I have had to be content with a sampling method. In any investigation of this kind it is difficult, perhaps impossible, to achieve absolute objectivity in the evaluation and selection of material. The account is thus broad brush and impoverished by exclusion but, it is hoped, not more so than other work of this kind. Nevertheless, the panoramic explanatory power of discourse analysis has provided a process through which past policies can be evaluated and enabled the story of the development of further education to be told.

Bibliography

Adult Literacy and Basic Skills Unit (1983), *Adult Literacy and Basic Skills: A continuing partnership*, London: ALBSU.

Advisory Council for Adult and Continuing Education (1979), *A Strategy for Basic Education of Adults*, London: ACACE.

Allen, D. (1995), 'Modern Budgetary Control', *The Administrator*, April.

Andreski, S. (ed.) (1983), *Max Weber on Capitalism, Bureaucracy and Religion: A selection of texts*, London: Allen and Unwin.

Anthony, R. (1991), 'We Don't Have the Accounting Concepts we Need', *Harvard Business Review*.

Archer, M. (1979), *Social Origins of Educational Systems*, London: Sage.

Argles, M. (ed.) (1964), *South Kensington to Robbins: An account of English technical and scientific education since 1851*, London: Longmans.

Argyris, C. (1987), 'First and Second Order Errors in Managing Strategic Change: The role of organisational defensive routines', in Pettigrew, A. (ed.), *The Management of Strategic Change*, Oxford: Blackwell.

Aston, D. and Maguire, M. (1986), *Young Adults in the Labour Market*, Research Paper No. 55, London: Department of Education.

Aston, D. and Maguire, M. (1991), 'Patterns and Experiences of Unemployment', in Brown, P. and Scase, R. (eds), *Poor Work – Disadvantage and the Division of Labour*, Buckingham: Open University Press.

Atkinson, D. (ed.) (1993), *FE Funding and Delegation Schemes: An exegesis*, Mendip Papers.

Audit Commission (1985), *Obtaining Better Value from Further Education*, London: HMSO.

Auster, R. and Silver, M. (1979), *The State as a Firm: Economic forces in political development*, The Hague: Martinus Nijhoff.

Bachrach, P. (1969), *The Theory of Democratic Elitism*, London: University of London Press.

Bachrach, P. and Baratz, S. (1963), 'Decisions and Non-decisions: An analytical framework', *American Political Science Review*, No. 57.

Bachrach, P. and Baratz, S. (1970), *Power and Poverty: Theory and practices*, New York: Oxford University Press.

Bacon, F. (1966), 'Advancement of Learning. Book 1. 1605', in Jarman, L. (ed.), *Landmarks of Education: English Education as part of the European tradition*, London: John Murray.

Bains Report (1972), *The New Local Authorities: Management and Structure*, London: HMSO.

Ball, S. (1990), *Politics and Policy Making in Education*, London: Routledge.

Barrett, S. and Fudge, C. (eds) (1981), *Policy and Action: Essays on the implementation of public policy*, London: Metheun and Co. Ltd.

Baumol, W. (1982), 'Sales Maximisation Model', in Hardwick, P. et al. (eds), *An Introduction to Modern Economics*, London: Longman.

Becker, H. and Bennet, J. (1976), *Linguistic Behaviour*, London: Cambridge University Press.

Beck-Jorgenson, T. (1989), 'Strategic Stages in Cutback Management', in Dunshire, A. (ed.), *Cutback Management in Public Bureaucracies*, Cambridge: Cambridge University Press.

Beer, M. et al. (1990), 'Why Change Programmes Don't Produce Change', *Harvard Business Review*.

Beer, S. (1965), *Modern British Politics: A study of parties and pressure groups*, London: Faber and Faber.

Bennet, R., Glennerster, H. and Nevison, D. (1995), 'Investing in Skill: Expected returns to vocational studies', *Journals Oxford Limited: Education Economics*, Vol. 3, No. 2.

Bennett, N., Crawfor, M. and Riches, C. (1992), *Managing Change in Education*, London: PCP Publishing.

Benson, K. (1983), 'Inter-organisational Networks and the Policy Sector', in Rogers, A. and Whetton, D. (eds), *Interorganisational Co-ordination*, Iowa: Iowa State University Press.

Bentham, M. and Heck, R. (1994), 'Political Culture and Policy in State-controlled Education System: The case of educational politics in Hawaii, *Education Administration Quarterly*, Vol. 30, No. 4.

Benveniste, G. (1987), *Professionalising the Organisation: Reducing bureaucracy to enhance effectiveness*, California: Jossey-Bass.

Berle, A. and Mean, G. (1982), 'The Modern Corporation and Private Property', in Hardwick, P. et al. (eds), *An Introduction to Modern Economics*, London: Longman.

Bernstein, B. (1973a), *Class, Codes and Control. Applied Studies towards a Sociology of Language, Vol. 2*, London: Routledge and Kegan Paul.

Bernstein, B. (1973b), *Social Relationships and Language: Some aspects of the work of Basil Bernstein*, London: Open University Press.

Bernstein, B. (1974a), *A Brief Account of the Theory of Codes*, London: Open University Press.

Bernstein, B. (1974b), *Class Codes and Control: Rheoretical strides towards a sociology of language, Vol. 1*, London: Routledge and Kegan Paul.

Beveridge Report (1942), *Social Insurance and Allied Services*, Report by Sir William Beveridge, presented to Parliament by command of Her Majesty, November, Cmnd. 6406, London: The Macmillan Co.

Bishop, J. (1981), 'Briefing for Implementation', in Barrett, S. and Fudge, C. (eds), *Policy and Action: Essays on the implementation of public policy*, London: Metheun and Co. Ltd.

Black, M. (1962), *Models and Metaphors*, Ithaca: Cornell University Press.

Blaug, M. (1975), 'The Economics of Education in English Classical Political Economy: A re-examination', in Skinner, A. and Wilson, T. (eds), *Essays on Adam Smith*, Oxford: Clarendon Press.

Bloor, D. (1988), *Objectivity and Cultural Divergence*, Cambridge: Cambridge University Press.

Board of Education (1927), *The Education of the Adolescent: Report of the consultative committee*, London: HMSO.

Board of Education (1938), *Report of the Consultative Committee on Secondary Education*, London: HMSO.

Bottery, M. (1992), *The Ethics of Educational Management*, London: Cassell.

Bottomore, T. (1971), 'Class Structure in Western Europe', in Scotford, M. et al. (eds), *Contemporary Europe: Class, status and power*, London: Pitman.

Bradshaw, P. (1986), 'The Making of Public Policy', in *Politics, Legitimacy and the State*, Block Four, Course D208, Open University Press.

Bravermann, H. (1974), 'Labour and Monopoly Capitalism', *Monthly Review Press*.

Briault, E. (1976), 'A Distributed System of Educational Administration: An international viewpoint', *International Review of Education*, Vol. 22, No. 4.

Brown, P. and Scase, R. (eds) (1991), *Poor Work – Disadvantage and the Division of Labour*, Buckingham: Open University Press.

Bryce Report (1895), Report on the Royal Commission on Secondary Education.

Burns, N. (1993) [1991], in Maclure, S. (ed.), *Missing Links: The challenge to further education*, London: PSI Publishing.

Burns, T. (1973), 'Leisure in Industrial Society', in Smith, M. et al. (eds), *Leisure and Society in Britain*, London: Allen Lane.

Burns, T. and Stalker, G. (1961), *The Management of Innovation*, London: Tavistock.

Business and Technical Education Council (BTEC) (1983), *Guide to Organisation*.

Camerson, K. and Whetton, D. (1988), 'An Assessment of Salient Management Skills', in Quinn, R. (ed.), *Beyond Rational Management: Mastering the paradoxes and competing demands on high performance*, London: Jossey-Bass.

Campbell, J. (1988), *The Hero with a Thousand Faces*, London: Paladin Books.

Caplow, A. (1981) [1964], 'The Sociology of Work', in Johnson, T. (ed.), *Professions and Power*, 4th edn, London: Macmillan Press Ltd.

CBI (1980), *Training in Britain Survey*, London: HMSO.

CBI (1989), *Towards a Skills Revolution*, London: HMSO.

Charles Ames, B. and Hlavacek, J. (1991), 'Vital Truths about Managing your Costs', *Harvard Business Review*.

Cheal, D. (1991), *Family and the State of Theory*, London: Harvester Wheatsheaf.

Child, J. (1973), *Management and Organisation*, London: Harper and Row.

Cicourel, A. (1987), *Method and Measurement in Sociology*, New York: Free Press.

Citizen's Charter (1991), *A Guide: Raising the standard. A Message from the Prime Minister*, July, London: HMSO.

Clegg, S and Dunkerley, D. (1980), *Organisations, Class and Control*, London: Routledge and Kegan Paul.

Coates, D. (1981), 'Politicians and the Sorcerer: The problems of governing with capitalism in crisis', in Potter, D. (ed.), *Society and the Social Sciences: An introduction*, London: Routledge and Kegan Paul.

Cohen, M., March, J. and Olsen, J. (1972), 'A Garbage Can Model of Organisational Choice', *Administrative Science Quarterly*, Vol. 17, No. 1, March.

COI (1971), *Education in Britain*, London: Central Office of Information.

Common, R. Flynn, N. and Mellon E. (1992), *Managing Public Services*, London: Butterworth-Heinmann.

Conservative Manifesto (1992), *The Best Future for Britain*, London: Conservative Central Office.

Cooper, C. (1990), 'Meeting the Needs: Educational guidance within HE', *Educational Guidance News*, Spring.

Coote, A. and Pfeffer, N. (1993), 'Is Quality Good for you?', Institute for Public Policy Research, Social Policy Research Paper No. 5.

Cotgrove, S. (1958), *Technical Education and Social Change*, London: Allen and Unwin.

Cox, C. and Dyson, A. (eds) (1971), *The Black Papers on Education*, London: Davis-Poynter Limited.

Coyle, K. (1994), 'Post-modernism', in Clark, H. et al. (eds), *Organisations and Identities: Text and readings in organisational behaviour*, London: Chapman and Hall.

Crisp, P. (1991), *Strategic Planning and Management*, Bristol: FEFC.

Cross Report (1888), *Report of the Royal Commission on the Elementary Education Acts*.

Crossman, R. (ed.) (1963), *The English Constitution*, London: Fontana Books.

Crozier, M. (1964), *The Bureaucratic Phenomenon*, Chicago: University of Chicago Press.

Crozier, M. (1979), *The Minimum State*, London: Hutchinson.

Dahl, R. (1957), 'The Concept of Power', *Behavioural Science*, No. 2.

Dahl, R. (1961), *Who Governs?*, New Haven: Yale University Press.

Dahl, R. (1985), *A Preface to Economic Democracy*, Cambridge: Polity Press.

Davies, D. (1978), *Policies for Youth in the 1980s*, September, Further Education Unit.

Dean, C. (1991), 'Firms Unexcited by Evolution', *Times Educational Supplement*, 7 June.

Dearden, J. (1991), 'Measuring Profit Centre Managers, Getting Numbers you can Trust', *Harvard Business Review*.

DES, (1966a), *A Plan for Polytechnics and other Colleges*, Cmnd 3006, London: HMSO.

DES (1966b), *Report of the Study Group of the Government of Colleges of Education*, MoE/DES, London: HMSO.

DES (1966c), *Technical College Resources: Size of classes and approval of further education courses*, London: HMSO.

DES (1966d), *Training of Teachers for Further Education*, Circular 21, London: HMSO.
DES (1966e), *Annual Monitoring Survey*, London: HMSO.
DES (1967), *The Government of Colleges of Education*, February, Circular 2/67, London: HMSO.
DES (1970a), *Government and Conduct of Establishments of Further Education*, Circular 7/70, London: HMSO.
DES (1970b), *New Policies for Public Spending*, Cmnd 4515, London: HMSO.
DES (1971), *Tuition Fees in Further Education*, Circular 4/71, London: HMSO.
DES (1972a), *Central Arrangements for Promoting Educational Technology in the United Kingdom*, London: HMSO.
DES (1972b), *Education: A framework for expansion*, Cmnd 5174, London: HMSO.
DES (1972c), *Teacher Education and Training* (James Report), London: HMSO.
DES (1973a), *Adult Education: Plan for development* (Russell Report), London: HMSO.
DES (1973b), *Educating our Children – Four Subjects for Debate*, London: HMSO.
DES (1976a), *Tenth Report for the Expenditure Committee 1975–6: Policy making in the DES*, July, London: HMSO
DES (1976b), *Tenth Report of the Expenditure Committee: Policy making in the DES*, Cmnd 6678, London: HMSO.
DES (1977a), *Young People and Work* (Holland Report), May, London: HMSO.
DES (1977b), *Educating our Children – Four Subjects for Debate*, London: HMSO.
DES (1977c), *Education and Management: A discussion paper*, London: HMSO.
DES (1977d), *Further Education for Young Unemployed People*, Administrative Memorandum 4/77, London: HMSO.
DES (1977e), *Links between the Training and Further Education Services*, Administrative Memorandum 12/77, London: HMSO.
DES (1977f), *The Composition of School Governing Bodies*, Cmnd 7430, London: HMSO.
DES (1977g), *Unemployed YoungPeople: The contribution of the education service*, Circular 10/77, London: HMSO.
DES (1978), *Review of Educational Provision for Children and Young People with Special Needs* (Warnock Report), London: HMSO.
DES (1979a), *Sir William Pile*, London: George Allen and Unwin.
DES (1979b), *Aspects of Secondary Education in England*, December, London: HMSO.
DES (1981a), *A Framework for the School Curriculum*, March, London: HMSO.
DES (1981b), *A New Training Initiative: A programme for action*, Cmnd 8455, Circular 12/81, London: HMSO.
DES (1982a), *17+: A new qualification*, London: HMSO.
DES (1982b), *Experience and Participation*, Cmnd 8686, London: HMSO.
DES (1982c), *Further Education for Unemployed Young People*, Administrative Memorandum 2/82, London: HMSO.

DES (1982d), *The Youth Training Scheme: Implications for the education service*, Circular 6/82, London: HMSO.
DES (1983a), *Audit Inspectorate: Guide to resource efficiency*, February, London: HMSO.
DES (1983b), *The Work of the HM Inspectorate in England and Wales*, DES/Welsh Office.
DES (1984a), *Further Education for Unemployed People under the '21 hours rule'*, Administrative Memorandum 3/84, London: HMSO.
DES (1984b), *Records of Achievement: A statement of policy*, London: HMSO.
DES (1984c), *Training for Jobs*, Cmnd 9135, London: HMSO.
DES (1985a), *Better Schools*, Cmnd 9469, London: HMSO.
DES (1985b), *The Further Education Act 1985: Commercial activities in further education*, Circular 6/85, London: HMSO.
DES (1985c), *Annual Monitoring Survey*, London: HMSO.
DES (1986a), *Working Together – Education and Training*, Cmnd 9823, July, London: HMSO.
DES (1986b), *Annual Monitoring Survey*, London: HMSO.
DES (1987a), *Higher Education: Meeting the challenge*, Cmnd 114, London: HMSO.
DES (1987b), *Providing for Quality: The pattern of organisation to age 19*, Circular 3, London: HMSO.
DES (1987c), *Managing Colleges Efficiently*, DES/Welsh Office.
DES (1988a), *The Transfer of Responsibility for Education in Inner London*, Circular 6/88, London: HMSO.
DES (1988b), *Education Reform Act 1988: Local management of further and higher education colleges: articles of government*, Circular 9/88, London: HMSO.
DES (1989a), *Guide For College Governors*, London: HMSO.
DES (1989b), *Annual Monitoring Survey 1988/89*, London: HMSO.
DES/DOE/DTI (1985), *Education and Training for Young People*, Cmnd 9482, London: HMSO.
DfEE (1991a), *Education and Training for the 21st Century*, May, London: HMSO.
DfEE (1991b), *National Vocational Qualifications*, London: HMI.
DfEE (1993a), *The Charter for Further Education*, London: HMSO.
DfEE (1993b), *The Further and Higher Education Act 1992*, Circular 1/93, London: HMSO.
DfEE (1993c), *Full Time Student Equivalence*, Circular 93/09.
DfEE (1996a), *Funding 16–19 Education and Training: Towards convergence* (with a Foreword by the Secretary of State for Education and Employment), London: HMSO.
DfEE (1996b), *Review of the 16–19 qualifications Framework. Interim Report: The issues for consideration*, July, London: HMSO.
DfEE (1996c), *Competitiveness: Creating the enterprise centre of Europe*, Cmnd 3300, London: HMSO.
DfEE (1996d), *Competitiveness: Forging ahead*, Cmnd 2867, London: HMSO.

DfEE (1996e), *Training Statistics*, London: HMSO.
DfEE (1996f), *Education and Training*, Circular 96/30, London: HMSO.
DfEE (1997), *Public Expenditure Survey Settlement 1997–98 to 1999–2000*, (extrapolated forward one year), London: HMSO.
DfEE (1998), *Funding Methodology – Projections for 1998–99*, Circular 97/04, London: HMSO.
Djilas, M. (1957), *The New Class*, London: Thames and Hudson.
Donnison, D. (1986) [1970], 'Extract from Second Report of the Public Schools', in Maclure, S. (ed.), *Missing Links: The challenge to further education*, London: PSI Publishing.
Downes, D. and Flower, F. (1965), *Educating for Uncertainty*, Fabian Tract 364.
Downs, A. (1967), *Inside Bureaucracy*, Boston: Little Brown.
Doyal, I. and Harris, R. (1986), *Empiricism, Explanation and Rationality*, London: Routledge and Kegan Paul.
Dreyfus, H. and Rabinow, P. (eds) (1982), *Michel Foucault: Beyond structuralism and hermeneutics*, Hemel Hempstead: Harvester.
Drucker, P. (1995), 'The Information Tools Executives Truly Need', *Harvard Business Review*, January/February.
DTI (1994), *Competitiveness: Helping businesses to win*, Cmnd 2563, London: HMSO.
Dunleavy, P. (1981), 'Alternative Theories of Liberal Democratic Politics: The pluralist Marxist debate in the 1980s', in Potter, D. (ed.), *Society and the Social Sciences: An introduction*, London: Routledge and Kegan Paul.
Dunleavy, P. (1989), 'The Architecture of the British Central State', *Public Administration*, Vol. 67, Nos 3 and 4.
Dunn, J. (1980), *Political Obligation in its Historical Context: Essays in political theory*, Cambridge: Cambridge University Press.
Dunn, S. (1991), 'Root Metaphor in the Old and New Industrial Relations', *British Journal of Industrial Relations*, Vol. 28, No. 1, March.
Dunshire, A. and Hood, C. (1989), *Cutback Management in Public Bureaucracies*, London: Cambridge University Press.
Durkheim, E. (1973), *On Morality and Society: Selected readings*, ed. Bellah, R., Chicago: University of Chicago Press.
Dutton, S. (1998), 'Raising FEs' Teaching Standard', *FE Now*, Vol. 43, February.
Dyson, K. (1980), *The State Tradition in Western Europe*, Oxford: Martin Robertson.
Eccles, R. (1993), 'The Performance Measurement Manifesto, Getting Numbers you Can Trust', *Harvard Business Review*.
Education Act 1944.
Education Act 1976.
Education Act 1980.
Education Act (No. 2) 1986.
Education Act 1993.
Education (Handicapped Children) Act 1970.

Education Reform Act 1988.
Education (Further Education) Regulations (1975), SI:1975/1054, London: HMSO.
Education (Teachers') Regulations (1982), SI: 1982/106, London: HMSO.
Ekman, P. and Friesen, W. (1975), *Unmasking the Face*, Englewood Cliffs: Prentice Hall.
Emerson, R.M. (1962), 'Power Dependence Relations', *American Sociological Review*, No. 27.
Etzioni, A.(1961), *A Comparative Analysis of Complex Organisations*, New York: Free Press.
European Community (1985), *Transition of Young People from Education to Working Life*, working document, Brussels.
European Community (1990), *The Twenty-First Report. Vocational Training and Re-training*, Select Committee of the European Community.
FASB (1978–85), *Conceptual Framework*, FASB, USA.
Fayol, H. (1916), *Administration Industriale et Generale*, Paris.
FEFC Annual Report 1993–94.
FEFC Annual Report 1994–95.
FEFC Annual Report 1995.
FEFC Annual Statistics 1996/97.
FEFC (1994), *Measuring Achievement*, November, Circular 94131.
FEFC (1995), *Funding Allocation 1995–96*.
FEFC (1997a), *Widening Participation Committee: Pathways to success* (Kennedy Report), February.
FEFC (1997b), *Analysis of Institutions' Strategic Planning Information for the Period 1998–99*.
FEFC (1997c), *Convergence of Average Levels of Funding*, Circular 97/09.
FEFC (1997d), *Fundamental Review of the Funding Methodology*, Circular 97/31.
FEFC (1997e), *Sector Accounting Policies and Financial Statements: Guidance on the Requirements of the Council*.
FE, Now (1998), Issue 43, February.
FESC (1983), *College Government in the 1980s*, Coombe Lodge Report, Vol. 16, No. 12.
FEU (1978), *The Further Education Unit: A basis for choice*, FEU.
FEU (1985), *The Changing Face of Further Education, Part Two*, FEU.
FEU (1988), *The Statutory Framework of Further Education*, Coombe Lodge Report, Vol. 19, No. 8.
FEU (1990), *Challenges for Colleges: Developing a corporate approach to curriculum and strategic planning*, FEU.
FEU (1991), *Quality Matters*, June.
FEU (1994), *Colleges and TECs: Funding by outputs*, February, FEU.
Field, M. (1993) [1991], 'Funding Framework', in Atkinson, D. (ed.) (1993), *FE Funding and Delegation Schemes: An exegesis*, Mendip Papers.

Fielder, F. (1994), 'Leadership: A contingency model', in Clark, H. et al. (eds), *Organisation and Identities*, London: Chapman and Hall.
Fineman, S. (1993), 'Organisations as Emotional Arenas', in Fineman, S. (ed.), *Emotions in Organisations*, London: Sage.
Finer, S. (1970), *Comparative Government*, London: Allen.
Fleming Report (1944), *The Public Schools and the General Educational System*, London: HMSO.
Floud, J. (1973), 'Social Class and Educational Opportunity', in Lawson, J. et al. (eds), *A Social History of Education in England*, London: Methuen and Co. Ltd.
Foot, M. (1970), *Aneurin Bevin 1945–1960*, London: Davis Poynter.
FORCE (1990), *Community Action Programme*, FORCE, May.
Foucault, M. (1977), *Discipline and Punish: The birth of the prison*, Harmondsworth: Penguin.
Foucault, M. (1982), 'After Word: The subject and "power"', in Dreyfus, H. and Rabinow, P. (eds) (1982), *Michel Foucault: Beyond structuralism and hermeneutics*, Hemel Hempstead: Harvester.
Foucault, M. (1990), *Politics, Philosophy and Culture*, ed. Kitzman, L., London: Routledge.
Foucault, M. and Binswanger, L. (1991), *Dream and Existence*, London: Humanities Press.
Fox, A. (1965), *Industrial Sociology and Industrial Relations*, Research Paper, London: HMSO.
Fraser, D. (1984), *The Evolution of the British Welfare State*, London: Macmillan.
Freidman, M. (1962), *Capitalism and Freedom*, Chicago: University of Chicago Press.
French, J.P. and Raven, B. (1959), 'The Bases of Social Power', in Cartwright, D. (ed.), *Studies in Social Power*, Michigan: Ann Arbor.
Fryer, R. (1997), *Learning for the Twenty-first Century. First Report of the National Advisory Group for Continuing Education and Lifelong Learning*, Nagcelli, November.
Further Education Act 1985.
Further and Higher Education Act 1992.
Gabriel, Y. (1993), 'Organisational Nostalgia – Reflections on the Golden Age', in Fineman, S. (ed.), *Emotions in Organisations*, London: Sage.
Galatians, ch. 3, v. 28.
Gardner, H. (1993), *Multiple Intelligences go to School: The theory in practice*, New York: Basic Books.
Gardner, K. (1968), *Crisis in the Classroom*, New York: Basic Books.
Garvin, D.A. (1988), *Managing Quality*, New York: Free Press.
Geoffe, R. (1995), *Corporate Realities: The dynamics of large and small organisations*, London: Routledge.
George, V. and Miller, S. (eds) (1994), *Social Policy towards 2000: Squaring the welfare circle*, London: Routledge.

Giddens, A. (1987), *Social Theory and Modern Sociology*, Cambridge: Polity Press in association with Blackwell.

Giddens, A. (1996), *In Defence of Sociology: Essays, interpretations and rejoinders*, Cambridge: Polity Press.

Glatter, R. (1989), *Educational Institutions and their Environment: Managing the boundaries*, Milton Keynes: Open University Press.

Glennerster, H. (1995), *British Social Policy since 1945/1995*, London: Blackwell.

Glennerster, H. and Bennett, R. (1995), 'Investing in Skill: Expected returns to vocational studies', *Education Economics*, Vol. 3, No. 2.

Glennerster, H. and Le Grand, J. (1995), 'The Development of Quasi-markets in Welfare Provision in the United Kingdom', *International Journal of Health Services*, Vol. 25, No. 2, New York: Baywood Publishing Company Inc.

Gleick, J. (1987), *Chaos: Making a new science*, New York: Cardinal, Sphere Books.

Goleman, D. (1996), *Emotional Intelligence: Why it can matter more than IQ*, London: Bloomsbury Publishing Ltd.

Goleman, D. (1997), *Vital Lies, Simple Truths: The psychology of self-deception*, London: Bloomsbury.

Goold, M. and Campbell, A. (1987), *Strategies and Styles*, Oxford: Blackwell.

Gosden, P. (1983), *The Education System since 1944*, Oxford: Martin Robertson.

Gouldner, A. (1964), *Patterns of Industrial Bureaucracy*, New York: Free Press.

Greenwood, R. (1982), 'Attributes of a Profession', in Wilding, P. (ed.), *Professional Power and Social Welfare*, London: Routledge and Kegan Paul.

Hall, P., Land, H., Parker, R. and Webb, A. (1975), *Change, Choice and Conflict in Social Policy*, London: Heinman Educational Books.

Hall, S. (1994), 'The Changing Face of Politics in the 1990s', in Clark, H. et al. (eds), *Organisations and Identities: Text and readings in organisational behaviour*, London: Chapman and Hall.

Hall, V. (1994), 'NVCQ and Further Education', *Coombe Lodge Report*, Vol. 20, No. 5.

Hallinger, P. and Heck, R. (1996), 'Reassessing the Principal's role in School Effectiveness: A review of empirical research, 1980–1995', *Education Administration Quarterly*, Vol. 32, No. 1.

Halsey, A. (1981), *Change in British Society*, 3rd edn, Oxford: Oxford University Press.

Ham, C. and Hill, M. (eds) (1987), *The Policy Process in the Modern Capitalist State*, London: Wheatsheaf Books.

Hammersley, M. (1993), *The Dilemma of Qualitative Data: Herbert Blaumer and the Chicago tradition*, London: Routledge.

Hammersley, M. and Atkinson, P. (1983), *Ethnograpy: Principles in practice*, London: Tavistock.

Hancock, J. (1998), 'The Search for Skills', *FE Now*, 43, February.

Handy, C. (1996), *Beyond Certainty*, London: Hutchinson.

Hansard (1988), 'The Re-organisation of Further Education'.

Hansard (1991a), Prime Minister, House of Commons Statement, 21 March.
Hansard (1991b), Statement on the reorganisation of further education.
Hargreaves, D. (1984), *Improving Secondary Schools: Report of the committee on the curriculum and organisation of secondary schools*, London: ILEA.
Hargrove, E. (1983), 'The Search for Implementation Theory', in Zeckhauser, R. and Leebaert, D. (eds), *What Role for Government? Lessons from Policy Research*, London: Duke Press, Policy Studies.
Harris, J. (1993), *Private Lives, Public Spirit: Britain 1870–1994*, London: Penguin.
Harrison, M. (1993), *Operations Management Strategy*, London: Pitman Publishing.
Haslegrove, H.L. (1969), *Technician Courses and Examinations*, National Advisory Council on Education for Industry and Commerce, London: HMSO.
Hayek, F.A. (1960), *The Constitution of Liberty*, London: Routledge and Kegan Paul.
Hayek, F.A. (1967), *Studies in Philosophy, Politics and Economics*, London: Routledge and Kegan Paul.
Heck, R. (1996), 'Leadership and Culture', *Journal of Educational Administration*, Vol. 34, No. 5.
Heck, R. (1991), 'Towards the Future: Re-thinking the leadership role of the principal as philosopher', *Journal of Educational Administration*, Vol. 29, No. 3.
Helco, H. and Wildavsky, A. (1974), *The Private Government of Public Money*, London: Macmillan.
Henderson, A. and Parsons T. (eds) (1947), *Theory of Social and Economic Order: Weber 1864–1920*, New York: Free Press.
Hill, M. (ed.) (1993a), *New Agendas in the Study of the Policy Process*, London: Harvester Wheatsheaf.
Hill, M. (ed.) (1993b), *The Policy Process: A reader*, London: Harvester Wheatsheaf.
Hiromoto, T. (1991), 'Another Hidden Edge: Japanese management accounting', *Harvard Business Review*.
Hitchcock, G. (1988), *Education and Training 14–18: A survey of major initiatives*, Harlow: Longman.
Hochschild, A. (1983), *The Managed Heart*, Berkeley: University of California Press.
Hoffman, L. (1984), 'Empathy, Social Cognition and Moral Action', in Kurtines, W. and Gerwitz, J. (eds), *Moral Behaviour and Development: Advances in theory, research and applications*, New York: John Wiley.
Hogwood, W. and Lewis, A. (1984), *Analysis for the Real World*, New York: Oxford University Press.
Hoy, W.K. and Miskel, C.G. (1987), *Educational Administration: Theory, research and practice*, New York: McGraw Hill.
Huff, A.S. and Ranney, J.M. (1981), 'Assessing the Environment for an Education Institution', *Long Range Planning*, Vol. 14, No. 3.
Hutton, W. (1997), 'Lack of Welfare State Causes Poverty', *Guardian*, 21 December.
Innaconne, L. (1977), *Three Views of Change in Education Politics*, Chicago: Society for the Study of Education.
International Review of Education (1976), Vol. 22, No. 4.

Jarman, T. (ed.) (1963), *Landmarks in the History of Education: English as part of the European tradition*, London: John Murray Ltd.

Jefferson, G. (1973), 'A Case of Precision Timing in Ordinary Conversation', *Semiotica*, Vol. 9.

Johnson, G. and Scholes K. (1989), *Exploring Corporate Strategy*, London: Prentice Hall.

Johson, W. (1991), 'Global Workforce 2000', *Harvard Business Review*, April.

Jones, P. (1992), 'Post-modernism', *Social Science Teacher*, Vol. 21, No. 3, Summer.

Keenoy, T. (1991), 'The Roots of Metaphor in the Old and New Industrial Relations', *British Journal of Industrial Relations*, June.

King, M. (1980), 'Reason, Tradition and the Progressiveness of Science', in Gutting, G. (ed.), *Paradigms and Revolutions*, Notre Dame, Indiana: University Press.

Kuhn, K. (1981), 'The Sciences as Puzzle Solving Traditions', in Brown, S. et al. (eds), *Conceptions of Inquiry*, London: Methuen and Co Ltd.

Labour Party (1992), *Your Good Health: A White Paper for a Labour government*, London: Labour Party.

Lakoff, G. and Johnson, M. (1980), *Metaphors we Live by*, Chicago: University of Chicago Press.

Land, H., Parker, R. and Webb, A. (1975), *Change, Choice and Conflict in Social Policy*, London: Heinemann Educational Books.

Larson, M.S. (1982), 'The Rise of Professionalism', in Wilding, P. (ed.), *Professional Power and Social Welfare*, London: Routledge and Kegan Paul.

Liberal Democrat Party (1992), *Changing Britain for good: the Liberal Democrat Manifesto*, Dorchester: Liberal Democrat Publications.

Leach, A. (1970), 'English Schools at the Reformation', in Jarman, T. (ed.), *Landmarks in the History of Education*, London: John Murray.

Lee, D. (1991), 'Poor Work and Poor Institutions: Training and the youth labour market', in Brown, P. and Scase, R. (eds), *Poor Work: Disadvantage and the Division of Labour*, Bristol: Open University Press.

Lewellen, T. (1992), *Political Anthropology: An introduction*, Westport: Bergen and Garvey.

Lindblom, C. (1968), 'The Science of Muddling Through', *Public Administration Review*, No. 45.

Lipsky, M. (1980), *Street-level Bureaucracy: Dilemmas of the individual in public services*, London: Russell Sage Foundation.

Loabsy, B. (1967), 'Long Range Formal Planning in Perspective', *Journal of Management Studies*, October.

Local Government Act 1972.

Local Government Planning and Land Act 1980.

Locke, J. (1970), 'Essay Concerning Human Understanding, 1690', in Jarman, T. (ed.), *Landmarks in the History of Education*, London: John Murray.

Locke, M. et al. (1980), *College Administration Handbook*, London: Longman.

Lukes, S. (1974), *Power: A radical review*, London: Macmillan.

Lukes, S. (1977), *Essays in Social Theory*, London: Macmillan.
Lukes, S. (1993), 'Three Distinctive Views of Power Compared', in Hill, M. (ed.), *The Policy Process: A reader*, New York: Harvester Wheatsheaf.
Lynch, R. (1997), *Corporate Strategy*, London: Pitman.
Lyotard, J.F. (1992), 'Postmodernism', ed. Coyle, K., *Bulletin of the Marx Memorial Library*, Spring, The Marx Memorial Library.
Macaskil, E. (1997), 'Benefit Row Splits Government', *Guardian*, 22 December.
Macey, D. (1993), *The Lifes of Michael Foucault*, New York: Pantheon Books.
Mackney P. (1998a), 'FE must Unite Forces to Fight for a Better Deal', *FE Now*, Vol. 43, February.
Mackney P. (1998b), 'Ways Forward', *The Lecturer*.
Maclure, S. (ed.) (1988a), *Educational Documents: England and Wales 1816 to the present day*, London: Chapman and Hall.
Maclure, S. (1988b), *Education Re-formed*, 3rd edn, London: Hodder and Stoughton.
Marx, K. and Engels, F. (1988), *Collected Works*, Vol. 30, Lawrence and Wishart.
Maslow, A. (1959), *Motivation and Personality*, New York: Harper.
Maude, A. (1971), 'The Egalitarian Threat', in Cox, C. and Dyson, A. (eds), *Fight for Education*, London: The Critical Quarterly Society.
Mayo, E. (1960), *The Human Problems of an Industrial Civilisation*, New York: Viking Press.
McCullock, G. (1944), *Education Reconstruction: The 1944 Education Act and the 21st century*, London: Woburn Press.
McGrath, J.E. (1962), *A Summary of Small Group Research Studies*, Arlington: Human Sciences Research Inc.
McGregor, D. (1960), *The Human Side of Enterprise*, London: Mcgraw Hill.
Merton, R.K. (1957), *Social Theory and Social Structure*, New York: Free Press.
Michels, R. (1987), 'Political Parties', in Ham, C. and Hill, M. (eds), *The Policy Process in the Modern Capitalist State*, London: Wheatsheaf Books.
Milton, J. (1932), *Private Correspondence and Academic Exercises*, trans. Phyllis Tillyard, Rolls Series.
Ministry of Labour and National Service (1958), *Training for Skill: Recruitment and training of young workers in industry*, National Joint Advisory Council, London: HMSO.
Mintzberg, H. (1973), *The Nature of Managerial Work*, London: Harper and Row.
Mintzberg, H. (1984), *The Case for Configuration Organisation: A quantum view*, New York and London: Prentice Hall.
Mintzberg, H. (1989), *Mintzberg on Management*, New York: The Free Press.
Mintzberg, H. (1994), *The Rise and Fall of Strategic Planning*, New York and London: Prentice Hall.
Mintzberg, H. and Quinn, S.B. (1991), *The Strategy Process*, Englewood Cliffs: Prentice Hall.
MoE (1943), *Education Reconstruction*, Cmnd 6458, London: HMSO.
MoE (1944), *Further Education*, No. 8, London: HMSO.

MoE (1945), *Higher Technological Education* (Percy Report), London: HMSO.
MoE (1946), *Further Education, 1946–1947 Major Establishments(other than Arts)*, London: HMSO.
MoE (1947), *Education for Management. Report of a Special Committee*, London: HMSO.
MoE (1948), *Technical Colleges and other Further Education Establishments Arrangements for the Deferment of Students in the Calendar Year 1948*, Administrative Memoranda, 274/48.
MoE (1949a), *Expenditure of Local Education Authorities*, Circular 210, October, London: HMSO.
MoE (1949b), *Recognition of Schools and other Educational Establishments as Efficient*, Administrative Memorandum No. 327.
MoE (1950), *National Advisory Council on Education for Industry and Commerce. The Future Development of Higher Technological Education*, London: HMSO.
MoE (1952), *Further Education – Income from Fees*, Administrative Memorandum No. 410.
MoE (1954), *The English Advisory Council's Report on Premature School Leaving*, London: HMSO.
MoE (1955), *Advisory Council on Scientific Policy. Report on the Recruitment of Scientists and Engineers by the Engineering Industry*, Cmnd 9703, London: HMSO.
MoE (1956a), Circular 305/56, London: HMSO.
MoE (1956b), *Fees for Further Education*, Circular 307, London: HMSO.
MoE (1956c), *Technical Education*, Cmnd 9703, London: HMSO.
MoE (1958), *Public Relations in Further Education*, Circular 343, London: HMSO.
MoE (1959a), *15–18 Year Olds. Report of the Central Advisory Council for Education* (Crowther Report), London: HMSO.
MoE (1959b), *Governing Bodies for Major Establishments of Further Education*, Circular 7, London: HMSO.
MoE (1959c), *Report of the Advisory Committee on Further Education for Commerce*, Ministry of Education: National Advisory Council for Education for Industry, London: HMSO.
MoE (1959d), *The Further Education Regulations*, Circular 351, London: HMSO.
MoE (1961), *Better Opportunities in Technical Education*, Cmnd 6458, London: HMSO.
MoE (1962), *Fees in Establishments of Further Education*, Administrative Memorandum 5/62, London: HMSO.
MoE (1963a), *Organisation of Further Education Courses*, Circular 3, London: HMSO.
MoE (1963b), *Half our Future*, Central Advisory Council for Education, London: HMSO.
MoE (1963c), *Committee of Enquiry 16–18 Year Olds*, Committee Paper, London: HMSO.

MoE (1963d), *Higher Education. Report of the Committee appointed by the Prime Minister* (Robbins Report), Cmnd 2154, London: HMSO.

MoE (1963e), *Report of the Special Committee on the Crowther Report*, National Advisory Council on Education for Industry and Commerce, London: HMSO; reprinted in Argles, M. (1964), *South Kensington to Robbins: An account of English technical and scientific education since 1851*, London: Longmans.

MoE (1963f), *Early Leaving*, Central Advisory Council for Education (England), London: HMSO.

MoE (1964a), *Day Release* (Hennicker Heaton Report), London: HMSO.

MoE (1964b), *The Public Relations of Further Education*, Circular 17, London: HMSO.

MoE (1964c), *Better Opportunities in Technical Education*, London: HMSO.

Moss Kanter, R. (1983), *The Change Masters*, New York: Simon and Schuster.

MSC (1975), *Vocational Preparation for Young People. A Discussion Paper*, Training Services Agency, May.

MSC (1981), *A New Training Initiative: An agenda for action*, December, London: HMSO.

MSC, TVEI Unit (1985), *Supporting TVEI*, London: HMSO.

MSC/DES (1986), *Review of Vocational Qualification in England and Wales: A report by the working group*, London: HMSO.

National Statistics Summary Tables 1975.

NEC (1984), *Competence and Completion: Training and Education in the Federal Republic of Germany, the United States and Japan*, National Economic Council.

Nisbet, R. (1969), *Social Change and History: Aspects of Western theory of development*, New York: Oxford University Press.

Niskanen, W. (1971), *Bureaucracy and Representative Government*, New York: Aldine-Atherton.

Nixon, J. (1980), 'The Importance of Communication in the Implementation of Government Policy at the Local Level', *Policy and Politics*, Vol. 8, No. 2.

Nolan Report (1996), *Second Report of the Committee on Standards in Public Life*, Cmnd 3270, London: HMSO.

Norwood Report (1943), *Curriculum and Examinations in Secondary Schools*, London: HMSO.

Norwood, C. (1965) [1943], 'Report of the Committee of Secondary Schools Examination Council', in Maclure, S. (ed.), *Educational Documents: England and Wales 1816 to the present day*, London: Chapman and Hall.

Nurian, D. (1993), *Introducing Discourse Analysis*, London: Penguin Books.

O'Hara, R. (1988), 'The Legal Structure of Further and Higher Education', in Waitt, I. (ed.), *College Administration*, London: Longman and NATFHE.

Ogawa, R. and Bossert, S. (1995), 'Leadership as an Organisational Quality', *Education Administration Quarterly*, Vol. 31, No. 2.

Oliver, M. (1991), 'Disability and Participation in the Work Force', in Brown, P. and Scase, R. (eds), *Poor Work – Disadvantage and the Division of Labour*, Buckingham: Open University Press.

OU (1982), *Politics, Legitimacy and the State*, Milton Keynes: Open University Press.

OU (1988), *Educational Evaluation*, Open University Course E811, Milton Keynes: Open University Educational Enterprises.

Ouchie, W. (1980), 'Markets, Bureaucracies and Clans', *Administrative Science Quarterly*, Vol. 25, March.

Oxford Department of Education (1964) [1963], 'Technology and the Sixth Form Boy', in Argles, M. (ed.) (1964), *South Kensington to Robbins: An account of English technical and scientific education since 1851*, London: Longmans.

Parker, S. (1991), in Thurton, S. (ed.), *Behaviour in a Business Context*, London: Chapman and Hall.

Parkes, D. (1982), *The Changing Face of FE*, FEU.

Parkes, D. (1983), 'College Government – a Valediction', *The Further Education Staff College*, Vol. 16, No. 12.

Parkin, F. (1979), *Marxism and Class Theory: A bourgeoisie critique*, London: Tavistock Publications.

Payne, J. (1987), 'Does Unemployment Run in Families: Some findings from the the General Household survey', *Sociology*, Vol. 21, No. 2.

Peters, E. (1991), *Chaos and Order in the Capital Markets: A new view of cycles, prices and market volatility*, New York: Wiley.

Peters, T. (1989), *Thriving on Chaos: A handbook for a managerial revolution*, London: Macmillan.

Peters, T. (1992), 'Rethinking Scale', *California Management Review*, Vol. 7, No. 29, Autumn.

Pettigrew, A. (1987), *The Management of Strategic Change*, Oxford: Blackwell.

Popper, K. (1981), 'The Rationality of Scientific Revolutions', in Brown, S. et al. (eds), *Conceptions of Inquiry*, London: Methuen and Co Ltd.

Porter, M.E. (1979), 'How Competitive Forces Shape Strategy', *Harvard Business Review*, May.

Potter, D. (1986), 'Competing Theories of the State', in *Politics, Legitimacy and the State*, Block Four, Course D208, Milton Keynes: Open University Press.

Poulantzas, N. (1993), 'State, Power, Socialism', in Hill, M. (ed.), *The Policy Process: A reader*, London: Harvester Wheatsheaf.

Prais, S. (1981), *Productivity and Industrial Structure*, Cambridge: Cambridge University Press.

Prais, S. and Wagner, K. (1983), *Schooling Standards in Britain and Germany*, National Institute of Economic and Social Research.

Pressman, J. and Wildavsky, A. (1973), *Implementation*, Berkeley: University of California Press.

Pressman, J. and Wildavsky, A. (1993), in Hill, M. (ed.), *New Agendas in the Study of the Policy Process*, London: Harvester Wheatsheaf.

Putman, L. and Mumby, D. (1993), 'Organisations, Emotion and the Myth of Rationality', in Fineman, S. (ed.), *Emotions in Organisations*, London: Sage.
Quinn, J. (1980), *Strategies for Change: Logical incrementalism*, London: Irwin.
Quinn, R. (1988), *Beyond Rational Management*, London: Jossey-Bass.
Reid, W. (1989), *The Meaning of Company Accounts*, London: Gower.
Robbins, Lord. (1965) [1963], 'Report of the Committee on Higher Education', in Maclure, S. (ed.), *Educational Documents: England and Wales 1816 to the present day*, London: Chapman and Hall.
Romans, ch. 13, v. 1.
Rousseau, J.-J. (1963) [1970], 'L'Education Publique', in Jarman, T. (ed.), *Landmarks in the History of Education: English as part of the European tradition*, London: John Murray Ltd.
Royal Commission on Secondary Education 1894–85.
Sandretto, M. (1991), 'What Kind of Cost System do you Need?', *Harvard Business Review*.
Schein, E.H. (1992), *Organisational Culture and Leadership*, San Francisco: Jossey-Bass.
Schumpeter, J. (1947), *Capitalism, Socialism and Democracy*, London: Allen and Unwin.
Schwartz, H.(1993), 'Narcissistic Emotion and University Administration: An analysis of "political correctness"', in Fineman, S. (ed.), *Emotions in Organisations*, London: Sage.
Seldon, A. (ed.) (1996), *Privatising Welfare after the Last Century*, London: Institute of Economic Affairs.
Sengee, P. (1990), *The Fifth Discipline: The art and practise of the learning organisation*, New York: Century Business.
Sengee, P. (1996), 'The Learning Organisation', *Management Journal*, October.
SI (1982), Education (Teachers') Regulations, SI 1982/106, London: HMSO.
Sikka, P. (1995), 'The Mountains are Still There: Accounting academics and the bearings of intellectuals', unpublished paper, University of East London.
Silvermann, D. (1993), *Interpreting Qualitative Data: Methods for analysing talk, text and interaction*, London: Sage.
Silvermann, D. (1997), *Qualitiative Research – Theory, Method and Practice*, London: Sage.
Simon, H. (1945), *Administrative Behaviour: A study of decision making in organisations*, London: Free Press.
Sinclair, J. and Coulture, M. (1975), *Towards an Analysis of Discourse*, London: Oxford University Press.
Skinner, A. and Wilson, T. (1975), *Essays on Adam Smith*, Oxford: Clarendon Press.
Skocpol, T. (1993), 'Bringing the State Back', in Hill, M. (ed.), *The Policy Process: A reader*, London: Harvester Wheatsheaf.
Slatter, B. and Tapper, T. (1981), *Education, Politics and the State: The theory and practice of educational change*, London: McIntyre Ltd.

St Mark, ch. 12, v. 17.
Stacey, R. (1993), *Strategic Management and Organisational Dynamics*, London: Pitman.
Stacey, R. (2000), *Strategic Management and Organisational Dynamics: The challenge of complexity*, Harlow: Prentice Hall.
Sticht, T. (1996/97), 'Functional Context Education', *Basic Skills*, December/January.
Stone, N. (1991), 'Does Business have any Business in Education', *Harvard Business Review*, April.
Sui, R. (1980), *The Master Manager*, New York: Wiley.
Sweezy, P. (1980), 'Capitalism and Democracy', *Monthly Review*, June.
Taylor, F. (1911), *The Principles of Scientific Management*, New York: Harper.
Taylor-Goody, P. (1994), 'Education National Success and Individual Opportunity', in George, V. and Miller, S. (eds), *Social Policy towards 2000: Squaring the welfare circle*, London: Routledge.
The European Social Charter (1961), Cmnd 2643, Member States of the Council of Europe, October.
The Teachers' Pay and Conditions Act 1987.
The Treasury (1986), *The Government's Expenditure Plans 1986–87 to 1988–89*, Cmnd 9702, London: HMSO.
Thurton, S. (ed.) (1991), *Behaviour in a Business Context*, London: Chapman and Hall.
Times Education Supplement (1991), 'Vocational Work Feels the Quality', 7 June.
Titmus, R.M. (1982) [1971], 'Goals of Welfare State', in Wilding, P. (ed.), *Professional Power and Social Welfare*, London: Routledge and Kegan Paul.
Tooley, J. (1996), *The Ethics of Markets in Education: Policy process and practice*, Southampton: University of Southampton Centre for Education Marketing Symposium, July.
Tullock, G. (199), 'The Economic Theory in Bureaucracy', in Hill, M. (ed.), *New Agendas in the Study of the Policy Process*, London: Harvester Wheatsheaf.
Turner, V. (1974), *Dramas, Fields and Metaphor: Symbolic action in human society*, Ithaca: Cornell University Press.
Vallance, E. (1995), 'Moral Support for Making Profits', *Management Today*, October.
Vollmer, H. and Mills, D. (eds) (1966), *Professionalisation*, London: Prentice Hall.
Waldron, V. and Krone, K. (1991), 'The Experience and Expression of Emotion in the Workplace: A study of a corrections organisation, *Management Communications Quarterly*, Vol. 4.
Webb, S., 'Labour and the New Social Order', adopted by the Labour Party conference in 1918.
Weiner, M. (1992), *English Culture and the Decline of the Industrial Spirit*, London: Penguin Books.
West, E. (1996), 'Education after the State', in Seldon, A. (ed.), *Privatising Welfare after the Last Century*, London: Institute of Economic Affairs.
White Paper (1956), *Technical Education*, Cmnd 9703, London: HMSO.

White Paper (1980), *Special Needs in Education*, Cmnd 7996, London: HMSO.
Wilding, P. (ed.) (1982), *Professional Power and Social Welfare*, London: Routledge and Kegan Paul.
Wiley, N. (1987), *The Marx–Weber Debate*, London: Sage Publications.
Williams, F. (1989), *Social Policy: A critical introduction*, Cambridge: Polity Press.
Williams, R. (1957), *Whose Public Schools?*, London: Bow Group.
Williams, S. (1986), *The Times*, 25 March.
Williamson, O. (1975), *Markets and Hierarchies: Analysis and anti-trust implications*, New York: Free Press.
Wolfe, A. (1977), *The Limits of Legitimacy*, New York: Free Press.
Wood, F. and Townsley, J. (1986), *Finance*, London: Pitman.
Wootton, A. (1975), *Dilemmas of Discourse: Controversies about the sociological interpretation of language*, London: Allen and Unwin.
Youth Service (1960), *Report of the Departmental Committee in the Youth Service in England and Wales* (Albemarle Report), London: HMSO.

Index

Advisory Council for Adult and Continuing Education (ACACE) 72, 90
Advanced Further Education 186
Allen, D. 265
Annual Monitoring Survey 190
Anthony, R. 180
Argles, M. 60
Argyris, C. 205, 209, 267, 268
Aston, D. and Maguire, M. 72, 74
Atkinson, D. 190–92
Audit Commission 44, 143, 188, 219

Bachrach, P. 16, 202, 217
Bachrach, P. and Baratz, S. 2, 202, 217, 269
Bacon, F. 28
Ball, S. 65, 69
Barrett, S. and Fudge, C. 2, 15, 16, 202, 217, 262
Beer, M. 212
Bennet, R., Glennerster, H. and Nevison, D. 4
Bennett, N., Crawfor, M.and Riches, C. 89, 198
Benson, K. 2
Bentham, M. and Heck, R. 29, 209, 218
Bernstein, B. 152
Beveridge Report 32
Bishop, J. 16
Black, M. 94, 148, 153
Blaug, M. 30
Bottomore, T. 60
Bravermann, H. 13
Braiult, E. 10
British Education Council (BEC) 37, 76
Brown, P. and Scase, R. 67, 84, 206, 266
Bryce Report 37
Burns, N. 3
Burns,T. and Stalker, G. 204, 207
Burnham Further Education Funding Document 43
Business and Technical Education Council (BTEC) 24, 52, 76

Campbell, J. 148
Central Office of Information (COI) 134
Certificate of Pre-vocational Education (CPE) 77
Certificate in Secondary Education (CSE) 67, 78
Charles Ames, B. and Hlavacek, J. 182
Chief Executive Officer 187
Child, J. 209
Confederation of British Industry (CBI) 5, 15, 40, 49
Conservative Manifesto 139
Cooper, C. 185, 199, 265
Coote, A. and Pfeffer, N. 198
Cotgrove, S. 56
Council for National Academic Awards (CNAA) 37
Cox, C. and Dyson, A. 64, 87
Crisp, P. 198
Crozier, M. 2, 71, 202, 217

Dahl, R. 11
Davies, D. 72
Dearden, J. 181, 182, 265
Department for Education and Employment (DfEE) 25
  1991a 5, 78, 111, 116, 129, 192
  1993a 82, 97, 102, 115
  1993b 97, 134, 188
  1996a 142, 196
  1996b 142, 143
  1996c 113, 129, 140
  1996d 25
  1998 25
Department of Education and Science (DES) 5, 17, 37, 38, 40, 43, 46, 52, 72
  1966a 60
  1966b 63
  1966c 138
  1966d 43
  1966e 63
  1967 63
  1970a 65

1970b 118
1971 118
1972a 66
1972b 64, 66, 67, 101, 118, 186
1972c 66, 70, 102
1973a 67
1976b 70, 135
1977a 73
1977b 71, 109
1977d 70, 103
1977f 131
1977g 73
1978 104
1979a 71
1979b 71
1981a 72, 73
1981b 74
1982a 75
1982b 75
1982c 74, 101, 119
1982d 74, 104
1983a 109
1983b 122
1984a 76, 78, 119
1984c 48, 118, 186
1985a 78, 128
1985b 120, 122
1985c 105
1986a 136, 141
1986b 77, 78
1987a 42, 44, 46, 112
1987b 79, 123, 129, 137
1987c 131
1988a 131, 192, 219
1988b 128, 132
1989a 188
1989b 188
Donnison, D. 87
Downes, D. and Flower, F. 61
Drucker, P. 182, 265
Dunleavy, P. 4, 269
Dunn, J. 148
Dunn, S. 154, 264
Dutton, S. 87

Eccles, R. 181
Education Act
   1902 32, 37
   1921 30
   1944 32, 34, 37, 41, 52, 99
   1976 136
   1980 70
Education Reform Act 1988 188, 190
Ekman, P. and Friesen, W. 212
Emerson, R.M. 198
Etzioni, A. 11, 205
European Community (EC) 46, 47, 49, 181

Fayol, H. 204
Field, M. 190
Fielder, F. 208
Financial Accounting Standards Board
   (FASB) 180, 184
Fineman, S. 211, 212, 267
Finer, S. 11
Floud, J. 56
Foot, M. 55
Foucault, M. 153, 202, 269
Fox, A. 208
Freidman, M. 15, 204
Fryer, R. 85
Further Education Funding Council (FEFC)
   5, 84, 86, 106, 113, 188, 192, 193, 197,
   234, 239, 266
   1994, 82, 112
   1997a, 144
   1997b, 121
   1997c, 84
   1983, 72, 80
   1978, 74
   Annual Report
      1993–94 194
      1995 141, 194, 195
   Annual Statistics 1996/97 197
Further Education Staff College (FESC) 37
Further Educational Statistical Record 190
Further Education Unit (FEU) 25, 37, 42,
   111, 138
   1985 74
   1988 25
   1994 193
full-time equivalent (FTE) 190

Gabriel, Y. 255

Gardner, H. 267
Gardner, K. 69
Garvin, D.A. 198, 266
General Certificate in Secondary Education (GCSE) 78, 242, 249
General National Vocational Qualification (GNVQ) 82, 139, 140, 241, 249
Giddens, A. 16 149, 264
Glatter, R. 198
Glennerster, H. 88
Glennerster, H. and Le Grand, J. 244
Glieck, J. 206
Goleman, D. 267
Goold, M. and Campbell, A. 209
Gosden, P. 60
Gouldner, A. 2, 202, 217

Hall, P., Land, H., Parker, R. and Webb, A. 1
Hall, V. 13
Hallinger, P. and Heck, R. 266
Halsey, A. 245
Ham, C. and Hill, M. 1, 12, 13
Hammersley, M. and Atkinson, P. 1
Hansard
   1988 123
   1991a, 81, 188
   1991b 132
Hargrove, E. 15
Harris, J. 30, 36, 88
Harrison, M. 198
Heck, R. 208, 244
Helco, H. and Wildavsky, A. 25
Henderson, A. and Parsons, T. 245
Her Majesty's Inspectorate (HMI) 41, 257
Higher National Diploma (HND) 24
Hiromoto, T. 183
Hitchcock, G. 69, 74
Hochschild, A.. 254
Hoffman, L. 211
Hoy, W.K. and Miskel, C.G. 198
Huff, A.S. and Ranney, J.M. 197
Hutton, W. 84

Innaconne, L. 208, 218
Inner London Education Authority (ILEA) 133

Jarman, T. 27

Keenoy, T. 208
King, M. 148

Labour Party 139
Larson, M.S. 202
Liberal Democrat Party 139
Leach, A. 27
Lee, D. 89
Lewellen, T. 209, 218
Lindblom, C. 16, 205, 209
Loabsy, B. 205, 209
Local Education Authority (LEA) 17, 25, 37–44, 61–3, 68, 71,75, 80, 99, 103, 106, 113, 118, 132, 134, 185, 187, 188, 191, 257
Locke, J. 29
Lukes, S. 11, 267
Lyotard, J.-F. 17

Macaskil, E. 86
Macey, D. 154
Maclure, S. 56, 77, 95, 217
Manpower Services Commission (MSC) 17, 37, 40, 41, 46, 68, 70, 103, 185
   1975 68, 103, 128, 134
   1981 73
   Technical and Vocational Education Initiative Unit 75
Maslow, A. 205
Maude, A. 64, 137
Mayo, E. 204
McGrath, J.E. 208, 218
McGregor, D. 205
Merton, R.K. 207
Milton, J. 29
Mintzberg, H. 202, 205, 245
Ministry of Education (MoE)
   1943 33, 95, 96, 107, 121, 124, 131
   1944 38
   1945 55, 56
   1946 35
   1948 38, 99
   1949a 55, 117, 118, 185
   1949b 99
   1950 56

1952 118
1954 55
1955 56, 57
1956a 57
1956b 117, 118
1956c 57, 58, 63
1959a 36, 43, 58, 61, 123, 124, 128, 131
1959b 39, 58, 99, 131, 219
1959d 39, 99, 143
1961 59, 60
1962 62
1963a 61, 108, 127
1963b 61, 100, 101, 127
1963c 59
1963d 60, 62
1963e 58
1963f 59
1964a 61, 62, 100
1964c 100
Moss Kanter, R. 206, 209

National Advisory Body for Higher Awards (NAB) 37, 52, 190
National Association of Teachers in Further and Higher Education (NATFHE) 43, 54, 86
National Council for Vocational Qualifications (NCVQ) 50
National Economic Council (NEC) 48
National Joint Committee (NJC) 43, 44
National Union of Teachers (NUT) 65
National Vocational Qualifications (NVQs) 44, 79, 82–4, 241, 251, 258
Nisbet, R. 148, 264
Norwood, C. 87

O'Hara, R. 23, 37
Ogawa, R. and Bossert, S. 208
Oliver, M. 70
Ouchie, W. 9

Parker, S. 211, 267
Parkin, F. 14
Peters, T. 206
Polytechnics and Colleges Funding Council (PCFC) 42, 80

Planning Programming Budgeting System (PASB) 180
Parkes, D. 65, 88
Payne, J. 74
Poulantzas, N. 269
Peters, T. 206
Prais, S. 76
Pressman, J. and Wildavsky, A. 15

quality management 112
Quinn, J. 205, 206

Reid, W. 181, 191
return on investment 181
Robbins, Lord 87
Rousseau, J.-J. 29

Sandretto, M. 184
Sengee, P. 206, 267, 268
Sikka, P. 181
Stacey, R. 206, 209, 268
Sticht, T. 36
Sui, R. 212
Sweezy, P. 14

Taylor, F. 204
Taylor-Goody, P. 87, 148
Training and Education Council (TEC) 192, 193, 197
Technical and Vocational Education Initiative (TVEI) 40, 75, 76, 79
The Treasury 186
Thurton, S. 211
Titmus, R.M. 245
Tooley, J. 4
Trades Union Congress (TUC) 15, 37, 65
training occupation classification 190
total quality management 111
Turner, V. 94, 153

Unit for Development of Adult Continuing Education (UDACE) 68
University Funding Council (UFC) 42

vocational qualifications 48
Vallance, E. 4

Waldron, V. and Krone, K. 211, 259
Webb, S. 33
weighted full-time equivalent students 193
Weiner, M. 30, 36
Wilding, P. 202

Williams, R. 60
Wood, F. and Townsley, J. 180, 195

Youth Training Scheme (YTS) 40, 80